POLITICS, ECONOMICS,
AND THE PUBLIC

AMERICAN POLITICS RESEARCH SERIES

POLITICS, ECONOMICS, AND THE PUBLIC

Policy Outcomes in the
American States

THOMAS R. DYE

UNIVERSITY OF GEORGIA

RAND McNALLY & COMPANY
Chicago, Illinois

AMERICAN POLITICS RESEARCH SERIES

Aaron Wildavsky, Series Editor

BARBER, *Power in Committees: An Experiment in the Governmental Process*

DYE, *Politics, Economics, and the Public: Policy Outcomes in the American States*

SCHLESINGER, *Ambition and Politics: Political Careers in the United States*

STEINER, *Social Insecurity: The Politics of Welfare*

Copyright © 1966 by Rand McNally & Company
All Rights Reserved
Printed in U.S.A. by Rand McNally & Company
Library of Congress Catalog Card Number 66:19442

To

MY MOTHER

TABLE OF CONTENTS

List of Tables

List of Figures

CHAPTER I

A Model for the Analysis of Policy Outcomes

MODEL-BUILDING FOR POLICY RESEARCH

THE STUDY OF PUBLIC POLICY OUTCOMES is one of the major responsibilities of political science. While the structure and functioning of political systems have always been a central concern of political science, the content of public policy is also an element of political life which political science must endeavor to explain. Policy outcomes express the value allocations of a society, and these allocations are the chief output of the society's political system. Policy outcomes, like election returns, roll-call votes, or court decisions, must be assembled, described and explained. That is the task of this volume.

A central problem facing students of American state politics is not only *describing* the great variation in policy from state to state but, more importantly, *explaining* these policy differences. This volume endeavors both to describe and to explain the policy choices of the fifty states in five of the most important areas of state policy-making: education, welfare, highways, taxation, and the regulation of public morality. A great deal of effort has been given over in the book to the systematic description of the end product or output of the state political systems in these areas. But our central purpose is the explanation of these policy outcomes, and this involves examination of the relationships between policy outcomes and those social, economic, and political conditions which operate to shape them. No doubt many of the specific policy choices made by any state are a product of unique historical circumstances in that state. But this does not excuse students of state politics from searching for those conditions which appear most influential in determining public policy over time in all of the fifty states and for generalizations which help to explain why state governments do what they do.

What accounts for differences among the states in education, welfare, highways, taxation, and the regulation of public morals? What roles do urbanization, industrialization, wealth, and adult education play in determining state policies? What difference does it make in public policy whether a state is under Democratic or Republican party control? whether a state is a one-party or a two-party state? or whether its voters turn out in large numbers on election day or stay at home? What are the policy consequences of malapportionment of state legislatures? These are some of the questions which must be dealt with in explaining public policy in the states.

The explanation of public policy can be aided by the construction of a model which portrays the relationships between policy outcomes and the forces which shape them.[1] A model is merely an abstraction or representation of political life: it should order and simplify our thinking about politics. Models appear in prose or in diagram or in mathematical notation, but often they are not made explicit. There seem to be many advantages, however, to developing an explanatory model of policy outcomes at the outset of any research into this area. Such a model can provide hypotheses about what policy outcomes should be under given circumstances. These hypotheses can then be tested against data derived from real political systems. If the hypotheses are proved correct, the model can be retained; if not, then the model can be modified or replaced by one that more closely corresponds to the real world of politics. For example, if a model indicates that welfare policy outcomes are partly a function of party competition, data on party competition and welfare policies can be examined to see if differences in the levels of competition produce differences in welfare policies. If it turns out that party competition and welfare policy are not related, then this relationship can be dropped from the original model and some other model can be constructed which does not hypothesize such a relationship.

The basic dilemma in model-building is how much to simplify reality. Certainly the utility of a model lies in its ability to simplify

---

[1] For a thorough discussion of the utility of models, see Herbert A. Simon and Allen Newell, "Models, Their Uses and Limitations," in Leonard D. White, ed., *The State of the Social Sciences* (Chicago: University of Chicago Press, 1956); Paul Meadows, "Models, Systems, and Science," *American Sociological Review*, XXII (1957), 3-9; and James M. Beshers, "Models and Theory Construction," *American Sociological Review*, XXII (1957), 32-38.

political life so that we can think about it more clearly and understand the relationships which we find in the real world. Yet too much simplification may lead to inaccuracies in our thinking about reality. If we include too few variables in our model or posit only superficial relationships, we may not be able to explain the policy outcomes which occur in the real world. On the other hand, if we include too many variables or posit overly complex relationships, our model becomes so complicated that it is not an aid to understanding. A model must simplify the relationships between policy outcomes and the forces which determine them, but it must at the same time be congruent with the real world of American state politics.

Another consideration in model-building is the ability of a model to aid in the design of policy research. A model should point out where to look for explanations of public policy and suggest the conditions under which we should expect to observe particular policy outcomes. A model should contain propositions about politics and public policy which can be directly tested in political research. It should be possible to devise operations using data from state political systems that will establish or discredit the validity of the model. In short, a model must be "researchable." Of course, no model will ever predict policy outcomes with unerring accuracy, but we should be able to develop predictions from models, so that, when results deviate from predictions, attention will be focused on the limitations of the model and the factors included in it.

Generally one thinks of any outcomes, including policy outcomes, as a result of *forces* brought to bear upon a *system* and causing it to make particular *responses*.[2] A model for the explanation of public policy outcomes, therefore, may describe relationships between socio-economic inputs (forces), political system characteristics (systems), and policy outcomes (responses). These relationships can be diagrammed as in Figure I-1.[3] This particular model assumes that the socioeconomic character of a society, that is, any condition defined as external to the boundaries of its political system, determines the nature of its political system. The political system is that group of inter-related structures and processes which functions to authoritatively allocate values within a society. Policy outcomes are viewed as the

[2] Hubert M. Blalock, Jr., *Causal Inferences from Nonexperimental Research* (Chapel Hill: University of North Carolina Press, 1964), pp. 7-9.
[3] This conceptualization is based upon David Easton's "An Approach to the Analysis of Political Systems," *World Politics*, IX (1957), 383-400; and his *A Framework for Political Analysis* (New York: Prentice-Hall, 1965), pp. 23-76. See also Richard E. Dawson and James A. Robinson, "Inter-Party Competition, Economic Variables, and Welfare Policies in the American States," *Journal of Politics*, XXV (1963), 265-89.

FIGURE I-1

**A Model for Analyzing Policy Outcomes
in American State Politics**

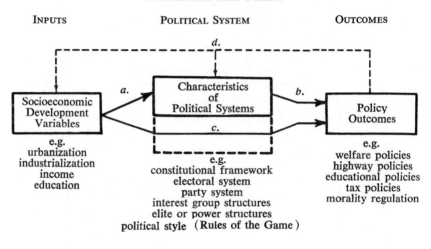

INPUTS   POLITICAL SYSTEM   OUTCOMES

d.

Socioeconomic Development Variables

a.

Characteristics of Political Systems

b.

Policy Outcomes

c.

e.g.
urbanization
industrialization
income
education

e.g.
constitutional framework
electoral system
party system
interest group structures
elite or power structures
political style (Rules of the Game)

e.g.
welfare policies
highway policies
educational policies
tax policies
morality regulation

value commitments of the political system, and as such they are the chief output of that system.

Inputs are received into the political system in the form of both demands and support. Demands occur when individuals or groups, in response to perceived environmental conditions, act to promote goals, interests, or actions. Support is rendered when individuals or groups accept the outcomes of elections, obey the laws, and pay their taxes. The political system includes all of those institutions, structures, and activities which function to transform demands into authoritative decisions requiring the support of society. Any system absorbs a variety of often conflicting demands, and, in order to transform these demands into outputs (public policies), it must arrange settlements. The political system receives support insofar as it provides satisfying outputs and activates deeply rooted attachments to the system itself.

Linkages *a* and *b* suggest that socioeconomic variables are inputs which shape the political system and that the character of the political system in turn determines policy outcomes. These linkages represent the most common notions about the relationship between socioeconomic inputs, political system variables, and policy outcomes. They suggest that system variables have an important independent effect on policy outcomes by mediating between socioeconomic conditions and these outcomes. Linkage *c*, on the other hand, suggests that socioeconomic variables affect public policy directly, without being mediated by system variables. Of course, public policy is still formu-lated through the political system, but linkage *c* suggests that the character of that system does not independently influence policy outcomes. Hence the linkage between socioeconomic inputs and policy outcomes is unbroken. Feedback linkage *d* suggests that policy out-comes have some reciprocal impact on socioeconomic conditions and system characteristics.

Already the task of model-building has succeeded in directing our attention to an important problem in the explanation of policy out-comes. In exploring the relationships between socioeconomic varia-bles, political system characteristics, and policy outcomes, we must ask whether or not differences in policy outcomes are *independently* related to system characteristics. Do system characteristics mediate between socioeconomic inputs and policy outcomes (as suggested by linkages *a* and *b*), or are policy outcomes determined without regard to system characteristics (as suggested by linkage *c*)? To state the problem in another fashion: Assuming that socioeconomic variables influence both system characteristics and policy outcomes, can system characteristics be shown to influence policy outcomes once socioeco-nomic variables are controlled? Of course, political systems are, by definition, the structures and processes which function to make public policy, but do the characteristics of these systems have any indepen-dent influence on policy outcomes? This is one of the central questions with which this book is concerned.

POLICIES AND PREFERENCES

To explain policy outcomes in state politics we have selected an essentially *empirical* model, rather than a *normative* or a *prescriptive* model.[4] Policy outcomes, even though they express the value commit-ments of political systems, are treated in our model as facts. Our model does not enable us to proceed beyond *explanations* of state policies; that is, it does not provide *justifications* for state policies. Nor will it provide a basis for determining preferences among alternative state policies. It will not tell us what we *ought* to do in state government; at best it can only help us to understand *why* state governments do what they do. The failure to provide a guide for policy-making is a serious limitation of any empirical model. One must turn to normative models —models of "good government," "good welfare programs," "good

[4] The distinction between normative and empirical models is discussed in Vernon Van Dyke, *Political Science: A Philosophical Analysis* (Stanford: Stanford University Press, 1960), pp. 6-13, 104-7.

educational systems," "good highway programs," "sound tax systems," and so forth—in order to find help in determining policy preferences.

This is not to claim that policy analysis can ever be completely value-free. Values play an important part in selecting the policies to be examined, in selecting the system characteristics to be studied, and in identifying the socioeconomic variables to be considered; indeed, values play a part in deciding to study state policy in the first place. The important distinction between an empirical and normative model is that the utility of the former is in helping to *explain* public policy, while the utility of the latter is in helping to *guide* public policy. By choosing to employ an empirical model, we are committing ourselves to the task of explanation rather than recommendation.

Our explanatory model is also distinct from the prescriptive model of Harold Lasswell and others of the "policy science" approach of a few years ago.[5] The policy science scholars were aware of the logical distinction between empirical and normative models. Yet they contended that the *relationships* between policies and preferences, that is, the relationships between instrumental policies and end values, were essentially empirical questions. As such, they were amenable to systematic inquiry not unlike the type of inquiry proposed in our model. They argued that, if certain end values are postulated, then the question of what policies would best implement these ends would be a question capable of scientific inquiry. They urged that prescriptive models be developed which would express the relationships between given end values and a particular course of public action. By clarifying relationships between means and ends, policy tools could be fashioned to help alter the course of "the world revolution of our time," whatever that phrase meant. While normative models would continue to concern themselves with definitions of "the good life," prescriptive models would describe the relationships between specific public policies and various definitions of the good life.[6]

In contrast to the models advanced by Lasswell and other proponents of a policy science, our explanatory model of public policy seeks merely to identify the major determinants of public policy choices. It does not consider what state policy ought to be, or even when it should be given a specified set of end values. It merely seeks to describe and account for differences in policy outcomes among the fifty states in

[5] Daniel Lerner and Harold D. Lasswell, eds., *The Policy Sciences* (Stanford: Stanford University Press, 1960).
[6] See Harold D. Lasswell, "The Policy Orientation," in Lerner and Lasswell, pp. 3-15.

relation to socioeconomic input variables and political system characteristics. If an understanding of the determinants of policy outcomes contributes in any way to rational decision-making, this is a by-product of the explanatory model and not its central purpose. In this regard our explanatory model differs from the prescriptive model of the policy scientists as well as other normative models.

ECONOMIC DEVELOPMENT AND POLICY OUTCOMES

Since a model is an abstraction from reality, it will never be completely congruent with conditions in the real world. It is inevitable that, in the process of simplifying reality, a model will fail to reflect all of the complexities of the real world. Simplification involves a reduction in the number of variables which are seen as relevant to the political process. From the almost unlimited number of real world conditions which influence public policy outcomes, we can choose only a limited number for inclusion in our model, and, since it is impossible to consider all the environmental conditions which might influence policy outcomes, we shall never be in a position to explain completely the policy choices of all of the fifty states. In testing our model we shall be content to learn *to what extent* our model explains actual policy choices.

Students of politics from Aristotle to the present have recognized that a society's economic development helps to shape its political life. Economic development as defined here includes four closely related components of economic development: urbanization, industrialization, wealth, and education. Industrial societies require and support concentrations of people in urban centers in contrast to agricultural societies which are more extensive users of land. An industrial economy increases worker productivity and produces a surplus of wealth. And a highly developed industrial economy requires educated rather than uneducated workers. In our model of public policy determination, economic development – urbanization, industrialization, wealth, and education – is viewed as the crucial input variable which shapes the character of the political system and the kinds of policy outcomes it produces. There are good theoretical reasons as well as considerable empirical evidence to justify the selection of economic development, rather than any number of other environmental variables, as the principal input variable in our model.

Economic theory provides solid justification for postulating that economic development influences political system characteristics and

7

policy outcomes.[7] Industrialization, whether in a planned or unplanned society, is said to result in increased specialization and demands for coordination. Coordination in a free enterprise economy is provided by the market mechanism and by corporate bureaucracies, but a great deal is also provided by government. Industrial development mandates the growth of public regulatory activity. The coordination demanded in our industrial society always involves certain inescapable difficulties: the expansion of some industries and contraction of others, overestimates and underestimates of economic conditions, and errors of judgment resulting in economic imbalances. In response to these dislocations, collective remedial action tends to increase, and added responsibilities are placed upon government. In addition, urbanization is understood to lead to a variety of social problems which are presumed to be amenable to collective action. This too implies added governmental responsibilities. Migration from rural to urban areas in response to the development of industry, the decline of agriculture, and the general search for economic opportunity by individuals and businesses also create governmental responsibilities. Economic development also involves expansion, at the state and local levels, of education, transportation, and welfare services, which are largely the responsiblity of governments, as a result of dislocations and as an integral part of economic growth. Such expansion involves not only adjustment of state policies in these areas but also adjustment of the government tax and revenue systems which must finance all of these new responsibilities.

These linkages in economic theory appear to be well supported by empirical research. Recently, students of comparative government have attempted to isolate the *functional prerequisites* of political democracy and the socioeconomic conditions generating political stability and instability. Seymour Lipset in *Political Man* first used the term "economic development" to refer collectively to four related socioeconomic variables — industrialization, urbanization, wealth, and education.[8] Lipset studied the relationship between these economic

[7] See the discussion of economic development by James R. Elliot, "A Comment on Inter-Party Competition, Economic Variables, and Welfare Policies in the American States," *Journal of Politics,* XXVII (1965), 185-91. In establishing the theoretical linkages between economic development and political systems, Elliot cites the work of Bruce R. Morris, *Problems of American Economic Growth* (New York: Oxford, 1961); Walter Krause, *Economic Development* (San Francisco: Wadsworth, 1961); Charles P. Kindleberger, *Economic Development* (New York: McGraw-Hill, 1958); Benjamin Higgins, *Economic Development* (New York: Norton, 1959); Henry H. Villard, *Economic Development* (New York: Holt, Rinehart, and Winston, 1960); and W. W. Rostow, *The Process of Economic Growth,* 2nd ed. (New York: Norton, 1962).

[8] Seymour Martin Lipset, *Political Man* (New York: Doubleday, 1960); and "Some Social Requisites of Democracy: Economic Development and Political Legitimacy," *American Political Science Review,* LIII (1959), 69-105.

development variables and the character of political systems in Western Europe and Latin America. Economic development variables and rates of change in these variables were shown to be related to stable democratic government as opposed to unstable democratic government or dictatorships. Robert Alford suggests that industrialization and urbanization encourage national political integration.[9] National political integration in turn affects other political system variables such as federalism, secularism in government, the emergence of national political parties, and class polarization in voting. Lyle Shannon correlated indices of economic development with self-government and non-self-government and showed that the latter type of political system is related to economic underdevelopment.[10]

Daniel Lerner utilized economic development variables to explain the stability of political systems in the Middle East and also introduced an additional dimension which affects stability, namely the disproportionate development of one or another of the indices of economic development. His views of the relationships between economic development and political system characteristics have already been cited by Lipset but they are worth quoting again at length:

The secular evolution of a participant society appears to involve a regular sequence of three phases. Urbanization comes first, for cities alone have developed the complex of skills and resources which characterize the modern industrial economy. Within this urban matrix develop both of the attributes which distinguish the next two phases—literacy and media growth. There is a close reciprocal relationship between these, for the literate develop the media which in turn spread literacy. But, literacy performs the key function in the second phase. The capacity to read, at first acquired by relatively few people, equips them to perform the varied tasks required in the modernizing society. Not until the third phase, when the elaborate technology of industrial development is fairly well advanced, does society begin to produce newspapers, radio networks, and motion pictures on a massive scale. This, in turn, accelerates the spread of literacy. Out of this interaction develop those institutions of participation (e.g., voting) which we find in all advanced modern societies.[11]

These studies in comparative government have focused on the relationship between socioeconomic inputs and political system characteristics, but very few cross-cultural studies have explored the relationship between system variables and policy outputs. Phillips Cutright comments on this void in comparative research:

[9] Robert R. Alford, *Party and Society* (Chicago: Rand McNally, 1963).
[10] Lyle W. Shannon, ed., *Underdeveloped Areas* (New York: Harper, 1957); and "Is Level of Development Related to Capacity for Self-Government?" *American Journal of Economics and Sociology,* XVII (1958), 367-82.
[11] Daniel Lerner, *The Passing of Traditional Society* (Glencoe, Ill.: Free Press, 1958), p. 60.

Unfortunately, an inventory of the activities of national governments, or even a conceptual scheme to aid in their classification, is not at hand. Comparative studies of the outputs of national governments are limited by the lack of scales of these activities, and relatively little attention has been given to classification of the activities. Available indicators of government activities are not, however, being fully exploited.[12]

Cutright himself studied social security policy outcomes in 76 nations and the effect of economic development and national political organization on these outcomes. He found that, in spite of very great differences among nations in ideological orientation and type of political system, policy outcomes in the area of social security were strongly related to economic development. "Nations with high levels of economic development but with less than 'perfect' (i.e., democratic) political systems had government activities highly similar to those undertaken by democratic governments. . . . Similar levels of social security coverage are found in nations whose governments are thought to act in response to the popular will as occurs in nations whose governments are thought to act with less regard to public demands. It appears that the level of social security in a nation is a response to deeper strains affecting the organization of a society."[13] In terms of our model, Cutright is saying that social security policy outcomes among nations are more a product of economic development inputs than they are a product of political system characteristics.

Later we shall return to a closer examination of the ideas set forth by Lipset, Cutright, and others, but it is already clear that economic development merits inclusion in our model as a principal input variable. These studies in comparative national governments aid in the construction of our model of public policy outcomes, a model which hopefully can be transferred to the study of American state politics.

FIFTY STATES – A COMPARATIVE APPROACH

The development of an explanatory model of public policy, whether in international politics or American state politics, requires comparative analysis. Comparative analysis occupies a distinguished

[12] Phillips Cutright, "Political Structure, Economic Development, and National Security Programs," *American Journal of Sociology*, LXX (1965), 537-48. Reprinted by permission of The University of Chicago Press. See also Phillips Cutright, "National Political Development: Measurement and Analysis," *American Sociological Review*, XXVIII (1963), 253-64; U.S. Department of Health, Education, and Welfare, Social Security Administration, *Social Security Programs Throughout the World 1961* (Washington: Government Printing Office, 1961).

[13] Cutright, "Political Structure, Economic Development, and National Security Programs," p. 548.

place in all political inquiry. Aristotle's studies were truly comparative, particularly if we remember that his definition of "constitution" included not only the political system of a society but also its socioeconomic character – the distribution of wealth, religion, education, and leisure. Studies which merely describe one political institution or event, without identifying or explaining similarities and differences among political data, cannot contribute substantially to the development of any explanatory theory of politics. Even the most insightful descriptions of specific political events cannot provide explanations which rise above the level of hunches. Roy Macridis explains that comparative study "entails the comparison of variables against a background of uniformity either actual or analytical for the purpose of discovering causal factors that account for variations."[14] Comparison, in other words, is an integral part of explanation. And all meaningful description is comparative; that is, facts can only be perceived when they are contrasted with some other element in the environment. Comparison is really basic to perception, conceptualization, explanation, thought, and expression.

Since comparisons are so critical to explanation, it follows that the value of the comparative approach is not limited to the study of national political systems. The comparative potential in American state politics is enormous, and it is a potential in which the more recent literature in American state politics has displayed significant interest.[15]

The American states provide an excellent opportunity for applying comparative analysis in non-experimental research. These fifty separate political systems share a common institutional framework and cultural milieu. All states operate under written constitutions which divide authority between executive, legislative, and judicial branches. The structure and operations of these branches are quite similar from state to state. All states function within the common framework of the American federal system. All states share a national language, national symbols, and a national history. In short, important institutional and cultural factors may be treated as constants for analytical purposes.

This background of institutional and cultural uniformity in the American states makes it easier to isolate causal factors in our analysis of public policy outcomes. Comparative analysis of national political systems is made very difficult because of the many great institutional and cultural differences among national societies; it is difficult to isolate

[14] Roy C. Macridis, *The Study of Comparative Government* (New York: Doubleday, 1955), p. 2.
[15] See, for example, Herbert Jacob and Kenneth Vines, eds., *Politics in the American States: A Comparative Analysis* (New York: Little, Brown, 1965).

the reasons for variations in system characteristics or policy outcomes where vast differences exist in geography, climate, language, economy, history, religion, and so on. In contrast, when one focuses upon the American states many important independent variables are held constant, and the explanatory power of a single set of variables can be more clearly observed.

Of course the American states are not entirely alike, either with respect to socioeconomic development inputs, political system characteristics, or policy outcomes. And this too is an important asset in comparative research. In non-experimental research one cannot artificially manipulate variables in order to observe their effects; instead, one must find situations in the real world in which variations exist in the phenomena under study. The existence of variations from state to state in levels of economic development, political systems, and policy outcomes enables us to search for relationships between differences in policy outcomes and differences in levels of economic development or political system characteristics; and in order to test our model we must be able to observe the associated changes in these phenomena. It is the closeness of the relationships between variations in policy outcomes and variations in levels of economic development or political system characteristics which permits us to establish the utility of our model of policy outcomes. For example, if differences in policy outcomes are more closely associated with differences in economic development levels than differences in political systems, then we may infer that economic development is more of a determinant of policy outcomes than system characteristics. But if the closer association is between policy outcomes and system characteristics, then the opposite can be inferred. Chapter II will explain how this closeness can be measured.

Fortunately, if only for the sake of analysis, there are marked differences among the states in economic development levels.[16] In 1960 the median family income in Connecticut was two and one-half times what it was in Mississippi. Over 85 per cent of New Jersey residents lived in urban areas, while 65 per cent of North Dakota residents lived in rural areas. Only 1 per cent of the labor force in Massachusetts was engaged in agriculture, in contrast to 33 per cent in North Dakota. Kentucky adults averaged only an eighth-grade education, while adults in seven states averaged more than twelve years of schooling. This is sufficient variation to permit us to make observations about the impact of economic development levels on political systems and policy outcomes.

[16] U.S. Bureau of the Census, "United States Summary," *Census of Population 1960,* PC (1)-1C (Washington: Government Printing Office, 1960).

POLITICAL SYSTEMS AND POLICY OUTCOMES

Despite uniformity in constitutional framework, the political systems of the fifty states are remarkably varied. The comparative strength of the Republican and Democratic parties obviously differs. States can also be differentiated by the level of interparty competition and in the strength and functions of their party organizations. Furthermore, in some states conflict between rural and urban interests dominate state politics, while in other states conflict among regions, between legislature and governor, between liberal and conservative, or between labor and management may dominate the political scene. Some states are characterized by high levels of political participation, while in other states less than half of the eligible voters go to the polls. In some states the legislature makes the crucial decisions about public policy, while in other states the legislature simply rubberstamps the decisions of a strong governor, an influential party leader, or powerful interest groups in the state. In some states political alignments follow party lines, while in other states political battle lines reflect factional rivalries, competition among powerful interest groups, or conflict between liberals and conservatives or labor and industry. In short, state political systems can be quite different from one another.

Just as it was necessary to limit the number of environmental variables which could be included in our model, so also is it necessary to limit the number of system characteristics to be incorporated into it — another compromise with reality which we must make in the construction of a model.

Four sets of system variables have been chosen for inclusion in our model of policy outcomes, two reflecting characteristics of the party system and two reflecting characteristics of the electoral system. Party systems are represented in our model by several measures of the level of interparty competition in state politics and by measures of the division of Democratic and Republican party control of state government. Electoral systems are represented by several measures of the level of voter participation or turnout and by several measures of the degree of malapportionment in state legislative districts. All four of these system characteristics — the division of two-party control, the level of interparty competition, the level of voter participation, and the degree of malapportionment — have been hypothesized as influential in shaping policy outcomes in the American states. More will be said about these four variables in Chapters VIII and IX, but a few of the reasons for their inclusion in our model are discussed here.

What difference does it make in public policy outcomes whether a state is under Republican or Democratic party control? In the literature on American parties it has been argued that our two parties offer few policy alternatives.[17] American political parties are often regarded as "brokerage" organizations, devoid of ideology, and more inclined to adjust their policy positions to fit popular demands. Since parties in a two-party system must win a majority to hold office, each attempts to attract support from the moderate center of the electorate. In competing for this same market, parties are led to offer policy positions which are almost identical. This gives rise to the Tweedledee – Tweedledum image of American parties. In each state both parties tailor their policies to local conditions; politicians cater to the particular demands of their constituencies. The result is that the parties do not have any independent impact on policy outcomes. Parties merely reflect socioeconomic inputs, as do policy outcomes.

Herbert McClosky has challenged this view of the American party system. On the basis of survey material on the opinions of party leaders and rank-and-file members, he concludes that the parties are "distinct communities of cobelievers who diverge sharply on many important issues. . . . Republican and Democratic leaders stand furthest apart on the issues that grow out of their group identification and support – out of the managerial, proprietary and high status connections of the one, and the labor, minority, low status and intellectual connections of the other."[18] Of course this does not prove that these leaders act upon their divergent beliefs, but the implication in McClosky's work is that Democratic and Republican control of state government will independently affect policy. Support for this view is provided by Malcolm Jewell's compilation of data on party voting in state legislatures.[19] He found that on more than half of the non-unanimous roll-call votes in the legislatures of New York, Connecticut, Pennsylvania, Rhode Island, and Massachusetts, the majority of Democrats voted against the majority of Republicans. This is evidence of considerable party conflict in these states. William J. Keefe reported that in both the Pennsylvania and Illinois legislatures the parties differed substantially on roll-call votes on major issues.[20] In both legislatures the Democratic party was more interested than the Republicans in labor, minorities, and social legislation, while the Republican party showed greater concern for

[17]E.g., V. O. Key, Jr., *Politics, Parties, and Pressure Groups*, 4th ed. (New York: Crowell, 1958), ch. 8; and Maurice Duverger, *Political Parties* (New York: Wiley, 1958).

[18] Herbert McClosky, *et al.*, "Issue Conflict and Consensus among Leaders and Followers," *American Political Science Review*, LIV (1960), 426.

[19] Malcolm Jewell, *The State Legislature* (New York: Random House, 1962), p. 52.

[20] William J. Keefe, "Comparative Study of the Role of Political Parties in State Legislatures," *Western Political Quarterly*, IX (1956), 535-41.

fostering business and limiting the role of the government in regulating the economy.

On the other hand, there is evidence that in some states party voting is very infrequent and that the parties do not offer significantly different policy choices. The authors of *The Legislative System* obtained mixed results when they questioned legislators about what they thought the role of parties to be in legislative policy-making.[21] Over 90 per cent of New Jersey legislators perceived considerable party influence. Ohio legislators were more divided: 51 per cent perceived considerable party influence, but 31 per cent saw little or no party influence. In California and Tennessee only 6 and 21 per cent, respectively, of the legislators perceived considerable party influence, and 40 and 57 per cent felt that parties exercised little or no influence.

Another possibility is that in some states it does make a difference which party is in office while in other states it does not. Analysis of party influence on roll-call votes in state legislative chambers suggests that interparty conflict on policy questions is more likely to occur in the urban industrial states in which the parties represent separate socioeconomic constituencies.[22] Party conflict over policy occurs in those states in which Democratic legislators represent central-city, low-income, ethnic, and racial constituencies and Republican legislators represent middle-class, suburban, small-town, and rural constituencies. In these states parties clash over taxation and appropriations, welfare, education, and the regulation of business and labor—in short, over the major social and economic controversies which divide national parties. Party conflict on policy questions is much less frequent in rural states where the parties must appeal to more homogeneous constituencies. These studies suggest that at least in urban industrial states, where the parties represent separate socioeconomic constituencies, it does make a difference which party controls state government.

The inclusion in our model of measures of Democratic and Republican party control allows us to explore these questions about the effects of partisanship on public policy. But in addition to the question of Democratic or Republican control of state government, there is also

---

[21] John C. Wahlke, Heinz Eulau, William Buchanan, and Leroy C. Ferguson, *The Legislative System* (New York: Wiley, 1962), p. 425.
[22] Duncan MacRae, "The Relation between Roll Call Votes and Constituencies in the Massachusetts House of Representatives," *American Political Science Review*, XLVI (1952), 1046-55; and Thomas R. Dye, "A Comparison of Constituency Influences in the Upper and Lower Houses of a State Legislature," *Western Political Quarterly*, XIV (1961), 473-80.

the separate question of the impact of interparty competition on policy outcomes. What difference does it make in public policy outcomes whether a state is characterized by highly competitive two-party politics or non-competitive one-party dominance?

A number of scholars have described and classified state political systems according to their levels of interparty competition: Ranney and Kendall, Key, Schlesinger, and Golembiewski, for example.[23] It seems clear that economic development affects the level of interparty competition. Golembiewski, in a study of relationships between a variety of "sociological factors" and state party systems, reported statistically significant associations between urbanism, income, and industrialization, and classifications of party competition among the states. Ranney and Kendall, Key, and Schlesinger have also indicated that one or more of the measures of economic development correlates closely with party competition in the American states. These studies tend to confirm the existence of the linkage between economic development and political system characteristics postulated by our model (linkage *a* in Figure I-1).

On the other hand, the linkage between party competition and policy outcomes (linkage *b* in Figure I-1) has *not* been systematically established. "Conclusions" about the effect of party competition on policy are mainly derived from a priori analysis or from anecdotal data. For example, it is often argued that competitiveness results in increased benefits for citizens because the parties are forced to bid for votes. Students of state party systems also feel that it is more difficult to hold factions responsible for policy choices than it is to hold competitive parties responsible. One-party factional systems may obscure politics for most voters and permit conservative interests to manipulate factional alignments. A large number of people who have little knowledge about the policies of various factions may be easily misled. Even if policy differences between parties are vague, there is at least the distinction between an *in-party* and an *out-party* which voters can identify at election time, and this is not really true in a one-party system. All of this implies that the policy choices of competitive states are different from those of non-competitive states.

Empirical evidence to support speculation about the effect of party

---

[23] Austin Ranney and Willmoore Kendall, "The American Party System," *American Political Science Review*, XLVIII (1954), 477-85; Joseph A. Schlesinger, "A Two-Dimensional Scheme for Classifying the States According to Degree of Inter-Party Competition," *American Political Science Review*, XLIX (1955), 1120-28; V.O. Key, Jr., *American State Politics: An Introduction* (New York: Knopf, 1956), p. 99; and Robert T. Golembiewski, "A Taxonomic Approach to State Political Party Strength," *Western Political Quarterly*, XI (1958), 494-513.

competition on policy outcomes is meager. In *Southern Politics,* V. O. Key, Jr., finds that states with loose multi-factional systems with little continuity of competition tend to pursue conservative policies on behalf of upper socioeconomic interests.[24] States with cohesive and continuous factions pursue more liberal policies on behalf of less affluent interests. Duane Lockard observed among the six New England states that the two-party states (Massachusetts, Rhode Island, and Connecticut), in contrast to the one-party states (Maine, New Hampshire, and Vermont), received larger proportions of their revenue from business and death taxes, spent more on welfare services such as aid to the blind, the aged, and dependent children, and were better apportioned.[25] Neither of these studies, however, attempted systematically to hold constant for the impact of economic development while observing these policy outcomes. It was Dawson and Robinson who first attempted to sort out the influence of party competition on policy outcomes from the influence of economic development.[26] The focus of the Dawson and Robinson study was upon outcomes in welfare policy, particularly the average assistance payments to categories of welfare recipients. On the basis of rank orderings of the states, they found that increases in both party competition and levels of income, urbanization, and industrialization were usually accompanied by increases in welfare benefits. However, when wealth was held constant party competition no longer appeared to be closely related to increased welfare benefits. The authors concluded that "inter-party competition does not play as influential a role in determining the nature and scope of welfare policies as earlier studies suggested. The level of public social welfare programs in the American states seems to be more a function of socio-economic factors, especially per capita income."[27]

In short, there are good a priori reasons to believe that party competition does independently influence policy outcomes, but, on the other hand, there is some empirical evidence that suggests otherwise. There are some correlations between public policies and party competition, but they may be merely a product of the relationships between economic development and policy outcomes. The inclusion of party

[24] V.O. Key, Jr., *Southern Politics in State and Nation* (New York: Knopf, 1951), pp. 298-314.
[25] Duane Lockard, *New England State Politics* (Princeton: Princeton University Press, 1959), pp. 320-40.
[26] Dawson and Robinson, "Inter-Party Competition, Economic Variables, and Welfare Policies in the American States." See also the same authors' "The Politics of Welfare," in Jacob and Vines, pp. 371-410.
[27] Dawson and Robinson, "Inter-Party Competition, Economic Variables, and Welfare Policies in the American States," p. 289.

competition in our model of policy outcomes permits us to explore these questions.

The level of voter participation is also an interesting characteristic of political systems, and one which might reasonably be expected to influence public policy outcomes. Of course voting and non-voting have important meaning for the political system, since they represent levels of confidence in political institutions and degrees of support for the democratic rules of the game.[28] But we are more interested in the effect of high or low electoral participation on policy outcomes. Do states with consistently higher voter turnouts pursue policies noticeably different from those pursued by states with low turnouts, and can these policy differences be traced to the effect of voter participation?

There are good reasons to hypothesize that participation levels do influence policy choices.[29] Non-voting is most common among lower-income, lower-status, poorly educated groups. High voter participation is a characteristic of higher-status, higher-income, well educated groups. Non-voting is also characteristic of non-white populations; non-whites vote less often than whites even when income, status, and education attributes are the same. In addition, the Republican party draws its most reliable support from the higher socioeconomic groups who vote more frequently; low turnouts are said to hurt the Democratic party which draws its strength more heavily from lower socioeconomic groups. Certainly the outcomes of elections are vitally affected by turnout levels, and the presumption is that public policy is in turn influenced by the outcome of elections.

The final system variable to be included in our model of policy outcomes is malapportionment. Commentators on state politics have often implied that malapportionment seriously affects the policy choices of state legislatures. In the literature on state politics it is frequently argued that there are important policy differences between urban and rural constituencies and that malapportionment which overrepresents rural interests grants the rural constituencies a real advantage in policy-making. Charles Adrian has stated, "Malapportionment, in terms of population, has serious effects upon governmental policies,"[30] and V. O. Key has added, "it must be assigned a high rank"[31] among the factors which have led to the low status of state legislatures. Of course there is little doubt that malapportionment

---

[28] Lester W. Milbrath, *Political Participation* (Chicago: Rand McNally, 1965).
[29] See Dawson and Robinson, "The Politics of Welfare," pp. 406-7.
[30] Charles Adrian, *State and Local Governments* (New York: McGraw-Hill, 1960), pp. 306-7. See also Daniel Grant and H. C. Nixon, *State and Local Government in America* (Boston: Allyn and Bacon, 1963), pp. 204-5; and Jewell, pp. 30-33.
[31] Key, *American State Politics,* pp. 76-77.

affects the character of state political systems or processes, but determining its effects on the content of public policy is a more difficult problem.

Proponents of reapportionment have been very enthusiastic about its consequences for policy outcomes. They have frequently attributed a lack of party competition, unfair distributions of state funds, conservative tax schemes, unprogressive educational policies, and penny-pinching welfare programs to rural overrepresentation; they expect to see these policies changed by reapportionment. Reapportionment, it is said, will help the states to come to grips with the important domestic problems facing the nation and so resume their rightful place in the American federal system.[32]

In contrast, a few scholars have urged more caution regarding predictions about the policy consequences of reapportionment. Duane Lockard referred specifically to the effect of malapportionment on policy outcomes in Massachusetts and Connecticut: "Do states with fair apportionment respond to urban appeals more readily? If anyone has made a systematic study of this, I am unaware of it, but limited evidence does not seem to indicate that the states with fair apportionment are any more considerate of urban problems than states with malapportionment."[33] Herbert Jacob was equally skeptical about the effect of reapportionment on public policy. In a study of the effects of malapportionment on party competition, highway funds distribution, and certain welfare expenditures, he found that conditions in malapportioned states were not noticeably different from conditions in well-apportioned states. He concluded, "it is improbable that it [reapportionment] will substantially invigorate state governments or dissolve the stalemates which sap public confidence in them."[34]

The impact of apportionment practices on policy outcomes in no way affects the moral or constitutional issues involved in state legislature reapportionment. The federal courts are committed to a policy of insuring to each citizen the equal protection of apportionment laws, regardless of whether or not, or how, reapportionment affects policy outcomes. But inclusion of apportionment measures in our model of policy outcomes enables us to predict the policy changes which may occur in the wake of court-ordered reapportionment.

[32] See footnotes 30 and 31; in addition, see Commission on Intergovernmental Relations, *A Report to the President for Transmittal to Congress* (Washington: Government Printing Office, 1955), p. 39.

[33] Duane Lockard, *The Politics of State and Local Government* (New York: Macmillan, 1963), p. 319.

[34] Herbert Jacob, "The Consequences of Malapportionment: A Note of Caution," *Social Forces*, XLIII (1964), 261.

There is considerable variation among the states in these four system characteristics, and this variation enables us to search for associated differences in policy outcomes. Methods of measuring Republican and Democratic control of state government, the level of interparty competition, the level of voter participation, and the extent of malapportionment will be described in Chapter III; variations among the states in these four system characteristics and the inter-relationships among the system characteristics will be described, and the effect of economic development levels on these system characteristics will also be analyzed.

POLICY OUTCOMES IN THE AMERICAN STATES

In the 1960-1961 legislative biennium more than 104,000 bills were introduced in American state legislatures,[35] and over 33,000 of them were enacted into state law. Each of these bills, rejected or enacted, represents a separate policy choice. Even the continuation of laws written earlier into the statute books represents public policy. What policies are to be selected from this universe of policy choices in order to assess the impact of economic development levels or political system characteristics on public policy?

In this study we have selected a variety of policy outcome measures in five of the most important areas of state politics — education, health and welfare, highways, taxation and revenue, and the regulation of public morality. Education, highways, and health and welfare are the three largest categories of state spending, in that order. Our judgment that these are the principal functional areas of state policy-making is defended in the introductory sections of the chapters dealing with these topics. It has also been decided that tax and revenue policies are vital outcomes of any political system and deserve systematic examination. Finally, it has seemed desirable to analyze policy outcomes in police protection, crime control, correctional policy, the character of state bureaucracy, and the level of general social control. These policies are considered together under the title "the regulation of public morality."

The explanation of these policy outcomes provides an excellent challenge for systematic comparative research in state politics. Over 90 different outcomes in state politics are described and analyzed in these five separate fields. Marked differences can be found among the states in these outcomes: for example, per pupil educational

[35] Council of State Governments, *Book of the States 1962-63* (Chicago: Council of State Governments, 1963).

expenditures in New York are over two and one-half times what they are in Mississippi; average monthly welfare benefits in Connecticut are three times as much as they are in Arkansas; per capita expenditures for highways in Wyoming are four times higher than in New Jersey; per capita taxes in California are over twice as high as per capita taxes in South Carolina; Nevada provides three times the number of policemen per population that South Dakota provides. In short, there are very significant differences among the states in a wide variety of policy outcomes. This presents both an opportunity and a challenge for comparative, systematic, policy research.

CHAPTER II

The Design of Policy Research

MODELS AND OPERATIONS: BRIDGING THE GAP

OUR RESEARCH DESIGN stems directly from the explanatory model of public policy which we constructed in Chapter I in order to organize and simplify our thinking about the complex relationships among socioeconomic forces, political system characteristics, and policy outcomes. The model provides us with hypotheses about the forces shaping public policy which the research design must test against data derived from the real political systems of the American states. If the hypotheses generated by the model prove correct, the model can be retained. If not, then the model must be modified or replaced by one which conforms more closely to the real world of state politics.

The function of the research design is to tie the model down to this real world. The research design must *operationalize* the model: it must give empirical meaning to the several elements of the model, and it must describe the empirical conditions which would confirm or disconfirm the relationships among these elements that our model has postulated. Thus, the initial task in our policy research is to give empirical referents to economic development, political system characteristics, and public policy outcomes. Then tests must be designed to prove or disprove the validity of the kinds of linkages suggested by the model.

Our model assumes, first of all, that the socioeconomic character of a state affects the nature of its political system. In order to operationalize this linkage, we must develop measures of socioeconomic development among the states and measures of the variations in the character of their political systems. Then we must systematically examine the linkages which exist in the states between these socioeconomic measures and the political system variables. This is the principal task of Chapter III. Since the model also assumes that the socioeconomic character of a state influences its public policy outcomes, Chapters IV through VIII are devoted to the measurement of policy outcomes and the identification of linkages between these outcomes and socioeconomic conditions in the states. Moreover, the model hypothesizes that political system variables influence the public policy outcomes in a state; Chapters IX and X will examine the linkages between political system variables and measures of policy outcomes. Finally, Chapter XI presents a summary of the effects of all of our economic development and political system variables on policy outcomes.

There is a serious gap, however, between the language of explanation and the language of research operations. This means there is a serious gap between the explanatory model and the research design. This gap can never be bridged in a completely satisfactory manner. One *thinks* about public policy in terms of a conceptual language of explanation that contains notions of inputs, forces, systems, and characteristics. But one *tests* hypotheses about public policy by means of indices, measures, operations, correlations, frequencies, and regressions. These statistical operations are not synonymous with explanation. For example, in testing for the existence of a linkage between socioeconomic inputs and policy outcomes, we shall refer to *correlations* between socioeconomic *indices* and policy outcome *measures*. Yet, the existence of correlations between indices of economic development and measures of public policy outcomes does not prove the validity of an explanatory model. There are a number of problems which prevent us from finding research operations which are completely symmetrical with our explanatory model.[1]

There is, first of all, the problem of determining the meaning of various indices or measures and their relationship to the concept which they are presumed to describe. Is it valid to assume that an index or measure can describe any phenomenon in the real world broader than that to which it directly refers? For example, does "median family income" refer simply to the median figure received by the census-taker when he asks a respondent what his family income was last year? Or can median family income be employed as an index to a larger phe-

---

[1] The most enlightening essay on this topic is Hubert M. Blalock, Jr., *Causal Inferences in Nonexperimental Research* (Chapel Hill: University of North Carolina Press, 1964).

nomenon, namely economic development, the central input variable in our model? Do figures on "per pupil expenditures" mean only the quotient one obtains by dividing pupil attendance figures by educational expenditures? Or can per pupil expenditures be employed as a measure of public policy in the field of education, an important output of state political systems? In short, to what extent can indices and measures be given meaning beyond the particular operations which were used to obtain these measures?

This particular question is part of a larger dispute between theorists and operationalists in the social sciences. Although we have no intention of joining in this debate, it should be stated at the outset that we have given a great deal of emphasis in this study to the development of a conceptual model of public policy determination. Throughout the study a distinct theoretical bias leads us to assume that indices and measures *represent* concepts such as socioeconomic development, political system characteristics, and public policy. In the interest of developing and testing our model of public policy determination, we have made great inferential leaps from data to concepts and back again. While we insist that all concepts in our model have operational meaning, that is, that they have empirical referents, our central focus is upon the concepts themselves rather than upon measures or operations.

Another problem is that of making inferences from correlations and other statistical operations. The statistical correlation and regression analysis employed in this study is described in a later section of this chapter. But it should be recognized at the outset that there is a serious gap between the language of correlation and regression analysis and the language of explanation. In describing the linkages between economic development and public policy, explanatory language implies that economic development "determines," "accounts for," "produces," "results in," "explains," public policy outcomes. Yet statistical correlations can at best tell us only how close the association is between variations in economic development and variations in public policy outcomes. It is quite clear that the causal language of our model is not the same as the relational or associative language of correlation analysis. Concomitance of occurrence is part of the causality, but it is not all of it. Day is always followed by night, but we do not infer from this concomitance that days "produce," "determine," or "explain" nights. There is a high degree of association between rainfall in Philadelphia and rainfall in Trenton, but we do not say that rain in Philadelphia "causes" rain in Trenton, or vice versa. Even Mill covered himself on this point by adding a ten-word clause at the end of his cannon of concomitant variation:

Whatever phenomenon varies in any manner whenever another phenomenon varies in some particular manner, is either a cause or an effect of that phenomenon, or is connected with it through some fact of causation.[2]

The realization that concomitance is not the same as cause, however, does not rule out the utility of correlation analysis. For even though the existence of a correlation does *not* demonstrate the existence of a causal relationship, nonetheless the absence of a correlation *does* demonstrate the absence of a causal relationship. Mill's cannon of concomitant variation has withered under the attack of logical positivists, operationalists, and other empirical philosophers, but the converse of Mill's cannon remains more or less intact: "Nothing can be the cause of a phenomenon if when the phenomenon varies that thing does not or when the phenomenon does not vary that thing does."[3] Public policy cannot be determined by levels of economic development or political system characteristics if public policy does not vary when the levels of economic development vary or the political system characteristics change. In short, the converse of Mill's cannon can be used to reject explanatory hypotheses. This means that negative or null explanatory hypotheses can be rejected, that is, hypotheses which assert that there is no relationship between public policy and economic development or the character of the political system. It is possible to test these null hypotheses about the factors which influence public policy, and, if these null hypotheses are disproved, then at least the *probability* is increased that a positive explanatory relationship exists. This study makes a great deal of use of the converse of Mill's cannon in attempting to see if presumed relationships disappear under particular circumstances.

Another problem stemming from the gap between the language of explanation and the language of research involves the differentiation of *independent* from *dependent* variables. In our explanatory model, public policy is designated as the dependent variable. It is public policy which we hope to describe, analyze, and explain. Economic development variables and political system characteristics are treated as independent variables. This differentiation is a product of the structure of our model. However, in mathematics, including correlation analysis, there is no basic differentiation between independent and dependent variables. Whatever happens to appear on the left-hand side of an

---

[2] J. S. Mill, *A System of Logic* (New York: Harper, 1887), p. 279. See also Blalock, pp. 27-60; Morris R. Cohen and Ernest Nagel, *An Introduction to Logic and Scientific Method* (New York: Harcourt, Brace, 1934), ch. 13; and Mario Bunge, *Causality* (Cambridge: Harvard University Press, 1959), pp. 46-48.

[3] Mill, p. 280.

equation or on the *y* axis in a regression, is conventionally referred to as the dependent variable. Yet, by definition, things that appear on the left- and right-hand sides of an equation are equivalent and inter-changeable. Thus, in an equation which postulates that variations in public policy are a function of variations in the levels of economic development, it is algebraically possible to turn the equation around and state that variations in economic development levels are a function of variations in public policy. However, while this interchangeability is algebraically possible, it is not possible in our conceptual model or in the real world which our model depicts. Again the language of explana-tion is not congruent with the language of research operations.

Deciding which phenomena are to be treated as independent and which as dependent variables would create no real difficulties if we knew enough about the real world to be able to say for certain whether a phenomenon were a dependent or an independent variable. But in policy research, and indeed in most social science research, there is at least some doubt as to which variables can be considered independent. We shall assume that levels of economic development and political system characteristics determine public policy outcomes. This is the direction of the arrows in our model. But our statistical operations provide no certain way of deciding whether levels of economic devel-opment determine policy outcomes or policy outcomes determine the levels of economic development. Correlations do not tell us whether system characteristics produce policy outcomes or policy outcomes produce system characteristics. The direction of causality is a product of our model and not of research operations.[4]

Another serious problem in operationalizing our explanatory model involves the classification of real world phenomena as socioeco-nomic inputs, political system characteristics, and policy outcomes. The model establishes these classifications of data as a means of ordering reality, so that our thinking about political life can be sim-plified. But in the real world data are not labeled inputs, system characteristics, or outcomes. Data can be obtained from the real world, for example, on "median family income," "percentages of legislative seats won by Democrats," and "per pupil educational expenditures." But it is only in the context of our explanatory model that these data are neatly categorized as socioeconomic inputs, political system char-acteristics, and policy outcomes respectively. There is no way to justify empirically the designation of any particular variable as an input, a system characteristic, or an outcome—these designations spring from our model. Someone else, using some other model, might

[4] Blalock, pp. 35-38.

classify the variables of the real world in some other manner. The only criterion for determining whether the classification of variables in this study is any better than some alternative one, is which classification contributes most to our understanding of the real world of state politics. In other words, the only criterion for evaluating our model and its classification of variables is its utility in explanation.

Since our classification of variables is a function of our model and not really an attribute of the real world, it is not really useful at the outset of our study to debate whether or not any particular variable should be designated a policy outcome, a socioeconomic input, or a system characteristic. Later, of course, on the basis of empirical findings, we will want to make modifications in our model, including its classification scheme, in order to improve its usefulness in explanation. But it is inappropriate to debate at the outset whether or not "per capita state tax revenues" or "high school drop-out rates," for example, should be designated as socioeconomic inputs or policy outcomes, since there is no empirical way of demonstrating that these variables should fall in one classification or the other. If classifying these as policy outcomes makes our task of explanation any easier, then they should remain as such until some better model of state politics is proposed.

Another problem in operationalizing our explanatory model is the possibility that the design developed out of that model will tend to confirm the model, regardless of whether or not it is congruent with the real world. This might easily occur in the designation of variables as inputs or outcomes. If measures which are clasified as inputs and as outcomes are really only slightly different measures of the same phenomenon, the high correlation which will exist between these particular input and outcome measures may appear to confirm the model. However, the correlations may actually be a mere artifact of the research design, a product of a classification scheme which designated measures of the same phenomenon as two different elements. For example, the "educational level of the adult population" is a socioeconomic input while the "high school drop-out rate" is an educational policy outcome. Our model chooses to view drop-outs as a product of state educational systems, that is, as a phenomenon separate from, although influenced by, the educational level of the state's population. If a high correlation is obtained between these two variables, the model views this as confirmation of a linkage between a socioeconomic input and an educational policy outcome. However, it may be that both measures are indices of the same phenomenon, perhaps a general commitment to education; and the confirmation of the linkage is really meaningless. There is no empirical way to determine whether a high correlation between two measures is a product of the fact that both measures measure the same thing or the confirmation of a genuine relationship between two separate phenomena.[5]

In summary, transforming the language of explanation into the language of research is a difficult task. No explanatory model can ever be fully demonstrated empirically. But this does not mean that it is not helpful to think in terms of an explanatory model or to develop a model which will produce testable hypotheses. In working with models it is always necessary to make use of a whole series of untestable simplifying assumptions. Even when a model yields correct empirical predictions, this does not mean the model itself has been empirically verified. But unless we permit ourselves to make simple assumptions, we shall never be able to generalize beyond the single or unique political event. Without making the kinds of assumptions that an explanatory model requires, we shall never be able to explain political life.

In this volume we assume that political science, like other sciences, employs two distinct languages, the explanatory and the operational, and recognize that there is no empirical or logical way of completely bridging the gap between the two. However, we shall move freely from operational to explanatory language and back again as necessary, largely on the basis of convention.[6]

MEASURING ECONOMIC DEVELOPMENT[7]

Choosing from an almost infinite number of environmental conditions which could be viewed as input variables, we have constructed a model which focuses upon the impact of economic development. Economic development is viewed as the principal input variable shaping the character of state political systems and the kinds of policy outcomes encountered in state politics. This reduction in the number of inputs to be considered insures that our model will fail to explain

---

[5] See Blalock, pp. 61-94.

[6] "We shall take the commonly accepted position that science contains two distinct languages or ways of defining concepts, which will be referred to simply as theoretical and operational languages. There appears to be no purely logical way of bridging the gap between these languages. Concepts in one language are associated with those in the other merely by convention or agreement among scientists." Blalock, p. 6. See also F. S. C. Northrop, *The Logic of the Sciences and the Humanities* (New York: Macmillan, 1947), chs. 3-7.

[7] All operational measures of economic development, political system characteristics, and policy outcomes are described in the Appendix, together with the source for each measure. This greatly reduces the need for extensive footnotes. The absence of a footnote for factual data presented in the text indicates that the data and their sources are given in the Appendix.

completely the political systems or the policy choices of all fifty states. Certainly there are other environmental conditions in the states which help to shape their political systems and public policies; race, ethnicity, size, region, climate, history are just a few of the input variables which might be, but which are not, included in our formal analysis. The self-imposed limitations of our study require that we be content to learn to what extent economic development explains policy choices.

For this study economic development has been defined as a composite of four functionally interrelated phenomena: urbanization, industrialization, wealth, and education. Economic development involves, first of all, industrialization. America's transformation from an agricultural to an industrial society is perhaps the most prominent development in its history. As late as 1870, over 53 per cent of America's work force was engaged in agriculture, forestry, or fisheries.[8] Only 17 per cent of the work force was directly engaged in manufacturing, and less than 30 per cent of the work force was engaged in supporting economic activities: transportation and public utilities, finance, wholesale and retail trade, and service activities including government. By 1900 these proportions had changed: 38 per cent of the work force in primary economic activities — agriculture, forestry, and fisheries; 22 per cent in direct manufacturing activity; and 40 per cent in supporting activities. The history of the twentieth century describes the declining role of primary activities and the increase in manufacturing and in the trade, finance, and service activities which become increasingly important as an economy matures. By 1960 only 7 per cent of the labor force was employed in agriculture, forestry, and fisheries, 27 per cent was employed in manufacturing, and 66 per cent in supporting activities.

One minus the percentage of the work force engaged in agriculture, fisheries, and forestry has been selected as our measure of industrialization. This definition of industrialization centers upon the occupational activities of the working population. It is felt that this aspect of industrialization may be politically more relevant than any dollar measures of industrial activity, since this measure focuses upon the meaning of industrialization to the work experiences of the people. This measure of the non-agricultural work force lumps together manufacturing, mining, construction, transportation, trade, finance, and service employees, including government employees. Of course not all of these employees owe their jobs to industrialization, yet any other

[8] Historical data are drawn from U.S. Bureau of the Census, *Historical Statistics of the United States: Colonial Times to 1957* (Washington: Government Printing Office, 1960), p. 74.

categorization would probably introduce more error than this one. To use manufacturing employees as a percentage of the work force would associate all the other categories of employees with agricultural activity. If one prefers, he can consider our measure of industrialization to be principally a measure of non-agricultural employment.

Not all of the states share the same high level of industrial activity which characterizes the nation as a whole. In 1960 only 63.1 per cent of the population of North Dakota was in non-agricultural employment, while in five states (Connecticut, Massachusetts, New Jersey, New York, and Rhode Island) non-agricultural employment accounted for over 98 per cent of the work force. Because of the industrial character of the nation as a whole, the distribution of the states along this measure is heavily skewed toward non-agricultural employment. Ideally one would wish for a more normal curve to aid in analysis, but variation among the states on this measure of industrialization is sufficient to permit meaningful regression analysis.

Most economists have come to regard urbanization as an integral part of economic development. Industrial activities require the concentration of people in urban centers, while agricultural activities are more extensive users of land area. There is the possibility that a population center can grow without industrialization, but this does not contradict the converse – that industrialization requires urbanization.

The definition of urbanization employed in this study is based on the percentage of the population living in urban areas, that is, in incorporated places of 2500 or more or in the urban fringe of cities of 50,000 or more. This is the standard Census Bureau definition. In 1790 the urban population of the United States was only 5.1 per cent of the total population.[9] By 1900 this figure had grown to 39.7, and in 1960 69.9 per cent of the population lived in urban areas. Here again not all the states share in this high degree of urbanization. Alaska has the smallest proportion of urban residents of any state in the nation (37.9 per cent), while New Jersey has the largest proportion of urban residents (88.6 per cent). The distribution of states according to the percentage of their population living in urban areas is shown in Figure II-1.

Most economists treat rising income as a basic component of economic development. An industrial economy means increased worker productivity and the creation of surplus wealth. Median family income in the United States rose from $1231 in 1939 to $5660 in 1959.[10] But this wealth was not evenly distributed throughout the states. Median family income in Mississippi in 1959 was $2884 while median

[9] U.S. Bureau of the Census, p. 14.
[10] U.S. Bureau of the Census, p. 167.

family income in Connecticut was $6887. In other words, family income in the richest state was over two and one-half times what it was in the poorest state.

An economically developed society requires educated rather than

FIGURE II-1

The Fifty States Distributed According to Industrialization, Urbanization, Income, and Education in 1960

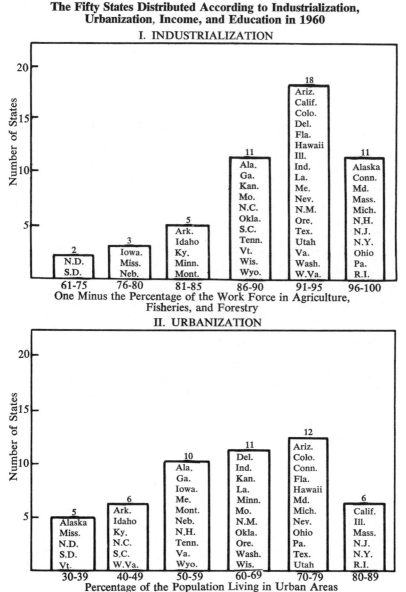

I. INDUSTRIALIZATION

II. URBANIZATION

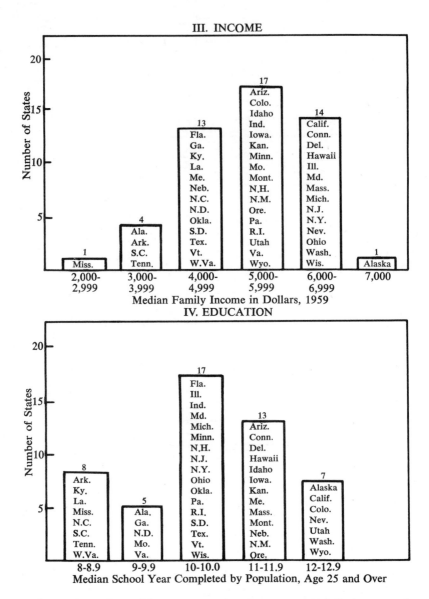

III. INCOME

Median Family Income in Dollars, 1959

IV. EDUCATION

Median School Year Completed by Population, Age 25 and Over

uneducated workers. Many economists have asserted that economic growth involves an upgrading of the quality of the work force, the development of professional managerial skills, and an increase in the volume of research. These developments obviously involve a general increase in the educational levels of the adult population. In 1940 the median school year completed by the adult population in the United

States was 8.6.[11] By 1960 the median school year completed had advanced to 10.6. Of course, this generally high level of educational attainment which characterized the nation as a whole did not prevail uniformly throughout the states. The median school year completed by the population over 25 years of age in Kentucky was only 8.7, while the median school year completed in Utah was 12.2

Economic theory, then, provides compelling a priori reasons for considering urbanization, industrialization, income, and education as facets of a single phenomenon—economic development. Some economists have asserted that economic development *means* urbanization, industrialization, income, and education. It is the presumed functional interrelatedness of these variables which justifies collective reference to them as economic development. However, in the construction of our research design, it has been decided to keep these measures analytically separate and not to combine them into a single index. Ordinarily, multiple measures of the same phenomenon would be combined into a single index, but, although there are good theoretical reasons for considering these measures as indices of the same phenomenon, it

TABLE II-1

The Relationships among Urbanization, Industrialization, Income, and Education in the Fifty States

	Urbanization	*Industrialization*	*Income*	*Education*
Urbanization	1.0			
Industrialization	.67*	1.0		
Income	.66*	.59*	1.0	
Education	.41*	.21	.74*	1.0

These figures are simple correlation coefficients for the fifty states; an asterisk indicates a statistically significant relationship.

turns out in empirical observations of the fifty states that they are not as closely related in the real world as we might expect. While our measures of urbanization, industrialization, income, and education in the fifty states are significantly related, these relationships are not close enough to lend empirical support to the contention that they are measures of the same phenomenon. The simple correlation coeffieients for the relationships among these four measures are shown in Table II-1. All but one of the several interrelationships are above the level which this study considers significant; only the relationship between industrialization and the educational level of the adult population falls below the accepted significance level ($r = .21$). The closest relationship

[11] U.S. Bureau of the Census, p. 214.

is between income and education ($r = .74$). On the whole, however, these coefficients suggest that the separate measures of economic development may have different impacts upon politics and public policy in the states, and, as a result, we will treat them separately in our analysis. This enables us to distinguish among the effects of these four separate measures, although we refer to them collectively as economic development.

This chapter has described the measurement of economic development in the fifty states. In addition, our study employs 12 separate measures of political system characteristics, providing indices of political participation, malapportionment, the division between Democratic and Republican party control, and the level of interparty competition. There are also more than 90 policy measures employed, to provide indices of policy outcomes in the fields of education, health and welfare, highways, taxation, and the regulation of public morality. However, it is more convenient to describe and discuss these many operational measures of political systems and policy outcomes as they appear in the chapters devoted to their analysis.

DESCRIBING LINKAGES AMONG ECONOMIC DEVELOPMENT, POLITICAL SYSTEM CHARACTERISTICS, AND PUBLIC POLICY

The method chosen to describe the complex relationships among economic development levels, political system characteristics, and policy outcomes is that of simple and partial linear correlation analysis.[12]

All the measures in this study — economic development measures, political system measures, and policy outcome measures — are degree variables. Each variable is expressed as a numerical quantity for each state rather than a categorization. All variables are expressed in terms of the original data, for example, people, dollars, votes, school years completed, prisoners, high school dropouts, and so on. Of course, these data are often presented as percentages, averages, or medians of these units, but the use of complicated indexes, scales, or scores is avoided. It is also important to note that measures in this study are *not* expressed as rankings of the states. All measures are cardinal expressions of original data, rather than ordinal expressions of rankings among the states. All simple and partial correlations which are presented are based upon these cardinal measures; rank order correlations are not employed.

[12] The basic guide for the statistics employed in this study is Hubert M. Blalock, Jr., *Social Statistics* (New York: McGraw-Hill, 1960), especially chs. 17-19.

Simple and partial correlation coefficients are appropriate statistics for measuring the extent to which sets of degree variables are related. The *simple correlation coefficient* measures the closeness of the association between two measures. It can range from a +1.0, indicating a perfect positive relationship to a −1.0, indicating a perfect negative relationship; a coefficient of zero or near-zero indicates no relationship among the variables. The social sciences usually do not produce perfect relationships. The size of the correlation coefficient describes the strength or weakness of the relationship between two variables. The correlation coefficient is standardized so that differences in the size or range of the variables do not affect the coefficient. Correlation coefficients are always comparable; that is, a large coefficient indicates a closer relationship between two variables than a small coefficient, regardless of the kinds of units or amounts represented in the sets of measures. For example, if a coefficient of .75 is obtained between income and per pupil educational expenditures in the states and a coefficient of .50 between urbanization and per pupil educational expenditures, it can be inferred that per pupil educational expenditures are more closely related to income than to urbanization. Simple correlation coefficients can describe the relationship between any two variables in our study; they are used in this study to show the extent to which differences in levels of economic development, political system characteristics, and public policy outcomes are associated and to describe the strength of these associations.

Occasionally reference is made to the *coefficient of determination* which is simply the square of the correlation coefficient. While the correlation coefficient measures the closeness of the relationship between two variables, the coefficient of determination measures the proportion of variation in a dependent variable which can be accounted for or explained by variation in an independent variable. For example, if a correlation coefficient of .75 was obtained between income and per pupil educational expenditures in the states, the square of this figure, .56, represents the percentage of variation in per pupil expenditures among the states which can be explained by differences in income levels. In short, one could say that income levels explain 56 per cent of the variation among the states in per pupil expenditures. Of course, one minus the coefficient of determination is the proportion of *un*explained variation in the dependent variables; in our example, 44 per cent of the variation in per pupil expenditures among the states cannot be explained by income levels.

Any simple correlation coefficient presented in this study need only be squared to ascertain the extent to which the independent variable succeeds in explaining differences among the states in the dependent variable. Of course this requires some assumptions about which variable is the independent or explanatory variable; this problem was discussed in a preceding section. The substitution of explanatory thinking for the associative thinking of correlation analysis is a product of our model and not of any empirical operations. A near-zero correlation coefficient will, of course, produce an infinitesimal coefficient of determination, and there is no difficulty in interpreting this to mean that neither variable can explain variations among the states in the other variable.

While simple coefficients show the extent to which two measures are related, they do not deal with the possibility of *intervening variables* creating *spurious relationships* or obscuring *independent relationships*. There may be a close association between two variables which are not related in any explanatory way simply because both variables are related to some third variable. It may be that these first two variables have no effect upon each other, but they are associated because both are related to the same third intervening variable. In such a case this third variable is said to produce a spurious relationship between the first two variables, and no really independent or explanatory relationship exists between them.

For example, it may be that differences in the levels of party competition among the states are associated with differences in welfare benefits. However, if it is shown that there is more party competition in wealthy states than in poor states and that welfare benefits are higher in wealthy states than in poor states, it may be that the association between party competition and welfare benefits is really a product of the effect of wealth. In other words, there may be no real causal relationship between increased party competition and higher welfare benefits; their occurrence together may be merely a result of the fact that both are a product of wealth. Other intervening variables which might account for the association between a system characteristic and a policy outcome would be urbanization, industrialization, and education.

How can we control for the effect of intervening variables and distinguish between explanatory relationships and spurious associations? The *partial correlation coefficient* is the statistical tool for achieving this control over intervening independent variables. Partial correlation coefficients can show the relationship between two variables while controlling for the effect of one or more intervening variables. They do so by adjusting the values of the dependent and independent variables to take into consideration the effect of the controlled variables. Partial coefficients also range from a +1.0 to −1.0, with a zero or near-zero coefficient indicating that no independent relationship exists between the two variables if we control for the effects of specified intervening variables. The size of the partial coefficients describes the strength of a relationship under controlled conditions.

In this study we shall use partial coefficients to examine the relationships between system characteristics and policy outcomes while controlling for the effects of economic development, and those between economic development and policy outcomes while controlling for the effects of political system characteristics. If using partial coefficients to control for economic development results in the disappearance of a relationship between a system variable and a policy outcome, we can conclude that the association between these variables is merely a product of the fact that both are related to economic development. On the other hand, if the partial correlation coefficients between system variables and policy outcomes remain significant even after controlling for economic development, then we may more readily conclude that political system characteristics *do* have an independent effect on public policy. For example, if the relationship between party competition and welfare benefits shown in simple coefficients disappears when economic development is controlled in partial coefficients, then we can conclude that no explanatory relationship exists between party competition and public policy.

Partial correlation coefficients are also used to examine relationships between economic development and policy outcomes while controlling for the effect of system variables. If the relationships between economic development and public policy which appear in simple coefficients are noticeably weakened or disappear when a system variable is controlled, then we can readily conclude that system characteristics *do* influence public policy. In such a case it can be said that economic development affects public policy only as it operates through changes in political system characteristics. On the other hand, if relationships between economic development and public policy outcomes remain the same even after controlling for the effect of system characteristics, then we may conclude that economic development independently influences public policy and that system characteristics do not alter the relationships between economic development variables and policy outcomes.

Thus, partial correlation analysis enables us to go one step beyond identifying the existence of associations and describing their strength, as in simple correlation analysis, to the identification and description of relationships under controlled conditions. By observing the disappearance, weakening, or continued strength of partial coefficients we can come much closer to establishing the validity of our explanatory model. Associations can be distinguished from explanatory linkages.

Of course, even a high partial correlation coefficient is not synonomous with explanation. Empirically, all that is shown by a significant partial coefficient is that an association between variables exists even under controlled conditions. The absence of a significant partial coefficient can demonstrate the absence of an explanatory linkage, but the existence of a significant partial coefficient merely increases the probability that an explanatory linkage may exist. The substitution of explanatory language for associations revealed by partial correlation analysis is still only a product of our model.

One final set of statistics — multiple and multiple-partial correlations — is employed in Chapter XI to summarize the total effect of *all* of the economic development and political system variables on policy outcomes in the states. The multiple correlation coefficient is employed to show the total amount of variation in policy outcomes which can be explained by all of the economic development and political system variables acting together. This analysis enables us to summarize the full explanatory power of our model.

Moreover, multiple correlation analysis also permits us to weigh the relative influence of our economic development and political system variables in our explanatory model. Multiple-partial correlation coefficients can show us the explanatory power of *all* of the economic development variables while controlling for *all* of the political system variables, and the explanatory power of *all* of the political system variables while controlling for *all* of the economic development measures. This will enable us to compare the effects of economic development and of political variables on policy outcomes. It can help us to determine whether the character of the political system or the nature of the socioeconomic environment is the most important influence on public policy.

THE QUESTION OF SIGNIFICANCE

The question of what is or what is not a significant correlation in the social sciences does not lend itself to generalization. A correlation coefficient of .90 indicates that 81 per cent of the total variation in a dependent variable has been explained by the independent variable. A correlation of .30 indicates that only 9 per cent of the variation in the dependent variable has been explained by the independent variable.

Obviously, from an explanatory point of view a coefficient of .90 is more disirable than one of .30, for it indicates an increase in our power of explanation. But does this mean that a coefficient of .30, that is, the ability to explain a very small percentage of the total variation in the dependent variable, is worthless? Obviously not. The ability to explain some variation in the dependent variable is more desirable than an inability to explain any variation.

The valuation placed upon low coefficients is inversely associated with the development of the science. It seems safe to say that the systematic study of public policy is a very underdeveloped field of inquiry. Any ability to explain public policy outcomes represents an increase in our level of knowledge. Perhaps students in more developed disciplines in the social sciences will be uncomfortable with the value placed upon low coefficients in this study. But those familiar with the difficulties of systematic comparative study of policy outcomes will probably be more satisfied with the identification of any explanatory relationships, however weak they may be.

Interpreting the significance of a particular finding, then, is really an exercise in personal judgment. The tables in this study report all coefficients, whether they are interpreted in the text as significant or not, so that the reader can exercise his own judgment as he wishes.

However, it has been necessary to arrive at a standardized practice of assigning significance to findings for the purpose of developing our explanatory model. It is especially necessary to find some criteria, however arbitrary, for rejecting explanatory hypotheses. Therefore, in interpreting correlation coefficients in this study, it has been decided to dismiss as insignificant those coefficients which might easily have occurred by chance. Even though the fifty states represent a universe rather than a sample, the theory of sampling has been employed to determine which coefficients might have occurred by chance if the American states were a sample from an imaginary infinite universe of political systems. The allusion to sampling is a hypothetical one. An analysis of variance test for the significance of r permits us to identify those coefficients which could occur by chance more than five out of one hundred times in the correlation of random numbers. For the purposes of this study, such coefficients are defined as *in*significant. Hypotheses which assert a relationship between variables which do not correlate any more closely than random numbers might be expected to correlate are rejected.

All calculations are made on the basis of observations about all fifty states (except with regard to party variables, where Nebraska and Minnesota are dropped from the analysis because of their non-partisan character). Given a constant number of observations in all correlations, it is possible to state that only simple coefficients above .30 and partial coefficients above .35 are significant at the .05 level. Since smaller coefficients could be the product of chance, hypotheses asserting a relationship for which the simple and partial coefficients are below .30 and .35 are rejected.

It should be emphasized that a test of significance is distinct from a measure of the strength or closeness of a relationship. A simple coefficient of .30 still means that an explanatory variable has accounted for only 9 per cent of the dependent variable. The test of significance merely makes us more confident that there is a real relationship, however slight, between these two variables.

EXPLANATION AND PREDICTION

Simple and partial correlations in themselves do not permit prediction of the dependent variable. For example, knowing the *closeness* of the relationship between urbanization and police expenditures does not in itself permit us to predict the police expenditures required at a given level of urbanization. Predictions such as this can only be made with the use of regression coefficients, often referred to as *slopes* or *b* values. However, as a result of our decision to deal in explanations rather than predictions, this study has not dealt in regression coefficients; correlation coefficients are presented, but not slopes, *b* values, or predicted values of our dependent variables. Inquiry is directed to identifying and explaining relationships among variables. Prediction, through the use of slopes and expected values, has little real meaning in the analysis of policy outcomes. It is true that regression equations can give us hypothetical statements about how much one variable (police expenditures) should change if a given variable (urbanization) changes by a particular amount; but where unexplained variance is quite high, these predictions are unreliable. As Blalock points out: "In most problems in social sciences, attention is rightly focused on locating the important variables. In explanatory work of this sort, correlational analysis becomes more important than regression analysis."[13] Our concern is basically with the explanation of actual policy outcomes and with assessing the relative importance of economic development and political system characteristics in determining these outcomes. For these purposes simple and partial coefficients are most appropriate.

Where it is useful to distinguish between those states which do conform to a particular hypothesis and those which do not, the scatter diagram is employed. The scatter diagrams in this study are visual

[13] Blalock, *Causal Inferences*, p. 51; see also his *Social Statistics*, p. 285.

presentations of the relationship between two variables as they occur in the fifty states. For example, Figure II-2 shows the relationship between urbanization and industrialization in all the states. Each state is represented by a dot placed upon a scatter diagram in which the measures of urbanization and industrialization are the coordinates. The hypothesis that urbanization and industrialization are related is represented by the broken line, the line of regression. The more the states cluster about that line, the more they support the hypothesis. The degree to which each state conforms to, or deviates from, the hypothesis is represented by the distance between that state and the line of regression. For example, if the relationship between any two variables were a perfect one (if the simple correlation coefficient were plus or minus 1.0), then all of the dots would lie directly on the line of regression. If there were no relationship between two variables (if the simple correlation coefficient were zero or near-zero), then the dots would be so randomly scattered on the diagram that no line of regression around which dots would cluster could be drawn.

Usually the dependent variable is placed on the y axis, and the independent or explanatory variable is placed on the x axis. If one insists upon predicting the dependent variable, given a certain value of the independent variable, he can read up from the point on the x axis which represents a given value to the line of regression and then read the value on the y axis which intersects the line of regression at that point. This value on the y axis is the expected or predicted value of the dependent variable, given a certain value of the independent variable. For example, let us assume that industrialization explains urbanization and that we insist on predicting urbanization levels from given levels of industrialization. In Figure II-2 the 90 per cent industrialization measure intersects the line of regression at the 60 per cent urbanization level. Thus states with 90 per cent of their work force in non-agricultural employment *should* have 60 per cent of their population living in urban areas. Such a prediction assumes that industrialization alone explains urbanization. Since we know from the square of the coefficient of determination (.67) that industrialization *explains* only 45 per cent of the variation in urbanization in the states, we know that this *prediction* is empirically unreliable. However, it is useful to identify those states lying above and below predicted levels so that additional explanatory questions may be asked. For example, in Figure II-2 five states are clearly shown not to conform to the hypothesis that industrialization leads to urbanization: Alaska, Maine, New Hampshire, Vermont, and especially West Virginia. All of these states lie markedly below the line of regression, indicating that they are not very urban even though their work force is industrial.

FIGURE II-2
The Fifty States Arranged According to Urbanization and Industrialization

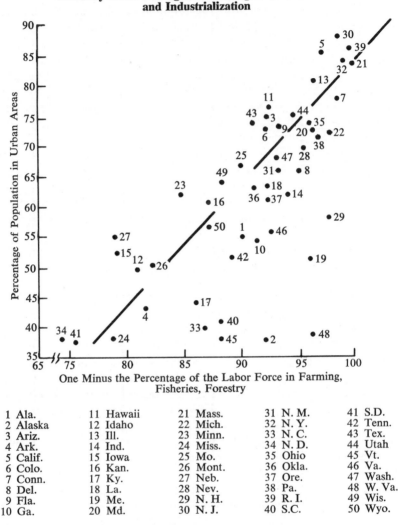

1 Ala.	11 Hawaii	21 Mass.	31 N. M.	41 S.D.
2 Alaska	12 Idaho	22 Mich.	32 N. Y.	42 Tenn.
3 Ariz.	13 Ill.	23 Minn.	33 N. C.	43 Tex.
4 Ark.	14 Ind.	24 Miss.	34 N. D.	44 Utah
5 Calif.	15 Iowa	25 Mo.	35 Ohio	45 Vt.
6 Colo.	16 Kan.	26 Mont.	36 Okla.	46 Va.
7 Conn.	17 Ky.	27 Neb.	37 Ore.	47 Wash.
8 Del.	18 La.	28 Nev.	38 Pa.	48 W. Va.
9 Fla.	19 Me.	29 N. H.	39 R. I.	49 Wis.
10 Ga.	20 Md.	30 N. J.	40 S.C.	50 Wyo.

THE FIFTY STATES AS UNITS FOR COMPARATIVE ANALYSIS

In our design for policy research, the fifty states are the principal units of analysis. Socioeconomic inputs, political system characteristics, and policy outcomes are expressed as attributes of the fifty states. This requires us to think of the states as separate political systems and the national government as a common element in the environments of these state political systems. This is not to say that the national government can be treated as a constant, for it impinges on state political systems in a very uneven fashion. In fact, the differing impact of the federal government on the several states is one of the principal concerns in the chapters to follow.

Local government is viewed as an integral part of state political systems. It is important to remember that a state political system is more than the formal institutions of state government itself; it includes state and local government structures, state party organizations, interaction among the parties, the level of political participation, the apportionment system, and any number of other structures and processes which help to transform social demands into public policy. Since local governments—their character, activities, finances, and relationships to state government—are treated as attributes of state political systems, policy outcomes which depend in whole or in part upon decisions made at the local level are also treated as attributes of state political systems. The degree to which a state relies on local governments for the provision of public services or for financial support for public functions is viewed as a policy outcome of the state political system.

Our commitment to comparative analysis requires that explanatory hypotheses be tested with reference to all fifty states. Since the object of comparative study is to develop general explanations which will apply to political systems universally, the universe of American state politics must include all the states. If we excluded any group of states from our analysis, or if we tested explanatory hypotheses with reference to regional groupings of states, we would be engaged in something other than genuine comparative analysis. Dividing the states into particular regional groupings based upon peculiar regional conditions, unique historical conditions, or special cultural patterns represents a serious compromise with efforts to achieve generality of explanation. It is sometimes argued that groupings are unavoidable and that explanatory statements which are meaningful in one region of the country are inappropriate in another region. This argument is similar to the position of the area specialists in international studies. But if regional conditions, historical circumstances, or cultural patterns prevent the development of explanatory statements which apply to all fifty states, then genuine comparative study is impossible and general explanatory models have little value. We are certainly not prepared to admit this at the outset of a study which is devoted to exploring the usefulness of a general explanatory model of policy outcomes in the American states. If we divided states into regional groupings, we would be discarding our explanatory model before it was even tested. Very often the eleven states of the Old Confederacy are, however, set apart in studies of the American states, and we are familiar with such phrases as "with the exception of the southern states," or "outside of the South." Certainly no part of the country has a greater claim to regional identity, unique historical conditions, or special cultural patterns than those states which declared their independence from the nation only a century ago. Yet so long as the southern states remain in the Union, and so long as we insist upon genuine comparative study in American state politics, we must include the southern states in testing our explanatory hypotheses. Certainly the inclusion of the 11 southern states in our research operations will affect the results: but so does the inclusion of any other 11 states.

On the other hand, it would be helpful to know which of our explanations of public policy are dependent upon the inclusion of the southern states in our analysis. The southern states generally stand at the lower end of the indices of economic development, and at the extreme end of three political system measures — the degree of Democratic success in state politics, the level of interparty competition, and the level of voter participation. Because we want to be able to identify those explanatory relationships which *are* a product of the inclusion of the southern states and those which also occur in the 39 non-southern states considered separately, all simple and partial correlation analysis which is performed on the 50 states is also performed separately on the 39 non-southern states. This allows us to check whether the relationships which occur in the 50 states also occur when the southern states are not considered.

As it turns out, nearly all of the significant relationships between economic development and public policy which occur in the fifty states also occur when the southern states are removed from analysis. Removing the 11 southern states very often alters the coefficient, but it seldom changes the finding. In those few places in the text where removing the southern states significantly affects the results, this fact is reported. Generally, however, only coefficients based on the fifty states are shown. If the effect of the southern states is not mentioned, it means that excluding the southern states has not substantially altered our findings. For the most part, the socioeconomic relationships which are reported for the fifty states do not depend upon the southern states.

In contrast to the coefficients which have been obtained with the measures of economic development, it turns out that the coefficients obtained with the political system measures are heavily influenced by the southern states. Many of the relationships between policy outcomes and Democratic success, party competition, and voter participation depend upon the southern states. Throughout the text we will indicate which relationships disappear when the southern states are removed from analysis.

The decision to use all fifty states for comparative analysis involves certain other methodological assumptions. First of all, since the fifty states constitute the universe of American states, there is no sampling problem in this study. Inferences about the state political systems are made from data derived from all the states; the limits of generalization are quite clear. As explained earlier, the theory of sampling is used to establish a standard by which we can reject hypotheses. However, tests of significance designed to ascertain the probability that the sample is an accurate representation of the universe are unnecessary.

The designation of the fifty states as units of analysis also means that inferences derived from this analysis apply to states as units rather than to individuals or groups within states. W. S. Robinson has shown that ecological correlations cannot validly be used as substitutes for individual correlations.[14] This means, for example, that if we find that welfare benefits increase with increases in state income levels, we cannot conclude that people with higher incomes favor more liberal welfare benefits. Of course, correlations based upon the fifty states may be of great value without reflecting on individual correlations. These correlations can validly be employed to test explanatory hypotheses framed in terms of state political systems.[15]

Finally, there are several methodological advantages in not changing the units of analysis in correlation studies and in avoiding correlations based upon groupings of data. All correlations in this study are based upon fifty observations; states are not grouped or ranked. As Hubert Blalock explains, this avoids the possibility of generating artificial correlations by grouping or collapsing the units of analysis.[16]

---

[14] W. S. Robinson, "Ecological Correlations and the Behavior of Individuals," *American Sociological Review*, XV (1950), 351-57.

[15] L. A. Goodman, "Ecological Regression and the Behavior of Individuals," *American Sociological Review*, XVIII (1953) 663-64; and H. Menzel, "Comment on Robinson's Paper," *American Sociological Review*, XV (1950), 674.

[16] Blalock, *Causal Inferences*, pp. 95-126.

CHAPTER III

Economic Development and State Political Systems

STATE POLITICAL SYSTEMS

GOVERNMENT AGENCIES IN THE STATES—legislatures, executive offices, and courts—serve as arenas for political activity, but politics involves much more than the operations of government agencies. Every individual, group, or organization which makes a demand upon government becomes involved in the political system by so doing. Every voter who casts a ballot becomes involved in politics. The political system includes the whole network of relationships among individuals, groups, organizations, and government institutions which functions to transform demands into public policy outcomes.

The explanation of policy outcomes in American state politics is the central task of this study. However, to accomplish this task we must first explore the character of state political systems and the forces which shape these systems. It has been suggested that policy outcomes are a function of levels of economic development and political system characteristics and that the job of policy research is to describe the independent effect of these phenomena on particular policy outcomes. Before turning directly to the analysis of policy outcomes, it is important, therefore, to understand the relationships between levels of economic development and political system characteristics. Understanding this linkage is a prerequisite to sorting out the effects of each on policy outcomes.

Students of comparative national politics have been increasingly concerned with the linkages between economic development and the

46

character of political systems. The work of Seymour Lipsit, Robert Alford, Lyle Shannon, Daniel Lerner, and Phillips Cutwright was described in Chapter I as an example of the burgeoning literature dealing with these linkages. Of course there is much less variation in the character of state political systems than in the character of national political systems.[1] The institutional framework of the fifty states is quite similar. All states have written constitutions which divide power between executive, legislative, and judicial branches. The structure, authority, and procedures of these branches of government are similar from state to state. The principle of checks and balances is found in every state constitution. Moreover, every state constitution has a bill of rights, which is remarkably similar from state to state. The political culture of the fifty states varies only slightly. This uniformity in political culture includes belief in the principles of democracy, in free elections and popular participation, in the legitimacy of competition for public office and criticism of public officials, in an economic system based on free enterprise, and in the legitimacy of political parties. The rules of the political game in every state prefer voting, lobbying, and persuasion to riots, rebellion, and revolution. These beliefs and rules may be more widely accepted in principle than in particular application, but there is certainly a broader consensus throughout the American states than in international politics.

However, despite these institutional and cultural similarities, the political systems of the fifty states are remarkably varied. State political systems can be differentiated by the relative strength of the Democratic and Republican parties, by the level of interparty competition, and by the strength and function of party organizations. Some states are dominated by a single party and there is little likelihood of the minority party ever capturing control, while in other states a more competitive situation exists. Some states have party-oriented political systems, where political demands are expressed by competing political parties, while other states have interest-group-oriented political systems, where political demands are conveyed by organized interests. The nature of the participants and the character of their demands also vary from state to state. In some states conflict between rural and urban interests dominates state politics, while in other states conflict between regions, between ethnic groups, between liberals and conservatives, between labor and management, or between competing business interests may dominate the political scene.

State political systems can also be differentiated by the degree of

[1] For a broad discussion of the similarities and differences in politics from state to state, see Herbert Jacob, "State Political Systems," in Herbert Jacob and Kenneth Vines, eds., *Politics in the American States* (New York: Little, Brown, 1965), pp. 3-4.

participation or non-participation. In some states feelings of political alienation, distrust, and inefficiency permeate large segments of the population, while in other states citizens' groups are hyperactive. In some states scandal and corruption in government are widespread, while in other states politics is so honest that it is dull. Leadership styles in state politics also vary considerably. For example, New York governors are likely to concern themselves with national and international issues as often as state issues, while politics in Arkansas is folksy and provincial.

The list of both obvious and subtle differences in politics among the fifty states is boundless. Yet only a limited number of political variables can be systematically investigated at any one time. Four sets of political system variables have been selected for inclusion in our model of policy outcomes. These are the division between Democratic and Republican control of state government, the level of interparty competition, the level of voter participation, and the degree of legislative malapportionment. These system variables have been chosen for their expected impact on policy outcomes, and all are hypothesized to be influential in shaping policy outcomes in the American states. In this chapter we will indicate how these variables are measured, describe the distribution of the states along these variables, and, more importantly, explore the relationships between the measures of economic development and these political system variables.

THE DIVISION OF TWO-PARTY CONTROL

In measuring the extent of Democratic or Republican domination of state politics we are concerned principally with control of the offices of governor and of the upper and lower houses of the state legislatures.[2] Fifty governors and 48 state legislatures are selected on partisan ballots (only the Nebraska and Minnesota legislatures are elected on a non-partisan ballot). Because we are concerned with public policy outcomes in the states, our measures of partisanship center on these *state* offices, and not upon a state's congressional delegation, its United States senators, or its vote in presidential elections. Other students of state politics have included a wider range of offices in their measures of party success, but our measures are directly related to the overall

[2] For a discussion of the problems involved in measuring political party strength, see Robert T. Golembiewski, "A Taxonomic Approach to State Political Party Strength," *Western Political Quarterly*, XI (1958), 494-513; Joseph P. Schlesinger, "A Two-Dimensional Scheme for Classifying States According to Degree of Inter-Party Competition," *American Political Science Review*, XLIX (1955), 1120-28; and Joseph P. Schlesinger, "The Structure of Competition for Office in the American States," *Behavioral Science*, V (1960), 197-209.

purpose of our study—the explanation of *state* policy outcomes. We wish to focus upon those institutions which most directly function to formulate state policy.

In measuring partisanship we are directly concerned with party fortunes in the ten years between 1954 and 1964. This time span has been chosen because party success during these years would most directly affect policy outcomes in the early 1960's. Since our policy outcome measures are variously dated between 1960 and 1964, it seemed appropriate that the measures of partisanship should focus on the time period immediately preceding and during the period for which policy outcomes were observed. A ten-year time span is generally shorter than the time span used by many other students of state parties, because it is usually felt that a short base period may reflect "bumps" in a party's long-term strength. But we are concerned with a party's ability to influence policy outcomes at a particular point in time—the early 1960's—and this ability is a function of the bumps in its strength at that time.

In measuring the success of a particular party, one may choose to focus upon either its *proportion of success* or its *duration of success*. The proportion of success refers to the percentage of the vote won by each party for statewide offices and the percentage of seats held by each party in the legislature. The duration of success refers to the length of time each party has controlled the statewide offices and the legislature. Since the present study deals with only a ten-year period, it is not really feasible to measure the duration of success; this is a reliable measure only over a long period of time. Our measures of party success are in terms of the proportion of success achieved by each party in the years immediately preceding our policy outcome measures.

Three specific measures of partisanship are employed throughout this study:

1. The percentage of the total seats in the lower chamber of the state legislature held by the Democratic party from 1954 to 1964.
2. The percentage of the total seats in the upper chamber of the state legislature held by the Democratic party from 1954 to 1964.
3. The average percentage of success for Democratic candidates in gubernatorial elections held between 1954 and 1964.

Note that these measures of partisan success in state legislative chambers and gubernatorial elections are expressed as *Democratic* percentages. The inverse of these measures expresses Republican success. Policies which positively correlate with these measures of Democratic control will negatively correlate with Republican control to the same degree. Therefore, we do not need separate measures of Republican control; we have only to reverse the direction of our findings with our democratic measures in order to know what Republican measures of control would produce.

In recent years the Democratic party has dominated American state politics. Table III-1 shows the number of upper and lower houses in state legislatures controlled by Democrats and Republicans from 1954 through 1964. The Democratic party has fared very well in state senates; only in the 1954-1956 session did it control fewer senates than the Republican party. The Democratic party's control of lower houses has been even more pronounced: Democrats never controlled fewer than 26 lower houses at any one time and have controlled as many as 39. The Democratic party has also had great success in controlling governors' chairs. In that same period Democrats have held between 27 and 35 of the 50 governorships.

TABLE III-1
Governorships and State Legislative Chambers
Controlled by Democrats and Republicans, 1954-1962

	Upper Houses			Lower Houses			Governorships	
	Dem.	Rep.	Tie	Dem.	Rep.	Tie	Dem.	Rep.
1962	28	20	0	27	20	1	33	17
1960	30	18	0	31	17	0	34	16
1958	31	17	0	28	9	1	35	15
1956	25	21	2	28	20	0	31	19
1954	20	25	1	26	20	0	27	21

From U. S. Bureau of the Census. *Statistical Abstract of the United States, 1963* (Washington: Government Printing Office, 1963), pp. 379-80.

Because of these Democratic successes, our partisanship measures are skewed toward Democratic control. Figure III-1 shows the distribution of states along all three measures of partisanship. The simple correlation coefficients for the relationships among these three measures are: Democratic control of lower and upper houses = .92; Democratic control of lower houses and governorships = .76; Democratic control of upper houses and governorships = .71. Southern states account for much of the Democratic party's measured strength in state politics, while midwestern and New England states account for much of the Republican party's state victories. The regional pattern will influence the findings obtained with these partisanship measures.

It is not really surprising that this regional pattern is reflected in the partisanship measures. The Republican party was founded in 1854 to resist the spread of slavery, which, at the time, was the principal labor source in the Southern region. The War between the States was the deepest political cleavage in American history; 17 states fought for the Union and 11 states for the Confederacy. A Republican President wrote the Emancipation Proclamation and led the Union to victory in war against the Confederacy. A Republican Congress presided over

FIGURE III-1

**The Distribution of States by Democratic
and Republican Control of State Government, 1954-1964**

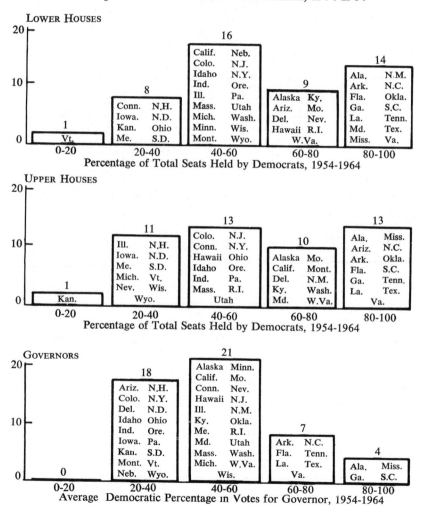

the military occupation of the Confederacy and wrote the Thirteenth, Fourteenth and Fifteenth Amendments. Most southerners were Democrats before the war, and the Democratic party of the South became the instrument for maintaining segregation as a substitute for slavery. Of course the Civil War ended a century ago, but these party identifications linger on in state politics as a product of the way in which individuals acquire party affiliations. Leading studies of voting behavior point out that most Americans acquire party preferences early in life from their parents, and they are usually reinforced by wife, friends, and work associates. A few individuals change party affiliation as a result of changes in their social or economic position in life or as a result of a move to a new community. But massive party switches take place only under such apocalyptic circumstances as the War between the States, or the Great Depression, or, perhaps, the Civil Rights Act of 1964.

Thus, the regional factor is still with us. In 1964 five states of the Old Confederacy voted for Republican presidential candidate Barry Goldwater, largely on the basis of his vote against the Civil Rights Act of 1964. Yet in these states over 90 per cent of both houses of the legislature are Democratic, and Democratic gubernatorial nominees receive little opposition in general elections. In Goldwater's home state of Arizona, Democrats controlled over 70 per cent of the seats in the legislature between 1954 and 1964. Florida voted for Republican presidential candidates in 1952, 1956, and 1960; but the Republicans never won the governorship or more than 7 per cent of the seats of either house of the Florida legislature in those years. It is important to remember, therefore, that our partisanship measures deal with state rather than national politics.

What is the relationship between economic development and Democratic and Republican party control of a state government? Table III-2 presents the simple correlation coefficients for the relationships between urbanization, industrialization, income and education, and all three measures of partisanship. Neither urbanization nor industrialization correlate significantly with Democratic or Republican party success. However, Democratic and Republican states differ significantly with respect to income and educational levels. The negative coefficients indicate that Democratic states tend to have lower income and educational levels than Republican states.

The relationship between higher income and educational levels and Republican success in state politics is one of those relationships which depends upon the inclusion of the 11 southern states in the 50 states. If we remove the 11 southern states, we find that there is really

TABLE III-2

**The Relationship between Economic
Development and Party Control of State Government**

| | Economic Development | | | |
	Urbanization	*Industrialization*	*Income*	*Education*
Democratic Control				
Lower houses	−.06	.11	−.46*	−.55*
Upper houses	−.15	.03	−.48*	−.51*
Governorships	−.22	−.03	−.56*	−.59*

Figures are simple correlation coefficients for 48 states; an asterisk indicates a statistically significant relationship.

no relationship in the 39 non-southern states between Democratic or Republican party success and urbanization, income, or education. There is, however, a significant relationship between Democratic success and industrialization in the non-southern states: an increase in industrialization (i.e., a decrease in farm employment) leads to an increase in Democratic success (i.e., a decline in the Republican proportion of legislative seats and gubernatorial votes).

These relationships between partisanship and income and education in the fifty states are important to keep in mind when exploring the effect of partisanship and policy outcomes. Republican states tend to be wealthier states with better educated adult populations, and Democratic states tend to be poorer states with less educated adult populations. This means that policy differences between Republican and Democratic states may not really be a product of party affiliation so much as a product of their differing wealth and education levels. To identify the independent effect of party affiliation on policy outcomes, it will be necessary to control for the effects of income and education.

Another way of showing the relationship between economic development and partisanship is simply to classify states according to their Republican or Democratic dominance in state politics, and to observe the socioeconomic attributes of states in various classifications of party affiliation. In Table III-3 the states are classified as Strong Republican, Moderate Republican, Divided, Moderate Democratic, and Strong Democratic. This classification is arrived at by combining roughly the three measures of partisanship. While Table III-3 is a somewhat cruder tool than correlation analysis, it does reveal some interesting relationships which are not shown in correlation coefficients.

Strong Democratic and Strong Republican states tend to resemble each other in socioeconomic composition more than they resemble the divided states. The income, education, urbanization, and industrialization levels of both Strong Republican and Strong Democratic states are

TABLE III-3

Economic Development and Party Affiliation in State Government

	Strong Republican	Moderate Republican	Divided	Moderate Democratic	Strong Democratic
Urbanization	47.8	64.0	72.9	64.8	54.5
Industrialization	83.0	90.2	93.8	93.2	89.0
Income	$4989	$5620	$6063	$5897	$4069
Education	11.0	11.1	11.0	11.0	9.2

Figures represent medians for the states in each category of party affiliation. *Strong Republican:* Kan., Idaho, Iowa, Me., N. D., Vt.; *Moderate Republican:* Ind., Ohio, N. H., N. Y., Neb., Pa., S. D., Utah, Wyo.; *Divided:* Ariz., Conn., Ill., Mich., Mont., Nev., N. J., Ore., R. I., Wis.; *Moderate Democratic:* Alaska, Calif., Colo., Del., Hawaii, Md., Mass., Minn., Mo., N. M., Wash., W. Va., Okla.; *Strong Democratic:* Ala., Ark., Miss., La., S. C., Tex., Ga., Va., Fla., N. C., Tenn., Ky.

lower than in the states under divided party control. Of course, since there are many more states with Strong Democratic party control than with Strong Republican party control, coefficients based upon all fifty states show a significant relationship between Democratic control and lower levels of income and education. However, Table III-3 suggests that economic development may be more closely related to party *competition* than to Democratic or Republican party success.

INTERPARTY COMPETITION

Interparty competition has received more attention from political scientists than any other system variable in state politics.[3] Many eminent political scientists from Woodrow Wilson to E. E. Schatt-schneider have contended that competitive, responsible parties are necessary for effective democratic control of government in modern society.[4] The ideal model of a party system is one in which competitive parties present alternative programs in election campaigns, and the party winning a majority of votes captures all the governmental power it needs to write its program into law. Moreover, in the ideal party system, the party's elected officials act cohesively so that the voters can hold the party collectively responsible for public affairs at the end of its term of office. The key to this normative political model is the existence of competitive parties which are roughly balanced in strength. In *The State Legislature,* Malcolm Jewell has extolled the

[3] For an excellent summary of research on state parties, see Austin Ranney, "Parties in State Politics," in Jacob and Vines, pp. 61-100.
[4] E. E. Schattschneider, *Party Government* (New York: Farrar and Rinehart, 1942); and Austin Ranney, *The Doctrine of Responsible Party Government* (Urbana: University of Illinois Press, 1954).

virtues of party competition: "If this book has a theme, it is that the best means of making the state legislature responsible to the voters is a viable two-party system."[5]

Other political scientists have been less enthusiastic about the competitive, responsible, two-party model.[6] But without weighing the merits of either position, we need to know the real extent of party competition in the fifty states and the forces which seem to bring about or inhibit this competition. Then we shall be in a better position to examine the effect of party competition on policy outcomes.

Our measures of party competition are very similar to our measures of Democratic and Republican party control of state government. The major difference is that our competition measures deal with the proportion of success achieved by the *majority* party in each state, regardless of whether the majority party is the Democratic or Republican party. Specifically our measures of interparty competition are:

1. One minus the percentage of seats in the lower house of the state legislature held by the majority party from 1954 to 1964.
2. One minus the percentage of seats in the upper house of the state legislature held by the majority party from 1954 to 1964.
3. One minus the average margin of victory in gubernatorial elections from 1954 to 1964.

Competition scores in lower houses range from 49 $(1-51$ per cent) in the Pennsylvania and Illinois lower houses (most competitive), to 0 $(1-100$ per cent) in the houses in Arkansas, Alabama, Louisiana, Mississippi, and South Carolina (least competitive). In state senates, competition scores range from 48 $(1-52$ per cent) in Connecticut and Michigan (most competitive), to 0 $(1-100$ per cent) in the senates in Alabama, Arkansas, Louisiana, Mississippi, South Carolina, and Texas (least competitive). Gubernatorial competition scores range from 48 $(1-52$ per cent) in Illinois, Iowa, Delaware, Wyoming, Massachusetts, Montana, New York, Michigan, New Jersey, Minnesota and Washington (most competitive), to under 10 $(1-90$ per cent) in Louisiana, Georgia, Mississippi, and South Carolina (least competitive).

The decision to use these particular measures of competition is based upon the same considerations that have influenced the choice of partisanship measures. Because we are concerned with state policy outcomes, our party competition measures center on competition for

[5](New York: Random House, 1962), p.6.
[6] Pendleton Herring, *The Politics of Democracy* (New York: Rinehart, 1940); and Herbert Agar, *The Price of Union* (Boston: Houghton Mifflin, 1959).

control of those institutions whose function it is to make public policy for the state—the governorship and the upper and lower chambers of the state legislature. The time span selected for measuring party competition is the decade immediately preceding the years selected for measuring policy outcomes. Competition is measured by the propor-

FIGURE III-2

**Distribution of States by Level of Interparty
Competition, 1954-1964**

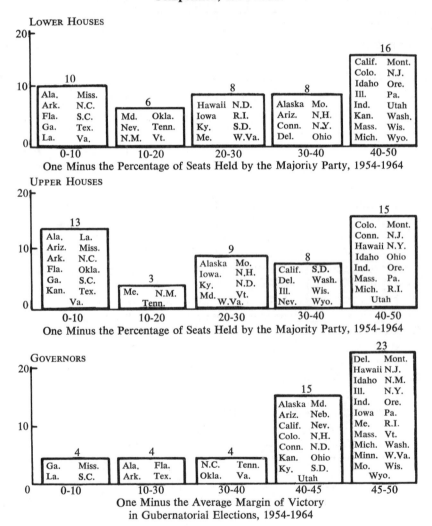

LOWER HOUSES

	10			8	8	16

16
Calif.	Mont.
Colo.	N.J.
Idaho	Ore.
Ill.	Pa.
Ind.	Utah
Kan.	Wash.
Mass.	Wis.
Mich.	Wyo.

10
Ala.	Miss.
Ark.	N.C.
Fla.	S.C.
Ga.	Tex.
La.	Va.

6
Md.	Okla.
Nev.	Tenn.
N.M.	Vt.

8
Hawaii	N.D.
Iowa	R.I.
Ky.	S.D.
Me.	W.Va.

8
Alaska	Mo.
Ariz.	N.H.
Conn.	N.Y.
Del.	Ohio

0-10   10-20   20-30   30-40   40-50

One Minus the Percentage of Seats Held by the Majority Party, 1954-1964

UPPER HOUSES

13
Ala.	La.
Ariz.	Miss.
Ark.	N.C.
Fla.	Okla.
Ga.	S.C.
Kan.	Tex.
Va.	

3
| Me. | N.M. |
| Tenn. | |

9
Alaska	Mo.
Iowa.	N.H.
Ky.	N.D.
Md.	Vt.
W.Va.	

8
Calif.	S.D.
Del.	Wash.
Ill.	Wis.
Nev.	Wyo.

15
Colo.	Mont.
Conn.	N.J.
Hawaii	N.Y.
Idaho	Ohio
Ind.	Ore.
Mass.	Pa.
Mich.	R.I.
Utah	

0-10   10-20   20-30   30-40   40-50

One Minus the Percentage of Seats Held by the Majority Party, 1954-1964

GOVERNORS

4
| Ga. | Miss. |
| La. | S.C. |

4
| Ala. | Fla. |
| Ark. | Tex. |

4
| N.C. | Tenn. |
| Okla. | Va. |

15
Alaska	Md.
Ariz.	Neb.
Calif.	Nev.
Colo.	N.H.
Conn.	N.D.
Kan.	Ohio
Ky.	S.D.
Utah	

23
Del.	Mont.
Hawaii	N.J.
Idaho	N.M.
Ill.	N.Y.
Ind.	Ore.
Iowa	Pa.
Me.	R.I.
Mass.	Vt.
Mich.	Wash.
Minn.	W.Va.
Mo.	Wis.
Wyo.	

0-10   10-30   30-40   40-45   45-50

One Minus the Average Margin of Victory
in Gubernatorial Elections, 1954-1964

tion of success posted by the majority party, rather than the number of times offices change party hands.

Figure III-2 shows the distribution of states by level of interparty competition in both houses of the legislature and in gubernatorial elections. The states with the least amount of competition are the one-party Democratic states of the South. Even the most Republican states in the nation do not approach the degree of one-partyism which exists in these southern states. Of course, the strong Republican states in New England and the Midwest — Maine, Iowa, Vermont, New Hampshire, North and South Dakota — are much less competitive than in the ideal two-party system. In only ten states are the parties reasonably balanced in *both* houses of the legislature, that is, with neither party controlling more than 60 per cent of the seats. In short, the southern states are not the only states with something less than a highly competitive party system.

Gubernatorial politics appear to be somewhat more competitive than legislative politics. In 38 states the average margin of victory in gubernatorial elections is less than 60 per cent, and in 23 states it is less than 55 per cent.

The relationship between economic development and party competition in the states has already been established in the literature on American state politics. Golembiewski, in a study of the relationships between a variety of sociological factors and state party systems, has reported statistically significant associations between urbanism, income, and industrialization, and classifications of party competition among the fifty states.[7] Ranney and Kendall, Key, and Schlesinger have also implied that one or more economic development measures correlate closely with party competition in the American states.[8] This linkage is reconfirmed in the measures used in the present study.

Table III-4 shows that party competition is significantly associated with income and education levels in the states. Parties are more evenly balanced in the legislatures of the wealthier states and the states with better educated adult populations; there is less competition in the legislatures of the poorer states and the states with less educated adult populations. This relationship between party competition and wealth and education is even more pronounced in gubernatorial elections. There is also a slight relationship between party competition and urbanization.

[7] See Golembiewski.
[8] Austin Ranney and Willmoore Kendall, "The American Party System," *American Political Science Review*, XLVIII (1954), 477-85; V. O. Key, Jr., *American State Politics* (New York: Knopf, 1956), p. 99; and Schlesinger, "Structure of Competition."

TABLE III-4

The Relationship between Economic Development and Party Competition

| | *Economic Development* | | | |
	Urbanization	*Industrialization*	*Income*	*Education*
Party Competition				
Lower houses	.26	.00	.52*	.57*
Upper houses	.30*	.03	.51*	.50*
Governorships	.29	.18	.66*	.62*

Figures are simple correlation coefficients for 48 states; an asterisk indicates a statistically significant relationship.

Party competition is more closely associated with income and education than our measures of Democratic party success. The coefficients for the relationship between economic development and party competition (Table III-4) are higher than those for the relationship between economic development and partisanship (Table III-2). This suggests that socioeconomic development does not consistently favor one party or the other. Rather, high levels of income and education tend to foster party competition. Both one-party Republican and one-party Democratic states tend to be states with populations possessing lower income and educational attributes.

Of course economic development does not explain all of the variation among states in levels of party competition. Income explains only 25 to 40 per cent of the variations in party competition, and all four measures of economic development combined can explain only about 50 per cent of the total variation among the states in competition levels. One-party Democratic domination in the southern states is not only a product of economic underdevelopment; it has its historical and racial roots as well. Midwestern states with many of the same economic characteristics as the southern states have somewhat more party competition than the southern states. Discounting the effects of economic development, southern states are still less competitive than non-southern states. If the southern states are excluded from the correlations, relationships between economic development and party competition can still be observed, but the coefficients are noticeably reduced. This means that the southern states will have an important influence on the findings obtained with the measures of party competition.

Since competitive states stand higher on measures of wealth and education than non-competitive states, policy differences between competitive and non-competitive states may not necessarily be a product of party competition itself. Policy differences between competitive and non-competitive states may really be a product of their differing levels of wealth and education rather than a direct product of party competition. It will be necessary to control for the effects of income and education in order to observe the *independent* effect of party competition on policy outcomes.

POLITICAL PARTICIPATION

Political participation may assume a variety of forms.[9] Individuals may participate in the political system by running for or winning election to public office; by participating in marches, demonstrations, or sit-ins; by making financial contributions to political candidates or causes; by attending political meetings, speeches, or rallies; by writing letters to public officials; by belonging to organizations which support or oppose particular candidates or legislative proposals; by wearing a button or putting a political sticker on a car; by attempting to influence friends regarding political candidates or issues; by voting; and by following an issue or campaign in the mass media. This listing probably constitutes a hierarchy of forms of participation; those forms most often engaged in are listed last, while those least often engaged in are listed first. Activities at the top of the hierarchy involve greater expenditures of time and energy and require greater personal commitment than those activities at the bottom. Less than 1 per cent of the American adult population runs for public office or engages in public demonstrations. Only about 5 to 7 per cent are active in parties and campaigns, while about 10 per cent make financial contributions. Larger proportions participate indirectly through clubs and discussion with their friends. About 65 per cent of the American people will vote in a hard-fought presidential campaign. Fully one-third of the population are politically apathetic and passive; they do not vote and they are largely unaware of the political life of the nation. All of these proportions apply to presidential elections in the United States. In state elections the ranks of participants diminish and the ranks of the apathetics grow.

It is impossible to obtain state-by-state figures on the proportions of persons who engage in each of the political activities mentioned above. The only reliable measures of political participation in each of the fifty states are voter turnout figures. These voter participation

[9] This discussion of political participation in the states relies upon Lester W. Milbrath, *Political Participation* (Chicago: Rand McNally, 1965); and his "Political Participation in the States," in Jacob and Vines, pp. 25-60.

figures are very important in comparative analysis. Voter participation itself is highly valued in American political theory and it is probably a good indicator of other forms of political participation.

Three measures of voter participation are employed in this volume:

1. The average percentage of eligible voters casting votes in gubernatorial elections between 1954 and 1964.
2. The percentage of eligible voters casting votes in the 1958 Congressional elections.
3. The percentage of eligible voters casting votes in the 1962 Congressional elections.

Only the first of these measures deals directly with state politics. Ideally we would also want to employ the average percentage of eligible voters casting votes for the upper and lower chambers of the state legislatures. Unfortunately, however, votes for state legislators are not centrally collected in the United States, and substitution has been unavoidable. It has been felt that off-year congressional election turnouts are better substitutes than turnouts in elections for the Presidency or the United States Senate. The use of congressional election turnouts in a study of state politics is not indefensible in view of the consistency of state-by-state voter turnout figures in all types of elections. If the states are ranked by voter turnout for different years and for different types of elections, the similarities in the rankings for the several years and elections is striking. Lester Milbrath reports that the *lowest* rank-order correlation coefficient in a matrix of percentages on voter turnout in presidential elections between 1940 and 1960 and gubernatorial and senatorial elections between 1952 and 1960 is strikingly high (.84). He concludes that voting turnout in the states is a patterned or habitual behavior.

It is often argued that since the Democratic party dominates state elections in the South, primary elections there are more vigorously fought than general elections. This is true, and turnout figures in the one-party southern states are slightly higher in primary elections than in general elections. However, the substitution of primary turnout figures for the southern states makes almost no change in the state-by-state rankings.[10] Southern states continue to rank at the bottom of the list.

The average participation rate in gubernatorial elections from 1954 to 1964 ranged from a low of 4.2 per cent in Mississippi to a high of 79.1 per cent in West Virginia. The distribution of states along the measures of voter participation are shown in Figure III-3. The simple

[10]Milbrath, "Political Participation in the States," p. 42.

correlation coefficients among these three turnout measures are: governors, 1954-1964, and congressional, 1958: .94; governors, 1954-1964, and congressional, 1962: .91; and congressional, 1958, with congressional, 1962: .94.

What is the effect of economic development on voter participation? It has been suggested that persons living in cities are more likely to participate in politics than persons living in the country. However,

FIGURE III-3

Distribution of States by Level of Voter Participation

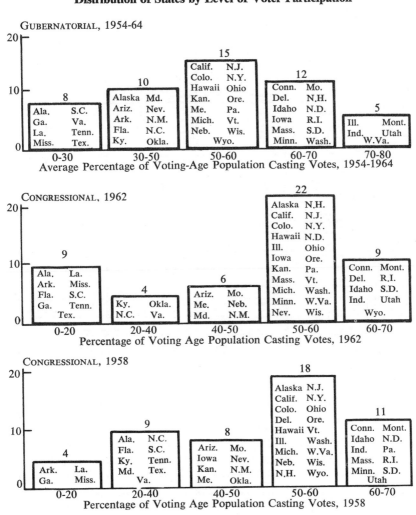

among the fifty states there is no discernible relationship between urbanization and voter turnout. Nor does the degree of industrialization, as measured by non-agricultural employment, appear to influence voter participation. The coefficients in Table III-5 indicate that there is no significant relationship between voter participation and urbanization or industrialization. However, voter participation is significantly related to income and educational levels in the fifty states. Participation is notably higher in states with higher median family incomes and well educated adult populations. If the southern states are removed, however, these relationships fall below the accepted levels of significance.

TABLE III-5
The Relationship between Economic Development and Voter Participation

| | Economic Development | | | |
	Urbanization	Industrialization	Income	Education
Voter Participation				
Gubernatorial, 1954-1964	.18	.05	.52*	.49*
Congressional, 1958	.21	.08	.61*	.59*
Congressional, 1962	.26	.10	.66*	.63*

Figures are simple correlation coefficients for the fifty states; an asterisk indicates a statistically significant relationship.

Certainly income and education do not themselves fully explain participation rates among the states. (At best these input variables explain about 25 per cent of the variation among the states in turnout percentages.) From other studies we know that voter participation rates are also affected by the exclusion of Negroes through social, political, and economic barriers; of lower educated groups through literacy tests and complicated registration procedures; of highly mobile people through residence requirements; and of lower income groups through poll taxes. Voter participation rates among the states are also affected by racial composition; Negroes vote less often than whites even when legal barriers are eliminated. Turnout figures are also affected by legal conventions in the states which define registration procedures, voting hours, absentee ballot rules, and so on. Voter participation rates can also be affected by the degree of interparty competition; this relationship is described in a later section of this chapter. Finally, voter behavior in some states defies systematic explanation. West Virginia has experienced considerable poverty in recent years; its adult educational level is one of the lowest in the nation; and its registration and voting laws are similar to those of most states. Yet West Virginia voters insist upon going to the polls in large numbers: perhaps voting in Appalachia is one form of recreation in an otherwise drab environment.

The relationships between participation and income and education are particularly important in the study of policy outcomes. Since states with high voter turnouts have wealthier and better educated populations than states with low voter turnouts, differences between the policy choices of states with high and with low voter turnouts cannot be automatically attributed to the effects of voter participation. It may be that differences in the policies of states with high and low voter turnouts are a product of wealth or education rather than voter turnout itself. In order to identify the independent effect of voter participation in policy outcomes, it will be necessary to control for the effects of income and education.

MALAPPORTIONMENT

Prior to *Baker* v. *Carr* in 1962,[11] American state legislatures were not apportioned equally on a population basis. By almost any standard, malapportionment was severe in the vast majority of legislative chambers. The federal courts have defined malapportionment as variation in the numbers of people in legislative districts which receive the same number of representatives. In the words of the Supreme Court: "... as nearly as practicable, one man's vote is to be worth as much as another's."[12] Operationally the courts have been computing the average population of single-member legislative districts on the basis of the last official decennial census, and insisting that actual districts should not deviate more than 15 (or 25) per cent from the average district in the numbers of persons represented by one legislator. This means, in effect, that the ratio of the largest single-member district to the smallest should not exceed 1.35 (or 1.66) to 1.00. By this standard every state legislative chamber in the nation in 1960 was malapportioned, as were both houses of the United States Congress.[13] The lowest ratio of largest-to-smallest district was 2.2 to 1 in the Hawaiian house of representatives. Forty-seven of the 99 legislative chambers in the nation (Nebraska has a unicameral legislature) had ratios in excess of

[11] *Baker* v. *Carr*, 369 U.S. 189 (1962).
[12] *Westberry* v. *Sanders*, 84 S. Ct. 526 (1964).
[13] Paul T. David and Ralph Eisenberg, *Devaluation of the Urban and Suburban Vote* (Charlottesville: Bureau of Public Administration, University of Virginia, 1961).

10 to 1, i.e., the largest district was ten times larger than the smallest. In nine chambers this ratio exceeded 100 to 1.

Malapportionment, or inequality of representation, can be objected to as a matter of principle, and this type of objection has been sustained by the federal courts. But we are more concerned with the effect of this system characteristic on policy outcomes. It is clear that malapportionment was an important characteristic of state political systems in the years preceding our measures of policy outcomes. Since malapportionment was more severe in some states than in others, it has been possible to explore the effects of malapportionment on policy outcomes.

Several measures of the malapportionment of state legislatures are available. Unfortunately the measure most frequently employed in court litigation is not one of the better measures. By focusing on the extent to which any actual district deviates from the state's average district, the courts emphasize extreme districts which may or may not be typical of most other districts in an apportionment plan.

Perhaps a better measure of malapportionment is the theoretical minimum percentage of a state's population that can elect a majority in each house.[14] Legislative districts for each house are placed in rank order from smallest population per member to largest, and a population count is made, beginning at the smallest-population end of the scale and proceeding until it includes all the legislative districts necessary to elect a majority of members of the house in question. The minimum number of people which can elect a majority in that house is then expressed as a percentage of the state's total population. The two minimum percentages of the population which can elect a majority in each chamber can be added to provide an index of malapportionment for the legislature as a whole. Percentages are additive in this case, since the real denominator is the power of each house to influence policy and this is assumed to be equal. In 1960 this index ranged from a low of 37 for Nevada with the least representative legislature to a high of 96 for Oregon with the most representative legislature. Hereafter this measure is referred to as the *index of representativeness*.

The index of representativeness measures malapportionment in the technical sense. But malapportionment becomes relevant in the study of policy outcomes only when it operates to discriminate against important political interests in a state. The theoretical minimum percentage of a state's population which can elect a majority of the legislature may not be an interest group in state politics; it is a more or

[14] See Manning J. Dauer and Robert G. Kelsay, "Unrepresentative States," *National Municipal Review*, XLIV (1955), 551-75.

less artificial grouping of persons based upon a method or measurement. It seems important to devise an apportionment measure which reflects discrimination against important political interests.

To date, research in malapportionment has centered on its impact on the conflict between rural and urban interests. In order to determine the degree of discrimination against urban areas, David and Eisenberg have undertaken to compute the *value* of a vote cast in the largest urban counties of each state.[15] Actual constituencies are then compared to these average constituencies: the value of a vote is represented by the ratio of an actual constituency to the average constituency in the state. For example, in a district with twice the population of the state's average district, the value of a vote would be .50. The value of a vote in the largest category of counties (by population size) in each state is computed for each house and then the measures for both houses are averaged to provide an *index of urban representation* for each legislature. In 1960 this index ranged from a low of .12 in Georgia, where the largest counties were most discriminated against in apportionment, to a high of 1.05 in Louisiana, where the largest counties were granted the greatest legislative representation.

Table III-6 shows national averages of the value of a vote in four categories of counties by population. Clearly the more populous counties in the nation are underrepresented in American state legislatures. And, prior to 1962, it did not seem that the situation was improving with time.

TABLE III-6
Relative Values of a Vote for State Legislators,
National Averages for Counties by Size, 1910-1960

Categories of Counties by Population Size	1910	1930	1950	1960
Under 25,000	1.13	1.31	1.41	1.71
25,000 – 99,999	1.03	1.09	1.14	1.23
100,000 – 499,999	.91	.84	.83	.81
500,000 and over	.81	.74	.78	.76

From Paul T. David and Ralph Eisenberg, *Devaluation of the Urban and Suburban Vote* (Charlottesville: Bureau of Public Administration, University of Virginia, 1961), p. 8.

A third measure of malapportionment is the technically sophisticated *apportionment score* proposed by Glendon Schubert and Charles Press.[16] The apportionment score combines inverted coeffi-

---

[15] See David and Eisenberg.
[16] Glendon Schubert and Charles Press, "Measuring Malapportionment," *American Political Science Review,* LVIII (1964), 302-27, and corrections, 968-70.

cients of variation for each state (divide the population of the average district by the standard deviation of all districts and subtract the dividend from 1.0) with statistical measures of skewness and kurtosis in the distribution of districts by size of population. The result is an index which measures this combination of variance, skewness, and kurtosis in the populations of legislative districts in each state. In 1962, according to this scale, Massachusetts, with the highest apportionment score, was technically the best apportioned legislature in the nation, and Indiana, with the lowest score, was the worst.

All three of these measures — the index of representativeness, the index of urban underrepresentation, and the apportionment score — are used in this study. Each measure depicts a slightly different aspect of malapportionment; each results in a slightly different ranking of states. The simple correlation coefficients between these three measures are as follows: index of representativeness and index of urban underrepresentation: .45; index of representativeness and apportionment score: .50; index of urban underrepresentation and apportionment score: .70. The first measure focuses on the theoretical minimum proportion of a state's population that can control the legislature, the second measure focuses on urban underrepresentation, and the third measure focuses on the degree to which a state's apportionment scheme approaches the statistical concept of normality. In the chapters to follow we shall evaluate the political relevance of each of these measures.

How does malapportionment come about? The task of districting a state generally falls upon the legislature itself. One explanation attributes urban underrepresentation to our rural heritage: districts drawn up when our nation was overwhelmingly rural remain because of the rural legislator's distrust of the growing city populations. Entrenched rural and small-town interests are reluctant to surrender control to city populations with their large blocks of ethnic, laboring, Catholic, and Negro voters. Rural interests are often allied with those urban interests who share this view of the urban electorate. Often revealingly frank defenses of rural overrepresentation are made on the grounds that rural and small-town people are "better" or "safer" citizens than big-city voters. In addition, there is always a natural reluctance for legislative bodies to perform major surgery on themselves; to expect a legislature to redistrict itself is to expect legislators to threaten their own incumbency. Therefore, many state legislatures simply refuse to reapportion or carry out only token reapportionment, despite increasing urbanization in their states. In 1961 Tennessee and Alabama had not reapportioned their legislatures in 60 years. In the last few decades only half of the states have reapportioned their legislatures during the ten years following a census.

In many cases, however, urban underrepresentation is a product of political compromises made in constitutional conventions, compromises similar to those made in the Convention of 1787 in which the United States House of Representatives was made representative of population, while the Senate was made representative of the states, regardless of their populations. Many state constitutions base representation, particularly in the upper chamber, upon some unit of govern-

FIGURE III-4

Distribution of States by Measures of Malapportionment

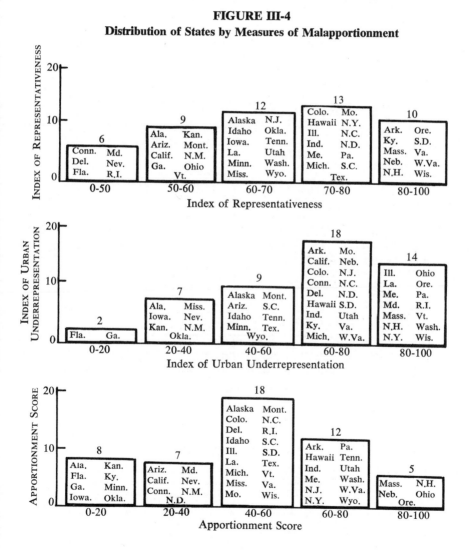

ment within the state, usually the county, rather than population. Two recent state apportionments show that these constitutional provisions are not necessarily a hangover from our rural heritage but represent political compromises of a recent vintage. In 1955 Cook County, with over half the population of Illinois, was given only 24 of that state's 58 senators. The new constitution of Hawaii gives Oahu only 40 per cent of the senators, although the island contains 80 percent of the state's population.

Is it possible to explain malapportionment in terms of socioeconomic characteristics? Are the rural agricultural states more likely to underrepresent urban areas than the urban industrial states? Table III-7 shows some slight relationships between measures of economic development and the index of urban underrepresentation. Urban, industrial, high-income states are less likely to discriminate against their urban areas than rural, low-income agricultural states. This

TABLE III-7

**The Relationship between Economic Development
and Malapportionment of State Legislatures**

| | | Economic Development | | |
	Urbanization	Industrialization	Income	Education
Index of representativeness	−.24	−.19	−.21	−.19
Index of urban underrepresentation	.27	.33*	.36*	−.06
Apportionment score	.01	.14	.14	.13

Figures are simple correlation coefficients for the fifty states; an asterisk indicates a statistically significant relationship.

relationship holds in the non-southern states as well as in all the fifty states. However, there is *no* relationship between economic development and malapportionment in the technical sense. There are no significant correlations between the index of representativeness or the apportionment score and any of the socioeconomic measures. The legislatures of rural farm states are just as likely to be unrepresentative in the technical sense as the legislatures of urban industrial states. The southern states are no more malapportioned than the non-southern states.

In short, findings obtained with the index of urban underrepresentation may be affected by intervening socioeconomic variables, but findings obtained with the index of representativeness and apportionment score are probably free from the effects of these intervening variables. In using the index of representativeness and apportionment score there is no fear that policy differences between malapportioned and well apportioned states are a product of socioeconomic levels. However, inasmuch as states which underrepresent urban areas tend to be the rural agricultural states, it may be that policy differences between states designated as malapportioned or well apportioned on the index of urban underrepresentation are really a product of differing levels of economic development and not malapportionment per se. In attempting to sort out the *independent* effect of urban underrepresentation it will be necessary to control for the effects of economic development.

PARTY COMPETITION AND POLITICAL PARTICIPATION

In analyzing the effect of system characteristics on policy outcomes, it is also important to understand the linkages among system characteristics. With four sets of system characteristics to be considered, there are six sets of relationships which could be described: competition and participation, competition and partisanship, competition and malapportionment, participation and partisanship, participation and malapportionment, and partisanship and malapportionment.

One of the more interesting of these relationships is that which occurs between party competition and voter participation. Lester Milbrath has argued that the more vigorous the competition between parties, the greater the interest of citizens in elections, and the larger the voter turnout. He reasons that:

When parties and candidates compete vigorously, they make news and are given a large play via the mass media. Thus a setting of competitive politics tends to have a greater amount of political stimuli available in the environment than does a setting with weak competition. Persons living in an environment containing a high level of politically relevant stimuli are a bit more likely to become active in politics than those living where there are relatively few political stimuli. Political interest tends to rise in an environment with competitive parties, not only because more stimuli are available for consumption, but also because interest rises with increasing conflict. People tend to follow a close contest with more interest. Furthermore in a close contest they are more likely to perceive that their votes count, and, thus, they are more likely to cast them. An additional factor is that, when parties are fighting in a close contest, their workers tend to spend more time and energy campaigning and getting out the vote.[17]

[17] Milbrath, "Political Participation in the States," p. 50. Copyright ©, 1965, by Little, Brown and Company and reprinted by permission of the publisher, Little, Brown and Company.

Of course, Milbrath recognizes that other factors also influence participation. We have already seen that income and education positively correlate with voter turnout in the fifty states. A variety of studies of individual behavior suggest that the correlations between participation and these socioeconomic variables also obtain at the individual level.[18] Socioeconomic status determines an individual's life situation, including his personality, beliefs, and attitudes, and through these factors it affects his political participation.

Since socioeconomic inputs have been shown to affect both party competition and voter participation, it becomes necessary to control for the effects of these input variables when attempting to assess the *independent* effect of party competition on voter turnout. Only if voter participation levels are higher in the competitive states than in the noncompetitive states and these differences in participation levels can be attributed to competition rather than to socioeconomic variables are we justified in inferring that party competition increases voter turnout.

The simple coefficients in Table III-8, which do not control for economic development, show that party competition and political participation are closely related in state politics. States with high levels

TABLE III-8

**The Relationship between Party Competition and Political Participation,
Controlling for the Effect of Economic Development**

| | Political Participation | | | | | |
| | *Gubernatorial* | | *1962 Congressional* | | *1958 Congressional* | |
	Simple	*Partial*	*Simple*	*Partial*	*Simple*	*Partial*
Party Competition						
Lower houses	.67*	.47*	.72*	.51*	.72*	.48*
Upper houses	.64*	.45*	.67*	.45*	.72*	.52*
Governorships	.85*	.75*	.87*	.75*	.84*	.66*

Figures are simple and partial correlation coefficients; partial coefficients control for the effect of urbanization, industrialization, income, and education; an asterisk indicates a statistically significant relationship.

of competition turn out more voters than states with low levels of competition. This is true outside of the South as well as within the South.

When economic development is controlled, the relationship between party competition and voter turnout continues to be significant

[18] Angus Campbell, *et al., The American Voter* (New York: Wiley, 1960); and Robert E. Lane, *Political Life* (New York: Free Press, 1959).

although not as close. The partial coefficients, which control for the effects of urbanization, industrialization, income, and education, are noticeably lower than the simple coefficients. This means that controlling for economic development weakens the relationship between competition and partisanship, but there is still a significant association between these two system variables. This evidence tends to substantiate the view that party competition does have an independent effect on voter participation. An increase in party competition results in an increase in voter turnout, even when socioeconomic factors are controlled.

OTHER RELATIONSHIPS AMONG SYSTEM CHARACTERISTICS

Table III-9 is a matrix of simple coefficients showing the relationships among all four sets of system characteristics — party competition, partisanship, voter participation, and malapportionment. Three of the four system characteristics are closely interrelated. A lack of party competition, low voter participation, and Democratic party success seem to constitute a syndrome. Malapportionment, at least in its technical sense, is not part of this syndrome; it appears to be a separate system variable.

The absence of party competition in the states is associated with success of the Democratic party, because the extreme one-party systems in the southern states are Democratic, and heavily Democratic states outnumber heavily Republican states. Outside of the South the competition measures are not related to the partisanship measures.

This association between one-partyism and Democratic success is not merely a product of economic development. Even when economic development is controlled, a lack of party competition remains significantly related to Democratic success. This indicates that one-partyism in the South is *not only* a product of the lower socioeconomic development levels in the southern states. The complete collapse of the Republican party in the southern states after the Civil War was not accompanied by an equivalent collapse of the Democratic party in the non-southern states. Non-southern states at the same economic levels as southern states still have more party competition than the southern states. The Civil War and its aftermath, the racial composition of southern states, and the determination of the South to keep its Negro population from exercising political power, all contribute independently to one-partyism in the South.

Malapportionment is not so closely tied to this syndrome of one-

TABLE III-9

Relationships among System Variables

	Party Competition			Democratic Control			Voter Participation		
	Lower Houses	Upper Houses	Governors	Lower Houses	Upper Houses	Governors	Governors	1958 Cong.	1962 Cong.
Party Competition									
Lower houses	1.00								
Upper houses	.93	1.00							
Governors	.66	.62	1.00						
Democratic Control									
Lower houses	−.64	−.59	−.63	1.00					
Upper houses	−.57	−.56	−.58	.92	1.00				
Governors	−.71	−.68	−.91	.76	.71	1.00			
Voter Participation									
Governors	.67	.64	.84	−.74	−.70	−.80	1.00		
1958 congressional	.72	.67	.87	−.83	−.78	−.87	.94	1.00	
1962 congressional	.72	.72	.84	−.79	−.75	−.81	.91	.94	1.00
Malapportionment									
Representativeness	.18	.13	.08	.13	.14	.12	.12	.07	.06
Urban underrepresentation	.32	.36	.40	.39	.37	.46	.42	.43	.39
Apportionment score	.24	.26	.27	.30	.29	.30	.30	.29	.31

Figures are simple correlation coefficients for the fifty states.

partyism, low participation, and Democratic politics. Malapportionment in its technical aspects appears unrelated to these other system characteristics. Coefficients obtained with the index of representativeness and apportionment score indicate that competitive Republican states with high rates of participation are just as likely to malapportion their legislatures as one-party, low-participation, Democratic states. On the other hand, significant relationships can be observed between urban discrimination and these system characteristics. There is a noticeable tendency for one-party, low-participation, Democratic states to underrepresent urban voters in apportionment. Moreover this relationship is not merely a product of the effects of socioeconomic variables. Even when the socioeconomic variables are controlled, urban underrepresentation remains significantly related to party competition, voter participation, and partisanship.

CHAPTER IV

Educational Policy

DiRECTIONS IN EDUCATIONAL POLICY

NEXT TO NATIONAL DEFENSE, education is the nation's largest public undertaking. Over $20 billion a year is spent on public schools in the United States. While this is less than Americans spend on alcohol and tobacco, it is more than is spent for highways, welfare, police and fire protection, agricultural subsidies, public health, space research, or any other governmental function outside of the national military establishment. The primary responsibility for public education rests with the fifty state governments and their subdivisions. It is the largest and most costly of state functions.

It was in 1647 that the Massachusetts colonial legislature first required its towns to provide for the education of children out of public funds, and by 1850 every state except Arkansas authorized the spending of tax monies for public schools. The rugged individualists of earlier eras thought it outrageous that one man should be taxed to pay for the education of another man's child. They were joined in their opposition to public education by those aristocrats who were opposed to arming the common man with the power that knowledge gives. But the logic of democracy led inevitably to public education. The earliest democrats believed that the safest repository of the ultimate powers of society was in the people themselves. If the people made mistakes, the remedy was not to remove power from their hands but to help them in forming their judgment through education. Congress passed the Northwest Ordinance in 1787, offering land grants for public schools in the new territories and giving succeeding generations words to be forever etched on grammar school cornerstones: "Religion, morality and knowledge being necessary to good government and the happiness of mankind, schools and the means for education shall ever be encouraged." When American democracy adopted universal manhood suffrage, it affected every aspect of American life, and particularly education. If the common man was to be granted the right of suffrage, he had to be educated to his task. This meant that public education had to be universal, free, and compulsory. Compulsory education began in Massachusetts in 1852 and was eventually adopted by Mississippi in 1918.

Yet as late as 1900 public education was a crude experience by today's standards and one which not every child was privileged to enjoy. Public school expenditures for the entire nation were less than $220 million, a figure exceeded today in many individual school districts. Less than $17 per year was spent on each child who attended school. Moreover, a smaller proportion of the nation's income was spent for education in 1900 than is currently being spent. America spent 1.5 per cent of its smaller national income on education then, compared to over 3.5 per cent of its vastly expanded income today. Teachers salaries were incredibly low. The average teacher's salary in 1900 was $325 per year. This was bad even by labor standards in 1900: the average annual earnings of industrial workers in that year were about $490. Teacher-pupil ratios in 1900 were large: there was, on the average, one teacher for every 37 pupils. Perhaps even more serious was the fact that most schools were ungraded. Over 80 per cent of the schools of the nation were one-room schools which contained children of all ages and levels of accomplishment and whose teachers taught eight grades at once. Many teachers had no professional training before entering the classroom. There was a vast proliferation of local school districts throughout the nation. An estimated 200,000 individual school districts rendered state control over educational standards an impossible task. Great variations existed in the quality of the public schools from one town to the next, depending on the availability of local taxable property and the willingness of local board members to spend money on schools. All but about 17 per cent of the costs of public education was borne by local communities. State governments shunted the responsibility for education onto their subdivisions, and the federal government did little for public education prior to World War I.

It is difficult to believe in the light of public education today that these conditions prevailed a scant 60 years ago. Recent decades have

TABLE IV-1
Trends in Public School Education, 1900-1964

	1900	1910	1920	1930	1940	1950	1960	1964
Public school enrollment	15,503	17,814	21,578	25,678	25,434	25,111	36,087	40,900
Enrollment as a percentage of children 5-17	71.9	74.2	78.3	81.7	84.4	83.2	82.2	84.0
Total instructional staff	423	523	678	880	912	962	1,464	1,778
Public school expenditures (in millions of dollars)	$215	$426	$1,036	$2,317	$2,344	$5,838	$15,613	$21,202
Expenditures per pupil	$17	$28	$53	$87	$88	$209	$375	$455
Expenditures as a percentage of personal income	1.5	1.6	1.4	3.0	3.0	2.6	3.8	4.3
State percentage of school revenues	17.4	14.9	16.5	16.9	30.3	39.8	39.1	40.1
Federal percentage of school revenues	0	0	0.3	0.4	1.8	2.9	4.4	3.5
Average teachers' salaries per year	$325	$485	$871	$1,420	$1,441	$3,010	$5,174	$6,164
Male teachers as a percentage of total	29.9	21.1	14.0	22.8	21.6	29.7	35.9	30.5
Pupil-teacher ratio	36.7	34.1	31.8	29.2	27.9	26.1	24.6	23.0
Graduation rate	8.8	16.8	29.0	50.8	50.8	59.0	65.1	70.7
Number of school districts	n.a.	n.a.	n.a.	127	117	84	41	32
One-room schools as a percentage of total	n.a.	n.a.	n.a.	62.6	56.2	46.5	22.0	12.9

Unless otherwise specified, figures are expressed in thousands. The principal sources for this table are: U. S. Office of Education, *Digest of Educational Statistics, 1964* (Washington: Government Printing Office, 1964); Department of Health, Education and Welfare, *Health, Education and Welfare Trends 1964* (Washington: Government Printing Office, 1964); and U. S. Bureau of the Census, *Historical Statistics of the United States, Colonial Times to 1957* (Washington: Government Printing Office, 1960).

witnessed profound changes in the role of public education in American society. Henry Steele Commager has listed four historic tasks of American education:

Democracy could not work without an enlightened electorate. The States and sections could not achieve unity without a sentiment of nationalism. The Nation could not absorb tens of millions of immigrants from all parts of the globe without rapid and effective Americanization. Economic and social distinctions and privileges, severe enough to corrode democracy itself, had to be overcome. To the schools went the momentous responsibility of inculcating democracy, nationalism, assimilation, and equalitarianism.[1]

Today the tasks of education are all that and more. Technological advances have changed the relationship between education and the economy. Many economists have come to classify education as a capital goods expenditure.[2] The National Education Association presses this point with legislators:

There is an intimate relationship between schooling and the economic health of a nation and of its citizens. Prosperity demands productivity and productivity demands trained talent. Education develops the intellectual and manual skills which underlie the productive abilities of individuals and nations today. Nations with the highest general level of education are those with the highest economic development. Schools, more than natural resources, are the basis of prosperity.

The modern economy demands not muscle but skill and intellect. As energy is produced increasingly by mechanical means, the man who has only his energy to sell is increasingly dispensable. . . .

Education does not guarantee health, wealth or civic virtue; but sickness, unemployment, and crime are most prevalent among the under-educated segments of the population, and all undermine prosperity. Their cost is expressed in human and social decay and in public expenditures for police, relief, and treatment of preventable illness. Where ignorance generates poverty, poverty perpetuates ignorance, and the whole nation is the weaker. . . .

A similar relationship appears in draft rejections. . . . Rejection rates cannot be attributed to lack of schooling alone, but they correlate highly with lack of education and with low expenditures for schools. . . .

The ability of American society to conduct its essential affairs, political, economic, and military, depends directly on education.[3]

---

[1] Henry Steele Commager, *Living Ideas in America* (New York: Harper & Row, 1951), p. 546.
[2] Harold M. Groves, *Education and Economic Growth* (Washington: National Education Association, 1961).
[3] Educational Policies Commission, *National Policy and the Financing of the Public Schools* (Washington: National Education Association, 1962), pp. 7-11.

The Supreme Court was acutely aware of the new role of public education in American life when it wrote its decision in *Brown* v. *Topeka* in 1954:

Today education is perhaps the most important function of state and local governments. Compulsory school attendance laws and the great expenditures for education both demonstrate our recognition of the importance of education to our democratic society. It is required in the performance of our most basic public responsibilities, even service in the armed forces. It is the very foundation of good citizenship. Today it is the principal instrument in awakening the child to cultural values, in preparing him for later professional training, and in helping him to adjust normally to his environment. In these days it is doubtful that any child may reasonably be expected to succeed in life if he is denied the opportunity of an education.[4]

In the last six decades, public educational policy has responded dramatically to the new demands placed upon it by our nation's rapid economic development. Public elementary and secondary schools enroll over 40 million students. Public expenditures for education now amount to over $20 billion, more than 3 per cent of the nation's total personal income. Over $400 per year is spent on the public education of each child. Teachers' salaries average more than $5700 per year. This salary range is lower than in most other professions, but it is more than the average industrial worker's and a vast improvement over the salaries of even a few years ago. Teacher-pupil ratios have been lowered on the average to one teacher for every 23 pupils. State governments have undertaken a greater share of the direct responsibility for public education than ever before. Over 40 per cent of the cost of public schools are paid for directly by state rather than local revenues. School administration has been streamlined. Consolidation of school districts has eliminated two out of every three school districts in the past 30 years.

This impressive record of progress in public education is a tribute to the capabilities of our fifty states. Yet national averages can obscure as much as they reveal about the record of the states in public education. Our federal system provides for the decentralization of educational policy-making. Fifty state school systems establish policy for the nation, and this decentralization results in variations from state to state in educational policy. Only by examining public policy in all fifty states can the full dimensions of American education be understood.

[4] *Brown* v. *Board of Education of Topeka, Kansas,* 347 U.S. 483 (1954).

ECONOMIC DEVELOPMENT AND PUBLIC EDUCATION

America's economic development, its increased demand for an educated work force, multiplication of the national wealth, expansion of the industrial work force, and the rapid shift from rural to urban living have all paralleled the development of public education. Between 1900 and 1960 the urban proportion of our population increased from 39.6 to 69.9 per cent, and the non-agricultural proportion of our work force expanded from 62.5 to 93.7 per cent. The median family income grew from approximately $400 to over $5,600, and the average educational level of the adult population increased from the fifth-grade to the eleventh-grade level.

Werner Z. Hirsch made a systematic study of the relationship between several socioeconomic conditions and changes in per pupil expenditures for public education from 1900 to 1958.[5] He found that per pupil expenditures rose with increased enrollments, expansion of public high school education, lengthening of the school term, increased urbanization, and increased national income. Of all these conditions, the closest relationship occurred between per capita income and per pupil expenditures. As the nation's income increased its school expenditures for each pupil also increased: on the basis of nationwide figures, Hirsch estimated that for every increase of 1 per cent in per capita income, per pupil expenditures rose 1.09 per cent.

The presentation of figures comparing the rate of economic development with advances in public education is informative, but it does not systematically isolate those aspects of economic development which have been responsible for changing the character of our public educational system. Only by a closer state-by-state analysis are we able to observe systematically the impact of economic development upon a wide variety of state educational policies. Nationwide figures and trends obscure great variations in the educational policies of the fifty states. The object of state-by-state analysis is to identify differences in the educational policies of the states and then to observe the kinds of social, economic, or political conditions which exist in states with differing educational policies. Only if the policy choices of wealthy, industrial, urban states consistently differ from the policy choices of poor, rural, agricultural states, can we attribute variations in educational policies to the influence of economic development.

While the existence of variations in educational policies among the fifty states may not be a healthy state of affairs for American education,

[5] Werner Z. Hirsch, *Analysis of the Rising Costs of Public Education* (Washington: Joint Economic Committee, 1959).

it does provide political science with a means to investigate the forces which influence public policy in this area.

THE COST OF TEACHING JOHNNY TO READ

Any analysis of public educational policies must begin by explaining educational expenditures. No doubt the most important element in explaining total dollar expenditures for education in each state is the number of children attending school. But this type of correlation belabors the obvious: the more children to be taught, the more money must be spent on education.[6] The number of children to be educated and, hence, total school expenditures are primarily a measure of the *need* for educational services. In explaining public policy, however, we are concerned with the *way* in which states meet their educational needs. By using *per pupil* expenditures rather than *total* expenditures, explanation can center on those factors which influence the amount of service provided per unit of need. Per pupil expenditures in effect hold constant for need and provide a measure of the state's willingness and ability to provide educational services. They may also be considered a rough measure of the quality of the educational services provided.

In the 1961-1962 school year public school expenditures per pupil ranged from Mississippi's $229 to New York's $628. The nationwide figure for per pupil expenditures was $418, but eight states joined with Mississippi in paying less than $300 per year per child. Fifteen states spent between $300 and $400 per pupil, twenty-five states spent between $400 and $500, and Alaska and New York spent over $600 per child. Why is it that some states spend over twice as much on the education of each child as other states?

Table IV-2 shows that economic development is an important determinant of a state's willingness and ability to provide educational services. All four measures of economic development correlate significantly with variations among the states in per pupil expenditures for public education. Partial correlations (not shown) indicate that increases in any one of the four measures of economic development — urbanization, industrialization, income, education — will bring about

[6] Correlation analysis which employed total dollar expenditures and total population as variables would find population dominating, and even obscuring, all other factors. Very high coefficients can be obtained from such analysis, but they possess little value for explanatory theory. A recent study in which total rather than per capita expenditures is the dependent variable is Robert C. Wood, *1400 Governments* (Cambridge: Harvard University Press, 1961). Most studies of public expenditures use per capita measures. See Jerry Miner, *Social and Economic Factors in Spending for Public Education* (Syracuse: Syracuse University Press, 1963).

TABLE IV-2
The Relationship between Economic Development and Educational Expenditures

	Urbanization	Economic Development Industrialization	Income	Education
Per pupil expenditures	.51*	.36*	.83*	.59*
Educational expenditures as a percentage of personal income	−.31*	−.44*	−.30*	−.05
Educational expenditures as a percentage of total state and local expenditures	−.10	−.03	.01	.17
Per capita educational expenditures	.20	−.04	.61*	.75*

Figures are simple correlation coefficients for the fifty states; an asterisk indicates a statistically significant correlation.

increases in per pupil expenditures, even when the effects of the other three measures are controlled. However, it is income which explains more about per pupil expenditures than any other variable. Almost 70 per cent of the total variation among the fifty states in per pupil expenditures can be explained with reference to median family income. The results are the same even if the southern states are excluded from the analysis. Clearly, wealth is the principal determinant of the amount of money to be spent on the education of each child.

How do these findings compare with previous studies? There is general agreement that educational expenditures are related to income. Solomon Fabricant and Glen Fisher in separate studies of state government expenditures in 1942 and 1957 broke down *per capita* state expenditures for education and showed these to be related to the *per capita* incomes in the states.[7] These scholars disagreed on the impact of urbanization: Fisher's study tended to confirm our findings that urbanization does contribute to increased educational expenditures, while Fabricant felt that urbanization had little independent effect. Sherman Shapiro correlated per pupil expenditures with per capita income, industrialization, urbanization, and eight other independent socioeconomic variables among the states. Industrialization, as measured by the non-agricultural work force, and urbanization were somewhat less important than income in determining per pupil expenditures. None of Shapiro's other variables, including race, total enroll-

[7] Solomon Fabricant, *The Trend of Government Activity in the United States Since 1900* (New York: National Bureau of Economic Research, 1952); and Glen W. Fisher, "Determinants of State and Local Government Expenditures: A Preliminary Analysis," *National Tax Journal,* XIV (1961), 349-55.

ment, attendance rate, proportion of school-age children in school, or high school enrollment, were independently related to school expenditures.[8] In short, scholars seem to agree that levels of public spending for education are overwhelmingly a product of income levels.[9]

Figure IV-1 is a scatter diagram which portrays visually the relationships between income and per pupil expenditures. The broken line represents the proposition that per pupil expenditures are a function of median family income. The closeness of a state to this line is directly proportionate to its conformity to this proposition. States which lie considerably above or below the line are states which spend more or less per pupil than one would expect, given the median family income of the state. For example, Hawaii, Utah, Idaho, and Ohio spend slightly less than we would expect on the basis of their income levels; while New York, North and South Dakota, Louisiana, Oregon, and Wyoming spend slightly more. On the whole, however, states conform quite closely to the proposition that school expenditures are a function of family income.

STATE EFFORTS IN EDUCATION

Per pupil expenditures measure both the willingness and the ability of a state to spend money for education. The next problem is to separate willingness to spend from ability to spend in order to determine roughly the sacrifice a state is making for education. The desire for education can be expressed in terms of school expenditures, relative to some measure of a state's ability to spend money. In this way states that spend more or less *relative to their ability* can be identified. The most appropriate measure of ability to pay for education is probably the total personal income of the state.[10] Therefore, the measure *total public school expenditures as a percentage of total personal income* really holds constant for a state's ability to spend and more directly measures a state's willingness to sacrifice personal income for public education. This is referred to here as a state's *educational effort.*

The nation as a whole spent about 3.9 per cent of its total personal

---

[8] Sherman Shapiro, "Some Socio-Economic Determinants of Expenditures for Education," *Comparative Education Review,* VI (1962), 160-66.

[9] The positive effects of urbanization, industrialization, and education and the close relationship between income levels and per pupil expenditures can also be observed by using local school districts rather than states as the units of analysis in a regression program. See Miner.

[10] See Advisory Commission on Intergovernmental Relations, *Measures of State and Local Fiscal Capacity and Tax Effort* (Washington: Government Printing Office, 1962).

income for public education in 1960. However, two states, Massachusetts and Rhode Island, spent less than 3.0 per cent of their total personal income for public schools, while two states, Arkansas and Wyoming, spent over 6.0 per cent. Some 23 states spent between 3.0 and 4.0 per cent of their personal income for public schools, 16 states

FIGURE IV-1

**The Fifty States According to
Median Family Income
and Per Pupil Expenditures, 1962**

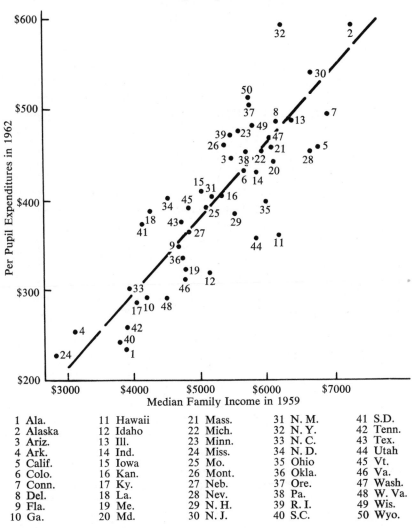

1 Ala.	11 Hawaii	21 Mass.	31 N. M.	41 S.D.
2 Alaska	12 Idaho	22 Mich.	32 N. Y.	42 Tenn.
3 Ariz.	13 Ill.	23 Minn.	33 N. C.	43 Tex.
4 Ark.	14 Ind.	24 Miss.	34 N. D.	44 Utah
5 Calif.	15 Iowa	25 Mo.	35 Ohio	45 Vt.
6 Colo.	16 Kan.	26 Mont.	36 Okla.	46 Va.
7 Conn.	17 Ky.	27 Neb.	37 Ore.	47 Wash.
8 Del.	18 La.	28 Nev.	38 Pa.	48 W. Va.
9 Fla.	19 Me.	29 N. H.	39 R. I.	49 Wis.
10 Ga.	20 Md.	30 N. J.	40 S.C.	50 Wyo.

spent between 4.0 and 5.0 per cent, and 7 states spent between 5.0 and 6.0 per cent.

Table IV-2 indicates that increased industrialization, urbanization, and income actually result in a reduction in educational effort. This is in striking contrast to the effect of these variables on per pupil expenditures: while per pupil expenditures increase with increasing income levels, school expenditures as a percentage of personal income decline. This means that the poorer, less industrialized, rural states are actually putting forth a greater effort in the educational field relative to their resources than the wealthy, urban, industrial states. But so great are the inequalities in wealth among the states that the poorer states, despite their greater effort, are unable to approach the wealthier states in per pupil expenditures. Even Mississippi's shockingly inadequate per pupil expenditure of $229 (5.8 per cent of that state's personal income) represents a greater effort than New York's expenditure of $628 per pupil (only 3.7 per cent of that state's personal income spent on education). In short, wealthier states can provide better educations for their children with less of an economic sacrifice than that required of poorer states to provide an inferior education for their children.

The National Education Association has been cognizant of this situation for some time and has used these conditions to support appeals for federal aid to education. It is argued that federal aid will help to equalize educational opportunities throughout the nation.

The operation of a national industrial economy appears to insure that average per capita incomes will be unequal among the states. The poorest states, if left to their own resources, have no reasonable prospect of raising the funds to provide adequate education. Some form of equalization is needed, because it is vital to the nation that the children in the poorest states also be well educated. Therefore, federal participation in the financing of their schools is essential.[11]

Educational expenditures as a percentage of total state and local government expenditures are a measure of the public effort in education *relative to other public efforts*. We have already noted that, for the nation as a whole, educational expenditures constitute the largest functional category of state and local government expenditures. In 1961 educational expenditures amounted to 37 per cent of all public expenditures at the state and local levels. Yet here again there is considerable variation among the states. Utah spent about 48 per cent of its public funds for education, while Massachusetts spent only 29 per cent of its state and local government funds for education.

[11] Educational Policies Commission, p. 23.

Does economic development affect the proportion of public funds going to education, relative to other public functions? In general the coefficients in Table IV-2 indicate that economic development does *not* affect the relative proportion of public funds devoted to education. Wealthy, urban, industrial states do not consistently spend more for education than for other public functions. These states simply spend more for *all* public functions without particularly favoring education. The variation which exists among the states in the proportion of public funds devoted to education cannot be traced to any of the indices of economic development.

One final expenditure variable deserves attention: per capita educational expenditures. Per pupil expenditures are probably a better measure of educational service per unit of need than per capita expenditures. However, it might be argued that not only the pupils but every member of society benefits from public education, and therefore it is appropriate to measure educational service on a per capita basis. Per capita educational expenditures are closely related to levels of income and adult education. It is interesting that the levels of adult education appear even more influential than income in determining per capita school expenditures.

Robert H. Salisbury has suggested that once a certain degree of affluence has been achieved within a state, educational expenditures become more closely associated with levels of adult education than with income.[12] Wealth determines a state's ability to achieve a certain plateau in its educational programs, but, once this has been realized, efforts to climb still higher depend on commitments to education. He cites the record of educational spending in the upper Midwest with its tradition of Progressivism and strong commitment to education.

ORGANIZING AND FINANCING PUBLIC SCHOOLS

The fifty state governments, by means of enabling legislation, establish local school districts and endow them with the authority to operate public schools. These state enabling laws create local school boards and provide a means for choosing their members, usually but not always by popular election. State laws authorize boards to levy and collect taxes, to borrow money, to engage in school construction, to hire instructional personnel, and to make certain determinations about local school policy. Yet in every state the authority of local school districts is severely circumscribed by state legislation. State law deter-

[12] Robert H. Salisbury, "State Politics and Education," in Herbert Jacob and Kenneth Vines, eds., *Politics in the American States* (New York:Little, Brown, 1965), p. 353.

mines the types and rates of taxes to be levied, the maximum debt which can be incurred, the number of days schools shall remain open, the number of years of compulsory school attendance, the minimum salaries to be paid to teachers, the types of schools to be operated by the local boards, the number of grades to be taught, the qualifications of teachers, and the general content of curricula. In addition, many states choose the textbooks, establish course outlines, fix styles of penmanship, recommend teaching methods, establish statewide examinations, fix minimum teacher-pupil ratios, and stipulate course content in great detail. Some states outlaw the mention of Communism in the classroom or the teaching of evolution. In short the responsibility for public education is firmly in the hands of our state governments.

State responsibility for public education is no mere paper arrangement. At one time there was no effective way for state governments to insure that local school districts conformed to state policies; there were no enforcement agencies or devices to guarantee that state regulations were enforced. But in recent years two devices have been utilized effectively by the states to help insure that local districts do not deviate from state standards. The first device is the statewide administrative agency, sometimes called the State Board of Education, State Department of Education, or the Superintendent of Public Instruction. All states except Michigan, Illinois, and Wisconsin have established these agencies and given them general supervisory authority over the administration of state educational programs.[13] Of the 47 state boards of education, 31 are appointed by the governor. The number of popularly elected boards has increased from three to nine in the past decade. The central task of these state administrative agencies is to oversee local school districts and insure that state policies are being implemented. While there are some variations among the states in the power vested in these agencies, one trend is common to all of the states: state educational agencies are centralizing state control over education.

The operating head of these state agencies, generally called a commissioner or superintendent of education, may exercise the most forceful influence over educational policy in the state. In 23 states these chief school officers are appointed by their boards, in 22 states they are directly elected, and in 5 states they are appointed by the governor. The department which this officer oversees provides specialized technical services and information to local school officials; and, more importantly, it establishes and enforces statewide minimum

[13] Council of State Governments, *The Book of the States 1962-63* (Chicago: Council of State Governments, 1963), p. 308.

standards in curriculum, teacher certification, school construction, and many other aspects of school policy and administration.

A second device for insuring the implementation of state educational policies are state grants of money to local school districts. Every state provides grants in one form or another to local school districts to supplement locally derived school revenue. This places the superior taxing powers of the state at the service of public schools operated at the local level. In every state an equalization formula in the distribution of state grants to local districts operates to help equalize educational opportunities in all parts of the state. Equalization formulas differ from state to state as do the amounts of the state grants involved, but in every state poorer school districts receive larger shares of state funds than wealthier districts. This enables the state to guarantee a minimum *foundation* program in education throughout the state. In addition, since state grants to local school districts are administered through state departments of education, state school officials are given an effective tool for implementing state policies, namely, withholding or threatening to withhold state funds from school districts which do not conform to state standards. The growth of state responsibility for school policy has been accomplished largely by the use of money — state grants to local schools.[14]

Increasing state participation in school finances, then, is an indication of the increasing centralization of education in the states. In 1900 the state proportion of total public school expenditures in the nation was only 17 per cent. By 1964, however, state governments contributed over 40 per cent of the total funds spent for the public schools.

One of the most dramatic reorganization and centralization movements in American government in this century has been the successful drive to reduce through consolidation the number of local school districts in the United States. In 1932, in the first official census of governments, there were over 127,000 school districts in the United States. But by 1964 this number had been reduced to 32,000. In a 30-year period three out of every four school districts were eliminated through consolidation. The one-room school house, so glorified in song and story, yet so inadequate by today's educational standards, had, by 1964, been reduced to less than 13 per cent of all schools. Support for school district consolidation has come from state school officials in every state. Opposition to consolidation has been local in character.

The extent of state participation in financing public schools and

---

[14] See Robert H. Salisbury, pp. 339-41; and Paul Mort, Walter Reusser, and John Polby, *Public School Finance,* 3rd ed. (New York: McGraw-Hill, 1960), p. 218.

the success of the movement to consolidate school districts are both important indices of educational centralization in the states. While it is clear from national trends along both of these indices that the states on the whole are centralizing education, nonetheless these trends are by no means uniform throughout the states. In Nebraska, New Hampshire, and South Dakota, the state government still provides less than 10 per cent of school revenues, while in Delaware, New Mexico, and North Carolina the state pays over 70 per cent of the cost of the public schools. There is also considerable variation among the states in the success of the movement for consolidation of the school districts. The extent of consolidation can be measured by the average size of a school district, as expressed by the number of pupils. The larger the average districts in a state, the further the movement toward consolidation has progressed. The average school district in the nation in 1962 enrolled 1073 pupils. However, the average school district in Florida, Hawaii, Louisiana, and Maryland had over 10,000 pupils, while the average district in North and South Dakota, Montana, and Nebraska had fewer than 200 pupils.

These two indices of centralization—the percentage of total school revenues from state sources and the average size of school districts—are related. States which pay the largest proportion of the public school bill have been the states which have been most successful in consolidating local school districts. In 1962 the simple correlation coefficient for the relationship between school consolidation and state participation in school finances among the fifty states was .57.

What is the relationship between centralization in school administration and finance and economic development? Table IV-3 shows a slight tendency toward increased centralization in the poorer states and the states with lower levels of education among adults. It is in these states that the state governments have played a greater role in the financing of public schools and the school consolidation movement has made the greatest progress. The negative coefficients indicate that state participation in school finances decreases among the wealthier states and the states with more educated adult populations. These coefficients are not very high, indicating that the relationship between economic development and educational centralization is not particularly close, but they are suggestive. Apparently the lack of economic resources is a stimulus toward state participation in school financing and school district consolidation. Affluence, on the other hand, enables smaller local school districts to function more effectively, reduces the need for state aid, and delays the movement toward school consolidation.

Still another question involving the organization of public educa-

TABLE IV-3

**The Relationship between Economic Development and
the Organization and Financing of State School Systems**

| | Economic Development | | | |
	Urbanization	Industrialization	Income	Education
Average size of school districts	.06	.26	−.18	−.37*
School revenues from state government as a percentage of total school revenues	−.10	.18	−.30*	−.35*
School revenues from federal government as a percentage of total school revenues	−.36*	−.08	−.32*	−.27

Figures are simple correlation coefficients for the fifty states; an asterisk indicates a statistically significant correlation.

tion in the nation is the role of the federal government. While, prior to 1965, plans for large-scale federal aid to education consistently floundered in the Congress, the federal government did contribute to public education through a number of specialized programs.[15]

The total financial contribution of the federal government to public elementary and secondary education through these programs was quite small. Federal funds amounted to only about 4 per cent of the total public school revenues in 1962. However, there is considerable variation among the states in the extent of their reliance on federal funds for public schools. In nine states in 1962 federal funds amounted to less

[15] In 1962 these programs included:
  (1) National Defense Education Act: financial assistance to the states to strengthen public school instruction in science, mathematics, and foreign languages, to strengthen guidance counseling and testing in secondary schools, and to improve the statistical services of state agencies (begun in 1958).
  (2) Aid to school districts in federally affected areas: where federal activities create a substantial increase in school enrollments or a reduction in taxable resources because of federally owned property, federal funds can be used for construction, operation, and maintenance of public schools in such districts (begun in 1950, but related to defense programs in World War II).
  (3) National school lunch and milk programs providing cash grants and commodity donations for non-profit lunches served in public and private schools (begun in 1946).
  (4) Federal funds for the purchase of educational materials for the blind (begun in 1879).
  (5) Federal grants for vocational education to help states and school districts provide training in agriculture, home economics, trades, and industries (begun in 1917).
See U.S. Department of Health, Education, and Welfare, *Handbook of Programs,* 1963 ed. (Washington: Government Printing Office, 1963).

than 3 per cent of total school revenues, while in New Mexico and Hawaii federal funds amounted to 13 and 14 per cent of the total school revenues and in Alaska federal funds paid 27 per cent of the total school bill. Federal participation in school finances does have a slight equalizing affect among the states. Table IV-3 shows that the federal government tends to pay a greater proportion of the cost of public education in the less wealthy, rural states. Thus, federal aid tends to equalize educational opportunity throughout the fifty states, although the small amounts involved and the low coefficients severely limit the equalizing effect of this aid. With the passage of the Elementary and Secondary Education Act of 1965, the role of the federal government in educational finance will be greatly expanded. This act, among other things, pledges important federal aid to poverty-stricken schools, those schools which enroll children from low-income families. It can be expected that the equalizing effect of federal aid will be more pronounced in the years ahead as the percentage of educational expenditures taken over by the federal government increases.

What is the effect of increased state and federal participation on public school systems? Since it is in the poorer states that the state government plays the greatest fiscal role, and since these states also have the lowest per pupil expenditures, simple coefficients seem to say that state participation brings about lower per pupil expenditures. The simple coefficient for the relationship between state participation in school financing and per pupil expenditures among all fifty states is —.26. However, once the effects of economic development are controlled, this coefficient disappears; the partial coefficient for the relationship between state participation and per pupil expenditures, while controlling for the effect of economic development, is —.03. Clearly, then, it is a lack of economic resources and not state participation which brings about lower per pupil expenditures in the less wealthy states. There is no visible relationship between federal participation in school finance and per pupil expenditures; the simple coefficient for this relationship is —.07 and the partial coefficient, controlling for economic development, is —.06.

It is noteworthy, however, that the partial coefficients do *not* permit us to conclude that state and federal participation leads to increases in per pupil expenditures. The partial coefficients are too low to assert any positive relationship between state or federal participation and per pupil expenditures. This tends to confirm the findings of a special study on the effect of state participation in school expenditures by Edward F. Renshaw.[16] Renshaw found that increasing ratios of

[16] Edward F. Renshaw, "A Note on the Expenditure Effect of Aid to Education," *Journal of Political Economy,* LXVII (1960), 170-74.

state aid do *not* necessarily bring about increased expenditures per pupil. State aid is more a substitute for local support than it is a stimulant to educational expenditures. The same is apparently true of federal aid in its present form.

STATES AND SCHOOL TEACHERS

The definition of quality in education is elusive. Nearly everyone can claim to have known at least one remarkable teacher. But it is difficult indeed to say what it is that makes this teacher remarkable. In addition to the problem of defining what makes for quality in education, there is also the problem of the availability of relevant data for all fifty states. For example, ideally one would wish to know the training and preparation that the teachers of each state bring to the classroom. In every state, control over entrance into the teaching profession is vested in the state boards and departments of education. These boards issue certificates for teaching in the public schools to persons meeting established requirements. State boards report the number of persons teaching with substandard credentials, but the definition of substandard credentials varies from state to state. As a result there is no way to make interstate comparisons of the credentials of teachers. In 1962 only 82,000 of the nation's 1.5 million teachers were reported to have substandard credentials, but undoubtedly many more were teaching with less than adequate training.[17]

Traditionally the public has thought that teachers need to know only a little more than the children they teach. Only recently have states begun to limit recruitment to persons with a bachelor's degree. Many persons without college degrees remain on teaching staffs in the public schools, and, in addition, many states grant provisional, temporary, or emergency certificates to persons with little preparation for teaching. Approximately three-quarters of the nation's elementary school teachers are reported to hold bachelor's degrees, while about one-third of the nation's secondary school teachers hold master's degrees. Let us assume that the proportion of elementary teachers with a B.A. or B.S. degree and the proportion of secondary school teachers with a M.A. or M.S. degree are rough measures of the adequacy of teacher preparation in a state school system. In 1963 the proportion of elementary teachers with a bachelor's degree varied from a low of 17 and 18 per cent in North and South Dakota to a high of over 90 per cent in eight states — Arizona, Florida, New Mexico, North Carolina,

[17]George B. Leonard, Jr. "The Truth about the Teacher Crisis," *Look,* February 21, 1956. Reprinted in C. Winfield Scott, *et al., The Great Debate: Our Schools in Crisis* (New York: Prentice-Hall, 1959).

Oklahoma, South Carolina, Texas, and Utah. The proportion of secondary teachers with master's degrees varied from a low of 9 per cent in North Dakota to a high of 76 per cent in Hawaii.

It is interesting to observe that the states which apparently place little emphasis on elementary teacher preparation are not necessarily the poorer states, but they are the more rural and agricultural states. The coefficients in Table IV-4 for elementary teacher preparation show that state income levels are not related to the number of teachers

TABLE IV-4

The Relationship between Economic Development and State Instructional Policies

| | Economic Development | | | |
	Urbanization	Industrialization	Income	Education
Average salary per member of instructional staff	.69*	.64*	.88*	.57*
Elementary teachers with B. A. degree	.42*	.60*	.11	−.04
Secondary teachers with M. A. degree	.54*	.42*	.55*	−.42*
Male teachers as a percentage of total school teachers	.48*	.26	.63*	−.63*
Pupil-teacher ratio: enrollment per member of instructional staff	−.13	−.19	−.43*	−.50*

Figures are simple correlation coefficients for the fifty states; an asterisk indicates a statistically signficant correlation.

with four years of college as preparation, but urbanization and industrialization are related to this measure. The reliance of many midwestern agricultural states upon the two-year normal school for teacher preparation may have retarded the development of four-year teachers' colleges which even the poorer states of the South have been able to provide. Apparently midwestern farm communities do not feel that their elementary teachers need to be college graduates.

The rural states also score low in the preparation of their secondary teachers. However, in the case of secondary teachers, income levels play an important role in the willingness and the ability of a state school system to obtain highly trained high school teachers. All four measures of economic development are related to the preparation of secondary teachers.

Not even the National Education Association claims that higher teachers' salaries are synonymous with quality teaching. Yet teaching cannot reach the full status of a profession until teachers are paid enough to live with dignity in their communities. Less than adequate salaries make it difficult to attract talented students into the teaching profession and to convince teachers that they should devote professional time and care to their jobs.

The average teacher's salary in the nation in 1962 was $5,710 per year. This was higher than the average salary of industrial workers ($5,087 for 52 weeks) but considerably lower than the average salary of professional groups. School teachers in Connecticut, California, and New York were the best-paid teachers in the nation in 1962, with average annual salaries in the neighborhood of $7,000 per year. School teachers in Arkansas, South Carolina, and Mississippi were the lowest paid in the nation, with average annual salaries in that year below $3,900. The range of differences among the states in teachers' salaries is striking: California pays its teachers twice the annual salary paid to teachers in Mississippi.

Economic development is an important determinant in teachers' salaries. Table IV-4 shows that all four measures of economic development were closely related to teachers' salaries in the fifty states in 1962. Partial coefficients (not shown) confirm that urbanization, industrialization, wealth, and education are all independently related to teachers' salaries; an increase in any one of these measures, while controlling for the effect of the other three, would result in an increase in teachers' salaries. It is wealth, however, which is the single most important determinant of teachers' salaries. Median family income explains almost 80 per cent of the variation among the states in average teachers' salaries.

Another important measure of the professionalization of teaching is the percentage of total classroom teachers who are men. According to the National Educational Association's Executive Secretary for Professional Development:

A serious obstacle to the professionalization of teaching is the predominance of women in teaching positions. This has been true of all professions in which a relatively large proportion of the practitioners were women; the reason is, of course, biological and not inferior ability. The interruption of careers, or the termination of them, for child bearing and rearing and family duties, inevitably dictates an in-and-out role for women. Not only does this cause instability in the teaching staff, it creates other adverse factors. Low pay, large turnovers, a high leaving rate, pressures for mass production instead of excellence in teacher education, and indifference to professional status and growth tend to result from the preponderance and impermanence of women in teaching.[18]

In 1962 the proportion of men among classroom teachers in the nation was 30 per cent. The steady rise in the proportion of male

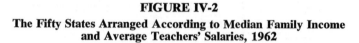

FIGURE IV-2

The Fifty States Arranged According to Median Family Income and Average Teachers' Salaries, 1962

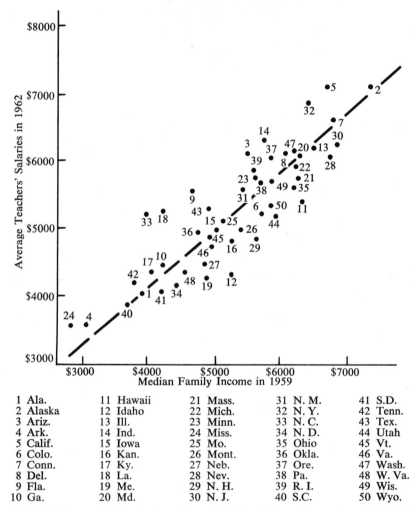

1 Ala.	11 Hawaii	21 Mass.	31 N. M.	41 S.D.
2 Alaska	12 Idaho	22 Mich.	32 N. Y.	42 Tenn.
3 Ariz.	13 Ill.	23 Minn.	33 N. C.	43 Tex.
4 Ark.	14 Ind.	24 Miss.	34 N. D.	44 Utah
5 Calif.	15 Iowa	25 Mo.	35 Ohio	45 Vt.
6 Colo.	16 Kan.	26 Mont.	36 Okla.	46 Va.
7 Conn.	17 Ky.	27 Neb.	37 Ore.	47 Wash.
8 Del.	18 La.	28 Nev.	38 Pa.	48 W. Va.
9 Fla.	19 Me.	29 N. H.	39 R. I.	49 Wis.
10 Ga.	20 Md.	30 N. J.	40 S.C.	50 Wyo.

[18] T. M. Stinnett, *The Profession of Teaching* (Washington: Center for Applied Research in Education, 1962), p. 38. Reprinted in Henry Ehlers and Gordon Lee, eds., *Crucial Issues in Education* (New York: Holt, Rinehart and Winston, 1964), p. 309.

teachers since 1910, when only 10.5 per cent were men, attests to the growing professionalization of public education. Of course there is wide variation among the states in their ability to attract men into public school teaching. Fewer than one-fifth of the public school teachers in South Carolina and Virginia were men in 1962, while 42 per cent of the teachers in Utah were men.

Table IV-4 indicates that economic development is positively related to the proportion of male teachers, although the relationship is less direct than the relationship between economic development and salary levels. Wealthy, urban states with well educated adult populations attract more men into their public educational systems than states lacking these attributes.

One final measure of instructional quality available for all fifty states is the pupil-teacher ratio, or the number of pupils enrolled per member of instructional staff. The assumption underlying the use of this index is that the close and personal attention of a teacher at the elementary and secondary school level is a positive factor in a pupil's mental development. A further assumption is that professional attention to individual needs can only be given by teachers who do not face large classes. Hence the smaller the teacher-pupil ratio, the greater the teacher's opportunity to contribute to the pupil's mental development through close professional attention. The teacher-pupil ratio for the nation as a whole in 1962 was 24 pupils per member of instructional staff. Teacher-pupil ratios in state school systems ranged from a low of 18.4 and 19.6 in North and South Dakota to a high of 28.5 and 29.3 in South Carolina and Mississippi.

Two indices of economic development, family income and the level of education among adults, correlate significantly with teacher-pupil ratios in the fifty states. Urbanization and industrialization appear to have little independent effect on teacher-pupil ratios. The signs of the coefficients in Table IV-4 indicate that teacher-pupil ratios decline with increases in the income and educational levels.

Teachers' salaries, the proportion of male teachers, teacher preparation levels, and teacher-pupil ratios all suggest the quality of the public education provided by a state. All these measures are closely linked to educational expenditures. The figures in Table IV-5 show that increases in per pupil expenditures are directly related to increases in teachers' salaries, increases in the proportion of men teachers, and decreases in teacher-pupil ratios. Per pupil expenditures are related to teacher preparation at the secondary level, although not at the primary level. Perhaps per pupil expenditures are simply another measure of quality in education. A deliberate policy to increase teachers' salaries

TABLE IV-5
The Relationship between Educational Expenditures
and State Instructional Policies

| | Per Pupil Expenditures | |
	Simple Coefficients	Partial Coefficients
Average teachers' salaries	.86*	.61*
Male teachers	.61*	.32*
Pupil-teacher ratio	−.65*	−.55*
Elementary teachers with B.A.	.02	.12
Secondary teachers with M.A.	.42*	−.08

Figures are simple and partial correlation coefficients for the fifty states; partial coefficients control for the effect of urbanization, industrialization, income, and education; an asterisk indicates a statistically significant relationship.

and teacher-pupil ratios automatically results in increased per pupil expenditures. Yet economic development, particularly wealth, remains the single most important determinant of both educational expenditures and educational quality. Wealth determines how much can be spent on education, how many men can be attracted to the teaching profession, and how many children each teacher must face in the classroom.

DROPOUTS AND MENTAL FAILURES

Evaluating the output of an educational system is at least as difficult as measuring the quality of instruction. Given conflicts over the objectives of public education, it is difficult to make any overall evaluation of educational output. Is the goal of public education college preparation, vocational skill, emotional happiness, psychological adjustment, academic excellence, the reduction of automobile accidents, the inculcation of spiritual values, the cultivation of patriotism, the production of engineers and scientists, the training of competent homemakers, or winning the Olympics? How can we tell whether the failure to achieve any one of these objectives is a product of our educational policies or an outgrowth of other national problems?

Two measures which seem to reflect public education and which are available on a state-by-state basis are the proportion of high school students who drop out of school before graduation and the proportion of selective service registrants who fail the mental examination prior to induction. Certainly the child who does not complete at least 12 years of education in a highly technological society represents a national liability, and so does the young man so feebly equipped with mental faculties that he is of no use to the armed services of the nation. On a nationwide basis, only about 727 out of every 1000 children who were ninth graders in 1959 managed to graduate from high school in 1963; some 273 of these 1000 children dropped out of school before gradua-tion. These figures are an improvement over comparable figures for high schoolers during earlier periods: the dropout rate per 1000 ninth graders from 1956 to 1960 was 379, and the dropout rate from 1946 to 1950 was 495 per 1000 ninth graders. There is considerable variation among the states in dropout rates. In 1963 California graduated all but 125 of each 1000 ninth graders in 1959, while in four states – Georgia, New Mexico, Kentucky, and Mississippi – the dropout rate during that same period was more than 400 out of every 1000 ninth graders.

In 1962, 24.5 per cent of all selective service registrants given examinations failed the mental test. (An additional 22.7 per cent were medically disqualified and 2.6 per cent were administratively disqual-ified, bringing the total disqualifications to 49.8 per cent of all exam-inees.) In South Carolina, Mississippi, and Louisiana, over 40 per cent of the selective service examinees failed the mental test, while in 11 states – Minnesota, Washington, South Dakota, Montana, Utah, Iowa, Oregon, Nebraska, Kansas, Wyoming, and Idaho – less than 5 per cent failed the mental test.

Table IV-6 summarizes a number of interesting relationships between economic development, educational expenditures, instruc-tional policies, and dropout rates and mental failures. First of all, on the basis of simple correlations, it appears that dropout rates and mental failures are inversely related to per pupil expenditures, teachers' salaries, the proportion of male teachers, and teacher-pupil ratios. States with high ratings on each of these measures have lower dropout rates and fewer mental failures. Furthermore, economic development, particularly the levels of wealth and education among adults, is directly related to dropout rates and mental failures. Thus, the simple correla-tions point to a familiar syndrome: wealthy states with well educated adult populations are the same states which spend more per pupil on their public schools, pay higher teachers' salaries, attract more male teachers, and have better teacher-pupil ratios; and these same states tend to experience fewer high school dropouts and selective service mental failures. In contrast, the less wealthy states with poorly edu-cated adult populations spend less per pupil on their public schools, pay lower teachers' salaries, attract fewer male teachers, and have poor teacher-pupil ratios, on the one hand, and experience more dropouts and mental failures, on the other. The question arises whether dropout rates and mental failures are a product of a state's economic development, its educational policies, or both.

In order to make this determination, partial correlation coefficients have been computed to show the relationship between educational policies and dropout rates and mental failures, while controlling for the effects of economic development. These are shown in Table IV-6. The decline in the size of the coefficients — once urbanization, industrializa-

TABLE IV-6
The Relationship between Economic Development and
Educational Policies, Dropout Rates, and Mental Failures

	High School Dropout Rates		Selective Service Mental Failures	
	Simple	Partial	Simple	Partial
Economic Development				
Urbanization	−.40*	−	−.05	−
Industrialization	.09	−	.13	−
Income	−.54*	−	−.46*	−
Education	−.60*	−	−.70*	−
Instructional Policies				
Average teachers' salaries	.67*	.19	.57*	.22
Teachers with B.A.	.36*	.34	.42*	.32
Teachers with M.A.	.35*	−.10	−.21	.03
Male teachers	.49*	−.01	−.51*	−.22
Pupil-teacher ratio	.63*	.22	.62*	.31
Educational Expenditures				
Per pupil expenditures	−.52*	.06	−.40*	.06
Expenditures relative to income	.02	.15	−.01	.22
Per capita expenditures	−.47*	−.03	−.59*	.00

Figures are simple and partial correlation coefficients for the fifty states; partial coefficients control for the effect of urbanization, industrialization, income, and education; an asterisk indicates a statistically significant relationship.

tion, wealth, and education are controlled — is striking. When economic development is controlled, there are no statistically significant relationships between educational policies and dropout rates and mental failures. The relationships between educational policies and dropout rates and mental failures which appear in simple correlations are a product of the influence of economic development. State educational policies in themselves have no noticeable independent effect on dropouts and mental failures. The most important determinant of these factors is the educational level of the adult population in the state: this variable explains over 50 per cent of the variation among the states in dropout rates and mental failures. These findings suggest that the parents rather than the public schools exert the most important influence on the child.

The scatter diagram in Figure IV-3 is a visual presentation of the proposition that dropout rates for the fifty states are a product of the

FIGURE IV-3

The Fifty States Arranged According to Adult Education Levels and High School Dropout Rates, 1963

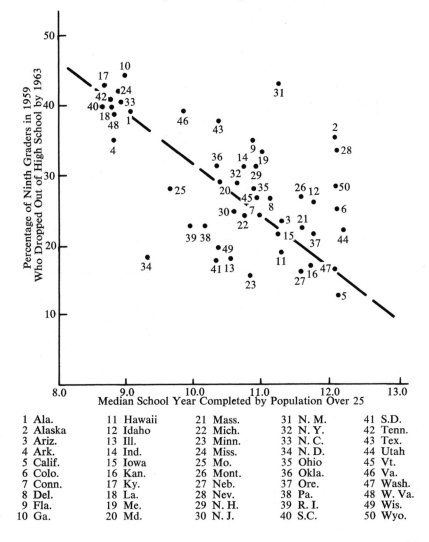

1 Ala.	11 Hawaii	21 Mass.	31 N. M.	41 S.D.
2 Alaska	12 Idaho	22 Mich.	32 N. Y.	42 Tenn.
3 Ariz.	13 Ill.	23 Minn.	33 N. C.	43 Tex.
4 Ark.	14 Ind.	24 Miss.	34 N. D.	44 Utah
5 Calif.	15 Iowa	25 Mo.	35 Ohio	45 Vt.
6 Colo.	16 Kan.	26 Mont.	36 Okla.	46 Va.
7 Conn.	17 Ky.	27 Neb.	37 Ore.	47 Wash.
8 Del.	18 La.	28 Nev.	38 Pa.	48 W. Va.
9 Fla.	19 Me.	29 N. H.	39 R. I.	49 Wis.
10 Ga.	20 Md.	30 N. J.	40 S.C.	50 Wyo.

levels of education in their adult populations. Dropout rates decrease with increases in the median school year completed by the population over 25. Most states are relatively close to the broken line, indicating that their dropout rates correspond rather closely to their levels of adult education. Georgia, Kentucky, Mississippi, South Carolina, Alabama, Tennessee, Louisiana, North Carolina, and West Virginia have high dropout rates, but no higher than we might expect, given the low educational levels of their adult populations. These states hug the upper end of the broken line, indicating that their high dropout rates correspond to the lower educational levels of their adult populations. In contrast, there are several deviant states considerably above and below the line of regression; the dropout rates in these states seem not to be related to the levels of education among their adult populations. The dropout rates in New Mexico, Alaska, Wyoming, and Nevada are extraordinarily high since these states have rather well educated adult populations. On the other hand, Arkansas, North Dakota, Rhode Island, Minnesota, Wisconsin, Illinois, Missouri, and Pennsylvania have lower dropout rates than one would expect on the basis of the levels of education among their adult populations.

STATES AND SCHOOL DESEGREGATION

When the United States Supreme Court decided in 1954 that "in the field of public education the doctrine of separate but equal has no place,"[19] it was the policy of 17 states to require the segregation of the races in the public schools. These 17 states were Alabama, Arkansas, Florida, Georgia, Louisiana, Mississippi, North Carolina, South Carolina, Tennessee, Texas, Virginia, Delaware, Kentucky, Maryland, Missouri, Oklahoma, and West Virginia. The Congress of the United States required the segregation of the races in the public schools of the District of Columbia. Four additional states — Arizona, Kansas, New Mexico, and Wyoming — authorized segregation upon the option of the local school boards.

Thus, in the decision of *Brown* v. *Topeka,* the Supreme Court struck down the laws of 21 states and the District of Columbia in a single opinion. Such a far-reaching decision was bound to meet with difficulties in implementation. In an opinion delivered the following year regarding the question of relief for Brown and others similarly situated, the Supreme Court said: "Full implementation of these constitutional principles may require solution of varied local school problems. School authorities have the primary responsibility for eluci-

---

[19] *Brown* v. *Board of Education of Topeka, Kansas,* 347 U.S. 483 (1954).

dating, assessing, and solving these problems; courts will have to consider whether the action of school authorities constitutes good faith implementation of the governing constitutional principles."[20] Thus, the court did not order immediate nationwide desegregation but instead turned over the responsibility for desegregation to state and local school authorities under the supervision of federal district courts. Thus, states which chose to resist desegregation could find recourse in extensive litigation, obstruction, and delay.

FIGURE IV-4
Segregation Pattern in 1954,
When the Supreme Court Declared Separate Schools Unconstitutional

Segregation pattern in 1954 when the Supreme Court declared separate schools unconstitutional.

Segregation required: 17 states and D.C.　　Segregation prohibited: 16 states

Local option on segregation: 4 states　　No specific legislation: 11 states
(*Wyoming has not exercised the option)

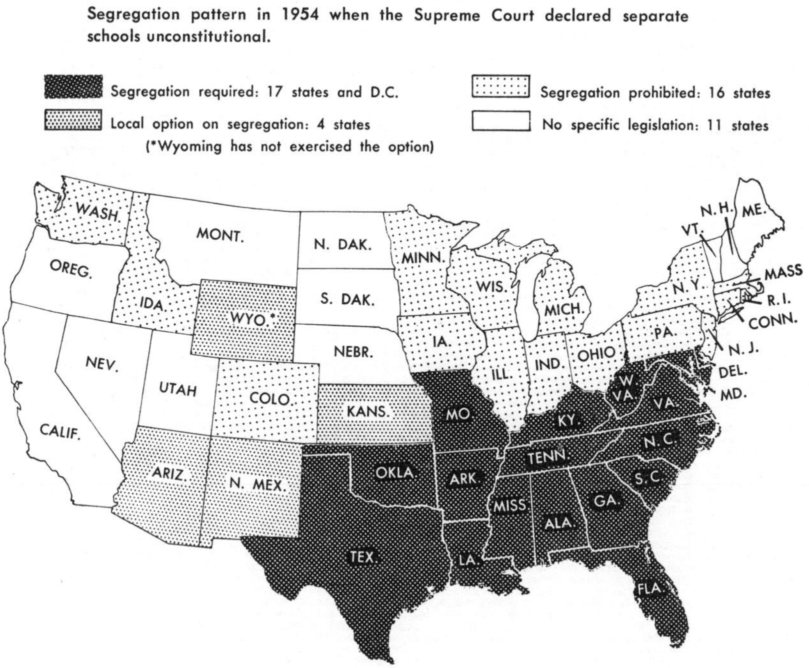

From *The New York Times*, May 17, 1954.

The six border states with segregated school systems — Delaware, Kentucky, Maryland, Missouri, Oklahoma, and West Virginia — together with the school districts in Kansas, Arizona, and New Mexico which had operated segregated schools chose not to resist desegregation formally. The District of Columbia also desegregated its public schools in the year following the Supreme Court's decision. Progress in desegregation in the border states is shown in Table IV-7. By 1964

[20] *Brown* v. *Board of Education of Topeka, Kansas,* 349 U.S. 294 (1955).

TABLE IV-7

Public School Desegregation, Fall, 1964

	School Districts			Negro School Enrollment		Negroes in School with Whites	
	Total	With Negroes and Whites	Desegregated	Numbers	Percentage of Total Enrollment	Numbers	Percentage of Total Negro Enrollment
Ala.	118	118	8	293,476	34.8	94	0.03
Ark.	412	228	24	114,651	25.6	930	0.8
Fla.	67	67	21	246,215	19.7	6,524	2.6
Ga.	196	180	11	354,850	32.0	1,337	0.4
La.	67	67	3	321,000	28.4	3,581	1.1
Miss.	150	150	4	295,962	49.0	58	0.02
N.C.	171	171	84	349,282	29.7	4,918	1.4
S.C.	108	108	16	260,667	41.2	260	0.1
Tenn.	152	141	61	173,673	19.3	9,265	5.3
Tex.	1,380	862	291	344,312	12.4	25,000	7.3
Va.	130	128	81	234,176	24.2	11,883	5.1
SOUTH	2,951	2,220	604	2,988,264	26.6	63,850	2.1
Del.	78	43	43	19,497	19.0	11,267	57.8
D.C.	1	1	1	123,906	87.6	106,578	86.0
Ky.	204	165	164	56,000	7.7	35,000	62.5
Md.	24	23	23	166,861	22.8	86,203	51.7
Mo.	1,542	212*	203*	102,000	10.0	44,000	44.1
Okla.	1,118	242	200	43,954	7.5	13,923	31.7
W. Va.	55	44	44	21,000	4.5	18,500	88.1
BORDER	3,022	730	678	533,218	14.8	315,471	59.2

*Estimated.

From Southern Education Reporting Service, *Southern School News*, X (1964), 1.

over half of the Negro children in the border states were attending integrated schools.

Resistance to school integration was the policy choice of the 11 states of the Old Confederacy. Segregationists pressed for states laws which would create an endless chain of litigation in each of the nearly 3,000 school districts in the South, in the hope that integration efforts would drown in a sea of protracted court controversy. In 1956, 96 members of the Congress from southern states signed a "Declaration of Constitutional Principles" in which they declared: "We commend the motives of those States which have declared their intention to resist forced integration by any lawful means."[21] Support for state resistance also came from conservative Republicans; Barry Goldwater wrote in 1960:

I have the greatest respect for the Supreme Court as an institution but I cannot believe that I display that respect by submitting abjectly to abuses of power by the Court, and by condoning its unconstitutional trespass into the legislative sphere of government. . . . I therefore support the efforts by the states, excluding violence of course, to preserve their rightful powers over education.[22]

Resistance has taken many forms. Refusal of a school district to desegregate until it is faced with a federal court injunction is the most common form of delay. Other schemes have included state payment of private school tuition in lieu of providing public schools, the amendment of compulsory attendance laws to provide that no child shall be required to attend an integrated school, the requirement that schools faced with desegregation orders cease operation, and the use of pupil placement laws to avoid or minimize the extent of integration. State officials have also attempted to prevent desegregation on the grounds that it will endanger public safety, although they have themselves precipitated and encouraged violent resistance through their attempts to "interpose" and "nullify" federal authority within their states.[23]

On the whole, those states which chose to resist desegregation were quite successful in doing so during the ten-year period from 1954 to 1964.[24] Table IV-7 indicates that in late 1964 only about 2 per cent of the Negro school children in the 11 southern states were attending

[21] *The New York Times,* March 12, 1956, p. 19.

[22] Barry Goldwater, *The Conscience of a Conservative* (Copyright ©, 1960, Victor Publishing Company, Inc., used by permission of MacFadden-Bartell Corporation, New York), p. 37.

[23] For an excellent review of resistance tactics, see Jack W. Peltason, *58 Lonely Men* (New York: Harcourt, Brace and World, 1961); see also Virgil T. Blossom, *It Happened Here* (New York: Harper, 1959); Don Shoemaker, *With All Deliberate Speed* (New York: Harper, 1957); and A. P. Blaustein and C. C. Ferguson, Jr., *Desegregation and the Law* (New Brunswick: Rutgers University Press, 1957).

[24] Southern Education Reporting Service, *Southern School News,* X (1964).

integrated schools. Only 604 of the South's 2,220 school districts which encompassed Negro students were officially desegregated; and most of these 604 districts experienced only token desegregation. It may be that in the second ten years after *Brown* v. *Topeka,* the southern states will not meet with quite so much success in opposing integration as in the first decade after that decision. However, the effectiveness of state policy in resisting the policy of the federal court up to 1964 is an important comment on the powers of the states in our federal system.

The decision of 11 southern states to resist desegregation is, of course, a product of the total cultural history of the region. The roots of racial attitudes in the South are too deep to examine here. However, progress in desegregation is not uniform throughout the southern states, and it is, therefore, possible to contrast the characteristics of those states which have made some progress toward integration with those that have not. For example, desegregation has been slow and painful in Mississippi, Alabama, and South Carolina, while changes have been somewhat easier in Texas, Tennessee, Virginia, and Florida. How do these states differ? What accounts for differences among southern states in their degree of resistance to desegregation?

Progress in desegregation is closely related to Negro political participation. The states which have resisted desegregation most effectively are also the states which do not encourage Negro political participation. Negro participation can be measured by the proportion of eligible adult Negroes who are registered to vote. The percentages of eligible Negroes who were registered to vote in the 11 southern states in 1964 were estimated to be: Alabama, 21.6; Arkansas, 41.5; Florida, 51.1; Georgia, 39.1; Louisiana, 31.6; Mississippi, 6.7; North Carolina, 45.0; South Carolina, 34.2; Tennessee, 67.2; Texas, 57.7; and Virginia, 27.7. Certainly Negro political participation and progress in school desegregation are closely related. The rank order correlation coefficient between the percentage of Negro children in school with whites and the percentage of eligible Negroes registered to vote was a highly significant .72 in 1964. However, while a politically active Negro electorate can provide an important stimulus to desegregation, Negro political participation cannot explain desegregation. Rather it is likely that both school desegregation and Negro registration are both a product of the same social conditions.

One hypothesis that we might test is that progress in desegregation and Negro registration are significantly affected by the states' proportion of Negro residents. Does a large proportion of Negroes in a state's population strengthen the integration movement or does it strengthen the resolve of segregationists to resist integration? The non-white population percentages in the 11 southern states in 1960 were as follows: Alabama, 30.1; Arkansas, 21.9; Florida, 18.0; Georgia, 28.6; Louisiana, 32.1; Mississippi, 42.3; North Carolina, 25.4; South Carolina, 35.0; Tennessee, 16.6; Texas, 12.6; and Virginia, 20.8. The evidence is very strong that a large Negro population strengthens the position of segregationists. In Table IV-8, the rank order correlation coefficient between non-white population percentages and progress in school desegregation in the 11 southern states is a highly significant —.87. The rank order coefficient for the relationship between non-white population percentages and Negro registration percentages is —.79. These high negative coefficients indicate that states with large Negro populations have made less progress toward desegregation than states with smaller proportions of Negro residents.

Table IV-8 also shows the relationship between economic development and progress in school desegregation and Negro registration in the southern states. While large Negro populations appear to stimulate resistance to desegregation, wealth and urbanization appear to have the

TABLE IV-8
Correlates of Progress in School Desegregation in 11 Southern States

| | Percentage of Population Which Is Non-White | Urban-ization | Economic Development | | |
			Industrial-ization	Wealth	Education
Percentage of negro school children in school with whites	—.87	.64	—.44	.76	.30
Percentage of eligible negroes registered to vote	—.79	.30	—.13	.37	.10

Figures give rank order correlation coefficients for 11 southern states.

opposite effect. These variables are not as influential as Negro population percentages in explaining progress toward desegregation; however, the wealth and urbanism of Texas, Florida, and North Carolina do help to explain the somewhat more progressive attitudes of those states toward desegregation. The ruralism and poverty in Mississippi, Alabama, and South Carolina help to explain their less progressive policies. Thus, economic development together with the racial composition of the population explain most of the variation among the southern states in their approach to school desegregation.

PARTISANSHIP AND EDUCATION POLICY

Thus far, attention has been focused upon the relationships between socioeconomic inputs and educational policy outcomes. Now we turn to the problem of assessing the influence of political system characteristics on educational policy.

Of course, in assessing the influence of political system variables on educational policy, it is necessary to take into account the effect of socioeconomic inputs, since these inputs have already been shown to influence both system characteristics and educational outcomes in the states. As explained in Chapter II, partial correlation analysis will enable us to explore the complex relationships between political system variables, socioeconomic inputs, and educational policy.

First of all, let us examine the effect of Democratic or Republican party control of a state government on its educational policy. Do the educational policies of states under Democratic and Republican control differ? In order to make this determination we have employed the same measures of partisanship that we described in Chapter III: the percentage of total seats in the upper and lower chambers of the state legislature held by the Democrats from 1954 to 1964, and the Democratic percentage of the two-party vote for the office of governor during that same period. Since these measures are expressed in terms of Democratic control, we need only reverse the signs of the coefficients obtained with these measures in order to observe the effect of Republican party control.

Table IV-9 presents both simple and partial correlation coefficients for the relationships between educational policy outcomes and Democratic dominance in the state legislatures and gubernatorial elections. The partial coefficients control for all four measures of economic development — urbanization, industrialization, income, and education.

As the coefficients indicate, there are many significant associations between partisanship and public policy outcomes. The simple coefficients show that states experiencing Democratic party control between 1954 and 1964 are the same states which have lower per pupil expenditures and lower per capita educational expenditures. While these Democratic states have *more* elementary teachers with B.A. degrees, on several other measures of the quality of instruction they rank low: they have fewer male teachers, higher pupil-teacher ratios, and higher dropout rates and mental failures. There is also some slight association between Democratic control and lower teachers' salaries. Finally, Democratic states tend to have larger school districts and to receive greater shares of educational revenues from state rather than local sources. Republican control of state government, on the other hand, is associated with the opposite educational outcomes.

When economic development is controlled, however, some of the association between partisanship and public policy disappears. This means that part of the association between Democratic party control

TABLE IV-9
The Relationships among Economic Development,
Partisanship, and State Educational Policies

| | Democratic Party Control | | | | | |
| | Lower Houses | | Upper Houses | | Governorships | |
	Simple	Partial	Simple	Partial	Simple	Partial
Per pupil expenditures	−.47*	−.06	−.43*	.06	−.58*	−.18
Expenditures relative to income	.15	.33	.20	.31	.07	.10
Per capita expenditures	−.39*	.30	−.34*	.29	−.51*	.05
Average teachers' salaries	−.23	.27	−.20	.05	−.42*	.02
Teachers with B.A.	.62*	.67*	.60*	.71*	.41*	.45*
Teachers with M.A.	−.15	.06	−.12	.16	−.24	.04
Male teachers	−.49*	−.25	−.48*	−.21	−.58*	−.29
Pupil-teacher ratio	.72*	.50*	−.67*	.44*	.72*	.51*
Dropout rate	.69*	.55*	.66*	.46*	.64*	.34*
Mental failures	.71*	.42*	.64*	.39*	.74*	.56*
Size of school district	.64*	.49*	.52*	.36*	.44*	.22
School revenues from state	.68*	.61*	.63*	.53*	.55*	.41*
School revenues from federal government	.27	.60*	.29	.51*	.18	.38*

Figures are simple and partial correlation coefficients; partial coefficients control for the effect of urbanization, industrialization, income, and education; an asterisk indicates a statistically significant relationship.

and educational outcomes is merely a product of the intervening effect of economic development. There seems to be no *independent* relationship between partisanship and per pupil expenditures, educational expenditures relative to income, per capita educational expenditures, average teachers' salaries, the preparation of secondary teachers, or the proportion of male teachers. These important educational outcomes are not affected by which party dominates state government.

On the other hand, even after controlling for economic development, significant associations continue to exist between partisanship and elementary teacher preparation, pupil-teacher ratios, dropout rates, mental failures, the size of school districts, and the extent of state and federal participation in school financing. The coefficients for these relationships are noticeably reduced when economic development is controlled, but we cannot reject the idea that there is some linkage between partisanship and these outcomes, a linkage which is not an artifact of economic development.

In spite of these controlled relationships, we are reluctant to infer that a direct causal relationship exists between Democratic politics and higher dropout rates and mental failures. It seems unlikely that Democratic politics brings about dropouts or mental failures or vice versa, especially in view of the fact that Democratic politics does not affect per pupil expenditures or teachers' salaries. The concentration of southern states among the most Democratic states accounts for these relationships; if the southern states are removed, the coefficients disappear. Rural midwestern Republican states, although they share many of the economic characteristics of the southern states, have fewer dropouts and mental failures. Likewise, the midwestern reliance of the two-year normal school in lieu of a B.A. degree as preparation for elementary teachers is probably not a product of Republican party affiliation.

The southern states stand high on dropout rates and mental failures. This standing is not merely a product of their lower levels of economic development, since southern states stand higher than non-southern states on these measures even after controlling for economic development. This suggests that some attribute of the southern states other than their levels of economic development or Democratic politics accounts for these generally undesirable educational outcomes. Unfortunately, our model cannot help us to explain policy outcomes which are not a product of the input variables or system characteristics included in our model. We can only speculate on what attribute of the southern states may be responsible for these educational failures. Certainly a plausible explanation is the system of segregated education in the southern states which deprives large numbers of children of educational and cultural opportunities. Negroes are heavily overrepresented among the dropouts and mental failures. It is probably not only segregated education which brings this about, but limitations on occupational and employment opportunities and general cultural deprivation as well.

It seems more plausible that Democratic politics may bring about increased federal and state support for education and decreased reliance upon local sources of educational revenue. Controlling for economic development actually increases the correlation between Democratic control and federal financial participation. Moreover, the removal of the southern states does not significantly affect the partial coefficients between Democratic politics and these particular outcomes. Differences between strong Democratic and strong Republican states in their degree of centralization in state educational administration must be related in some way to their differences in party affiliation. The midwestern and upper New England states, which in many ways resemble the South in economic resources, have resisted the consolidation of local school districts and have continued to place the heaviest financial burden for education on local rather than state governments. This suggests that in their policy adjustments to economic deprivation, strong Republican and strong Democratic states take separate courses. Strong Republican states in the Midwest and upper New England refuse to give up local control over education, while strong Democratic states of the South have consolidated their school districts and looked to the state and federal governments for financial support.

All we can really say on the basis of these operations, however, is that there is a linkage between the partisan character of state politics and several educational outcomes, and that this linkage does *not* depend upon economic development.

On several important measures of educational policy, strong Democratic and strong Republican states resemble each other more than they resemble states under divided control. For example, per pupil expenditures in both strong Democratic and strong Republican states are lower than per pupil expenditures in the divided states. School expenditures are a larger percentage of personal income in both strong Republican and strong Democratic states than in states with divided party control. Teachers' salaries in both strong Democratic and strong Republican states tend to be lower than salaries in states with divided party control. On these measures it appears that the existence of party competition is the important influence on policy, and that it does not matter whether the one-party dominance is Republican or Democratic in character.

PARTY COMPETITION AND EDUCATIONAL POLICY

Does it make any difference in educational policy outcomes whether a state has a competitive two-party system or a non-competitive one-party style of politics.

As explained in Chapter III, party competition can be measured as one minus the majority party's margin of legislative control and its margin of victory in gubernatorial elections (the party label of the majority party is irrelevant). In Table IV-10 these measures of party competition are correlated with the several measures of educational policy. In the simple coefficients, which do *not* control for the effects of economic development, party competition appears to be significantly related to many of the educational variables. States with a high degree of party competition tend to spend more money per pupil on their schools, pay higher teachers' salaries, attract more men teachers, and experience fewer dropouts and mental failures. These same states have larger school districts and raise more school revenue from local than from state or federal sources. But, since we already know that economic development affects both party competition and educational policies, it is necessary to sort out the influence of party competition on

TABLE IV-10

The Relationships among Economic Development, Party Competition, and State Educational Policies

| | Party Competition | | | | | |
| | Lower Houses | | Upper Houses | | Governorships | |
	Simple	Partial	Simple	Partial	Simple	Partial
Per pupil expenditures	.51*	.08	.48*	.00	.59*	.03
Expenditures relative to income	.07	−.14	−.16	−.21	−.24	−.27
Per capita expenditures	.43*	.07	.37*	.10	.46*	.14
Average teachers' salaries	.36*	.11	.35*	.18	.49*	.12
Teachers with B.A.	−.38*	−.34	−.39*	−.34	−.32*	−.34
Teachers with M.A.	.16	.16	.13	.22	.35*	.05
Male teachers	.50*	.14	.41*	.03	.57*	−.22
Pupil-teacher ratio	−.55*	−.21	−.50*	−.15	−.64*	−.34
Dropout rate	.74	−.53*	−.67*	−.40*	−.62*	−.38*
Mental failures	.64*	−.37*	−.57*	−.36*	−.75*	−.63*
Size of school district	−.51*	−.34	−.37*	−.18	−.43*	−.29
School revenues from state	−.50*	−.31	−.42*	−.21	−.47*	−.34
School revenues from federal government	−.24	−.30	−.26	−.34	−.14	−.34

Figures are simple and partial correlation coefficients; partial coefficients control for the effect of urbanization, industrialization, income, and education; an asterisk indicates a statistically significant relationship.

educational policy from the influence of economic development. When the effects of economic development are discounted, party competition does *not* explain differences among the states in per pupil expenditures, educational effort, teachers' salaries, teacher preparation, male teachers, or pupil-teacher ratios. Party competition appears independently related only to dropout rates and mental failures, but this relationship is a product of the peculiar influence of the southern states.

In short, while competitive states and non-competitive states differ somewhat in educational policy (as shown by the simple correlation coefficients), these differences can be traced to the effect of economic development rather than to party competition (as shown by the disappearance of significant coefficients). It is a state's economic development rather than its party system which is the principal determinant of its educational policy.

POLITICAL PARTICIPATION AND EDUCATIONAL POLICY

What is the effect of voter participation levels on educational policies in the states? Are educational policies in states with high participation rates any different from policies in states with low participation rates? Can policy differences between states with high and low rates of voter participation be traced directly to participation, or are they a product of intervening socioeconomic conditions? Of course, in order to assess the independent effect of participation on educational outcomes, it is again necessary to control for the effect of economic development.

The simple coefficients in Table IV-11 show that there is considerable association between voter turnout and educational outcomes. States with high levels of voter participation are the same states which had generally higher per pupil and per capita educational expenditures, higher teachers's salaries, better prepared secondary teachers, more male teachers, smaller pupil-teacher ratios, and fewer dropouts and mental failures. They are also the same states which had smaller school districts and placed greater reliance on local school revenue rather than state or federal school aid. However, since we know that these states are also the most wealthy, urban, and industrial states with the better educated adult populations, we cannot attribute these educational outcomes to voter participation levels until we control for the effects of economic development.

When economic development is controlled, most of the associations between voter participation and educational outcomes disappear. Voter participation has no independent effect upon educational expenditures, average teachers' salaries, the proportion of male teachers, pupil-teacher ratios, teacher preparation, the size of school districts, or the extent of state or federal participation, and what determines these educational outcomes is the relationships of these two sets of variables to a third intervening variable—economic development.

Interestingly, the coefficients between voter participation and dropout rates and mental failures remain significant, even after controlling for economic development. This relationship does not depend upon the southern states. It may be that the relationship between voter participation and dropout rates and mental failures is a feedback linkage. Voter participation may not affect educational outcomes, but educational outcomes, particularly dropouts and mental failures, may

TABLE IV-11

**The Relationships among Economic Development,
Political Participation, and State Educational Policies**

	Governorships		1962 Congressional		1958 Congressional	
	Simple	Partial	Simple	Partial	Simple	Partial
Per pupil expenditures	.49*	.18	.58*	.08	.58*	.05
Expenditures relative to income	−.19	−.23	−.17	−.22	.19	−.25
Per capita expenditures	.38*	−.08	.47*	−.10	.52*	−.09
Average teachers' salaries	.35*	−.16	.42*	−.17	.44*	−.26
Teachers with B.A.	−.37*	−.37*	−.43*	−.50*	−.38*	−.44*
Teachers with M.A.	.31*	.11	.25	−.05	.34*	.06
Male teachers	.49*	.22	.63*	.32	.61*	.30
Pupil-teacher ratio	−.63*	−.30	−.70*	−.39	−.63*	−.32
Dropout rate	−.66*	−.53*	−.68*	−.49*	−.71*	−.49*
Mental failures	−.73*	−.63*	−.78*	−.63*	−.77*	−.60*
Size of school district	−.45*	−.29	−.53*	−.41*	−.46*	−.28
School revenues from state	−.46*	−.31	−.56*	−.46*	−.48*	−.33
School revenues from federal government	−.26	−.29	−.24	−.28	−.14	−.34

Figures are simple and partial correlation coefficients; partial coefficients control for the effect of urbanization, industrialization, income, and education; an asterisk indicates a statistically significant relationship.

affect participation. Coefficients do not tell us which way the causal arrows point, but we cannot reject the possibility that there is some causal linkage between dropout rates and mental failures and voter participation.

MALAPPORTIONMENT AND EDUCATIONAL POLICY

Malapportionment of state legislatures has been successfully challenged before the Supreme Court on the grounds that it denies to citizens the equal protection of the laws. This was a normative challenge stemming from deeply held values about political equality; our empirical model cannot help us to examine its merits. The moral case for reapportionment cannot be tested empirically. However, proponents of reapportionment have occasionally made statements about the effect of malapportionment on public policy and predictions about the policy consequences of reapportionment; these *can* be tested empirically. It is often argued that there are important policy differences between urban and rural constituencies and that malapportionment, by overrepresenting rural areas, grants them a real advantage in policy-making. In the field of education it is possible that the overrepresentation of rural areas may deemphasize public education. It may be argued that reapportionment, by increasing urban representation, will lead to more financial support for public education and improvement in the quality of instruction.

It is possible to examine systematically the effect of malapportionment on the educational outcomes in the fifty states.Table IV-12 shows the relationships between malapportionment and educational outcomes. The malapportionment measures are the same as those described in Chapter III.

TABLE IV-12

The Relationships among Economic Development, Malapportionment, and State Educational Policies

	Index of Representation		Malapportionment Index of Urban Under-representation		Apportionment Score	
	Simple	Partial	Simple	Partial	Simple	Partial
Per pupil expenditures	−.12	.07	.36*	.12	.09	.15
Expenditures relative to income	.10	−.06	−.27	−.07	−.10	−.06
Per capita expenditures	−.19	−.01	−.03	.01	−.06	−.25
Average teachers' salaries	−.29	−.20	.30*	−.17	−.01	−.28
Teachers with B.A.	−.24	−.19	−.13	−.29	−.12	−.24
Teachers with M.A.	−.07	.10	.14	−.07	.10	−.04
Male teachers	−.22	−.09	.15	−.01	−.01	−.10
Pupil-teacher ratio	−.11	−.23	−.31*	−.41*	−.15	−.21
Dropout rate	.06	.29	.37*	.54*	.15	−.29
Mental failures	−.09	−.27	−.15	−.27	−.16	−.14
Size of school district	−.24	−.31	−.10	−.20	−.13	−.15
School revenues from state	−.25	−.34	−.32*	−.43*	−.23	−.28
School revenues from federal government	−.06	−.13	−.33*	−.39*	−.07	−.18

Figures are simple and partial correlation coefficients; partial coefficients control for the effect of urbanization, industrialization, income, and education; an asterisk indicates a statistically significant relationship.

On the whole, the policy choices of malapportioned legislatures are *not* noticeably different from the policy choices of well-apportioned legislatures. None of the coefficients under the index of representativeness or the apportionment score are statistically significant. There is no evidence that malapportionment in its technical sense has any relevance in educational policy decisions. Only six of the simple coefficients under the index of urban underrepresentation are above the level of significance, and only four of these hold up well once socioeconomic variables are controlled. School expenditures decline with increases in malapportionment, yet this relationship is clearly a product of the fact that expenditures are lower in the rural, less wealthy, agricultural states. Once economic development is controlled, the relationship between malapportionment and educational expenditures disappears. The same is true regarding average teachers' salaries. Urban underrepresentation is slightly related to higher pupil-teacher ratios, higher dropout rates, and increased state and federal participation in school finance. These relationships do not disappear when the southern states are removed from the correlation analysis.

CHAPTER V

Welfare Policy

DEVELOPMENT OF PUBLIC HEALTH AND WELFARE POLICY

GOVERNMENTS MAKE INNUMERABLE DECISIONS which authoritatively allocate values pertaining to the health and well-being of individuals. But the term *welfare* is generally used in a more restricitve sense to refer to assistance to the indigent and to programs designed to protect individuals against indigency. Concern for public health and welfare has been a recognized responsibility of government in English-speaking countries since at least 1572. In the Poor Relief Act of 1601 the English Parliament codified legislation regarding public care of the destitute and formally set forth principles of public welfare which were to influence governments in England and the United States for three-and-a-half centuries. Elizabethan law reflected the judgment that poverty was a product of moral and character deficiencies in the individual, and this view prevailed well into the twentieth century. Conditions of acceptance were made sufficiently onerous to discourage all but the most desperate. Primary reliance was placed on institutional relief—county workhouses and poor houses or almshouses. The "able-bodied poor," that is, the unemployed, were sent to county workhouses; while the "worthy poor," widows, aged, and handicapped, were sent to poor houses, frequently the same institution. Often the mentally and physically ill were kept in these same institutions; destitute children were kept in county orphanages or farmed out to foster homes. Some home relief was provided, often in food or clothing, but it could never exceed in value the income of the lowest paid persons not on relief. Poor rolls were made public, and relief was forthcoming only if there were no living relatives who could legally be required to support the destitute members of the family.

Under Elizabethan law the care of the destitute was clearly a responsibility of local governments rather than state or national governments. The parish in England, and the township or county in the United States, was required to collect a poor tax to be spent by overseers of the poor. Residence and settlement requirements meant that each parish or township or county was responsible only for indigents who had been born in the area or who had established residence there.

Industrialization and urbanization intensified health and welfare problems. In the late nineteenth century state governments began to build and operate specialized state institutions for the insane, the deaf, the blind, and the orphaned. This marked the first assumption of direct state responsibility for welfare. By 1931 all but five states had a department concerned with public welfare and the administration of state institutions. State involvement in home relief grew more slowly. In 1934, just prior to the passage of the Social Security Act, only 34 states assisted the blind, 28 states assisted the aged, and 42 states gave aid to mothers with dependent children. However, even many of these state programs for aid were only paper programs, and they rendered little effective assistance. The federal government provided only for needy veterans, Indians, and merchant seamen; the prevailing view was that there was no legitimate national interest in public health and welfare.

The Great Depression radically altered the attitudes toward and the structure and policy of public health and welfare. When poverty was experienced by millions of people, the myth that destitution was a product of personal failure was badly shaken. Millions who had previously considered relief only the desperate recourse of the unworthy joined in the breadlines. With one out of four Americans unemployed and one out of six receiving relief, there was a noticeable weakening of support for Herbert Spencer's view that the poor "are themselves the causes of their own poverty; that the means for redress are in their own hands; that the society in which they live and the government which presides over it, are without any direct power in this respect."[1] This change in public attitude, although by no means universal, was a prerequisite to altering Elizabethan policy.

[1] Herbert Spencer, "The Coming Slavery," in *The Man Versus the State* (London: Williams and Norgate, 1892), pp. 18-19. See also T. R. Malthus, *An Essay on the Principle of Population*, 6th ed. (London, 1826), pp. 287-288. Both statements are cited in Sidney Fine, *Laissez Faire and the General Welfare State* (Ann Arbor: University of Michigan Press, 1956), p. 7.

By 1932 the traditional structure of local relief had collapsed. Local governments were quickly drained of financial resources to aid the indigent. Direct state participation in welfare activities increased rapidly and a majority of states distributed money to local relief agencies. But state governments were also running out of money. In some states 40 per cent of the people were on relief and in some counties the figure rose to 80 per cent. Frantic appeals for help from the national government were made by states and localities. Even Herbert Hoover was forced into approving limited federal relief programs. The Roosevelt administration very early launched large-scale emergency relief and public works programs. In time these emergency programs were abandoned, but the precedent of federal responsibility for public welfare had been established.

The degree to which the Great Depression altered the structure of welfare financing can be observed in Table V-1 in the changing percentages of federal and state participation in the financing of health and welfare programs. The Great Depression also significantly influenced the nation's total welfare effort. The total amount expended for social insurance, public assistance, and public health increased substantially, and fiscal responsibility shifted from local governments to state governments and especially to the national government. Today the federal government finances the greatest share of social insurance programs; over $16 billion was spent in 1962 on OASDI, Railroad Retirement System, and the U. S. Employment Service. The states spent over $6 billion in the social insurance field, including expenditures for unemployment compensation, workmen's compensation, and state and local retirement systems. In the public assistance field, including aid to the aged, the blind, the disabled, dependent children, and those requiring general assistance, the federal government pays about half and the states and localities about half of the total bill. The states continue to carry the largest share of the cost of institutional care.

INTERACTION OF FEDERAL AND STATE WELFARE POLICIES

The Great Depression was also responsible for the Social Security Act of 1935, the most important piece of legislation in the welfare field since the Poor Relief Act of 1601. In the Social Security Act the national government undertook to establish the basic framework for public welfare policies for all levels of government. The Depression forced the national government to assume responsibility for the problems of economic insecurity and want and to deal with these problems on a permanent basis. Unlike policy in the field of education, in which

TABLE V-1

Health and Welfare Expenditures of Federal, State, and Local Governments, 1929-1962

	Social Insurance			Public Assistance			Other Welfare			Health		
	Total	Federal Per-centage	State and Local Per-centage	Total	Federal Per-centage	State and Local Per-centage	Total	Federal Per-centage	State and Local Per-centage	Total	Federal Per-centage	State and Local Per-centage
1929	340	21	79	500	01	99	---	---	---	455	10	90
1935	384	26	74	2,998	79	21	139	01	99	544	11	89
1940	1,216	29	71	3,599	63	37	114	09	91	697	14	86
1945	1,388	53	47	1,031	41	59	195	45	55	1,937	64	36
1950	4,911	42	58	2,496	44	56	402	42	58	2,344	28	72
1955	9,845	65	35	3,003	50	50	580	42	58	2,914	33	67
1960	19,292	74	26	4,101	52	48	1,161	35	65	4,342	36	64
1962	22,357	72	28	4,441	53	47	1,248	35	65	4,757	38	62

From U.S. Department of Health, Education, and Welfare, *Health, Education and Welfare Trends 1963* (Washington: Government Printing Office, 1963), pp. 106-8. Figures in *Total* columns are expressed as millions of dollars.

the role of the federal government is minimal, state policy in the health and welfare field is deeply influenced by federal policy. Any examination of the determinants of state welfare policy outcomes must first describe the effects of federal policy in this field.

Government programs in health and welfare can be classified according to the clientele they aid, their methods of finance, and the level of government providing the service.[2] The clientele may include the aged, the blind, dependent children, the unemployed, the disabled, the mentally ill or retarded, wards of the state, and the "needy." If the beneficiaries of a program are required to have made contributions to it before claiming its benefits, and if they are entitled to the prepaid benefits regardless of their personal wealth, then the program is said to be financed on the insurance principle. If the program is financed out of general tax revenues, and if recipients are required to show that they are indigent before claiming benefits, then the program is said to be financed on the welfare principle. In the American federal system, welfare programs can be wholly federal in financing and administration, cooperatively sponsored by both federal and state governments, or wholly financed and administered by the states and their subdivisions.

The Social Security Act placed great reliance on *social insurance* to supplement and, it was hoped, eventually to replace *public assistance*. The Old Age Survivors' and Disability Insurance (OASDI) program is a federally administered, compulsory, social insurance program, financed by regular deductions from earnings, which gives covered individuals a legal right to benefits in the event of specific occurences causing a reduction in income — old age, death of the provider, or disability. It is based on the same principle as private insurance — the sharing of risks — except that it is compulsory and the benefits may be changed by law. OASDI provides monthly retirement benefits to fully insured workers at age 65 or over and supplementary benefits to their wives, if they are aged or have a child of the earner in their care, to aged dependent husbands, and to dependent children under age 18. Monthly survivor benefits are payable to certain dependents of fully or currently insured workers. Monthly disability benefits are payable to fully insured workers with a prolonged disability and to their dependents. The OASDI program is designed to protect individuals against indigency. As a wholly federal program, OASDI will not be included in our analysis of state welfare policy outcomes.

The Social Security Act has also induced the states to enact unemployment insurance programs through the imposition of a payroll

[2]Wayne Vasey, *Government and Social Welfare: Roles of Federal, State and Local Governments in Administering Welfare Services* (New York: Holt, 1958).

tax on employers. A federal unemployment tax of 3.1 per cent of the first $3,000 paid to each employee is levied on the payroll of employers of four or more workers. Employers who pay into state insurance programs which meet federal standards may use these payments to credit 90 per cent of their federal unemployment liability. The federal government collects the remaining 10 per cent but gives it back to the states to help them pay for the administration of their programs. Although this federal program has succeeded in inducing all fifty states to establish unemployment insurance programs, the federal standards are flexible, and the states have had considerable freedom in shaping their own programs. In all cases unemployed workers must report in person and show that they are willing and able to work, and states cannot deny workers benefits for refusing to work as strikebreakers or refusing to work for wages below prevailing rates. But basic decisions concerning the amount of benefits, eligibility, and the length of time for which benefits can be drawn are left to the states. Variations among the states in average unemployment benefits will be used as a measure of state welfare outcomes.

The public assistance provisions of the Social Security Act authorize the national government to provide matching funds to states which provide assistance to the needy aged, the needy blind, the needy disabled, and dependent children. Federal contributions are in the form of grants-in-aid to the state and are based on the proportion of money paid by the state to each recipient. The federal share is determined by a formula which attempts to equalize welfare efforts among the states by having the federal government pay a larger share to states with higher needs and less wealth. The formula influences the size of benefits by authorizing the federal government to pay a large share of minimum benefits, and a lesser share of the remainder, up to a maximum amount above which it pays no share. The federal government also pays half of the cost of administering these programs.

The act was designed to induce greater participation in welfare programs by the states, and in this regard it has been successful. All of the states provide welfare assistance to the four categories of recipients aided by the federal government. Within the broad outlines of federal policy, however, the states retain considerable discretion in public assistance policy in terms of the amounts of money appropriated, the benefits to be paid to recipients, the rules of eligibility, and the means by which the programs will be administered. Each state may choose to grant assistance beyond the limits supported by the national government or it may choose to have no welfare programs at all. Each state establishes its own standards to determine need. Variations in average benefit payments in categorical assistance programs will be employed as a measure of state welfare policy outcomes.

In 1960 Congress passed the Kerr-Mills bill, amending the old age assistance (OAA) program. Under the amendment, the federal government will match, on a roughly 3-to-1 ratio, funds which are spent on the medical care of needy persons over 65 years of age. States have been slow to respond to this program; by 1963 only 23 had reported expenditures for the needy aged under Kerr-Mills provisions. This is a clear indication that the states are not necessarily forced into federally financed assistance programs and that they can remain outside of federal aid programs to which they object. Even among states which provide Kerr-Mills assistance there is wide variation in the number of recipients, the amount of benefits, and the standards of eligibility. State participation in the Kerr-Mills program, and average monthly payments made under it, are employed as measures of state policy outcomes.

The federally aided state assistance programs for the needy aged, the blind, the disabled, and dependent children are referred to as the *categorical assistance programs.* Only persons who fall within these categories of recipients are eligible for federal support. Aid to persons who do *not* fall into any of these categories but who, for one reason or another, are needy is referred to as *general assistance.* General assistance programs are entirely state-financed and state-administered. Without federal participation, these programs differ radically from state to state in terms of the persons aided, the criteria for eligibility, the amount and nature of the benefits, and financing and administration. Many of these programs continue to resemble Elizabethan welfare policy. The average general assistance payment is much lower than comparable payments in federally supported programs.

States also continue to maintain institutions for the care of individuals so destitute, alone, or ill that money payments do not suffice. These are the state orphanages, homes for the aged, and homes for the ill. They are for the most part state-financed as well as state-administered. Persons living in tax-supported institutions normally are not eligible for federal assistance, although they may receive old age payments for medical care received in a nursing home; and this provides incentive for the states to turn their indigent institutions into nursing homes. The quality of these homes and of the people employed to care for their residents varies enormously from state to state. Variations among the states in the overall quality of welfare services can be roughly measured by the per capita expenditures of state and local governments for public welfare.

The public health programs of state and local governments also vary a great deal from state to state. State health departments generally supervise local health programs, distribute state and local grants to local health departments, provide health services in areas where there are no local health facilities, and operate state hospitals. Local health officials provide most of the direct public services—the control of communicable diseases, environmental sanitation, protection of water and milk supply, air pollution control, laboratory services, the collection of vital statistics, and health education. The cost of providing for the medically indigent in America rests with state and local governments and private charity.

The federal government is becoming increasingly involved in public health. The U.S. Public Health Service, now a part of the Department of Health, Education, and Welfare, is one of the oldest agencies of the federal government, having been created in 1798 to provide medical and hospital care for merchant seamen. Today the service provides medical care and hospital facilities to certain categories of federally aided patients, enforces foreign quarantine regulations, licenses biological products for manufacture and sale, engages in and sponsors research, and administers federal grants-in-aid to the states for the improvement of health and hospital services. Federal grants-in-aid are available to promote the construction of hospitals, nursing homes, diagnostic centers, rehabilitation centers, medical schools, and other medical facilities. The Veterans Administration also provides extensive medical and hospital care.

It is important to note, however, that despite federal efforts in the field of health, state and local governments continue to spend over twice as much as the federal government for public health. Table V-1 indicates that, with the exception of the years of heavy postwar expenses for veterans' care, the federal government has always spent less in the health field than the states. State policies vary considerably in terms of per capita expenditures for health and hospitals, the number of patients in public institutions, the medical and hospital facilities available, and the relative reliance placed upon state versus local health care. All of these variables are employed as measures of state policy outcomes in the health field.

The passage of the Social Security Act Amendments of 1965, with Medicare provisions for prepaid hospital insurance for the aged under social security and low-cost voluntary medical insurance for the aged under federal administration, will mean a significant increase in the role of the national government in the health field. It may be that in the years ahead the national government, through the Medicare insurance programs, will come to spend as much or more than state governments for health care purposes. But in the early 1960's, when the data for this study was collected and analyzed, state and local governments carried the heaviest responsibility for the nation's public health.

ECONOMIC DEVELOPMENT AND PUBLIC HEALTH AND WELFARE POLICY

The federal government plays a major role in the shaping of state health and welfare programs. However, the states continue to exercise major responsibilities in the determination of health and welfare policy.[3] States retain the right to determine whether they will participate in federal programs. Within broad federal regulations, the states determine the benefits to be allocated to each recipient, the eligibility requirements, and the ways in which the programs are to be administered. In 1961 the average weekly benefits per recipient of unemployment compensation ranged from a low of $22 in Maine and North Carolina to a high of $110 in Connecticut. Similar variations in benefits are reported for other welfare programs. Wide variations among the states in per capita health and welfare expenditures can also be observed: per capita welfare expenditures ranged from a low of $75 in Virginia to a high of $506 in Louisiana, and per capita expenditures for health and hospitals ranged from a low of $12 in California to a high of $265 in Alaska. In addition, states have different eligibility requirements and different standards of determining need; as a result, states vary considerably in the number of welfare recipients per unit of population. States also vary with respect to the medical and hospital facilities available. Finally, the states differ in the extent to which health and welfare services are state rather than locally administered and financed.

What accounts for difference among the states in welfare policy? It is commonly assumed that the modern welfare state is a product of the industrialization and urbanization of Western society. There is little doubt that the levels of economic development affect the demand for health and welfare services. But only by a closer, state-by-state analysis can we observe systematically the impact of economic development on specific health and welfare policies. The object of this chapter is to describe differences among the states in health and welfare outcomes and then to identify the socioeconomic conditions associated

[3] See Richard E. Dawson and James A. Robinson, "The Politics of Welfare," in Herbert Jacob and Kenneth Vines, eds., *Politics in the American States* (New York: Little, Brown, 1965), pp. 371-410.

with differing outcomes. Because of the important role played by the federal government in public welfare, we also wish to identify the effect of federal policy on the specific choices of state governments in this field. As a result we must explore the complex relationships among economic development, federal policy, and state welfare outcomes.

ECONOMIC DEVELOPMENT AND WELFARE BENEFITS

Decisions about the amount of benefits to be paid welfare recipients are made primarily by state legislatures and state and local administrative agencies. These decisions obviously involve the allocation of values within the state political system. Welfare benefits are measured here by the average cash welfare payments made to six categories of needy individuals — the unemployed, the aged, the blind, the disabled, dependent children, and those on general assistance. Using benefits per recipient as our measure holds constant for the number of recipients and indicates the state's willingness and ability to provide welfare aid. This measure also gives a rough indication of the care provided to the indigent by the state.

In 1961 weekly unemployment benefits averaged over $40 in Ohio, California, Wisconsin, and Wyoming, almost twice as much as the average weekly unemployment benefits in Alabama, Arkansas, Maine, West Virginia, and North and South Carolina, all of which paid less than $24 to their average unemployed. The average nationwide unemployment check was $34 per week.

The range of differences among the states in federally financed public assistance benefits has been as great or greater than differences in unemployment compensation. Monthly OAA checks averaged about $68 for the nation, but ranged from a low of $35 in Mississippi to a high of $110 in Connecticut, a difference of over 300 per cent. Monthly benefits to the blind averaged $74 for the nation but varied from $38 in Mississippi to $118 in Massachusetts. The average monthly payment per family under the aid to dependent children (ADC) program was about $121; but the range of variation among the states in this program is tremendous. The average family ADC payment in Mississippi was $36, while the average payment in Illinois was $199. And, if we prefer to examine ADC payments on a per child rather than per family basis, the range of variation among the states is even greater; Mississippi paid $9 per child, while Illinois paid $46, and Connecticut, Minnesota, and New Jersey paid between $47 and $48.

Thirty-three states reported no payments at all under the Kerr-Mills program for medical care for the needy aged in 1961. Among those states reporting payment, average payments varied from $16 to

$457, with a national average of $193 per recipient. Disparities among the states in this program do not seem to be lessening with time, as we might expect. By 1963, four years after the program had been adopted by Congress, 22 states still had not made any payments under the program. Among participating states, average payments varied from $22 to $439.

We expect wide variation among the states in general assistance payments, since general assistance programs are wholly a responsibility of state and local governments. Figures in 1961 confirm this expectation: the average monthly payment per case was $68 for the nation, but average payments ranged as low as $13 in Alabama and as high as $114 in New Jersey.

Table V-2 indicates that urbanization, income, and education are significantly related to welfare benefits. These measures of economic development are closely associated with benefit levels in all major programs, with the single exception of the Kerr-Mills program of medical care for the needy aged. Discontent with the Kerr-Mills program is apparently not related to levels of economic development; states which participate in the program are not noticeably different in socioeconomic character from states which do not participate. Income is the single most important variable explaining welfare payments. Median family income explains between 40 and 65 per cent of the total variation among the states in the average benefits paid out to various categories of welfare recipients. It is far better to be indigent in a wealthy state than in a poor one.

TABLE V-2

The Relationship between Economic Development and Welfare Benefits

	Urban-ization	*Economic Development* Industrial-ization	Income	Education
Unemployment compensation, average weekly payment	.55*	.30*	.80*	.67*
Old age assistance, average monthly payment	.49*	.15	.63*	.61*
Aid to dependent children, average monthly payment	.51*	.26	.74*	.55*
Aid to the blind, average monthly payment	.59*	.28	.71*	.64*
Kerr-Mills medical assistance, average monthly payment	.17	.19	.15	.01
General assistance, average payment per case	.58*	.39*	.76*	.43*

Figures are simple correlation coefficients for the fifty states; an asterisk indicates a statistically significant relationship.

Figure V-1 is a scattergram picturing the relationship between income and average OAA payments in the fifty states. The broken line represents the hypothesis that the size of the payments is a function of income levels within the states. The scattering of states about the line

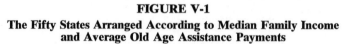

FIGURE V-1

The Fifty States Arranged According to Median Family Income and Average Old Age Assistance Payments

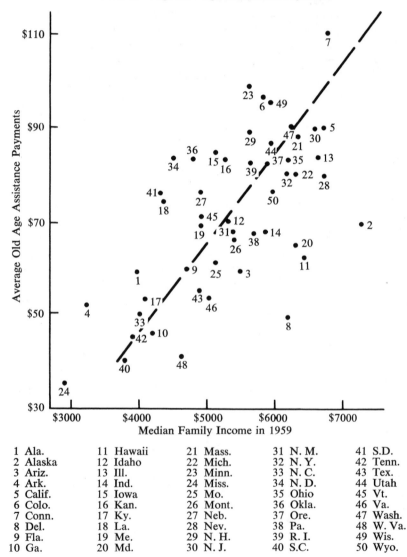

1 Ala.	11 Hawaii	21 Mass.	31 N. M.	41 S.D.
2 Alaska	12 Idaho	22 Mich.	32 N.Y.	42 Tenn.
3 Ariz.	13 Ill.	23 Minn.	33 N. C.	43 Tex.
4 Ark.	14 Ind.	24 Miss.	34 N. D.	44 Utah
5 Calif.	15 Iowa	25 Mo.	35 Ohio	45 Vt.
6 Colo.	16 Kan.	26 Mont.	36 Okla.	46 Va.
7 Conn.	17 Ky.	27 Neb.	37 Ore.	47 Wash.
8 Del.	18 La.	28 Nev.	38 Pa.	48 W. Va.
9 Fla.	19 Me.	29 N. H.	39 R. I.	49 Wis.
10 Ga.	20 Md.	30 N. J.	40 S.C.	50 Wyo.

shows that the states conform reassuringly well to the hypothesis. Only a few states are at a considerable distance from the line of regression, thus failing to conform to our hypothesis about the effect of economic development on benefit payments. Alaska, Delaware, Florida, and Maryland appear to pay somewhat less than we might expect on the basis of their income levels, while some of the midwestern states — Iowa, Oklahoma, Minnesota, and North and South Dakota — pay somewhat more than we would expect on the basis of their modest income levels.

It is not surprising that economic development levels are closely related to benefits paid to recipients of general assistance, since relief in this area is paid for exclusively from state and local fiscal sources; but it is surprising that economic development has such a great impact on benefit payments in those programs in which the federal government bears half the costs. We would expect federal participation to help reduce disparities among the states.

The reason why federal participation does not equalize benefit payments among the states is to be found in the formula which allocates federal money to the states for public assistance. When the categorical assistance programs were first created in 1935, federal grants-in-aid matched state contributions on a dollar-for-dollar basis. Later Congress amended its formula for matching federal funds in order to equalize welfare efforts among the states. Under the new formula the federal government pays a larger share of minimum benefits, and a lesser share of additional benefits up to a certain maximum benefit level, after which it pays nothing. The object of the formula is to help poorer states provide a minimum level of welfare service. However, since the formula means that the federal government pays a higher proportion of lower benefits, the federal government actually rewards states for low payments per recipient. Poorer states can get the most federal aid by paying small amounts of money to large numbers of people.

These findings about the important impact of the measures of economic development on benefit payments confirm the findings of previous research by Dawson and Robinson in state welfare policy.[4] Dawson and Robinson computed correlations between rankings of the states by size of benefit payments in 1961 and rankings of the states by urbanization, industrialization, income, and the proportion of population which was foreign born. Rank order correlation coefficients are

[4] See Dawson and Robinson, "The Politics of Welfare," and "Interparty Competition, Economic Variables, and Welfare Politics in the American States," *Journal of Politics,* XXV (1963), 265-89.

usually higher than simple coefficients, but the congruence between Dawson and Robinson's rank order coefficients and the simple coefficients in Table V-2 is striking. These researchers have reported coefficients between average rankings of the states by payment per recipient in six programs and rankings of the states by four socioeconomic variables as follows: urbanization = .62; industrialization = .39; income = .75; and foreign born = .75. They have also reported close relationships between socioeconomic development variables and welfare payments for the years 1941 and 1950, indicating that these relationships have persisted over time.

WELFARE RECIPIENTS

Benefit payments measure the care provided to each welfare recipient; they constitute a rough measure of the quality of welfare services. In contrast, the number of welfare recipients per 1000 population is a measure of the comprehensiveness of welfare care. Throughout the nation about 13 persons in 1000 were receiving OAA in 1961; about 20 persons in 1000 were receiving ADC payments; aid to the blind was distributed to less than one person in 1000; and aid to the disabled was given to 2 persons in 1000. In addition, the states estimated that there were 2.2 general assistance cases per 1000 population in that year. West Virginia, Louisiana, Mississippi, Alabama, and Oklahoma were among the states with the largest proportions of their population receiving public assistance; Hawaii, Wyoming, and New Hampshire were among the states with the lowest public assistance rates.

Table V-3 indicates that poorer states have larger proportions of

TABLE V-3
**The Relationship between Economic Development
and Welfare Recipients per Population**

| *Recipients per 1000 Population* | *Urbanization* | Economic Development | | |
		Industrialization	*Income*	*Education*
Old age assistance	−.22	−.36*	−.55	−.35*
Aid to dependent children	−.15	.16	−.30*	−.42*
Aid to the blind	−.33*	−.13	−.53*	−.51*
Aid to the disabled	−.20	−.14	−.64*	−.54*
Unemployment compensation	.39*	.69*	.58*	.23
General assistance	.38*	.34*	.40*	.25

Figures are simple correlation coefficients for the fifty states; an asterisk indicates a statistically significant relationship.

their populations on public assistance rolls. They pay smaller amounts of money to larger numbers of people. Having a large proportion of the population on public assistance rolls may be a natural concomitant of economic underdevelopment. However, as we have noted, federal formulas for the distribution of public assistance grants-in-aid accentuate this pattern by rewarding states which distribute money to larger numbers of people.

Additional evidence to support the inference that federal policy encourages poorer states to distribute public assistance to larger numbers of people can be found in the contrast in Table V-3 between the federal-state public assistance programs and state-financed general assistance care. The number of recipients of state general assistance per 1000 population is *greater* in the wealthy, urban, industrial states. In the absence of federal involvment, poorer states do *not* provide aid to as many people as the wealthier states.

The coefficients in Table V-3 clearly indicate that unemployment is a product of industrialization. Unemployment compensation payments were made to about 40 persons per 1000 in the nation in 1961. Unemployment compensation rates among the states are significantly related to levels of economic development, particularly industrialization. The greater the degree of industrialization, the more serious the problem of unemployment in terms of the percentage of the population affected.

HEALTH CARE

Seven variables have been selected for our overall evaluation of the health care offered in the several states. These variables include measures of both public and private health care. Public policy — federal, state, and local — is an important determinant of hospital facilities; a large number of hospitals are heavily subsidized by state and local governments and by the federal government. Figures on the number of hospital beds per population and the number of patients in public hospitals for the mentally ill and the retarded are heavily influenced by public decisions. On the other hand, the number of physicians per 1000 persons and the proportion of the population with hospital insurance is largely a product of private decisions about health care. Finally, infant death rates are proposed as measures of the overall quality of public and private health care.

On the whole, health care is not as closely associated with the levels of economic development as we might expect. Of course levels of economic development are closely related to the number of physicians per population and to the proportion of the population with health insurance; these measures are relatively uninfluenced by public programs of any kind. Table V-4 shows that health care in these terms is primarily a function of urbanization. There were approximately 14 physicians for every 1000 persons in the nation in 1961, and this ratio varied from a high of 17, 18, and 19 in the urban states of California,

FIGURE V-2

The Fifty States Arranged According to Urbanization and the Availability of Physicians

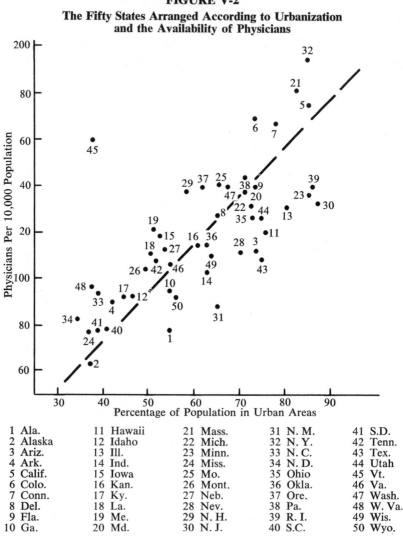

1 Ala.	11 Hawaii	21 Mass.	31 N. M.	41 S.D.
2 Alaska	12 Idaho	22 Mich.	32 N. Y.	42 Tenn.
3 Ariz.	13 Ill.	23 Minn.	33 N. C.	43 Tex.
4 Ark.	14 Ind.	24 Miss.	34 N. D.	44 Utah
5 Calif.	15 Iowa	25 Mo.	35 Ohio	45 Vt.
6 Colo.	16 Kan.	26 Mont.	36 Okla.	46 Va.
7 Conn.	17 Ky.	27 Neb.	37 Ore.	47 Wash.
8 Del.	18 La.	28 Nev.	38 Pa.	48 W. Va.
9 Fla.	19 Me.	29 N. H.	39 R. I.	49 Wis.
10 Ga.	20 Md.	30 N. J.	40 S.C.	50 Wyo.

Massachusetts, and New York to a low of 6 and 7 in rural Alaska, Alabama, Mississippi, and North Dakota.

Hospital facilities, on the other hand, do not appear to be a function of the levels of economic development. Public and private hospital facilities are in short supply throughout the nation; in 1961 there were 93 public and private hospital beds per 10,000 persons, and public facilities for 8 mental patients and 7 retarded patients per 10,000 persons. And there are inequalities among the states; hospital beds per 10,000 persons ranged from a low of 44 in Alaska to a high of 135 in New York. But Table V-4 suggests that these shortages and inequalities among the states are not directly related to levels of economic development.

TABLE V-4

The Relationship between Economic Development and Health Care

| | Economic Development | | | |
	Urban-ization	Industrial-ization	Income	Education
Physicians per population	.71*	.53*	.54*	.39*
Population with hospitalization insurance	.49*	.37*	.35*	.05
Hospital beds per population	.27	.07	.22	−.03
Patients in public mental hospitals	.04	.00	.06	.02
Patients in public institutions for the retarded	.04	−.08	.08	.19
Infant death rate, white	−.35	−.02	−.16	.03
Infant death rate, non-white	.23	−.21	−.18	−.23

Figures are simple correlation coefficients for the fifty states; an asterisk indicates a statistically significant relationship.

Surprisingly, levels of economic development have no affect on variations in infant death rates among the states. In 1961 there were 22 deaths of white infants under one year old per 1000 live births, and there was not much variation among the states on this white infant death rate: Utah had the lowest rate, 20 deaths per 1000 live births, and New Mexico was highest with 28 deaths. Table V-4 indicates that economic development is not related to the variation which does occur among the states.

The non-white infant death rate in America is about twice as great as the white infant death rate. About 41 non-white infant deaths per 1000 live births occured in 1961. There is greater variation among the states in this rate than in the rate for white infants: Vermont and New

Hampshire experienced 17 non-white infant deaths per 1000 live births, while Alaska experienced over 60. But this variation among the states is not associated with levels of economic development. Nor are non-white infant deaths associated with region: southern states are above the national average, but none of the five states with the highest ratios are in the South.

PUBLIC EFFORTS IN HEALTH AND WELFARE

Benefit levels are measured in terms of payments to recipients, but effort is measured in terms of per capita expenditures, expenditures relative to personal income, and expenditures relative to other public expenditures. On the whole, Americans do not spend a great deal on public health and welfare. Combined federal, state, and local expenditures in America for both health and welfare services amounted to only $10 billion in 1961. This figure, which breaks down to about $56 per capita or about 8 per cent of all government expenditures, indicates that Americans spent only 2.5 per cent of their total personal income for public welfare and health purposes. Of course an additional $22 billion is spent by federal, state, and local governments on social insurance programs, including OASDI, bringing the overall bill for social insurance, public welfare, and public health programs to $32 billion or about $177 per capita.

The welfare expenditures of the states amounted to about $26 per person in 1961. This figure includes state and local expenditures of federal monies as well as expenditures of state funds. In 1961 this measure of welfare effort, the per capita welfare expenditures in the states, ranged from a low of $11 in Virginia to a high of over $50 in Oklahoma, Colorado, and Louisiana. State and local governments spent an additional $22 per person for public health. Per capita expenditures for health ranged from a low of $10 and $11 in South and North Dakota to a high of over $40 in Wyoming and Nevada.

What is the effect of economic development on public health and welfare efforts? Table V-5 reveals an interesting difference between patterns of welfare expenditures and patterns of health expenditures. State efforts in public welfare, as measured by per capita welfare expenditures, apparently are *not* a function of the levels of economic development. None of the measures of economic development correlate with per capita welfare expenditures. But, on the other hand, all four measures of economic development are significantly related to the per capita health expenditures. Public health expenditures increase with increasing urbanization, industrialization, education, and particularly income.

What accounts for the fact that economic development affects per capita health expenditures but not per capita welfare expenditures? The answer appears to lie in the extensive federal involvement in the welfare field and the nature of this involvement. Earlier we have noted that the federal government contributes over half of the money used in public assistance programs but only about a third of the money spent for public health. Furthermore, we have noted that the formula for federal welfare contributions rewards poorer states which keep benefit payments low and thereby receive a larger proportion of their funds from the federal government. A glance ahead to Table V-6 indicates that the federal government carries a larger share of the costs of public welfare in poorer states. In terms of per capita expenditures, the federal government has been successful in equalizing welfare efforts among the states. Federal participation under its present formula, although it tends to perpetrate differences in benefit payments among the states which are based upon wealth, does overcome the influence of wealth on per capita welfare expenditures.

Dawson and Robinson provide additional evidence for attributing to federal policy the failure of economic development to affect welfare efforts. They observed that in 1941, prior to the time the federal government devised its present formula for overcoming the influence of wealth, per capita welfare expenditures were related to state per capita income. When the federal government contributed money on a simple dollar-for-dollar matching basis, state welfare efforts tended to reflect state per capita income. The rank order correlation coefficient for the relationship between per capita welfare expenditures and per capita income was .50; this rank order coefficient fell to .24 in 1950 and .03 in 1960. Dawson and Robinson attributed this decline to changes in the federal fund-matching formula which succeeded in eliminating inequalities among the states based upon wealth.[5]

In contrast to the absence of its impact on welfare expenditures, Table V-5 indicates that economic development does have an important impact on per capita health expenditures. In the health field, federal participation is not so extensive, and the formulas under which various grants are made do not result in the same equalizing effect. State efforts in the health field, as measured by per capita expenditures, are heavily influenced by the levels of economic development. Among the fifty states, increases in per capita health expenditures are related

[5] Dawson and Robinson, "The Politics of Welfare."

to increases in all four measures of economic development, particularly income.

Another measure of the health and welfare effort is the percentage of a state's personal income devoted to this field. This measure tends to hold constant for ability to pay and measures more closely a state's willingness to sacrifice personal income for health and welfare services. In 1961, the nation as a whole spent about 1 per cent of its total personal income on public health and welfare programs. In a number of states the proportion of personal income spent for health and welfare was less than one-half of 1 per cent, while in Oklahoma and Louisiana over 3 per cent of the state's personal income went for these purposes.

TABLE V-5

**The Relationship between Economic Development
and Public Health and Welfare Expenditures**

| | Economic Development | | | |
	Urban-ization	Industrial-ization	Income	Education
Per capita welfare expenditures	.19	.07	−.01	−.07
Per capita health expenditures	.45*	.39*	.56*	.42*
Health and welfare expenditures relative to personal income	−.16	−.19	−.44*	−.30*
Welfare expenditures as a percentage of total public expenditures	−.02	.02	−.39*	−.35*
Health expenditures as a percentage of total public expenditures	.31*	.43*	.12	−.12

Figures are simple correlation coefficients for the fifty states; an asterisk indicates a statistically significant relationship.

Just as increasing wealth lightens the burden of educational expenditures, so also does it lighten the burden of health and welfare services. Table V-5 shows that the proportion of personal income spent for health and welfare declines with increases in wealth. This inverse relationship between wealth and effort relative to income occurs in spite of the federal grant programs. Wealthier states provide much better benefits than poorer states, and yet poorer states tend to spend larger shares of their personal incomes for health and welfare services.

One final measure of the health and welfare effort is the proportion of public funds devoted to these programs. Only a little over 8 per cent of all state and local government expenditures in the nation were devoted to welfare purposes in 1961, while an additional 7 per cent went for public health services. A number of states spent less than 5

per cent of their public funds for welfare, while Oklahoma and Louisiana spent over 15 per cent. North and South Dakota spent less than 3
per cent of their public funds for health services, while several states
spent as much as 10 per cent of their funds for public health.

The coefficients in Table V-5 show that poorer states devote larger
shares of their public budgets to welfare services, while wealthier
states are able to reduce the proportion of their public funds going into
welfare programs. On the one hand, this situation may be a product of
the existence of poverty conditions in the poorer states which demand
greater relative attention of the government to welfare problems. On
the other hand, lower income levels do not seem to increase the
percentage of public money spent for health services. In fact, increased
urbanization and industrialization appear to require state and local
governments to devote larger shares of their budgets to health purposes, perhaps because federal matching funds induce poorer states to
spend public funds in the welfare field in order to bring more federal
money into the state. In our analysis of highway policy outcomes, too,
we seem to find that the lure of federal money is stronger in the poorer
states, and that they are, thus, motivated to devote larger shares of
their budgets to programs which receive federal monies.

FINANCING HEALTH AND WELFARE

If we are to attribute the equalization of per capita welfare expenditures among the states to the impact of federal contributions, we
must show that federal contributions to the states for welfare are
inversely associated with wealth. And Table V-6 shows this to be the
case. On a nationwide basis, the federal government provided about
half of all funds spent for public assistance in 1961, but the proportions
of public assistance funds coming from the federal government ranged
from 34 per cent in Connecticut to 77 per cent in Mississippi.

These varying proportions of federal public assistance funds are
closely related to all four measures of economic development, particularly wealth. The correlation coefficient of .83 in Table V-6 indicates
that median family income explains 70 per cent of the variation from
state to state in the federal proportion of public assistance funds. This
relationship between federal participation and state income levels is
shown graphically in Figure V-3. Federal percentages of total public
assistance expenditures decline with increases in state income levels.

Since the state-local percentages of total assistance expenditures
are actually one minus the federal percentage, we can merely reverse all
of the signs in Table V-6 relating to federal percentages in order to

know the relationship between economic development and *state-local* participation in public assistance financing. Thus, while federal percentages decline with increases in income levels, state-local percentages increase with increases in income levels. In short, increases among the states in the levels of economic development result in a shifting of financial support from the federal government to the states.

TABLE V-6

**The Relationship between Economic Development
and the Financing of Public Health and Welfare**

| | Economic Development | | | |
	Urban- ization	Industrial- ization	Income	Education
Federal percentage of public assistance funds	−.43*	−.35*	−.82*	−.59*
Federal health and welfare grants, per capita	−.31*	−.15	−.46*	−.31*
State percentage of state and local welfare expenditures	−.11	−.15	−.35*	.17
State percentage of state and local health expenditures	−.30*	−.07	−.08	−.15
Community Chest donations, per capita	.59*	.46*	.40*	.13

Figures are simple correlation coefficients for the fifty states; an asterisk indicates a statistically significant relationship.

The pattern of federal involvement in the whole health and welfare field can be revealed by totaling all federal grants for health, welfare, and related purposes and observing the distribution of these per capita grants among the states. As the negative coefficients in Table V-6 indicate, this measure of federal involvement is inversely related to economic development. The overall effect of federal policy in health and welfare is to help to offset disparities among the states based upon levels of wealth.

Participation of local governments in the financing of health and welfare programs also varies from state to state. Although federal policy requires that states participating in public assistance programs create an administrative board to oversee the administration of the state programs, it leaves open to the states the question of determining the relative degree of state, versus local, participation. The states can determine the extent of centralization or decentralization in both health and welfare financing.

On the whole, local governments in America participate more heavily in the financing of health services than in the financing of

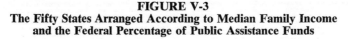

FIGURE V-3
The Fifty States Arranged According to Median Family Income
and the Federal Percentage of Public Assistance Funds

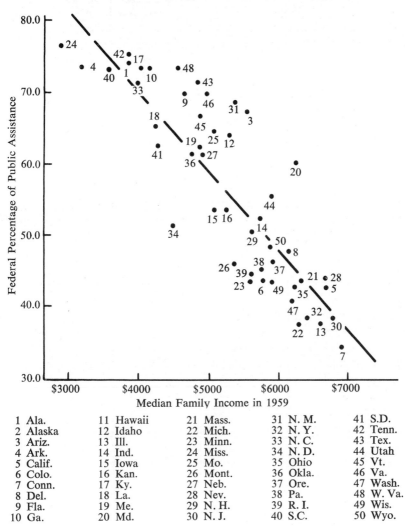

1 Ala.	11 Hawaii	21 Mass.	31 N. M.	41 S.D.
2 Alaska	12 Idaho	22 Mich.	32 N. Y.	42 Tenn.
3 Ariz.	13 Ill.	23 Minn.	33 N. C.	43 Tex.
4 Ark.	14 Ind.	24 Miss.	34 N. D.	44 Utah
5 Calif.	15 Iowa	25 Mo.	35 Ohio	45 Vt.
6 Colo.	16 Kan.	26 Mont.	36 Okla.	46 Va.
7 Conn.	17 Ky.	27 Neb.	37 Ore.	47 Wash.
8 Del.	18 La.	28 Nev.	38 Pa.	48 W. Va.
9 Fla.	19 Me.	29 N. H.	39 R. I.	49 Wis.
10 Ga.	20 Md.	30 N. J.	40 S.C.	50 Wyo.

welfare services. In 1961, local governments paid 43 per cent of the total state-local expenditures for public health while the states paid the remaining 57 per cent. However, in the welfare field, local governments paid only 15 per cent of the state-local bills while the states paid 85 per cent.

Table V-6 shows a slight tendency toward increased centralization in health and welfare financing in the poorer, rural states. The signs of the coeffieients all suggest that state governments tend to play a greater role in health and welfare financing than local governments in the less economically developed states. However, the coefficients are not very high, indicating that the relationship between economic development and centralization in health and welfare financing is not particularly close. It may be recalled that a slight tendency toward financial centralization at the state level among the poorer states has also been observed in the field of education. Southern states rely very little upon local governments for health and welfare services, while midwestern states rely heavily on these units for money. This reliance on local units in the Midwest prevails even in the poorer, less industrialized midwestern states.

Finally, it might be interesting to consider for a moment the pattern of private, in contrast to public, welfare effort. Complete information on private charitable activity is, of course, impossible to obtain. However, Community Chest donations are totaled for each state, and per capita Community Chest donations are here used as an index of private charitable activity. Table V-6 indicates that per capita contributions to Community Chest are closely related to levels of economic development. High levels of income, urbanization, and industrialization lead to increases in the per capita private charitable contributions. Community Chest activity is particularly well organized and well financed in urban areas. If welfare services were left completely in private hands, inequalities among the states, based on income levels, would be very great. While the effect of federal involvement in the care of the needy is to reduce inequalities among the states, the effect of private donations is to accentuate these inequalities.

RELATIONSHIPS AMONG POLICY VARIABLES

Up to now we have been concerned with the effect of economic development on health and welfare policy variables. We now turn to an examination of some of the important relationships *among* these policy variables.

Since we already know the relationships between levels of economic development and all of the policy variables listed in Table V-7, it is possible to predict most of the relationships among policy variables. For example, it has already been shown that benefit levels are positively correlated with economic development and that federal contributions are negatively correlated with economic development. This suggests that federal contributions are negatively correlated with economic development and, hence, with benefit levels, and Table V-7 shows this to be the case. Federal policy, through its formula for matching contributions, discourages high benefit levels. Federal grants per capita and the federal proportion of public assistance costs are negatively associated with the size of benefit payments. On the other

TABLE V-7
The Relationship between Public Health and
Welfare Expenditures and Benefit and Service Levels

	Per Capita Expenditures For Welfare	Per Capita Expenditures For Health	Federal Percentage Welfare	Federal Grants Per Capita	Local Percentage Welfare	Local Percentage Health
			Expenditures			
Per capita expenditures for welfare	1.00	.02	.04	.69*	−.23	.01
Per capita expenditures for health	.02	1.00	−.54*	−.21	.38*	.04
Unemployment benefits	.12	.59*	−.71*	−.31*	.32*	.21
OAA benefits	.38*	.29	−.57*	−.22	.31*	.28
ADC benefits	.18	.35*	−.64*	−.39*	.42*	.08
Blind benefits	.35*	.45*	−.65*	−.23	.27	.11
Kerr-Mills benefits	.26	.05	−.19	.03	−.13	−.15
General Assistance benefits	−.04	.42*	−.68*	−.49*	.41*	.10
OAA recipients	.67*	−.32*	.42*	.79*	−.40*	.03
ADC recipients	.27	−.24	.31*	.54*	−.39*	.04
Unemployment recipients	−.08	.47*	−.46*	−.29	.25	.03
General Assistance cases	.23	.12	−.34*	−.18	.14	−.04
Physicians	.34*	.39*	−.34*	.29	.24	.06
Hospitalization insurance	.16	.13	−.24	−.41*	.27	−.05
Hospital beds	.14	.26	−.27	−.33*	.36*	−.21
Mental patients	−.06	.09	−.08	−.24	.08	−.21
Retarded patients	.00	.02	−.10	−.24	.39*	−.10
Infant deaths, white	−.04	−.02	.23	.29	−.17	.11
Infant deaths, non-white	−.17	−.07	.16	.18	−.10	.06

Figures are simple correlation coefficients for the fifty states; an asterisk indicates a statistically signficant relationship.

hand, federal policy endeavors to insure that large numbers of people receive these minimum benefits. Thus, the federal aid measures are positively correlated with the number of recipients per population in the federal-state welfare programs. In contrast, federal participation is inversely associated with general assistance cases; this is because general assistance is a wholly state-administered program which depends upon state and local resources only. Since federal aid is granted inversely to state resources, it is negatively associated with state supported general assistance programs.

Since state-local percentages of total public assistance costs are really one minus the federal percentages, we can also say, on the basis of Table V-7, that benefit payments increase with increases in the state-local percentages of total public assistance costs. But the number of recipients per population decreases with increases in state-local percentages.

There is no significant relationship between federal proportions of total welfare expenditures and per capita total welfare expenditures — the federal formula does not encourage states to spend more money per capita for welfare purposes. If anything, an increase in welfare expenditures by a state (particularly as a result of an increase in benefit payments) will result in a decrease in the federal proportion of total welfare expenditures. Of course increases in either benefit payments or welfare recipients per population are associated with increases in total per capita welfare expenditures.

Earlier we noted that increases in the local proportions of state-local welfare efforts are related to increases in the levels of economic development. Furthermore, increases in the levels of economic development are related to increases in benefit payments. It follows that increases in the local percentages of state-local welfare efforts are associated with increases in benefit levels; this is shown in Table V-7. But this does not mean that local participation itself brings about higher benefit levels or that state administration is responsible for lower benefit levels. Rather it turns out that the levels of economic development determine both benefit payments and the degree to which states must take over welfare responsibilities from their localities. If the effect of economic development is controlled, no relationship can be observed between state and local participation and benefit levels or recipients per population.

Because per capita health expenditures are related to economic development, they too appear associated with the same outcomes which are related to economic development: benefit payments, recipients per population, and physicians per population. But per capita health expenditures are not related to hospital facilities or infant death rates.

PARTISANSHIP AND WELFARE POLICY

What effect does Democratic or Republican control of a state government have on its welfare policy outcomes? On the basis of questionnaires returned by over 3,000 Democratic and Republican national convention delegates. Herbert McClosky has concluded that Democratic and Republican leaders differ sharply over welfare issues: "... Republicans want not so much to abrogate existing social welfare or equalitarian measures as to keep them from being broadened. The Democrats, by comparision, are shown to be the party of social equality and reform, more willing than their opponents to employ legislation for the benefit of the underprivileged."[6] McClosky provides no evidence that Democrats or Republicans who occupy public office *act* in a manner consistent with their responses to questionnaires, however, nor does McCloskey claim that the policy choices of state governments under Democratic or Republican control will reflect these divergent views.

Perhaps policy outcomes are so influenced by socioeconomic conditions within the several states that neither Democratic nor Republican party control can significantly alter these outcomes. Perhaps the parties themselves are so much a product of their state constituencies that a change in the party in control of the state government does not produce any markedly different policy outcomes. Welfare policy outcomes, for example, may be determined by socioeconomic conditions rather than by the party which is in control of state government. The welfare policies of Democratic and Republican state governments in rural environments may resemble each other more than they resemble the policies of state governments with the same party label in urban environments.

Table V-8 shows the relationships among the fifty states between partisanship and several important health and welfare policy outcomes. In the simple coefficients, which do not control for the effect of economic development, Democratic party control is shown to be related to a number of welfare policy outcomes. This is not unexpected, since we already know that both Democratic party fortunes and welfare outcomes are related to economic development. Among the fifty states, Democratic control of state government is significantly associated with lower welfare benefit levels, larger numbers of welfare recipients, and increased state and federal participation in welfare finance. Is this association merely a product of the fact that many of the poorer states are Democratic states or are these outcomes really a product of low incomes and not of Democratic politics?

In general this seems to be the case. Most of the association between Democratic or Republican party control and welfare out-

---

[6] Herbert McClosky, *et al.,* "Issue Conflict and Consensus among Party Leaders and Followers," *American Political Science Review,* LIV (1960), 427.

comes appears to be a product of the intervening effect of economic development. Significant correlations between Democratic party fortunes and most welfare outcomes disappear once economic development is controlled in the partial coefficients. Partisanship appears to have little independent effect on the number of welfare recipients, the pattern of welfare financing, or welfare benefit levels. Of course, if the

TABLE V-8

The Relationships among Economic Development, Partisanship,
and State Health and Welfare Policies

| | Democratic Party Control | | | | | |
| | Lower Houses | | Upper Houses | | Governorships | |
	Simple	Partial	Simple	Partial	Simple	Partial
Per capita welfare expenditures	.01	−.08	.06	.02	−.12	−.23
Per capita health expenditures	−.10	.20	−.23	.02	−.13	.27
Expenditures relative to income	.24	.01	.28	.01	.16	−.18
State percentage of welfare	.37*	.26	.38*	.28	.33*	.19
State percentage of health	−.12	−.18	−.07	−.13	−.13	−.26
Federal grants per capita	.44*	.29	.48*	.31	.29	−.01
Federal percentage of welfare	.44*	−.07	.47*	.02	.47*	−.13
Unemployment benefits	.51*	−.13	−.51*	−.11	−.53*	.00
OAA benefits	−.65*	−.49*	−.63*	−.43*	−.59*	−.28
ADC benefits	−.64*	−.50*	−.65*	−.47*	−.68*	−.44*
Blind benefits	−.50*	−.26	−.51*	−.23	−.52*	−.14
Kerr-Mills benefits	−.23	−.34	−.21	−.25	−.03	−.01
General Assistance benefits	−.45*	−.26	−.51*	−.32	−.45*	−.07
OAA recipients	.38*	.13	.42*	.20	.30*	.04
ADC recipients	.39*	.10	.39*	.13	.15	−.00
Unemployment recipients	−.20	.26	−.26*	−.29	−.19	−.07
General Assistance cases	−.32*	−.32	−.29	−.22	−.30*	−.20

Figures are simple and partial correlation coefficients; partial coefficients control for the effects of urbanization, industrialization, income, and education; an asterisk indicates a statistically significant relationship.

southern states are removed from analysis, *all* significant coefficients between Democratic success and welfare policy disappear. The socio-economic relationships which were reported earlier can be observed in the non-southern states, but the partisanship relationships depend upon the inclusion of the southern states.

In short, there is little empirical evidence to support the view that Republican or Democratic party control seriously alters the welfare policy outcomes in the states. Welfare policy outcomes appear to be more closely tied to economic development than to partisanship.

PARTY COMPETITION AND WELFARE POLICY

What difference does it make in welfare policy outcomes whether a state has a competitive two-party system or a non-competitive one-party system? The Dawson and Robinson studies of welfare policy have dealt very effectively with this question, and the findings reported here provide further confirmation of their conclusions.

A common hypothesis in the literature is that the more competitive a state's party system, the greater its welfare effort; the hypothesis is based on the assumption that competition forces party candidates to appeal for electoral support to the numerically important lower socioeconomic groups. As a result, competitive parties advance policy positions reflecting the demands of these groups. Obviously, public assistance, unemployment insurance, public health care, and similar programs are of greater benefit to lower socioeconomic groups, and hence parties competing for their votes can be expected to support such programs. Competition brings about more liberal welfare policies, i.e., policies reflecting the interests of the "have-nots." In the absence of competition, a dominant party is more likely to reflect conservative welfare policies, i.e., policies reflecting the interests of powerful upper socioeconomic groups. Both V. O. Key and Duane Lockard have implied that competition leads to more liberal welfare programs.[7]

In order to investigate this hypothesis, Dawson and Robinson first ranked the states according to competition levels and several indices of welfare effort and then computed rank order correlation coefficients for the relationships between these variables.[8] They found moderate relationships between interparty competition and welfare outcomes, including benefit payments and per capita welfare expenditures, but these relationships were noticeably reduced when state income levels were held constant. They concluded that party competition is not as important in determining welfare policy outcomes as socioeconomic factors, especially per capita income.

As expected, the simple coefficients in Table V-9, which do *not* control for the effects of socioeconomic inputs, show that party competition is significantly related to a number of policy outcomes. Since the closest relationships occur between party competition and benefit payments, there is support for the hypothesis of Key and Lockard that competition brings about more liberal welfare policies. In addition,

---

[7] V. O. Key, Jr., *Southern Politics* (New York: Knopf, 1951), pp. 298-314; and Duane Lockard, *New England State Politics* (Princeton: Princeton University Press, 1959), pp. 320-40.

[8] Dawson and Robinson, "Interparty Competition, Economic Variables, and Welfare Policies in the American States."

increases in competition are related to decreases in federal involvement, decreases in the state proportion of state-local welfare expenditures, and decreases in recipients per population.

However, all of these relationships turn out to be a product of the effect of economic development. When the effect of economic development is controlled, the relationships between party competition and welfare outcomes disappear. None of the partial coefficients in Table V-9 indicate a statistically significant relationship. (Competition is not related to per capita welfare expenditures even in the simple coeffi-

TABLE V-9

**The Relationships among Economic Development,
Party Competition, and State Health and Welfare Policies**

| | Party Competition | | | | | |
| | Lower Houses | | Upper Houses | | Governorships | |
	Simple	Partial	Simple	Partial	Simple	Partial
Per capita welfare expenditures	.01	.02	.00	.00	.03	.01
Per capita health expenditures	.20	.11	−.27	−.01	−.20	.26
Expenditures relative to income	.27	.05	.28	.07	.36*	.08
State percentage of welfare	−.33*	−.20	−.30*	−.12	−.36*	−.19
State percentage of health	.10	.06	.06	.00	.06	.11
Federal grants per capita	.41*	.19	.41*	.17	.42*	.16
Federal percentage of welfare	−.49*	.02	−.50*	.08	−.52*	−.17
Unemployment benefits	−.52*	−.05	−.51*	−.04	−.52*	.11
OAA benefits	−.60*	−.01	−.57*	−.02	−.55*	−.02
ADC benefits	−.65*	−.04	−.60*	−.03	−.69*	−.07
Blind benefits	.61	−.11	.59*	−.11	−.53*	−.02
Kerr-Mills benefits	−.01	.01	−.04	−.00	−.04	.02
General Assistance benefits	−.56*	−.16	−.51	−.09	−.53*	−.05
OAA recipients	.32*	.07	.34*	.09	.48*	.12
ADC recipients	.28	−.06	.27	−.06	.17	−.02
Unemployment recipients	−.17	−.13	−.22	−.20	−.37*	−.16
General Assistance cases	−.32*	−.24	−.27	−.14	−.30*	−.12

Figures are simple and partial correlation coefficients; partial coefficients control for the effect of urbanization, industrialization, income, and education; an asterisk indicates a statistically significant relationship.

cients, because federal policy overcomes the effect of economic development in this measure.) Whenever there is association between competition levels and welfare outcomes in the American states, it occurs because economic development affects both competition and welfare outcomes. There is no empirical evidence to support the contention that party competition itself has any liberalizing effect on welfare policies.

POLITICAL PARTICIPATION AND WELFARE POLICY

What is the effect of political participation, as measured by voter turnout, on welfare policy outcomes? Convincing a priori arguments can be developed to support the view that increased levels of political participation should lead to increased welfare efforts and benefits. Survey researchers studying American voting habits are unanimous in concluding that the lower socioeconomic groups in the population exhibit less interest in politics and have lower voting rates. Historically these groups were the last to obtain the right to vote, and even today discrimination against Negroes, literacy tests, complicated registration procedures, and other devices deter members of the lower socioeconomic groups from exercising the franchise. In addition, these groups most often experience the political alienation, apathy, and feelings of political ineffectiveness which characterize non-voters. A low voter turnout usually means that higher socioeconomic groups are disproportionately represented among the voters; a high voter turnout that lower socioeconomic groups have gone to the polls and are more proportionately represented among the voters. When lower socioeconomic groups participate in politics, the assumption is that they will exercise some influence over public policy outcomes. Since lower socioeconomic groups are presumed to favor more liberal public assistance benefits, higher unemployment rates, and greater efforts in public health and welfare, their participation should be associated with these outcomes. In short, higher political participation levels among the states should be associated with more liberal welfare policies.

In order to explore this hypothesis systematically, it is again necessary to control for the effect of economic development. It is obvious that participation levels and welfare policy will be related, but the problem is to sort out the independent effect of participation on welfare outcomes.

The simple coefficients in Table V-10, which do not control for the effect of economic development, show that each of our indices of political participation is associated with several welfare policy outcomes. For example, participation levels are closely associated with benefit payments. Standing by themselves, these simple coefficients tend to confirm the chain of reasoning which has led to the proposition that increased participation by lower socioeconomic groups brings about more liberal welfare benefits. Voter participation is also associated with decreases in OAA recipients and increases in unemployment recipients and general assistance cases.

When the effects of economic development are controlled, however, *all* of these relationships disappear. The partial coefficients in

Table V-10 all indicate that there is no *independent* relationship between political participation and any of the welfare policies measured. The associations observed between participation and welfare policies are a product of the levels of economic development. Once urbanization, industrialization, income, and education are controlled, the relationship between voter participation and welfare policy disappears. There is no empirical evidence to support the view that increases in voter participation in the states bring about more liberal welfare policies.

TABLE V-10
**The Relationships among Economic Development,
Political Participation, and State Health and Welfare Policies**

	Governorships		Congressional 1962		Congressional 1958	
	Simple	Partial	Simple	Partial	Simple	Partial
Per capita welfare expenditures	.06	−.15	.64	.07	.03	.14
Per capita health expenditures	.07	−.29	.17	.03	.18	−.30
Expenditures relative to income	−.24	.05	−.19	.19	−.28	.08
State percentage of welfare	−.24	−.02	−.30	−.08	−.26	−.01
State percentage of health	.09	.05	.07	.09	.07	.11
Federal grants per capita	−.35*	−.12	−.31*	.00	−.39*	−.09
Fderal percentage of welfare	−.46*	.06	.54*	.00	.62*	.03
Unemployment benefits	.43*	−.04	.55*	.02	.58*	−.02
OAA benefits	.54*	−.02	.67*	.06	.63*	.02
ADC benefits	.64*	.02	.74*	.08	.73*	.06
Blind benefits	.50*	.04	.60*	.12	.57*	.04
Kerr-Mills benefits	.08	.07	.09	.08	.16	.18
General Assistance benefits	.47*	.04	.52*	.07	.50*	−.01
OAA recipients	−.40*	−.01	−.37*	−.02	−.46*	−.10
ADC recipients	−.10	.23	−.17	.22	−.19	.26
Unemployment recipients	.30*	.24	.31*	.23	.34*	.26
General Assistance cases	.37*	.20	.34*	.09	.34*	.23

Figures are simple and partial correlation coefficients; partial coefficients control for the effect of urbanization, industrialization, income, and education; an asterisk indicates a statistically significant relationship.

MALAPPORTIONMENT AND WELFARE POLICY

It is not unreasonable to assume that malapportionment of a state legislature may noticeably affect welfare policy outcomes. A number of writers on state government and politics have suggested that malapportionment results in conservative, penny-pinching attitudes toward welfare programs in state legislatures.[9] The failure of the states to come to grips effectively with the problem of indigency as well as other important domestic prolems, and the resulting necessity for increased federal involvement in policy areas once reserved to the states, has been attributed by informed persons to the debilitating effects of malapportionment in the state governments. Pressing problems of urbanization, including welfare problems, are left unattended by rural-dominated legislatures, it is argued, and the result is that the federal government must step in and take action.

There is no doubt that malapportionment has heavily overrepresented rural constituencies in state legislatures. And, since we generally attribute to rural constituencies conservative attitudes toward welfare programs, we may well expect malapportionment to correlate with decreases in benefit payments. Reapportionment which results in greater equality of representation on a population basis may be expected to bring about more liberal welfare policies.

Herbert Jacob, in a study appropriately entitled "The Consequences of Malapportionment: A Note of Caution," systematically examined the hypothesis that malapportionment directly affects welfare policy by comparative analysis.[10] Jacob noted that this hypothesis was largely the product of a priori reasoning and generalizing from limited examples; he proceeded to rank order all fifty states according to several measures of malapportionment and several policy measures including average OAA benefit payments and per capita health expenditures. On the basis of low rank order correlation coefficients, he concluded that there was little difference in welfare policy measures between states which were malapportioned and states which were well apportioned. Jacob was not prepared to say that malapportionment never had an effect on state policies, but he could find no measurable effect on the policy indices he investigated, and these indices tested the most frequently asserted hypotheses.

Table V-11 shows the relationship between welfare policy outcomes and the three measures of malapportionment described earlier. There are no significant relationships between welfare outcomes and the index of representation and the apportionment score. Both of these indices measure malapportionment in an abstract sense, and this form of malapportionment is unrelated to policy outcomes either in simple or

<hr>

[9] V. O. Key, Jr., *American State Politics* (New York: Knopf, 1956), p. 76; Charles R. Adrian, *State and Local Governments* (New York: McGraw-Hill, 1960), pp. 306-7; and Malcolm Jewell, *The State Legislature* (New York: Random House, 1962), pp. 30-33.

[10] Herbert Jacob, "The Consequences of Malapportionment: A Note of Caution," *Social Forces*, XLIII (1964), 256-61.

partial correlation analysis. Malapportionment, expressed as discrimination against urban areas, is assoiciated in simple coeffieients with lower benefit payments and greater federal participation in health and welfare financing. But when the effects of economic development are controlled, these relationships between urban underrepresentation and welfare outcomes disappear. Whatever association there is between

TABLE V-11

The Relationships among Economic Development,
Malapportionment, and State Health and Welfare Policies

| | | | Malapportionment | | | |
| | Index of Representation | | Index of Urban Underrepresentation | | Apportionment Score | |
	Simple	Partial	Simple	Partial	Simple	Partial
Per capita welfare expenditures	.02	.07	−.03	.03	−.19	−.07
Per capita health expenditures	−.09	−.00	.30*	.09	.10	.04
Expenditures relative to income	.09	−.04	.10	.12	.22	−.18
State percentage of welfare	−.12	−.17	−.26	−.11	−.08	−.05
State percentage of health	.10	.06	.34*	.31	.17	.18
Federal grants per capita	.01	−.08	−.31*	−.18	−.28	−.29
Federal percentage of welfare	.08	.02	.36*	.24	.13	.09
Unemployment benefits	−.17	−.03	.30*	.10	.13	.03
OAA benefits	−.01	.07	.37*	.04	.02	.06
ADC benefits	.12	.12	.49*	.06	.14	.09
Blind benefits	−.08	.16	.32*	.09	.01	.02
Kerr-Mills benefits	.13	.18	.34*	.27	.05	.05
General Assistance benefits	.03	.19	.51*	.18	.17	.16
OAA recipients	.15	.08	−.15	.04	−.19	−.04
ADC recipients	.01	−.03	−.11	−.13	−.19	−.04
Unemployment recipients	−.11	.02	.41*	.18	.29	.23
General Assistance cases	.05	−.19	−.33*	−.08	−.19	−.17

Figures are simple and partial correlation coefficients; partial coefficients control for the effect of urbanization, industrialization, income, and education; an asterisk indicates a statistically significant relationship.

urban underrepresentation and welfare policy it is clearly a product of the fact that the levels of economic development influence both welfare policy and urban underrepresentation. In short, there is no empirical evidence that malapportionment itself affects welfare policy outcomes.

Malapportionment is an important political system variable, and the extent of malapportionment may be an important influence on state political processes. But reapportionment, in and of itself, is not likely to bring about a noticeable liberalization of welfare policy.

CHAPTER VI

Highway Policy

DEVELOPMENT OF PUBLIC HIGHWAY POLICY

THE PROVISION OF PUBLIC HIGHWAYS is the second most costly function of state and local governments. Highway policy outcomes are not only of interest to the automotive and oil industries and to the driving public, but also to the Portland Cement Association, the railroads, the American Motor Truck Federation, farmers, the outdoor advertising industry, patronage-minded party chairmen, taxpayer associations, conservationists, and neighborhood improvement associations. These interests are concerned with the allocation of money for highway purposes, the sources of funds for highway revenue, the extent of gasoline and motor vehicle taxation, the regulation of traffic on the highways, the location of highways, the determination of construction policies, the division of responsibility between federal, state, and local governments for highway financing and administration, the division of highway funds between rural and urban areas and sections of the state, and a host of other important outcomes in highway politics. In this chapter we shall examine a number of highway policy outcomes in the fifty states, the impact of federal highway policies on these outcomes, and, of course, the impact of our economic development variables.

No invention has had such a far reaching effect on the life of the American people as the automobile; nor has any invention ever been distributed so rapidly to so many people. Henry Ford built one of the first gasoline-driven carriages in America in 1893, and by 1900 there were 8,000 automobiles registered in the United States. Five years

TABLE VI-1
Development of Public Highways, 1921-1961

	Rural and Municipal Surfaced Mileage (Thousands of Miles)	Motor Vehicle Registration (Millions)	Miles Traveled by Motor Vehicles (Millions)	State and Local Expenditures for Highways (Millions of $)	% of Total	State Highway Revenues from Highway-User Taxes (Millions of $)	Highway-User Taxes as % of State Highway Revenue	State Highway Revenues from Federal Funds (Millions of $)	Federal Funds as % of State Highway Revenue
1921	387	10,494	55,027	1,294	22.9	128	10	77	17.9
1930	694	26,750	206,320	1,741	20.6	851	49	94	7.3
1940	1367	32,453	302,188	1,573	14.0	1,321	84	196	11.0
1950	1939	49,162	450,216	3,803	13.7	2,587	68	426	11.9
1961	2179	75,847	737,535	9,835	17.5	5,511	56	2,729	30.5

From U. S. Bureau of the Census, *Historical Statistics of the United States* (Washington: Government Printing Office, 1960), pp. 456-64.

later, in 1905, there were almost 79,000 autos, and five years after that there were almost 500,000. The Model T was introduced in the autumn of 1908. By concentrating on a single unlovely but enduring model and by introducing assembly line processes, the Ford Motor Company produced automobiles for the masses. In 1921 there were over ten million cars in existence and the auto industry was the single largest manufacturing industry in the United States. In 1961 there were over 75 million registered motor vehicles in the nation, one for every 2.5 persons. Not only did the number of autos increase rapidly, but there were also important increases in the amount of driving that was being done. The miles traveled by motor vehicles increased at an even faster rate than the number of vehicles: it is estimated that 55 billion miles were driven in 1921, compared with 737 billion miles in 1961.

In addition to its economic and sociological significance, the invention of the automobile has had an important impact on government activity.[1] Governments spent very little for public roads at the beginning of the century; only $175 million was reported spent for roads by all state and local governments in 1902. The only hard-surfaced roads to be found were provided by big-city governments, a total of about 100,000 miles. But the automobile has brought about an insatiable demand for bigger and better highways. The automobile owner provides the broad base of political support for highway construction, but the leadership has come from the automotive and oil industries, the construction industry, the cement and equipment manufacturers, the organized farm interests seeking farm-to-market roads, and the newly created trucking industry. The railroad industry has provided the only substantial opposition to highway building, but all of the victories have gone to the supporters of highway transportation. By 1921 there was an estimated total of 387,000 miles of surfaced roads in America, and about $1.3 billion per year was being spent by state and local governments for highways. This represented over 20 per cent of all state-local expenditures at the time. Surfaced mileage doubled between 1921 and 1930, and highways expenditures continued to rise. The depression curtailed state-local highway expenditures just as it did automobile production, but, with the aid of federal public works programs, surfaced mileage doubled again by 1941. Highway expenditures, however, declined slightly as a proportion of total state-local expenditures.

By 1961 there were over two million miles of surfaced roads in

[1] For a complete description of highway policy in the United States, see Philip H. Burch, Jr., *Highway Revenue and Expenditure Policy in the United States* (New Brunswick: Rutgers University Press, 1962).

America and state-local expenditures for highways totaled nearly $10 billion annually. Highways expenditures were back up to almost 18 per cent of all state-local expenditures. In about half of the fifty states, expenditures for highway purposes exceeded one-fifth of all state-local expenditures, and in no state was the proportion less than one-eighth. Some states spent as much as one-third of their public funds on highways. We shall examine the states' highway expenditures in some detail later in this chapter.

Prior to the rise of the automobile, expenditures for public roads came out of general revenues, primarily the revenue from property taxation. The automobile changed public highway financing by providing governments with revenue sources from highway users. The first of these sources was motor vehicle registration fees, but after World War I excise taxes on gasoline were initiated. In 1921 motor vehicle taxes provided state governments with $122 million in revenue, while gasoline taxes contributed only $5 million. But by 1930 gasoline taxes contributed over half of the total highway-user receipts, which amounted to a respectable $851 million. Today gasoline taxes provide twice as much revenue as motor vehicle taxes. By 1940 highway-user taxes were the largest source of highway funds (84 per cent). The theory is that such taxes insure that the cost of highways is paid by the user. In fact, most states exempt gasoline purchased for vehicles which do not use the highways, such as farm equipment, from taxation. By 1961 all states taxed gasoline at a rate of from $.05 to $.07 per gallon. The federal government, which began taxing gasoline at $.01 per gallon in 1932, now collects $.04 per gallon. All fifty states obtain revenue from motor vehicle registration fees, ranging from $3 for passenger cars in Louisiana to $70 in Oklahoma. Usually heavier vehicles, trucks and buses, pay higher fees on the grounds that they inflict greater damage on the highways. More will be said about highway financing later, but it is interesting to note here that, by 1961, state highway revenue from gasoline and motor vehicle taxes amounted to over $5.5 billion and provided 56 per cent of all state highway funds.

At the beginning of the century, most road expenditures were made by local governments, particularly cities. Cities had very early created hard-surfaced street networks capable of servicing motor vehicles reasonably well. The greatest increase in surfaced mileage prior to World War II came in rural areas, which were, to say the least, unprepared for the advent of the automobile. State after state established state highway departments charged with the task of constructing highways in rural areas. State highway systems came into being, and state governments assumed direct responsibility for the construction and maintenance of a large proportion of public roads. States also began to distribute aid to local governments for highway purposes. State highway departments very often classified streets and highways in an effort to develop a rational scheme for dividing responsibility between state and local governments. In rural areas the primary state highway system connected cities, the secondary system connected primary highways with local land-service roads, and land-service roads provided direct access to farms and homes. In urban areas the primary street system connected state highways and major sectors of a city, the secondary street system connected primary streets with local streets, and local streets provided direct access to residences, businesses, and so on. Since the states generally financed the primary system, local communities often pressured state highway departments to classify more roads as primary state highways in order to shift the burden of finance onto the state. As a result, the proportion of roads designated as primary state highways gradually increased. Very often the criterion for inclusion in the primary state highway system favored rural areas, for example, the stipulation that the primary system connect county seats. The rural bias of some state highway departments lingers even today; we will return to this topic later in the chapter.

FEDERAL HIGHWAY POLICY

It was in the Federal Aid Road Act of 1916 that the federal government, through its Bureau of Public Roads, first provided regular funds for highway construction under terms which gave the bureau considerable influence over state policy. For example, in order to get federal money states were required to have a highway department, and to have their plans for highways construction approved by the Bureau of Public Roads. In 1921 federal aid was limited to a connected system of principal state highways, now called the federal aid primary highway system. Uniform standards were prescribed and even a uniform numbering system added, such as "U.S. 1" or "U.S. 30." Federal aid was to be limited to a maximum of 7 per cent of the total road mileage of the state and was to connect major cities. The emphasis of the program was clearly rural. The federal aid formula appropriated funds one-third on the basis of population, one-third on the basis of area, and one-third on the basis of total mileage of postal routes in the state. States were required to match federal monies, dollar for dollar. As Table VI-1 indicates, federal funds for state highways amounted to $77 million dollars in 1921, or about 18 per cent of all state revenue spent for highway purposes.

FIGURE VI-1
The National System of Interstate and Defense Highways

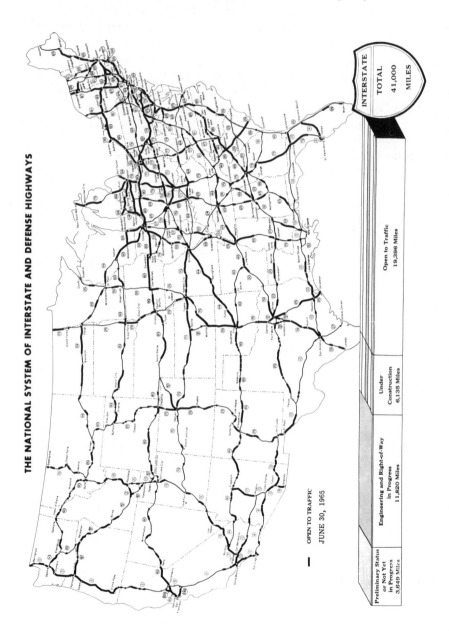

Federal aid flucuated considerably before World War II as a result of the depression and government countercyclical measures. In 1930 federal aid was only $94 million or 7.3 per cent of all state revenue devoted to highways, but in 1931 it was $218 million or 16 per cent of state highway revenue. In some depression years federal aid amounted to over 25 per cent of state highway revenue. During these years federal aid was based upon work relief policies rather than highway policies. It was not until 1944 that the federal government redefined its role in highways.

The Federal Highway Act of 1944 designated a federal aid secondary system of farm-to-market roads and provided for urban extension of primary roads, in addition to the federal aid appropriations for the primary highway system. Federal funds for primary, secondary, and urban extension roads, commonly call ABC funds, are determined by three separate formulas but all take into account area, population, and postal route mileage. These ABC funds are matched fifty-fifty by the states. In the use of federal funds, states make the surveys and plans, let the contracts, and supervise the construction, but only with the approval of the Bureau of Public Roads. All ABC roads remain under the administrative control of the states, who are responsible for their operation and maintenance. In 1961, ABC federal funds amounted to about $700 million. All payments to contractors for work done on any federal aid project are made from state revenues; the Bureau of Public Roads makes very few direct payments.

The Federal Highway Act of 1944 also authorized the national system of interstate and defense highways (I), now the dominant feature of federal highway policy. However, prior to 1956 only modest funds were provided for the I system and these were provided on a fifty-fifty matching basis. It was not until the Federal Highway Act of 1956 that Congress became serious about the I system, provided for its completion by 1972, and changed the matching basis to 90 per cent federal, 10 per cent state. This Act authorized 41,000 miles of highway designed to connect principal metropolitan areas, cities, and industrial centers, thereby shifting the emphasis of the federal activity from rural to urban needs. Figure VI-1 shows the I highway system as it will look upon its completion. Although the system will constitute less than 2 per cent of the total surfaced mileage in the nation, it is expected to carry over 20 per cent of all highway traffic. The Bureau of Public Roads has been given strong supervisory powers, including selection of routes (it could even transfer interstate mileage and funds out of a non-cooperating state), but administration, budgeting, and execution are still left to state highway departments. Federal monies are paid to the states, not to the contractors, as work progresses. The Federal Highway Trust Fund in the Bureau of Public Roads is responsible for the orderly scheduling of federal aid fund obligations and the phasing out of reimbursement requests of the states. A state can proceed at a more rapid rate in building its I highways if it chooses to do without federal reimbursement for a period of time; but in practice this is not done, and the bureau makes the real determination of who gets what, when, and how in the interstate highway program. The 1956 act has established uniformity in construction and engineering specifications and maximum size and weight limits for I highway users. It has also agreed to reduce by 0.5 per cent the state share of the cost of I highways if a state prohibits advertising on I highway rights-of-way. However, with only garden clubs available to battle with the billboard industry, only 16 states had adopted the ban by 1962, despite the federal incentive.

The federal interstate highway program reasserted federal interest in the highway field. By 1961 federal interstate funds amounted to over $2 billion annually, bringing the federal aid highway total (interstate plus ABC funds) to over $2.7 billion each year. Federal funds for highway construction now amount to over 30 per cent of all state highway revenue.

Occasionally specific highway issues are raised in particular states, issues which appear to center on mundane technical questions but which are actually highly charged political issues. A classic example of this type of policy decision was the dispute in Pennsylvania over the weight limitations on trucks.[2] The Pennsylvania Railroad, whose advice is not lightly dismissed in Pennsylvania politics, indicated its concern for the deleterious effects that heavy trucks had on highway surfaces. The "Pennsy" enlisted the support of the Automobile Association of America (AAA) and secured a law limiting truck weights to 45,000 pounds, while most other states had load limits of 60,000 to 70,000 pounds. Pennsylvania is the keystone state in east-west traffic in the nation, and the weight limitation seriously affected truck transportation. But the trucking industry was no patsy either, particularly under a Democratic administration that owed very little to the Pennsylvania Railroad. A titanic political struggle was fought for a period of years over the technical results of road tests, accident statistics, and court records, not to mention public charges and countercharges of vote buying, influence peddling, and libel. Eventually truck load limits were raised. As interesting as case studies such as these may be,

[2] Andrew Hacker, "Pressure Politics in Pennsylvania: The Truckers vs. the Railroads," in Alan F. Westin, ed., *The Uses of Power* (New York: Harcourt, Brace and World, 1962), pp. 323-76.

however, they do not permit comparative analysis of the underlying economic conditions and political system characteristics which influence policy outcomes in all fifty states.

Finally, interstate comparisons in highway policy are complicated by differences in area, geography, soil, and terrain among the states. Expansive but thinly populated states must maintain more miles of highway in relation to their populations than smaller, heavily populated states. It is relatively cheap to build highways in deserts but expensive to do so in mountains. Highways built in climates which are subject to heavy freezes, snowfalls, and rainfalls require more maintenance and repair than highways located in less rigorous climates. In short, it can be expected that natural factors will contribute to variations in highway outcomes among the states, and that socioeconomic or political factors will not explain all of the differences among the states in highway matters.

PUBLIC HIGHWAY EXPENDITURES

Public highways represent the second most costly function of state governments. About $10 billion were spent for highways in the United States in 1961, or about $54 per person. These expenditures are exceeded only by the cost of public education. Like educational expenditures, highway expenditures vary a great deal from state to state. Since federal highway funds flow through state highway departments, state expenditure figures include federal highway money. Per capita state-local highway expenditures in the states in 1961 ranged from a high of $143 in Wyoming to a low of $35 in New Jersey. Like educational expenditures, highway expenditures do not guarantee a good highway system, but they do provide a rough index of the extent to which supporters of highways have succeeded in obtaining public funds for their objectives.

Per capita highway expenditures in the states are significantly related to urbanization and industrialization. The relationship is an inverse one: the negative coefficients in Table VI-2 indicate that increases in urbanization and industrialization result in a decrease in per capita highway expenditures. Rural agricultural states spend more per capita on highways than urban industrial states. This is true whether we examine total state-local highway expenditures or only state highway expenditures.

Not only do the rural farm states spend more *per capita* on highways, but they also spend more in relation to their personal income. Highway expenditures amount to about 2.4 per cent of personal income for the nation as a whole. In North Dakota, however, highway expenditures amount to over 6 per cent of personal income, while New Jersey highway costs take only 1.3 per cent of that state's personal income. These varying amounts of personal income spent on highways are very closely related to urbanization and industrialization. Table VI-2 shows negative coefficients of .67 and .76 for the relationships between highway expenditures relative to income and urbanization and industrialization. The tendency for rural farm states to spend more per capita for highways than the urban states results in an even more pronounced tendency for these rural farm states to dig deeper into their personal incomes to support these expenditures. We will see in the next section that the federal government relieves some of the burden of highway financing in the rural states by giving them proportionately more funds than it gives to urban states. But federal monies notwithstanding, rural states still expend more of their personal income for highways than urban states.

One other measure of highway effort is the percentage of all state-local public funds devoted to highway purposes. This is a measure of highway effort relative to other publicly financed activities. Highway expenditures amounted to about 17.5 per cent of all state-local expenditures in the nation in 1961; only educational expenditures (36.6 per cent of all state-local expenditures) were greater. The proportion of public funds devoted to highways ranged from a low of 9.8 per cent in Hawaii to a high of 34.3 per cent in South Dakota, which was the only state which spent as much on highways as it did on education.

TABLE VI-2
The Relationship between Economic Development
and State and Local Highway Expenditures

| | | Economic Development | | |
	Urban-ization	Industrial-ization	Income	Education
State and local highway expenditures per capita	−.37*	−.51*	.02	.04
State highway expenditures per capita	−.39*	−.40*	.00	.04
Highway expenditures relative to income	−.67*	−.76*	−.50*	−.14
Highway expenditures as percentage of total expenditures	−.65*	−.65*	−.47*	−.10
Discrimination against urban areas in state highway expenditures	−.30*	.15	.24	−.16

Figures are simple correlation coefficients for the fifty states; an asterisk indicates a statistically significant relationship.

Levels of economic development are closely related to the proportion of public funds spent on highways. There is a pronounced tendency for rural farm states to spend greater proportions of public funds on highways than urban industrial states.

FIGURE VI-2

The Fifty States Arranged According to Urbanization and Highway Expenditures

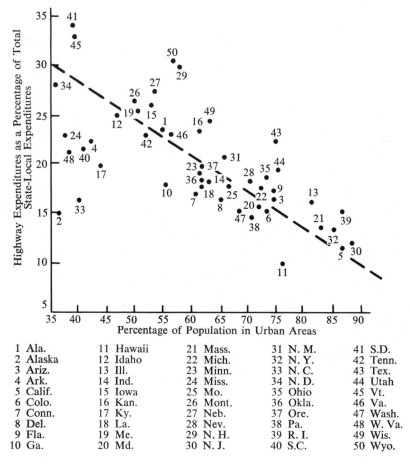

1 Ala.	11 Hawaii	21 Mass.	31 N. M.	41 S.D.
2 Alaska	12 Idaho	22 Mich.	32 N. Y.	42 Tenn.
3 Ariz.	13 Ill.	23 Minn.	33 N. C.	43 Tex.
4 Ark.	14 Ind.	24 Miss.	34 N. D.	44 Utah
5 Calif.	15 Iowa	25 Mo.	35 Ohio	45 Vt.
6 Colo.	16 Kan.	26 Mont.	36 Okla.	46 Va.
7 Conn.	17 Ky.	27 Neb.	37 Ore.	47 Wash.
8 Del.	18 La.	28 Nev.	38 Pa.	48 W. Va.
9 Fla.	19 Me.	29 N. H.	39 R. I.	49 Wis.
10 Ga.	20 Md.	30 N. J.	40 S.C.	50 Wyo.

In short, whether one prefers to measure highway efforts in per capita expenditures or in relative terms, the tendency for rural agricultural states to emphasize this particular function of state government is unmistakable. Figure VI-2 shows the fifty states arranged according to urbanization and the proportion of public funds spent on highways.

Only Alaska and North Carolina deviate markedly from the proposition that ruralism results in increased highway spending.

If levels of highway expenditures are influenced by economic development, what effect does economic development have on the character of these expenditures? Does urbanization and industrialization affect the distribution of highway program expenditures between rural and urban areas? From an engineering standpoint we might expect the distribution of expenditures to be determined primarily by highway use. But observers of state highway programs have contended that in practice this is not usually the case. Phillip H. Burch argues effectively that "the American city is being woefully short-changed in the allocation of state highway department money."[3] It is difficult to measure the extent to which urban or rural areas are not receiving a fair share of state highway expenditures. Burch notes that unpublished U.S. Bureau of Public Roads data show that about 44 per cent of all traffic occurs in urban areas, while state highway departments spend only about 25 per cent of their highway funds in urban areas. Of course, the degree of discrimination against urban areas varies from state to state. With Burch's data it is possible to rank the states according to *proper* expenditures for urban areas.[4] The urban percentage of total highway department expenditures can then be subtracted from the urban percentage of total traffic in each state; the larger the difference, the more discrimination against urban areas. In every state except California and Arizona, the differential favors rural areas; i.e., in every state except California and Arizona, urban traffic percentages are larger than urban highway expenditure percentages. California is reported to have 49 per cent of its highway expenditures going to urban areas, where 48 per cent of its total traffic is located. Ratios are also rather close in Rhode Island, Illinois, New Jersey, Connecticut, Massachusetts, and Ohio. In contrast North Dakota is reported to have 30 per cent of its traffic in urban areas, but it is spending only 4 per cent of its state highway funds in these areas.

Discrimination against urban areas in state highway expenditures is only slightly related to ruralism in the states. The most flagrant discrimination occurs in rural states, and the fairest ratios occur in urban states. But throughout the fifty states, urbanization is not as closely related to fairness in highway fund distribution as we might expect. We shall see in a later section that urban areas are also discriminated against in state grants to localities for local roads, and both discrimination against cities in direct expenditures and discrimina-

[3] Burch, p. 165.
[4] *Ibid.*, pp. 166-67.

tion in state grants for local roads turn out to be slightly greater in the rural states. It is important to note, however, that in recent years discrimination against urban areas in highway expenditures has been modified to some extent. Burch has noted that significant gains have been made by the urban areas in most states in the percentages of state highway funds they receive. The federal interstate highway program has also improved the relative position of urban areas in highway fund allocations.

Quite clearly, rural politics are much more highway-oriented than urban politics. Part of this phenomenon may be a product of the historical problems of rural isolation; "Let's Get Out of the Mud" was a familiar battlecry in rural politics a few years ago. Rural roads disturb relatively few individuals, while a metropolitan highway involves uprooting thousands of outraged residents and irate businessmen. Freeways are only a good idea when they run through someone else's backyard! Mileage is much cheaper and faster to build in rural areas; urban highways require more years and more money per mile. As Burch points out, "urban highways are poor politics for a governor when his successor will be cutting all the tapes."[5] Finally, it may be that urban dwellers have come to accept traffic jams as facts of life: they have never known anything better, so they fail to fight for highways with quite the same zest as their country cousins.

THE FEDERAL EFFECT

What is the impact of federal highway programs on highway policy in the fifty states? Federal highway aid to the states totaled about $15 per capita in 1961. However, federal aid distribution decisions insured that per capita federal aid varied considerably from state to state. Hawaii received about $2 per capita from the Bureau of Public Roads and four other states received less than $10 per capita (New York, Pennsylvania, Delaware, and North Carolina). In contrast, Wyoming received about $97 per capita in federal highway aid.

Reliance placed upon federal funds in highway finance also varies from state to state. In 1961, federal highway funds as a percentage of total state highway expenditures ranged from a low of 10 per cent in Delaware to a high of over 50 per cent in Alaska, Montana, Vermont, and Wyoming.

Both the per capita amount of federal highway aid and the extent of state reliance upon federal funds vary inversely with the levels of economic development. The impact of federal aid is greater in rural

[5] *Ibid.*, p. 173.

farm states than in urban, industrial states. Table VI-3 shows that per capita federal highway aid and federal aid as a percentage of total highway funds decrease with increases in urbanization and industrialization. These relationships are not particularly close, suggesting that federal aid decisions are influenced by factors other than urbanization and industrialization, but there is an identifiable tendency for federal highway funds to play a greater role in rural farm states. Note also that in the highway field federal funds do *not* tend to offset income differences among the states. There is no significant relationship between state income levels and federal highway aid.

TABLE VI-3
The Relationship between Economic Development and Public Highway Finance

	Economic Development			
	Urban-ization	*Industrial-ization*	*Income*	*Education*
Federal highway funds per capita	−.39*	−.31*	.07	.22
Percentage of state highway funds from federal government	−.45*	−.42*	.10	.23
Highway-user revenues as a percentage of total state revenue	−.32*	−.35*	−.27	−.10
Highway-user revenues as a percentage of state highway funds	.04	.20	−.32*	.26
Diversion percentages of highway-user revenue	.42*	.29	.07	.06
State percentage of total highway expenditures	−.30*	.05	−.15	−.04
Percentage of state highway funds granted to localities	.01	−.34*	−.08	−.01
Percentage of state road grants going to county rather than municipal roads	−.35*	−.45*	−.38*	.07

Figures are simple correlation coefficients for the fifty states; an asterisk indicates a statistically significant relationship.

STATE HIGHWAY ORGANIZATION AND FINANCE

The political importance of highway construction and the millions of dollars spent on highway building contracts each year have resulted in a tendency in some states to set highway departments and highway funds apart from the other functions of state government. Interests favorable toward highway construction (road builders, oil and gas companies, automobile associations, and so on) have generally argued for the organization of independent highway departments or commissions, free from direct gubernatorial control. They have also supported a system of earmarking certain state revenues, generally gasoline taxes, motor vehicle registration fees, and other highway-user revenues, for use on highways only. Of course not all states have been willing to remove highways from the regular channels of public control, and the pattern of highway organization and finance varies considerably from state to state.

Robert S. Friedman has classified the fifty states according to their degree of organizational independence from the governor in highway policy.[6] He has defined a dependent highway department as one in which the governor is free to name without restrictions his own highway department head who would serve at the pleasure of the governor. In contrast, an independent department is governed by a multimember board or commission who would choose the department head. The board may be chosen by the governor under certain restrictions, but its term of office would not coincide with that of the governor and its members could not easily be removed from office. Very often these board members or commissioners are chosen to represent geographic areas in the state, in formal recognition of the pork-barrel character of much highway work; this localism is opposed by proponents of coordinated planning for the state highway network.

Using these definitions, Friedman has roughly classified states into three categories of organizational independence in highway policies.[7] In contrast to the arguments of those defending highway interests, he does not feel that highway programs in states in which independence prevails are any more favored than in states in which the governor exercises significant control. However, our analysis reveals that the average per capita highway expenditures of Independent states is $64, and of Partially Independent states $69, while in Dependent states this figure is only $56. These figures suggest a slight relationship between organizational independence and increased highway expenditures, although there is no evidence that this is a causal relationship. Many of the states with gubernatorial control are the most urban, industrial states in the nation. This leads us to believe that ruralism produces both increased highway spending and independent highway boards.

The principal source of highway finance is highway-user revenue. Federal highway aid constitutes about 30 per cent of all state highway funds, but most of the remaining 70 per cent comes from taxes and fees

[6] "State Politics and Highways," in Herbert Jacob and Kenneth Vines, eds., *Politics in the American States* (New York: Little, Brown, 1965).

[7] *Independent:* Ariz., Ark., Colo., Del., Fla., Ga., Idaho, Ind., Iowa, Me., Mass., Mich., Miss., Mo., Mont., N.H., N.M., N.C., S.C., Tex., Utah, Wash., Wis., Wyo.; *Partially Dependent:* Calif., Conn., Kan., La., Md., Minn., Nev., Okla., Ore., S.D., Vt., Va., W. Va.; *Dependent:* Ala., Alaska, Hawaii, Ill., Ky., Neb., N.J., N.Y., N.D., Ohio, Pa., R.I., Tenn. (Friedman, p. 423).

levied upon highway users. In only a few states are any general revenues used for highway purposes. The state gasoline tax alone accounts for approximately half of all highway receipts. State gasoline tax rates are surprisingly uniform from state to state; all states levy gasoline taxes of from $.05 to $.07 per gallon. The second most important highway-user revenue source is the motor vehicle registration fee. In some states, particularly in the South, this fee is primarily a regulatory device with yearly charges running from only $3 to $5. In other states fees for passenger cars are $15 or more, with higher fees for heavier vehicles, particularly trucks and buses. Some states prorate fees on trucks and buses according to both weight and miles traveled. Toll road receipts constitue a major highway revenue source in some states. Tolls extract revenue from *through* traffic which has originated in another state and is destined for still other states. New York, New Jersey, and Pennsylvania collect over half of all the toll receipts in the nation.

Reliance upon highway-user revenue is only slightly related to economic development levels. Two measures of reliance upon highway-user revenues have been analyzed: the percentage of total *state revenue* from highway user-taxes in 1961, and the percentage of state *highway funds* from highway-user taxes in that year. The percentage of total state revenue from highway users varies from a low of 3.0 per cent in Nevada to a high of 49.0 per cent in Missouri. The percentage of state highway funds derived from highway users ranges from a low of 21 per cent in Alaska to a high of 62 per cent in Texas and New Mexico. Table VI-3 indicates that reliance upon highway-user revenue declines with increases in economic development.

The segregation of highway funds from general state revenues and receipts is an article of faith among highway interests. Prior to the rise of the automobile, highway expenditures came out of general revenue. But automobile travel has made it possible to place heavy reliance on highway-user revenues as a source of highway funds. Proponents of the benefits principle of taxation very early supported the earmarking of revenue from gasoline taxes and motor vehicle registration for highway purposes. As these revenues have grown, highway interests have pressed for legal and even constitutional provisions preventing the use of these revenues for anything except highway purposes. Today more than half of the states have constitutional provisions restricting the diversion of highway-user revenue to non-highway purposes, and many other states restrict diversion by statute or administrative practice. This guarantees the continued flow of road-building funds and, in effect, gives highways preferential treatment over other public functions.

It is possible to measure the degree to which the states permit or restrict the diversion of highway-user revenue to non-highway purposes. The United States Bureau of Public Roads reported in 1961 that 18 states permitted no diversion of highway revenue receipts whatsoever in that year, while 10 states permitted a diversion of over 10 per cent of their highway receipts. New Jersey diverted 28 per cent of highway receipts to other public purposes, more than any other state.

The tendency to divert highway receipts is related to urbanization and industrialization. The urban industrial states are more likely to divert larger proportions of highway receipts to non-highway purposes than the rural agricultural states which are more likely to guarantee the flow of highway receipts into highway expenditures. If success in preventing the diversion of highway receipts to other areas is a valid measure of strong interest in highway policy, then this interest has been significantly more successful in rural than in urban states.

STATE-LOCAL HIGHWAY RELATIONS

We noted earlier that local road systems in many cities were in operation long before state highway departments began building state highway networks. However, over time the trend has been to shift responsibility for road construction and maintenance from local governments to state governments, and local governments have come to rely increasingly on state funds for even their local roads. This has led to increased centralization, supervision, and control over local roads by state highway departments. City street and highway departments are somewhat freer of state supervision than their rural counterparts since they participate somewhat less in state aid programs, but, with urban extension of the state and federal highway systems receiving more attention in the past few years, cities too have been required to coordinate their street and highway planning with planning at other levels of government.

In 1961 state highway expenditures amounted to almost 80 per cent of all state-local expenditures for highways. This degree of centralization in state highway finance varied, however, from state to state: in New York state highway expenditures accounted for only 54 per cent of all state-local highway expenditures; while in 14 states state highway expenditures accounted for over 90 per cent of all state-local highway expenditures. This particular measure of centralization in state highway finance has turned out to be significantly related only to urbanization. Table VI-3 shows a significant, although not very close, inverse relationship between urbanization and the state percentage of total highway expenditures. This means that there is some tendency for state centralization in highway financing to proceed further in rural states than in urban states. Local highway efforts are slightly more important in the urban states.

Another facet of state-local relationships in the highway field involves state financial aid programs to localities. We have just considered state highway expenditures in relation to local expenditures, but part of state highway expenditures are in the form of grants-in-aid to local subdivisions. In 1961 states disbursed $1.6 billion to localities for road purposes. This amount was part of a total $9.6 billion disbursed by state highway departments in that year. This means that about 17 per cent of all state highway expenditures were grants to localities. The justification for such grants centers on the need for minimum road conditions throughout the state, the inadequacy of local revenue sources, and the desire to equalize financial burdens throughout the state. In 1961 two states made no grants to their localities out of state highway funds (Alaska and West Virginia), while Iowa gave away 40 per cent of these funds to local subdivisions. The tendency to grant varying proportions of state highway funds to localities is unrelated to the levels of economic development. Rural and urban states cannot be differentiated according to the proportion of state highway funds disbursed for local roads and streets.

Perhaps, however, the important question in state highway politics is not how much is given to localities, but to which localities it is given. In other words, are rural or urban areas favored in the distribution of state highway aid? Many observers of state highway politics have contended that urban areas are consistently short-changed in state highway grants-in-aid. The formulas for these state grants are often quite complex. Formulas utilizing vehicle miles traveled, gasoline consumption, population, and motor vehicle registrations generally favor urban areas, while formulas based on road mileage, area, or equal-dollar amounts to political subdivisions generally favor rural areas. The evidence seems quite conclusive that, across the nation, urban areas are heavily discriminated against in state highway grants-in-aid. The United States Bureau of Public Roads reports that in 1961 71 per cent of all state grants to localities went to county and township roads and only 29 per cent went to municipal streets.

Discrimination against municipalities in state highway grants is not uniform throughout the states. Only four states (Florida, Kentucky,

South Carolina, and Texas) were reported to have made *no* grants to municipalities in 1961 and distributed all of their grant money to counties and townships. In contrast, five states (Connecticut, Maryland, Missouri, Rhode Island, and Virginia) gave more than 50 per cent of their highway grants to municipalities, leaving less than half of their grant money for counties and townships. The proportions of state grants going to rural counties and townships in contrast to municipalities is significantly related to levels of economic development. Urban industrial states give larger proportions of their state highway grant money to municipalities, while rural agricultural states give larger proportions to counties and townships.

HIGHWAY MILEAGE IN THE STATES

Since over the years the number of automobiles has increased at a much faster rate than road mileage, it has been necessary to engineer and construct road systems which can carry more traffic at faster speeds. In 1961 there were about 76 million registered motor vehicles, including 63 million private autos. Two years later, in 1963, there were nearly 83 million registered motor vehicles, an increase of about 3.5 million yearly. While people continue to outnumber motor vehicles in the United States, the ratio is now down to about 2.4 persons for each vehicle.

It was expected that levels of economic development among the states would influence the number of automobiles per person and thereby indirectly influence the character and extent of highway building. However, this has not been the case: the ratio of people to motor vehicles in 1961 was as low as 1.6 to 1 in Wyoming and as high as 3.2 to 1 in New York. But this variation in the number of motor vehicles from state to state is surprisingly *unrelated* to any of the measures of economic development. None of the simple coefficients in Table VI-4 regarding motor vehicle registration are significant. While levels of economic development among nations affect motor vehicle registration, the automobile has apparently become a necessity in American life for both rich and poor. Automobile ownership appears to be more a function of geography than income levels among the states. You need a car in Wyoming more than you need one in New York.

The total surfaced mileage in a state is another element in the state highway system which is *not* a function of levels of economic development. There were 2.25 million miles of surfaced roads in the nation in 1961. The distribution of this mileage is clearly a function of size of the area rather than any socioeconomic condition: Texas has 120,000 miles of surfaced roads, while Rhode Island has only 1,224 miles. Only Alaska shows the effect of economic underdevelopment in its road mileage: there only 2,279 surfaced miles serve an area larger than Texas. The coefficients in Table VI-4 show no relationship between total road mileage and economic development. Federal primary system mileage and interstate mileage in the states also appear to be unaffected by economic development levels. There are over 266,000 miles of federal interstate highways. The increases in highway mileage which are created by population densities in urban states appear to be balanced by the greater distances, and therefore mileage, between cities in rural states. Land area again appears to be a more important influence on federal highway mileage than economic development. Texas, with over 17,000 miles of federal primary highways and over 3,000 miles of interstate highways, has the largest totals in the nation; in contrast, Rhode Island has only 478 miles of federal primary highways, the lowest federal total in the nation and Delaware has only 40 miles of interstate highway, the lowest interstate highway mileage in the nation.

All of this suggests that many of the demands placed upon state highway departments are not really a function of economic development. The absence of any significant coefficients in Table VI-4 indicates that factors other than economic development determine the total numbers of automobiles and highway miles which must be serviced by state governments. Area and terrain appear to be very important in determining state highway activities.

TABLE VI-4
The Relationship between Economic Development and Highway Mileage

	Urban-ization	Industrial-ization	Income	Education
Motor vehicle registration, persons per vehicle	−.03	.05	−.19	−.06
Total highway mileage	.09	−.27	−.16	−.08
Federal primary system mileage	.08	−.17	−.16	−.15
Interstate highway system mileage	.23	.08	.04	.05

Figures are simple correlation coefficients for the fifty states; an asterisk indicates a statistically significant relationship.

SOME RELATIONSHIPS AMONG HIGHWAY OUTCOMES

While our chief concern has been with the relationships between economic development and highway policy outcomes, there are some interesting relationships among highway outcome variables which deserve notice. Table VI-5 is a matrix of simple correlation coefficients showing the interrelationships among seven highway policy outcomes. The relationship between any two variables can be found in the cell in which they intersect.

All three measures of the level of state-local highway spending are positively related. "Per capita state and local highway expenditures" correlates with "highway expenditures as a percentage of total expenditures" (r = .78), and both of these measures correlate with "highway expenditures relative to personal income" (r = .64, r = .80, respectively). The states which spend more on highways do so by digging deeper into state treasuries and into personal incomes. This is in contrast to the states which spend more on education and welfare; we have found that these states are wealthier and able to spend more on these functions without using a larger share of personal income to do so. But the price of the emphasis on highways in the rural agricultural states can be measured in terms of reduced personal incomes and reduced public funds for other functions.

The availability of federal highway money is positively associated with increased state-local highway expenditures. "Federal highway funds per capita" correlates significantly with "per capita state-local highway expenditures" (r = .81) and with "highway expenditures as a percentage of total expenditures" (r = .56). "Federal percentage of state highway funds" also correlates with these two measures of state-local highway expenditures (r = .61, r = .49, respectively). These relationships are not merely a product of the intervening effects of economic development. Even when urbanization, industrialization, income, and education are held constant, federal highway money remains positively correlated with state-local highway expenditures. No doubt the correlations between federal highway funds coming into the states and the levels of state highway expenditures are built into the matching formulas of federal highway aid. States which spend more for highways automatically collect more federal matching money. But undoubtedly the availability of federal aid also stimulates state highway expenditures: the rural states which spend so much on highways become dependent on federal highway funds and thus are induced to spend even more for highways.

Earlier we noted that highway interests vigorously oppose the diversion of highway-user revenue to non-highway functions. It is interesting to note that there is a negative relationship between diversion and highway spending. States which divert larger proportions of highway-user revenue to non-highway purposes are the same states which spend less per capita on highways and which devote smaller

TABLE VI-5
Relationships among Highway Policy Outcomes

	1 *Per Capita Highway Expenditures*	*2* *Expenditures Relative to Income*	*3* *Highway Expenditures as a Percentage of Total Expenditures*	*4* *Urban Discrimination*	*5* *Federal Highway Aid Per Capita*	*6* *Federal Percentage of Highway Funds*	*7* *Diversion of Highway-User Revenue*
1. Per capita highway expenditures	1.0						
2. Expenditures relative to income	.64*	1.0					
3. Highway expenditures as a percentage of total expenditures	.78*	.80*	1.0				
4. Discrimination against urban areas in grants to localities	.22	.44*	.25	1.0			
5. Federal highway aid per capita	.81*	.39*	.56*	.15	1.0		
6. Federal percentage of highway funds	.61*	.45*	.49*	.13	.76*	1.0	
7. Diversion of highway-user revenue	−.35*	.35*	−.38*	.10	−.30*	−.45*	1.0

Figures are simple correlation coefficients for the fifty states; an asterisk indicates a statistically significant relationship.

percentages of their total public expenditures and personal incomes to highways. States with large highway expenditures, both in per capita amounts and relative terms, are more likely to prevent the diversion of highway revenue. The earmarking of highway revenue and antidiversion provisions are symptomatic, therefore, of the general success of highway interests. Of course most of these relationships are a product of the intervening effect of urbanization and industrialization; for the most part these relationships disappear when socioeconomic variables are controlled.

PARTISANSHIP, PARTY COMPETITION, AND HIGHWAY POLICY

Now that we have observed the effects of socioeconomic inputs on highway policy, particularly the important effects of urbanization and industrialization, let us examine the impact of some political system characteristics on highway policy.

First of all, what is the effect of Democratic or Republican party control of a state government on its highway expenditures, on the diversion of highway-user revenue, on state road grants to localities, or on discrimination against urban areas? If partisanship really affects highway policy, states under Democratic party control should exhibit noticeably different highway policies from states under Republican party control. Furthermore, differences between Democratic and Republican states in highway outcomes should remain, even after controlling for the effect of economic development. We have already seen that Democratic party control is inversely associated with economic development among the fifty states, and, of course, economic development affects highway policy. Therefore, economic development must be controlled in order to assess the independent effect of partisanship on highway policy.

Republican party success appears significantly related to increased highway expenditures. The simple coefficients in Table VI-6 show Democratic control to be inversely related to per capita highway expenditures in the states. This can be interpreted to mean that Republican party control is positively related to increased highway expenditures.

What is even more remarkable, however, is the closeness of the relationship between Republican control of state legislatures and state expenditures devoted to highways, even after controlling for the effects of economic development. Apparently Republican legislatures are more prone to spend public monies for highways in lieu of spending it for education, health and welfare, or other public functions. Democratic legislatures do not give as much priority to highway expenditures relative to other public functions. Significant partial coefficients indicate that differences between Republican and Democratic legislatures in the proportion of state expenditures devoted to highways is not merely a product of the effect of economic development. Moreover,

TABLE VI-6

The Relationships among Economic Development, Partisanship, and State Highway Policy

| | Democratic Party Control | | | | | |
| | Lower Houses | | Upper Houses | | Governorships | |
	Simple	Partial	Simple	Partial	Simple	Partial
Per capita highway expenditures	−.54*	−.33	−.49*	−.37*	−.37*	−.15
Expenditures relative to income	−.24	−.35*	−.16	−.34	−.03	−.16
Highway expenditures as a percentage of total expenditures	−.31*	−.51*	−.25	−.51*	−.05	−.21
Discrimination against urban areas in expenditures	−.01	−.18	−.07	−.24	.18	.07
Per capita federal highway aid	−.30*	.06	−.22	.05	−.18	.12
Federal percentage of highway funds	−.26	.17	−.16	.01	−.14	.04
State percentage of highway expenditures	.16	.14	.24	.21	.08	−.03
Diversion of highway-user revenue	.30*	.21	.25	.22	.32*	.26
Percentage of highway funds granted to localities	−.11	−.03	−.12	−.06	.00	.12
Rural percentages of state road grants	.05	.05	.07	.02	.24	.26
Total highway mileage	.01	−.03	.03	.02	.09	.11
Federal highway mileage	.11	.03	.14	.10	.21	.19

Figures are simple and partial correlation coefficients; partial coefficients control for the effect of urbanization, industrialization, income, and education; an asterisk indicates a statistically significant relationship.

these differences do not depend upon the southern states; even in non-southern states Republican legislatures are more prone to spend money for highways than Democratic legislatures. Partisanship in state legislatures (although not in governorships) appears to be independently related to emphasis on highways in state budgets.

However, partisanship does not appear to be independently related to other highway policy variables. In the simple coefficients,

Democratic party fortunes are slightly related to reduced federal highway aid and slightly related to increased diversion of highway-user revenue to non-highway purposes. However, once the impact of urbanization and industrialization are controlled, these relationships disappear. Deomcratic or Republican party control appears to have no independent effect on federal highway aid, the diversion of highway-user revenue, state road grants to localities, or discrimination against urban areas.

Party competition appears to have even less effect on highway policy outcomes than partisanship. One might hypothesize that highway expenditures will be higher in the one-party states. Highway departments in these states often take on the form of a party organization, rewarding the friends and punishing the enemies of a victorious candidate. The absence of parties may be expected to increase the

TABLE VI-7
The Relationships among Economic Development, Party Competition, and State Highway Policy

| | Party Competition | | | | | |
| | Lower Houses | | Upper Houses | | Governorships | |
	Simple	Partial	Simple	Partial	Simple	Partial
Per capita highway expenditures	−.20	.15	−.18	.06	−.25	−.05
Expenditures relative to income	.13	.19	.14	.13	.15	.00
Highway expenditures as a percentage of total expenditures	.05	−.17	.08	−.05	.06	−.19
Discrimination against urban areas in expenditures	.04	−.09	.09	−.02	.22	.09
Per capita federal highway aid	−.08	.22	−.07	.12	−.14	.16
Federal percentage of highway funds	−.13	.02	−.10	−.02	−.08	−.09
State percentage of highway expenditures	.18	.06	.15	−.01	.09	.00
Diversion of highway-user revenue	.19	.20	.14	.18	.21	.23
Percentage of highway funds granted to localities	−.18	−.10	−.16	−.06	.07	.20
Rural percentages of state road grants	.12	.08	.12	.04	.36*	.34
Total highway mileage	−.12	−.15	−.02	−.02	.13	−.07
Federal highway mileage	−.02	.08	.07	.07	.21	.14

Figures are simple and partial correlation coefficients; partial coefficients control for the effect of urbanization, industrialization, income, and education; an asterisk indicates a statistically significant relationship.

influence of highway departments and thereby lead to increased highway expenditures, less diversion of highway-user revenue, and other policies which favor highway interests.

In order to show that party competition independently influences highway policy, it would be necessary to show that highway outcomes in one-party states are significantly different from highway outcomes in two-party states, and that these differences can be traced to party competition rather than socioeconomic variables. But all available empirical evidence indicates that party competition has no effect on highway policy. Table VI-7 shows the relationships between party competition in the upper and lower houses of state legislatures and in gubernatorial elections and the twelve measures of highway outcomes. There are few significant differences between highway outcomes in one-party and two-party states. Not one of the partial correlations in Table VI-7 suggests a significant relationship between party competition and highway policy. Party competition has no apparent independent effect on highway expenditures, state road grants to localities, federal aid, the diversion of highway-user revenue, or discrimination against urban areas in highway expenditures. Whatever may be the effect of party competition on the style and character of state politics or any other policy outcomes, there is no evidence to support the view that party competition itself has any impact on highway policy outcomes.

MALAPPORTIONMENT, VOTER PARTICIPATION, AND HIGHWAY POLICY

Earlier we noted that in only a handful of states do cities receive state highway expenditures commensurate with highway use. In addition, we noted that cities receive relatively little financial aid in the way of state road grants to localities. One of the most frequent explanations of discrimination against urban areas in state highway policy is the underrepresentation of urban areas in malapportioned legislatures. There is little doubt that in the past malapportionment has indeed underrepresented urban areas. But whether or not discrimination against urban areas in highway policy is a product of malapportionment remains an interesting question.

We might also hypothesize that malapportionment results in an increase in highway expenditures. We have already seen that rural politics is extremely favorable toward highway building. The over-representation of rural areas in legislatures through malapportionment might be expected to result in larger highway expenditures. Malapportioned states may well spend more for highways, in both per capita and relative terms, than well-apportioned states.

However, despite good a priori reasons for believing that malapportionment affects highway policy, there is little empirical evidence to support this contention. Table VI-8 shows the relationships between highway policy outcomes and the three separate measures of malap-

TABLE VI-8

The Relationships among Economic Development, Malapportionment, and State Highway Policy

	Index of Representation		Index of Urban Underrepresentation		Apportionment Score	
	Simple	Partial	Simple	Partial	Simple	Partial
Per capita highway expenditures	.05	−.01	−.06	.16	.04	.04
Expenditures relative to income	.14	−.05	−.19	.20	.07	.00
Highway expenditures as a percentage of total expenditures	.21	.10	−.12	.28	.08	.18
Discrimination against urban areas in expenditures	−.08	.04	−.05	.05	.02	.07
Per capita federal highway aid	−.04	−.12	−.15	−.07	.06	−.02
Federal percentage of highway funds	.08	.04	−.11	.04	.15	.13
State percentage of highway expenditures	−.29	−.04	−.22	−.19	−.08	−.18
Diversion of highway-user revenue	−.29	−.03	−.17	−.32	−.21	−.20
Percentage of highway funds granted to localities	.02	.00	−.10	−.05	−.15	−.06
Rural percentages of state road grants	.06	.03	−.37*	−.18	−.09	−.05
Total highway mileage	.21	.23	−.23	−.19	−.23	−.13
Federal highway mileage	.16	.16	−.26	−.25	−.25	−.17

Figures are simple and partial correlation coefficients; partial coefficients control for the effect of urbanization, industrialization, income, and education; an asterisk indicates a statistically significant relationship.

portionment described in Chapter III. There are no significant relationships between highway outcomes in the states and either the David and Eisenberg index of representativeness (the smallest proportion of the population which can control a majority of the legislature) or the Schubert-Press apportionment score (degree to which legislative districts approach the normal statistical curve). Malapportionment in these terms has no identifiable effect on discrimination against urban areas in state highway department expenditures or on discrimination against urban areas in state road grants to localities, nor does it have any identifiable effect on any other highway policy outcome, including any of the measures of highway expenditures.

Malapportionment, when expressed in terms of discrimination against urban areas in representation, is associated in simple coefficients with only one highway policy variable: discrimination against urban areas in state road grants to localities. If our analysis went no further it would be easy to conclude that malapportionment did explain part of the discrimination against urban areas in highway policy. However, if the effects of economic development are controlled as they are by partial coefficients in Table VI-8, it turns out that the relationship between malapportionment and discrimination against urban areas

TABLE VI-9

The Relationships among Economic Development, Political Participation, and State Highway Policy

	Political Participation					
			1962		1958	
	Governorships		Congressional		Congressional	
	Simple	Partial	Simple	Partial	Simple	Partial
Per capita highway expenditures	.27	.03	.35*	.15	.33*	.11
Expenditures relative to income	.03	.04	−.01	.15	−.02	.17
Highway expenditures as a percentage of total expenditures	.17	.16	.05	.27	−.01	.21
Discrimination against urban areas in expenditures	−.06	−.08	−.05	−.02	−.19	−.05
Per capita federal highway aid	.12	−.18	.22	−.07	.23	−.06
Federal percentage of highway funds	.23	−.20	.08	−.17	.12	−.09
State percentage of highway expenditures	.02	.10	.02	.12	−.04	.13
Diversion of highway-user revenue	−.20	−.15	−.19	−.13	−.22	−.21
Percentage of highway funds granted to localities	−.11	−.23	−.05	−.05	−.04	−.17
Rural percentages of state road grants	−.19	−.13	−.17	−.08	−.12	−.03
Total highway mileage	.09	.06	−.10	−.06	−.14	−.14
Federal highway mileage	−.20	−.15	−.21	−.15	−.24	−.22

Figures are simple and partial correlation coefficients; partial coefficients control for the effect of urbanization, industrialization, income, and education; an asterisk indicates a statistically significant relationship.

in highway policy disappears. Whatever connection exists between urban underrepresentation in state legislatures and highway policy is clearly a product of the intervening effects of economic development. We can say only that it is true that urban areas are underrepresented in state legislatures, and it is true that urban areas are discriminated against in highway policy.

Political participation, measured in terms of voter turnout, is another system variable which does not appear to have any independent effect on highway policy outcomes. Table VI-9 shows the relationships between our three measures of voter turnout and highway policy outcomes in the fifty states. Not one of the partial correlation coefficients shown in Table VI-9 are statistically significant. There is no apparent relationship between voter turnout and any of our measures of highway expenditures, federal highway aid, diversion of highway-user revenues, state grants to localities, highway mileage, or discrimination against urban areas. Whatever may be the impact of increased political participation on other characteristics of political systems or on other policy variables, there is no empirical evidence that increased participation affects highway policy in any noticeable fashion.

CHAPTER VII

Tax and Revenue Policy

DEVELOPMENT OF TAX AND REVENUE POLICY

THE AUTHORITATIVE ALLOCATION of values in society involves the transfer of monies from private to public purposes. Revenue-raising is a vital function in all political systems. In the United States government revenues amount to about 37 per cent of the national income. The largest share of this, about two-thirds, goes to the federal government, principally to pay for the costs of past, present, and future wars. But state governments and their subdivisions collect over one-third of all government revenues. Revenue-raising presents state political systems with important policy choices. Decisions must be made about how much revenue is to be raised, how it will be raised, from whom it will be raised, and how great a financial burden will be imposed, and these decisions constitute some of the most important policy outcomes in state politics.

Taxes are the largest source of public revenue, accounting for 72 per cent of all state and local revenue in 1961. The United States Constitution places very few restrictions on the power of the states to tax: it prohibits states, without the consent of Congress, from levying taxes on imports and exports; and by implication it prohibits states from using the taxing power to deny to citizens equal protection of the law or due process of law. State constitutions, however, restrict state taxing powers far more than the federal Constitution. These restrictions often include maximum rates, prohibitions on income or sales taxes, prohibitions against progressive rates, and prohibitions on classification schemes. State constitutional restrictions, of course, can be treated as policy outcomes. In addition to taxes, governments also derive revenue from compulsory insurance payments, income from public businesses, fines, rents, and charges, and grants-in-aid from other governments. As we shall see, these non-tax revenues can be quite substantial.

Important changes have occurred in public tax and revenue policies in America in the last few decades. Present-day tax policy outcomes must be understood in the context of the changing policies in federal, state, and local finance since the beginning of this century. Table VII-1 deals with total government revenues from all sources — federal, state, and local. In 1902 total government revenues amounted to only $1.7 billion. State and local governments collected more revenue than the national government: 61.5 per cent of all government

TABLE VII-1
Total Government Revenues, 1902-1961

	Amount in Billions	Federal Percentage	State-Local Percentage	Percentage of National Income
1902	1.7	38.5	61.5	8.2
1913	3.0	32.3	67.7	8.6
1922	9.3	45.7	54.3	14.7
1932	10.3	21.6	78.4	24.2
1940	17.8	39.3	60.7	21.8
1950	66.7	80.3	19.7	27.6
1960	153.1	65.2	34.8	36.7
1961	158.7	63.8	36.2	37.2

From U. S. Bureau of the Census, *Historical Statistics of the United States* (Washington: Government Printing Office, 1960), pp. 722, 726.

revenues were raised in the states, while the federal government accounted for only 38.5 per cent of all revenues. Total government revenues amounted to only 8 per cent of the national income. Five decades later, public revenue collections in the United States had risen to over $158 billion. Perhaps what is more important than dollar increases, governments in 1961 took 37 per cent of the national income. This means that the burden of government finance has grown much faster than the national income. Another important change is the change in the relative position of federal versus state-local revenue collections. Wars, depressions, and threats of war have resulted in a shifting of financial emphasis from the states to the national government. The national government in 1961 collected 63.8 per cent of all government revenues, while the states and their subdivisions collected the remaining 36.2 per cent. In very recent years, however, state

TABLE VII-2

Total State and Local Government Revenues by Source, 1902-1961

| | State-Local Revenue Sources by Level of Government | | | | | State-Local Revenue Sources by Character | | | | |
	Total Amount (in Billions of $)	Federal	State	Local	Property Taxes	Excise and Sales Taxes	Income Taxes	Other Taxes	Charges	Federal Grants	Insurance and Utility Receipts
1902	1.0	0.7	17.5	81.8	67.4	2.7	—	12.0	11.4	0.1	6.0
1913	2.0	0.6	17.7	81.1	65.6	2.9	—	10.8	14.3	0.6	5.8
1922	5.2	2.2	23.8	74.0	64.2	3.0	2.0	8.5	12.7	2.2	7.5
1932	7.9	3.0	28.8	68.2	56.9	9.5	1.9	9.8	11.0	3.0	7.9
1940	11.7	8.0	42.7	49.3	37.7	16.9	3.2	8.7	7.3	8.0	18.2
1950	25.6	9.7	44.8	45.5	28.7	20.1	5.4	7.9	9.8	9.7	18.4
1960	60.3	11.6	43.3	45.1	27.2	19.7	6.0	7.0	12.3	11.6	16.2
1961	64.5	11.1	43.1	45.8	27.9	19.3	6.0	7.0	12.5	1.1	16.3

Figures are in percentages, unless otherwise specified. From U. S. Department of Health, Education and Welfare, *Health, Education and Welfare Trends 1963* (Washington: Government Printing Office, 1963), p. 102.

revenues have gained back some ground vis à vis federal revenues. In the early 1960's states raised tax and expenditure levels faster than the federal government.

Important changes have also occurred in state and local taxes and revenues in the last fifty years. Table VII-2 deals exclusively with the sources of state and local government revenues. In 1902 local revenues far surpassed state revenues and the federal government provided very little help to the states or their subdivisions. Local governments collected 81.8 per cent of state-local revenues, state governments collected 17.5 per cent, and the federal government contributed only 0.7 per cent of state and local revenues. But the 1930's brought an increase in federal contributions to programs administered by the states, and by the 1960's over 11 per cent of all state and local government revenues came from the federal government. Even more striking were the changes which occurred over the years in state-local relations. By 1940 state governments had assumed direct responsibility for many public programs previously left to local communities or not undertaken at all. This trend toward centralized state government has meant that the states themselves collect an increasing share of the total state-local revenue. In 1961 state sources accounted for 43.1 per cent of total state-local revenue, while local sources accounted for 45.8 per cent.

Table VII-3 reveals even more about the changes in federal-state-local relations in revenue. It separates state government revenue from local government revenue. State governments rely more heavily upon federal grants than local governments. Federal grants constitute nearly 20 per cent of the revenue of state governments, while only about 2 per cent of local revenue comes directly from the federal government. However, local governments receive over 25 per cent of their revenue from state grants. This dependence of local governments upon state governments for revenue arose during the 1930's: in 1922 local governments received 7.5 per cent of their revenue from the states; by 1932 this figure had grown to 12.9 per cent, and by 1940 to 21.4 per cent. (These intergovernmental transfers of money mean that total state revenues and total local revenues in Table VII-3 add up to more than total state and local revenues in Table VII-2, since intergovernmental revenues are counted twice.) In short, today intergovernmental payments are a vital source of revenue for both state and local governments. In 1961, 27 per cent of local revenue came from intergovernmental transfers, and 20 per cent of state revenue from them.

In 1902 insurance payments and utility receipts constituted only 6.0 per cent of total state and local revenues. Most of this income came

TABLE VII-3

A Comparison of State and Local Sources of Revenue, 1902-1961

State Government Revenue by Source

	Amount (in Billions of $)	From Federal Government	From Local Government	Income Taxes	General Sales Taxes	Motor Fuel Taxes	Alcohol and Tobacco Taxes	Other Taxes Including Property	Charges	Insurance and Utilities Stores
1902	0.2	1.6	3.1	—	—	—	—	71.3	13.0	1.0
1913	0.4	1.6	2.7	—	—	—	0.5	79.5	15.7	0.0
1922	1.4	7.3	2.0	7.4	—	1.0	—	61.3	13.3	7.8
1932	2.5	8.7	1.8	6.0	0.3	20.7	0.7	46.6	10.5	4.6
1940	5.7	11.6	1.0	8.0	8.7	14.6	5.1	21.3	6.0	23.6
1950	13.9	16.4	1.1	8.4	12.0	11.1	6.0	18.5	6.5	19.0
1960	32.8	19.9	0.6	10.3	13.1	10.2	4.8	16.6	7.9	16.7
1961	34.6	19.0	0.6	10.5	13.0	9.9	4.9	16.7	8.2	17.1

Local Government Revenue by Source

	Amount (in Billions of $)	From Federal Government	From State Government	Income Taxes	Excise and Sales Taxes	Property Taxes	Other Taxes	Charges	Utility Receipts
1902	0.9	0.4	5.7	—	—	68.3	8.8	10.3	6.5
1913	1.8	0.3	5.2	—	0.2	67.9	6.4	13.2	6.8
1922	4.1	0.2	7.5	—	0.5	71.7	1.8	11.5	6.8
1932	6.2	0.2	12.9	—	0.4	67.2	1.4	9.8	8.1
1940	7.7	3.6	21.4	0.2	1.7	54.0	2.3	6.6	10.2
1950	16.1	1.3	26.1	0.4	3.0	43.7	2.4	9.9	13.2
1960	37.2	1.8	25.0	0.7	3.6	42.5	1.9	13.0	11.6
1961	40.5	2.0	25.0	0.6	3.5	42.9	1.8	12.8	11.3

U. S. Bureau of the Census, *Historical Statistics of the United States* (Washington: Government Printing Office, 1960), pp. 727, 729.

from local municipal utilities—principally water supply. State governments were not very much involved in public enterprise or social insurance. In recent years, however, both state and local governments have received substantial incomes from various public enterprises and insurance programs. Today many municipalities provide electric power, gas, recreation facilities, and transit and transportation facilities on a commercial basis, in addition to water supply. Liquor store revenues have become a major source of state revenues (these receipts accounted for over 3 per cent of total state government revenue in 1961). Today payments into unemployment compensation insurance funds, workman's compensation funds, and employee retirement funds are another important source of state government revenue, even though these payments are made to special funds. By 1961 insurance premiums, utility receipts and liquor store receipts amounted to over 16 per cent of total state-local revenue.

Charges and miscellaneous general revenue have remained a relatively constant proportion of total state-local revenues over the years. These include everything from children's school lunch fees and textbook charges, to interest from public investments, to highway tolls, sewerage charges, and public hospital service fees.

Because of the increase in intergovernmental payments and non-tax revenue sources over the years, tax revenues have actually declined since 1902 as a proportion of total state-local revenues. Both Tables VII-2 and VII-3 classify tax revenues by type of tax. Important changes have occurred in the last fifty years in the types of taxes relied upon by state and local governments.

At the turn of the century the general property tax reigned as the only really important source of state and local revenue. In theory at least, all property within a community—real, personal, tangible, and intangible—was assessed at market value and a single uniform rate of tax was applied. In practice, however, assessments fell far below market value and they were not uniform from one county or municipality to the next; assessments usually varied from as high as 75 per cent of fair market value to as low as 10 per cent. Some property was specifically exempted from taxation—for example, the property of government agencies and religious institutions, and other property, especially personal and intangible property, was simply hidden from the assessors. The property tax provided states as well as localities with most of their revenue. State property tax rates were simply added to local rates and the states depended on local assessments. As late as 1922 the property tax was the largest source of both state and local revenue.

The awkwardness of the property tax, its many inequalities and opportunities for evasion, eventually led to its demise as an important source of state revenue. However, this tax continues to be the major source of revenue for local governments. In 1961, property taxes provided 42.9 per cent of all local revenues (88 per cent of all local *tax* revenues). Intangible and personal property has gradually been dropped from local tax rolls, either legally or illegally, but real estate is relatively easy to find and it cannot easily be moved about. A local sales tax can result in consumers and merchants leaving town, and a city income tax can speed the exodus to suburbia. Because of the dependence of local governments on property taxation, the role of this tax in the total state-local revenue system in America remains significant, accounting for 27 per cent of total state-local revenues in 1961. More state-local revenue is collected through property taxes than any other single type of tax.

The degree to which the property tax is relied upon in the total state-local structure of a state is really a product of the degree to which local governments are relied upon to provide public services. States which turn over governmental functions to their subdivisions will have total tax structures which are heavily dependent on property taxation. States which assume more direct responsibility for public services will depend less upon property taxation.

Sales and excise taxes played a very small role in state-local revenues in 1902. When prohibition ended, however, alcohol and later tobacco became important sources of revenue. In addition to penalizing a recognized vice, these excise taxes have had the advantage of inelasticity: sales of tobacco and alcohol remain surprisingly constant even during recessions and depressions. The advent of the automobile and the heavy demand for road construction have made motor fuel taxes a natural object of taxation: the gasoline tax, first adopted in 1919, spread to all states within ten years. By 1932 motor fuel taxes supplied 20 per cent of all state revenue. In recent years the growth of other taxes has reduced state reliance on this tax, but it still supplies about 10 per cent of state revenue. Under the pressure of the automotive and trucking industries, however, revenues from this tax are often segregated from general revenues for use on highways only.

In 1921 West Virginia levied the first general sales tax on a wide variety of consumer items. The general sales tax spread very rapidly in the 1930's as a source of revenue. State legislators who had not heard of Lord Keynes were impressed by the ability of this tax to raise revenue even during hard times. Its broad base meant that low rates could return high revenues. Consumers are a notoriously weak pressure group, and opposition by retailers can be squelched by state kickbacks for their efforts in collecting the tax. It is difficult for taxpayers to count pennies dribbled away two and three at a time; the tax does not involve obvious payroll deductions or year-end tax bills. Its burden is not as visible as income or property taxes; even when large items are purchased, the purchaser simply considers the tax part of the item's cost. Of course the general sales tax is regressive (we shall examine this aspect of state tax systems in some detail in the pages to follow), but widespread affluence has tended to soften some of the hardships that low-income groups may encounter in paying this tax. In fact, many legislators like the sales tax because it guarantees that the beneficiaries of certain government services, e.g., welfare, share in the cost of these services. By 1961 the general sales tax had grown to be the most important single source of state government tax revenue. A total of 35 states had imposed a general sales tax in that year.

Perhaps the popularity of the sales tax with state legislatures is due to the fact that the federal government has preempted income taxation and the localities have preempted property taxation. There is nothing left for the states to tax except consumption. It seems natural that the three levels of government should have separate sources of revenue. Of course the notion of preemption involves a value judgment—that property taxes can or should go no higher and that the federal government is now taking as much income as can be spared for public purposes.

In 1911, two years before the passage of the Sixteenth Amendment, Wisconsin passed the first modern enforcible income tax. Many states fell in line after the national government began taxing income in 1913, and as early as 1922 states were receiving over 7 per cent of their total revenue from income taxes. As a broad-base low-rate tax, the income tax is an excellent producer of revenue, as is the general sales tax. Unlike the sales tax, however, it is generally progressive in character. Its adoption is generally hailed as a victory for *equity* in taxation, that is, taxation based upon the *ability to pay* principle. Most of the states which have adopted income taxation did so before World War II. But in recent years the popularity of income taxation in the states has ebbed. Perhaps this has been a result of the heavy federal income tax levies during and after World War II. Perhaps general affluence has taken the steam out of the tax reform and equity movement. Perhaps the opposition of the business community to income taxation has made states which were concerned with their competitive position wary of a tax which might drive industry away. What neighboring states are doing is a frequent subject of discussion among state legislators. Although economists assert that taxes are far down the list of locational considerations, the idea that income taxes discourage industry remains an article of conventional wisdom.

In 1961 34 states levied individual and corporate incomes taxes, and 5 states levied taxes on corporation incomes only (Connecticut, New Jersey, Pennsylvania, Rhode Island, and South Dakota). But out of this total of 39 states, 26 *also* levied sales taxes. Income taxes accounted for 10.5 per cent of all state revenue, and only 6.0 per cent of total state-local revenue. This has meant that, on the whole, income taxes produce less revenue than property taxes or sales taxes. Individual income tax rates are generally progressive, with ranges from 1 to 6 and even 10 per cent of taxable income. Most of the states with individual income taxes have provisions for withholding.

Thus, while property taxes continue to be the major source of local revenue, state governments have given up property taxation and have come to depend upon a combination of general sales taxes, excise taxes on motor fuels, alcohol and tobacco, and individual and corporate income taxes. In 1961 all states taxed motor fuels, alcohol, and tobacco. Twenty-six states levied both sales and income taxes, thirteen states levied income but not sales taxes, nine states levied sales taxes but not income taxes, and only two states had neither a sales tax nor an individual or corporate income tax. On the whole, states raise more revenue from general sales taxes than any other type of tax.

ECONOMIC DEVELOPMENT AND TAX AND REVENUE POLICY OUTCOMES

These trends over time suggest that economic development has brought about significant changes in state tax and revenue policy. But the effect of urbanization, industrialization, income, and education on taxes and revenues can be described in greater detail by a comparative analysis of the fifty states. There are wide variations among the states in tax and revenue outcomes. Some states rely heavily upon their local governments and upon property taxation to supply needed state-local revenue. Some states rely heavily on federal grants-in-aid. Some states impose high per capita tax levels while other states are able to keep tax levels low: in 1961 per capita tax levels among the states ranged from a high of $298 to a low of $120. This means that the per capita tax levels of some states are over twice as high as those of other states. Tax burdens, that is, taxes in relation to personal income, also vary considerably among the states. There are differences among the states in the types of taxes relied upon and in the incidence of their tax structures.

Some states choose to levy income taxes, rather than sales taxes, while others avoid income taxes in favor of sales taxes. The proportion of revenue raised from property taxes, sales taxes, motor fuel taxes, alcohol and tobacco taxes, and income taxes differs in every state.

What accounts for differences among the states in tax and revenue policy outcomes? Are the tax and revenue policies of urban industrial states noticeably different from those of rural agricultural states? What is the effect of economic development on tax burdens, sources of revenue, and types and incidence of taxation? Do political system variables influence tax and revenue structures? What is the effect of Republican or Democratic party control on tax and revenue policy? What is the effect of party competition and political participation on the choice of taxes to be levied and the total tax levied? Comparative analysis of the fifty states enables us to explore these and related questions about the forces influencing tax and revenue policy outcomes.

TAX AND REVENUE LEVELS

Levels of *revenue* refer simply to the amounts of money per person raised from all sources. Levels of *taxation* refer to the amounts of money per person raised through taxation and exclude monies from insurance premiums, federal grants-in-aid, rents and charges, and utility and store receipts. Total revenue per capita and tax revenue per capita both control for most of the effects of population size among the states, but neither measure controls for the effect of income or taxable capacity. The question of *burden,* that is, taxation relative to income, will be considered below; states with the highest *levels of taxation* are not necessarily the same states with the highest *tax burden.*

In 1961, the total general revenues of state and local governments amounted to $295 per person; the comparable figure for the federal government was $483 per person. Total state and local general revenues varied from a high of over $400 in California, Nevada, and Wyoming to a low of less than $210 in South Carolina, North Carolina, and Alabama. Over 72 per cent of the total state and local government revenues were collected by means of taxation, rather than by means of federal grants, insurance premiums, or charges. States and local tax revenues amounted to $212 per capita in 1961. These per capita tax levels varied from a high of $293 and $298 in New York and California to a low of $120 to $130 in Alabama, Arkansas, Mississippi, and South Carolina.

What is the effect of economic development on levels of taxation and revenue? Table VII-4 shows that levels of revenue among the states are significantly related to income, education, and urbanization levels. Tax levels are also closely related to these three measures of economic development. There is little doubt that the ability of the states to raise revenue is a function of their level of economic development. Figure VII-1 is a scattergram showing the closeness of the relationship between tax revenues and median family income among the states.

TABLE VII-4

The Relationship between Economic Development and State and Local Revenues

	Economic Development			
	Urban-ization	Industrial-ization	Income	Education
Total revenues per capita, state and local governments	.30*	.03	.64*	.75*
Tax revenues per capita, state and local governments	.59*	.23	.76*	.74*
State and local tax revenues relative to personal income	−.15	−.52*	−.17	−.16
Total state and local debt, per capita	.61*	.54*	.59*	.37*

Figures are simple correlation coefficients for the fifty states; an asterisk indicates a statistically significant relationship.

Economic development also contributes to the ability of a state to carry larger public debt loads. Table VII-4 shows that urbanization, industrialization, and income are positively related to increases in per capita state and local debt levels. Rural farm states with lower income levels do not experience the same demand for public capital investment that urban industrial states experience, nor do they have the same ability to carry heavy debt loads.

TAX BURDENS

The concept of tax burden generally refers to taxes paid in relation to personal income. It is assumed that taxes eventually come out of personal income, whether they are levied on income itself or on sales or property or some other base.[1] The total tax burden of a state is measured by "total state and local tax revenues as a percentage of personal income." A high tax burden, it should be noted, does not necessarily merit the connotations of "burdensome." A high tax bur-

[1] Advisory Commission on Intergovernmental Relations, *Measures of State and Local Fiscal Capacity and Tax Effort* (Washington: Government Printing Office, 1962), p. 10.

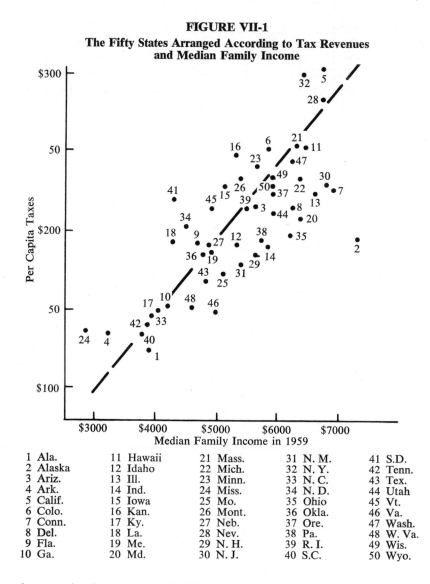

FIGURE VII-1

The Fifty States Arranged According to Tax Revenues and Median Family Income

1 Ala.	11 Hawaii	21 Mass.	31 N. M.	41 S.D.
2 Alaska	12 Idaho	22 Mich.	32 N. Y.	42 Tenn.
3 Ariz.	13 Ill.	23 Minn.	33 N. C.	43 Tex.
4 Ark.	14 Ind.	24 Miss.	34 N. D.	44 Utah
5 Calif.	15 Iowa	25 Mo.	35 Ohio	45 Vt.
6 Colo.	16 Kan.	26 Mont.	36 Okla.	46 Va.
7 Conn.	17 Ky.	27 Neb.	37 Ore.	47 Wash.
8 Del.	18 La.	28 Nev.	38 Pa.	48 W. Va.
9 Fla.	19 Me.	29 N. H.	39 R. I.	49 Wis.
10 Ga.	20 Md.	30 N. J.	40 S.C.	50 Wyo.

den may be the product of a high level of governmental services, and whether one considers a high level of government service burdensome or not depends upon personal values and preferences. A high tax burden may also reflect low personal income; a high tax burden in a poor state may not supply a satisfactory level of public service. In 1961, total state and local tax revenues in the United States amounted to $94 per $1000 of personal income. Among the states this measure of tax burden varied from a low of $71 in Delaware to a high of $128 in North Dakota.

What is the effect of economic development on tax burdens in the states? Table VII-4 shows a very striking relationship between higher levels of industrialization and lower state-local tax burdens. It is interesting that higher family incomes are not as closely associated with lower tax burdens as industrialization. Apparently the way to lower the tax burden in a state is to attract more industry. Our figures tend to confirm conventional wisdom in this regard.

FIGURE VII-2

**The Fifty States Arranged According to
Tax Revenues and Tax Burdens**

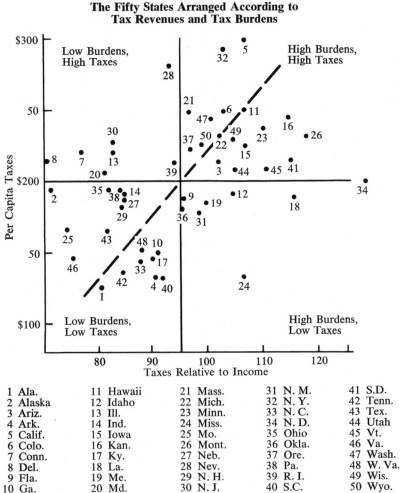

1 Ala.	11 Hawaii	21 Mass.	31 N. M.	41 S.D.
2 Alaska	12 Idaho	22 Mich.	32 N. Y.	42 Tenn.
3 Ariz.	13 Ill.	23 Minn.	33 N. C.	43 Tex.
4 Ark.	14 Ind.	24 Miss.	34 N. D.	44 Utah
5 Calif.	15 Iowa	25 Mo.	35 Ohio	45 Vt.
6 Colo.	16 Kan.	26 Mont.	36 Okla.	46 Va.
7 Conn.	17 Ky.	27 Neb.	37 Ore.	47 Wash.
8 Del.	18 La.	28 Nev.	38 Pa.	48 W. Va.
9 Fla.	19 Me.	29 N. H.	39 R. I.	49 Wis.
10 Ga.	20 Md.	30 N. J.	40 S.C.	50 Wyo.

The impact of industrialization can be observed in another fashion. High tax burdens are not necessarily a product of high tax levels, although a significant relationship exists between these variables in the fifty states. (The simple coefficient for the relationship between tax revenue per capita and taxes relative to personal income is .39; this relationship is represented by the broken line in Figure VII-2). It is possible to distinguish between those states in which a high tax level per capita is accompanied by a high tax burden and those states in which a high tax level per capita is not accompanied by a high tax burden. In Figure VII-2 all of the states above the solid horizontal line can be designated as states with high tax levels. In those states in the upper right quadrant, high tax level is accompanied by high tax burdens, but those states in the upper left quadrant (Delaware, Nevada, Connecticut, Illinois, and New Jersey) are in the enviable position of being able to collect high taxes per capita without imposing high tax burdens; they have sufficient industrial resources or other special tax sources (e.g., gambling and entertainment in Nevada) to enable them to collect high per capita taxes yet not take a large share of personal income. Even California and New York, which have the highest tax levels in the nation, rank below a number of other states in their tax burdens because of their surplus of taxable resources. In contrast, states in the lower right quadrant in Figure VII-2 (Mississippi, North Dakota, Louisiana, and Idaho) are in the most unenviable position of all: they have high tax burdens in spite of the fact that per capita taxes are low. Their tax resources are so limited that, even though per capita taxes and presumably public service levels are low, tax burdens are quite high.

FEDERAL, STATE, AND LOCAL PROPORTIONS OF REVENUE

The proportion of total revenue derived from federal, state, and local sources is an important attribute of the state revenue systems. The relative reliance placed upon state versus local sources of revenue is an index of centralization-decentralization in government and administration within the states. If local governments account for a large proportion of the total state and local government revenue in a state, this is an indication that local governments are providing a large share of the public services in that state. If, on the other hand, state governments account for the larger share of total state and local revenue, there is centralization in the provision of public services as well as in the revenue system. In addition, the relative reliance upon state versus local revenue is an index of the reliance placed upon property taxes, in contrast to income, sales, or motor fuel taxes. As noted earlier, the property tax is by far the largest source of *local* government revenue and this is true in every state. *State* governments, on the other hand, place major reliance on the sales, income, and motor fuel taxes as sources of revenue. Only Nebraska receives important revenues (about one-third) from the property tax. Thus, the proportion of state-local revenue collected by local governments is also an index of reliance on property taxes to finance public services. Finally, we will also note the relative reliance placed upon federal government grants as sources of state-local revenue among the states.

Because of duplicative transactions among levels of government, the revenues of state governments and the revenues of local governments add up to more than the total revenue of state and local governments. The measure employed in this study, "state percentage of total state and local revenues" is derived for each state by dividing the "general revenue of state government" by the "total general revenue of state and local governments." On a nationwide basis, in 1961 this "state percentage of total state and local revenues" was 54.2 per cent.[2] This ratio varied from a high of 87 per cent in Hawaii, where the state government rather than local governments performs most public services, to a low of 36 per cent in New Jersey, where local governments perform most public services.

Economic development is significantly related to decentralization in state-local finance and administration. Local governments tend to play a greater role in the state-local financial structure of urban high-income states, while state governments collect a greater proportion of the revenue in rural low-income states. Table VII-5 shows that these relationships are significant, although they are subject to many exceptions. The finding that state governments play a greater financial role vis à vis local governments in poorer rural states is consistent with findings reported earlier about greater state participation in public services in these states. Earlier we have observed that state governments in poorer rural states undertake more direct responsibilities in education, welfare, and highways than state governments in urban

---

[2] This is a slight overstatement of the states' fiscal role: if intergovernmental payments are disregarded and only "revenue from the states' own sources" considered, the states in 1961 raised $27.8 billion out of a total of $57.4 billion in state-local revenues from the states' own sources. This means that 48.4 per cent of total state and local revenues from the states' own sources was raised by state governments and 51.6 per cent by local governments. However, since it was felt that intergovernmental revenues should not be excluded from the analysis of state versus local financial roles, it was decided to use the figure described in the text.

high-income states. Low levels of economic development may tend to force centralization upon these states. Wealthier urban states can afford to let local governments shoulder more service responsibilities. This also means, of course, that the property tax is relatively more important as a state-local source of revenue in the wealthier urban states.

Federal monies are an important and growing source of revenue for state and local governments in the nation. In 1961 the federal government provided about 14 per cent of all state and local government revenue. The federal government turned over about $7 billion, almost $39 per capita, to states and localities. Alaska received over 35 per cent of its total state-local revenue from the federal government. Federal revenue is inversely related to economic development. Rural states receive significantly larger proportions of federal revenue than urban states.

TABLE VII-5
The Relationship between Economic Development
and Sources of State and Local Revenues

Revenue Sources, State and Local Governments	Economic Development			
	Urban-ization	Industrial-ization	Income	Education
State revenues as a percentage of total state and local revenues	−.30*	−.08	−.34*	−.24
Federal revenues as a percentage of total state and local revenues	−.59*	−.32*	−.33*	−.07

Figures are simple correlation coefficients for the fifty states; an asterisk indicates a statistically significant relationship.

TYPES OF TAXES AND THE INCIDENCE OF TAXATION

Earlier we analyzed tax burdens in terms of the proportion of a state's personal income devoted to taxes. This is a measure of the tax burden on the state's income considered in its entirety. But we are also concerned with the distribution of tax burdens among income groups within states. We want to have as clear a conception as possible about *who* actually bears the burden of a tax, that is, which income groups must devote the largest proportion of their income to taxes. Taxes which require high income groups to pay a larger percentage of their income in taxes than low income groups are said to be *progressive,* while taxes which take a larger share of the income of low-income groups than of high-income groups are said to be *regressive.*

TABLE VII-6

State and Local Tax Burdens by Income in 1958

Source	Family Personal Income							
	Under $2,000	*$2,000-$3,999*	*$4,000-$5,999*	*$6,000-$7,999*	*$8,000-$9,999*	*$10,000-$14,999*	*$15,000 and Over*	*Total*
Individual income	0.5	0.8	0.6	0.2	0.3	0.3	0.7	0.5
Corporation income	0.2	0.2	0.1	0.1	0.2	0.2	0.4	0.2
Excises and sales	4.8	3.9	3.7	3.6	3.2	3.2	2.1	3.3
Estate and gift	–	–	–	–	–	–	0.5	0.1
Property	5.9	4.6	4.1	3.7	2.8	2.8	2.1	3.5
Total, excluding social insurance	11.4	9.5	8.5	7.6	7.3	6.5	5.8	7.6

From George A. Bishop, "Tax Burden by Income Class," *National Tax Journal*, XIV (1961), quoted in staff report of the Advisory Commission on Intergovernmental Relations, *Measures of State and Local Fiscal Capacity and Tax Effort* (Washington: Government Printing Office, 1962), p. 23.

There are, however, very formidable difficulties in trying to determine the actual distribution of tax burdens among the income groups. Not only are there complex economic problems of tax shifting to be considered, but income and expenditure habits constantly change, making the most sophisticated computation of the incidence of a tax only a best estimate. Despite the difficulties, some scholars have attempted to make these estimates. Although no study has yet attempted to estimate tax incidence on a state-by-state basis (thus preventing a direct comparative analysis), economists have studied the incidence of the total state and local tax structure in the United States. Their general conclusion is that state and local tax systems are regressive.

Table VII-6 shows the estimates of economist George Bishop about the overall distribution by income classes of state and local taxes in 1958.[3] In that year total state and local tax collections amounted to 7.6 per cent of the nation's personal income. Bishop's estimates of the distribution of this burden show consistent decline with increases in personal income. The income group under $2000 per year was estimated to have paid 11.4 per cent of its personal income into state and local taxes, while the income group over $15,000 paid only 5.8 per cent of its personal income into these taxes.

Bishop also estimates the incidence of the various types of state and local taxes. Property taxes are quite regressive. This conclusion is based upon the assumption that the renter actually pays his property taxes through the increased rentals levied by the landlord, and the assumption that higher income groups have more wealth in untaxed forms of property. Since the property tax is the foundation of local tax structures in every state, it is reasonable to conclude that states which rely largely upon local governments for taxes and services are relying upon regressive tax structures.

State governments have generally given up reliance upon property taxes and have turned to individual and corporate income taxes, general sales taxes, and excise taxes on gasoline, alcohol, and tobacco. Bishop has estimated that state and local sales and excise taxes in the national aggregate are regressive, although not as steeply regressive as property taxes. This is based upon the assumption that low-income groups must devote most, if not all, of their income to purchases, while high-income groups devote larger shares of their income to savings. Many states exclude some of the necessities from sales taxation, packaged food, for example, in order to reduce the burden of this type

[3] George A. Bishop, "Tax Burden by Income Class," *National Tax Journal*, XIV (1961), 54; also cited in Advisory Commission on Intergovernmental Relations, p. 23.

of taxation on the poor. Yet excise and sales taxes have been estimated to take 4.8 per cent of the income of the under-$2000 group, but only 2.1 per cent of the income of the over-$15,000 group.

Individual and corporate income taxes seem to be the most progressive type of state and local taxation. Bishop estimates that in 1958 0.7 per cent of the income of the lowest-income class went to individual and corporate income taxes, while 1.1 per cent of the income of the highest class went into these taxes. This progressivity, however, is subject to some fluctuation in the middle-income groups. On the basis of Bishop's work, we can conclude that states which rely upon property taxes or sales taxes as principal sources of revenue are relying upon regressive sources, while states which rely more upon income taxes are relying upon more progressive sources.

What is the effect of economic development on the choice of a base for state taxes? This is a particularly important question because the type of taxes employed by a state determines the distribution of the tax burden. The conclusion that the total state and local tax structure in the nation is regressive does not mean that it is regressive in every state or that it may not be more or less regressive from state to state. We have no estimates of the incidence of the tax burden in every state, but we do know the extent to which the states rely upon various types of taxes, some of which are more regressive than others. Does economic development affect the type of taxes relied upon and therefore the progressivity or regressivity of the tax structure?

We expected that high levels of economic development would be associated with reliance upon income taxes, while lower levels of economic development would be associated with reliance upon more regressive sales and excise taxes. The original hypothesis was that urbanization and industrialization would result in the mobilization of liberal interests on behalf of "progressive," "modern" and "efficient" income taxation. Ruralism and economic underdevelopment were expected to result in greater reliance upon property and sales taxes, which are more compatible with conservative views on taxation. Conservatives argue that the broad base of sales taxation insures that the beneficiaries of public services share in the cost of them. Income taxes are said to discourage capital formation and investment incentives. Conservative views toward property, sales, and progressive income taxation were succinctly summarized by Barry Goldwater:

Government has a right to claim an equal percentage of each man's wealth and no more. Property taxes are typically levied on this basis. Excise and sales taxes are based on the same principle — although the tax is levied on a transaction rather than on property. The principle is equally valid with regard to incomes, inheritances, and gifts. The idea that a man who makes $100,000 a year should be forced to contribute ninety percent of his income to the cost of government, while the man who makes $10,000 is made to pay twenty percent, is repugnant to my notions of justice. I do not believe in punishing success.[4]

It was expected that these conservative views would be reflected in the tax policies of the rural, less industrialized states with less educated adult populations. In contrast, the principle of ability to pay and the theory of money based on marginal utility were expected to be represented in the policy outcomes of urban, industrial states with better educated adult populations. The principle of a graduated income tax based upon ability to pay, a principle accepted at the federal level in 1913 with the passage of the Sixteenth Amendment, together with the convenience, economy, and efficiency of income taxes were expected to appeal more to urban, industrial, educated populations.

Table VII-7 shows the relationship between economic development and state reliance upon the principal types of taxation. On the whole, our data fail to confirm our suspicions about economic development and progressivity in tax policy. Earlier we observed that urban states rely more upon their localities for tax revenue and the provision of public services than rural states. Since local governments rely upon the property tax, there is a close relationship between "local revenues as a percentage of total state-local revenues" and "percentage of state-local revenue derived from property taxation." The simple coefficient for this relationship is .66. This suggests that economic development is related to reliance upon property taxation in state-local revenue systems. And Table VII-7 shows this to be the case. Coefficients of .43 and .50 between property tax reliance and urbanization and industrialization indicate that reliance upon local government and property taxation is characteristic of the urban industrial states.

Since property taxation is considered regressive, these findings suggest that the urban industrial states have more regressive state-local tax structures than the rural farm states. The fact that centralization in state government has occurred more rapidly in rural America means that the total state-local tax structures of rural states may be less regressive than the total state-local tax structures of urban states. Urbanization and industrialization help local governments with their

[4]Barry Goldwater, *The Conscience of a Conservative* (Copyright ©, 1960, Victor Publishing Company, Inc., used by permission of MacFadden-Bartell Corporation, New York), p. 3. The quotation is used to illustrate conservative opinion. The misleading figures were supplied by Goldwater. In 1960 the actual federal income tax on $100,000 net taxable income was about 60 per cent while the tax on $10,000 net taxable income was about 24 per cent. Following the federal income tax reduction of 1964, the actual federal tax on $100,000 net taxable income was 48 per cent, while the tax on $10,000 was still about 24 per cent.

regressive property taxes to flourish. Our hypothesis that the tax structures of rural states are more regressive is demolished. This does not mean that urbanization leads to tax regressivity, but only that local governments provide more services and collect more taxes in urban states. And the tax structure of local governments is regressive.

But what if only state taxes are considered? Let us set aside the question of local taxes, and ask whether or not economic development affects the degree to which state governments rely upon one tax or another. Do urban industrial states choose progressive income taxation to finance state activities, while rural farm states choose sales taxation?

TABLE VII-7

The Relationship between Economic Development and Sources of State Tax Revenues

| | Economic Development | | | |
	Urban-ization	Industrial-ization	Income	Education
Income tax revenues as a percentage of state tax revenues	−.05	.02	.20	.19
Sales tax revenues as a percentage of state tax revenues	.03	.19	−.15	−.19
Alcohol and tobacco tax revenues as a percentage of state tax revenues	−.10	−.01	−.10	−.22
Motor fuel tax revenues as a percentage of state tax revenues	−.32*	−.35*	−.27	−.10
Property tax revenues as a percentage of total state and local tax revenues	.36*	−.11	.32*	.43*

Figures are simple correlation coefficients for the fifty states; an asterisk indicates a statistically significant relationship.

Table VII-7 shows that, contrary to our expectations, no significant relationships exist between reliance on sales tax or income tax and economic development. The proportion of state tax revenues derived from income taxes or sales taxes is not related to any of the measures of economic development. Urban states rely on sales taxation to the same degree as rural states, and rural states rely on income taxation to the same degree as urban states.

The rural farm states collect larger shares of motor fuel taxes than the urban industrial states. The relationship between ruralism and highway policy has already been discussed in Chapter VI. In contrast, reliance on taxes on alcohol and tobacco do not appear, in Table VII-7, to correlate with any of the indices of economic development. The moral arguments for discouraging the consumption of these "vices," or imposing penalties on those addicted to them, seem more compatible with the fundamentalism of America's hinterland than the cosmopolitanism of urban America. It is difficult to believe, however, that the failure to obtain significant correlations between taxes on alcohol and tobacco and urbanization and industrialization means that these phenomena do not affect the attitude of public policy toward such excise taxes. Rural states place very high tax rates on alcohol. The result, however, is often a reduction in consumption and hence in tax revenue, rather than an increase in such revenue. Urban states, in contrast, try to place alcohol tax rates at a level which will produce the highest revenue, not reduce consumption.

Not only is the proportion of tax revenue derived from sales and income taxes unrelated to economic development, but there are no significant differences in the levels of economic development between those states which have chosen to adopt sales taxes and those which have chosen to adopt income taxes. Table VII-8 shows no significant socioeconomic differences between the nine states with sales taxes and the thirteen states with income taxes. Nor are these states significantly different in socioeconomic character from the 26 states which have adopted both income and sales taxes.

TABLE VII-8
Economic Development and Sales and Income Tax Choices

	No Sales or Income Taxes (2 States)	Sales Taxes Only (9 States)	Income Taxes Only (13 States)	Sales and Income Taxes (26 States)
Urbanization	64.7	67.8	61.5	59.6
Industrialization	85.0	94.1	91.8	88.9
Income	$4873	$5914	$5886	$4941
Education	11.0	11.2	11.1	10.1

These findings suggest that the progressivity or regressivity of state tax structures is unrelated to levels of economic development. Although we have no measure of tax incidence in all fifty states which permit direct examination of the relationship between tax incidence and economic development, the fact that economic development has no apparent influence on the type of state tax employed is a strong indication that tax incidence is unrelated to levels of economic development. This is contrary to our initial hypothesis that urban states have more progressive tax structures than rural states, and vice versa. There is some additional evidence to help confirm the position that economic development does not affect tax incidence. In a recent comparative study of state tax policies, Professor Clara Penniman listed the ten state tax systems which, in her judgment, were the most progressive in the nation and the ten state tax systems which were the most regressive.[5] The following states were designated as most progressive: Alaska, Delaware, Idaho, Massachusetts, Minnesota, New York, Oregon, Vermont, Virginia, and Wisconsin. The most regressive states were Arizona, Arkansas, Hawaii, Illinois, Indiana, Michigan, Mississippi, Tennessee, Washington, and West Virginia. It is obvious that the states in each category cannot be differentiated by urbanization and industrialization: there are rural and urban states in both.

The choice of a sales or an income tax represents one of the most important policy choices facing a state government. Yet this major decision appears to be unaffected by levels of economic development. The sales tax seems to be emerging as the major source of state revenue in urban as well as rural states, in high-income states as well as low-income states. What accounts for this growing popularity of sales taxes in both developed and underdeveloped states?

Perhaps heavy federal income tax levies make it politically impossible for urban as well as rural state legislatures to rely heavily on income taxes for revenue. This view can be supported by noting the years in which the states with income taxes first adopted them. All of the major states relying on an income tax made their decision prior to World War II, three before 1920, and the others during the depression,[6] before federal income taxes became very heavy. No states have adopted income taxes since the end of World War II. Perhaps liberal opposition to sales taxation in urban industrial states is crumbling as a result of widespread affluence in postwar America. Or perhaps liberals have accepted the arguments of John K. Galbraith that their past opposition to sales taxation tended to reduce the amount of public funds available to support public improvements.[7] Galbraith argues effectively that the benfits to low-income groups which result from increased public expenditures outweigh whatever burdens are imposed on them by the regressivity of the sales tax. Galbraith's arguments may be used increasingly by liberals in urban as well as rural states as opposition to the sales tax declines and states come to rely more and more upon this source of revenue.

[5] Clara Penniman, "The Politics of Taxation," in Herbert Jacob and Kenneth Vines, eds., *Politics in the American States* (New York: Little, Brown, 1965), p. 312.
[6] *Ibid.,* p. 301.
[7] John K. Galbraith, *The Affluent Society* (Boston: Houghton Mifflin, 1956), ch. 22.

RELATIONSHIPS AMONG TAX
AND REVENUE POLICY OUTCOMES

So far we have been concerned with the relationships between economic development and tax and revenue policy outcomes. But there are also some interesting relationships among policy outcomes. Table VII-9 summarizes the relationships among ten policy outcomes in the tax and revenue field. Table VII-9 is a matrix of simple correlation coefficients which can be read very much like the mileage chart on a road map. To find the relationship between per capita taxes and per capita revenues, for example, simply locate the cell in which these variables intersect, in this case the second cell down in the far left column. As we might expect, this relationship is very close; it is described by a simple coefficient of .83.

Tax and revenue levels are positively related to tax burdens, as we noted this in our earlier section on tax burdens. Higher tax levels tend to be accompanied by higher tax burdens, as the simple coefficient of .39 indicates. But there are many exceptions to this proposition. It is possible in Figure VII-2 to identify states in which high tax levels are not accompanied by high tax burdens and to attribute these happy circumstances to high levels of industrialization. It is also possible to identify states in which low tax levels are accompanied by high tax burdens and to attribute these unhappy circumstances to a lack of industrialization.

Higher tax levels are significantly associated with lower federal and state financial participation. This does *not* mean, however, that federal and state participation tend to reduce tax levels. Actually these relationships are a product of the relationships between economic development and tax levels, and economic development and state and federal participation. High levels of economic development lead to high tax levels; high levels of economic development also reduce the need for state and federal financial assistance. And so it turns out that higher tax levels are associated with lower financial participation by federal and state governments.

Perhaps the most interesting relationships in Table VII-9 involve income and sales taxation and the tax burden. Reliance upon income and sales taxes for state revenue is related to higher tax burdens. Opponents of income and sales taxation have argued that resorting to these types of taxes has caused high tax burdens. But it seems more than likely that the causal connection is just the reverse; that is, states with high tax burdens have had to turn to sales or income taxation to

TABLE VII-9
Relationships among Tax and Revenue Policy Outcomes

	1	2	3	4	*Policy Outcomes* 5	6	7	8	9	10
Policy Outcomes										
1. Per capita total revenue	1.00									
2. Per capita tax revenue	.83*	1.00								
3. Taxes relative to income	.44*	.39*	1.00							
4. State percentage of state-local revenue	−.13	−.42*	.08	1.00						
5. Federal percentage of state-local revenue	.11	−.40*	.04*	.44*	1.00					
6. Income taxes	.19	.23	.66*	.01	.06	1.00				
7. Sales taxes	−.09	−.11	.66*	.03	.05	−.57*	1.00			
8. Alcohol and tobacco taxes	−.25	−.21	−.14	.02	.03	−.15	−.42*	1.00		
9. Motor fuel taxes	−.31*	−.38*	−.14	−.23	.19	−.23	.23	.32*	1.00	
10. Property taxes	.21	.43*	.18	−.66*	−.37*	−.13	−.29	.20	.05	1.00

Figures are simple correlation coefficients for the fifty states; an asterisk indicates a statistically significant relationship.

raise the necessary revenue. States with industry or other taxable resources sufficient to keep their tax burdens low have not been required to rely as heavily on income or sales taxation as states without taxable resources. States without industry who wish to maintain high levels of public service can do so only by increasing their tax burdens through the imposition of sales or income taxes. Only states which do not choose to provide high levels of public service, or states which are so wealthy that they can provide these services with little burden, can avoid reliance upon income and sales taxation. Reliance upon income taxation is inversely related to reliance upon sales taxation, even though half of the states have adopted both types of taxation.

Reliance upon property taxation is associated with increased state-local tax levels, but this does not mean that property taxation creates more revenue per capita. The association between property tax revenue and tax levels depends upon the relationships between economic development and tax levels and economic development and reliance upon local government and property taxation. Wealthy, urban, industrial states collect more tax revenue per capita, have lower tax burdens, and receive less money from state and federal governments. These same states depend more upon their local governments and the property tax. Thus reliance on the property tax appears to be associated with increased tax levels, lower tax burdens, and lower state and federal participation. Less wealthy, rural, farm states cannot rely upon their local governments or property taxation; since they cannot raise as much tax revenue per capita, they must rely more upon state and federal funds.

TAX POLICY AND PARTY POLITICS

To what extent does Republican or Democratic control of a state government influence the character of its tax and revenue structure? There are good a priori reasons for believing that the party in control of a state government does significantly influence its tax policy. At one time many liberal economists and tax experts favored increased public services but opposed financing these services through state sales taxes, because sales taxes were considered more regressive than income taxes. Liberals wanted to finance improved and expanded state services through state income taxes; conservatives, on the other hand, were by definition less enthusiastic about expanding public services and raising revenue levels, and they favored the sales tax because its broad base insured that the beneficiaries of public services would pay their share; they opposed the progressive income tax on the grounds that it penalized initiative. If the Democratic and Republican parties in the fifty states do represent liberal and conservative fiscal views, Democratic or Republican control of a state government should result in differences in tax and revenue levels and in the types of taxes relied upon by the state.

There are, however, equally good a priori reasons for believing that the state parties do *not* pursue markedly different tax policies when they occupy state offices. In the first place, as we have already mentioned, liberal opposition to the sales tax as a source of state revenue has been declining. John K. Galbraith has advised liberals that their opposition to sales taxation in the states has tended to reduce the amount of public funds available to support welfare efforts and other public activities which they favor. Sales taxes seem to be a less objectionable means of collecting revenue than income taxes to large segments of the voting public. Many liberal Democratic organizations in the states have now changed their position regarding sales taxes, feeling that the benefits of increased public funds raised from these taxes outweigh the burdens. In addition, it may be that the parties within each state are really a product of the characteristics of their local constituencies and not the representatives of liberal or conservative ideologies: state parties may be "brokerage" organizations, fitting their programs to popular demands rather than offering significantly different policy alternatives. For example, both Democrats and Republicans in a rural, low-income, agricultural state may pursue conservative revenue policies because their constituencies demand them; while both Democratic and Republican governments in wealthy, urban, industrial states may impose higher taxes and revenue levels to support improved public services because these are the kinds of policies demanded by constituents in that economic environment. Therefore, in order to test our hypothesis that Democratic or Republican control does influence state tax and revenue policy, we must decide whether the revenue policies of Democratic and Republican states are noticeably different and whether this difference can be traced to party control rather than to socioeconomic conditions.

Table VII-10 reveals that there is some tendency for Democratic and Republican states to differ in tax and revenue outcomes. Democratic states have had significantly lower tax and revenue levels than Republican states, and there is even a slight tendency for taxes in Democratic states to be lower in relation to personal income. Democratic states have relied less upon local sources of revenue than Republican states and more upon state sources of revenue, while Republican states have relied more upon property taxes than Democratic states; this reflects their increased reliance on local revenue. However, with regard to the sources of a state government's tax revenues, there are no significant differences between Democratic and Republican states in their reliance upon income taxes, state taxes on alcohol and tobacco, and motor fuel taxes. Thus, there is no empirical

TABLE VII-10

The Relationships among Economic Development, Partisanship, and State Tax and Revenue Policy

| | Democratic Party Control | | | | | |
| | Lower Houses | | Upper Houses | | Governorships | |
	Simple	Partial	Simple	Partial	Simple	Partial
Total revenue	−.46*	.18	−.46*	.09	−.53*	.04
Tax revenue	−.57*	−.29	−.60*	.32	−.62*	−.21
Taxes relative to income	−.31*	−.25	−.30*	−.28	−.23	−.20
Debt per capita	−.03	.17	−.01	.28	.15	.12
State revenue per capita	.03	.50	.03	.40	−.13	.23
Local revenue per capita	−.49*	.12	−.49*	.04	−.55*	.02
Federal revenue per capita	−.09	−.38	−.04	−.32	−.11	−.22
State percentage of total revenue	.54*	.53*	.55*	.47*	.42*	.29
Federal percentage of total revenue	.20	.39*	.26	.35*	.23	.27
Income taxes	−.06	.18	.01	.22	−.17	.00
Sales taxes	.12	−.06	.07	−.09	.19	.06
Alcohol and tobacco taxes	.04	−.08	.04	−.07	.20	.13
Motor fuel taxes	−.26	−.37	−.17	−.27	−.11	−.24
Property taxes	−.68*	−.64*	−.64*	−.54*	−.52*	−.36*

Figures are simple and partial correlation coefficients; partial coefficients control for the effect of urbanization, industrialization, income, and education; an asterisk indicates a statistically significant relationship.

evidence to support the view that Democratic or Republican control of a state government influences the selection of income or sales taxes as the principal source of state revenue.

Once economic development is controlled, most of the association between partisanship and tax and revenue policy disappears. Partisanship in state government has no independent effect upon per capita tax and revenue levels, tax burdens, debt levels, or the type of taxes employed to finance the state government. Whatever association has existed between Democratic party control and lower tax and revenue levels is merely a product of the fact that the Democratic party dominates state politics in the poorer states. Economic conditions and not Democratic politics keep down tax and revenue levels in these states.

The only fiscal outcome which partisanship may affect is the relative reliance placed upon state and federal sources of revenue as opposed to local sources. Even after controlling for economic development, there is still a significant relationship between Democratic politics and increased state and federal percentages of total state-local revenue and increased reliance upon property taxation. Moreover, these relationships remain significant even after removing the southern states from the correlation analysis. This means that Republican states place significantly greater reliance upon local sources of revenue, whether they are wealthy or poor. Democratic states, regardless of their level of economic development, place greater reliance upon state governments and the federal government as sources of revenue.

This finding is consistent with the findings in earlier chapters that partisanship is independently related to the proportions of local versus state and federal support for education and welfare. Even after controlling for economic development, and for the influence of the South, Republican states can be clearly differentiated from Democratic states in their financial reliance upon local units of government.

What is the effect of party competition on state tax and revenue structures? Correlation analysis has failed to produce any evidence that party competition *independently* affects tax and revenue outcomes. Two-party states have higher per capita tax and revenue levels than either one-party Democratic or one-party Republican states. There is also a tendency for two-party states to rely more upon local sources of revenue and less upon state sources in their total state-local revenue structure. However, with regard to every other tax and revenue measure employed in this study, no significant differences can be observed between states with competitive and non-competitive party systems. Since competitive and non-competitive states cannot be differentiated on most measures of tax and revenue outcomes, we can conclude that party competition has little independent effect on state fiscal policy. Table VII-11 shows that party competition is associated in simple correlations with only 5 of 14 summary tax and revenue measures.

When economic development is controlled, there are no significant relationships between party competition and tax and revenue outcomes. None of the partial coefficients in Table VII-11 are above the accepted levels of significance. The association between party competition and tax and revenue levels is merely a result of the fact that economic development produces both interparty competition and higher tax and revenue levels. Party competition has little independent effect on a state's tax and revenue outcomes.

TABLE VII-11

The Relationships among Economic Development, Party Competition, and Tax and Revenue Policies

| | Party Competition | | | | | |
| | Lower Houses | | Upper Houses | | Governorships | |
	Simple	Partial	Simple	Partial	Simple	Partial
Total revenues	.40*	.19	.40*	.13	.47*	.16
Tax revenues	.52*	.03	.53*	.02	.59*	.07
Taxes relative to income	.10	.05	.07	.03	.03	.01
Debt	.22	.02	.24	.01	.21	.02
State revenue per capita	−.07	−.34	−.02	−.24	−.07	−.23
Local revenue per capita	.43*	.12	.42*	.08	.49*	.10
Federal revenue per capita	−.01	−.27	−.01	−.19	−.07	−.28
State percentage of total revenue	−.53*	−.34	−.47*	−.30	−.44*	−.28
Federal percentage of total revenue	−.25	−.21	−.25	−.14	−.26	−.24
Income taxes	.12	.05	.10	.03	.18	.01
Sales taxes	.22	.13	.22	.15	.15	.00
Alcohol and tobacco taxes	.15	.04	.10	.02	.16	.02
Motor fuel taxes	−.15	−.06	−.05	−.03	−.10	−.10
Property taxes	−.61*	−.34	−.52*	−.31	−.48*	−.32

Figures are simple and partial correlation coefficients; partial coefficients control for the effect of urbanization, industrialization, income, and education; an asterisk indicates a significant relationship.

TAX POLICY AND CHARACTERISTICS OF ELECTORAL SYSTEMS

What is the effect of political participation on tax and revenue policy outcomes? In Chapter III we have shown that economic development has an important influence on political participation. Since economic development is also related to several important measures of tax and revenue policy, we expect to find some association between voter turnout and tax and revenue policy as a product of the relationships between these variables and economic development. The important question, of course, is whether political participation *independently* influences policy outcomes in the tax and revenue field.

The simple coefficients in Table VII-12, which do not control for the intervening impact of economic development, show that voter turnout is associated with several measures of tax and revenue outcomes. Voter turnout is associated with those outcomes which have been shown to be related to economic development — total revenue per capita, tax revenue per capita, the state proportion of total tax revenue, and reliance upon property taxation for state-local revenue. States with higher voter participation tend to collect more total revenue and more tax revenue per capita than states with lower voter participation. States with high voter turnout rely less upon state revenues and more upon local property taxes than states with low voter turnout.

When the effects of economic development are controlled, however, all of these relationships between political participation and tax and revenue policy disappear. None of the partial coefficients in Table VII-12, which control for the combined effects of urbanization, in-

TABLE VII-12

**The Relationships among Economic Development,
Political Participation, and Tax and Revenue Policies**

| | *Political Participation* | | | | | |
| | *Gubernatorial* | | *1962 Congressional* | | *1958 Congressional* | |
	Simple	*Partial*	*Simple*	*Partial*	*Simple*	*Partial*
Total revenue	.39*	−.09	.50*	−.09	.55*	−.07
Tax revenue	.52*	.14	.59*	.15	.63*	.12
Taxes relative to income	.14	−.05	.17	.00	.19	.00
Debt	.11	−.13	.13	−.19	.16	−.21
State revenue per capita	.17	−.25	.06	−.26	.16	−.18
Local revenue per capita	.41*	−.04	.52*	−.04	.57*	−.03
Federal revenue per capita	.28	−.25	.12	−.22	.16	−.15
State percentage of total revenue	−.42*	−.30	−.48*	−.34	−.40*	−.23
Federal percentage of total revenue	−.23	−.25	−.20	−.20	−.18	−.14
Income taxes	.08	−.10	.07	−.07	.11	−.07
Sales taxes	−.03	.13	−.14	.03	−.10	.10
Alcohol and tobacco taxes	−.21	−.08	−.19	−.04	−.20	−.04
Motor fuel taxes	.15	.04	.20	.12	.06	.05
Property taxes	.50*	.32	.48*	.29	.51*	.31

Figures are simple and partial correlation coefficients; partial coefficients control for the effect of urbanization, industrialization, income, and education; an asterisk indicates a significant relationship.

dustrialization, income, and education, indicate statistically significant relationships. Whatever relationships exist between political participation and tax and revenue outcomes are a product of the influences of economic development on both of these sets of variables. There is no empirical evidence to support the view that differences in voter participation among the states independently influence tax or revenue outcomes.

What is the effect of state legislative malapportionment on tax and revenue policy? There is no evidence that the tax and revenue policies of well apportioned states are significantly different from the tax and revenue policies of malapportioned states. Whether one prefers to measure malapportionment in a technical sense as in the index of representation and the apportionment score or whether one prefers to measure discrimination against urban areas as in the index of urban underrepresentation, the results are the same. Since there are no consistent differences between the tax outcomes of well apportioned and malapportioned states, there is no empirical evidence to support the inference that malapportionment affects tax or revenue policy. None of the partial coefficients in Table VII-13 indicate a statistically significant relationship.

TABLE VII-13

The Relationships among Economic Development, Malapportionment, and Tax and Revenue Policies

| | \multicolumn{6}{c}{*Malapportionment*} |
| | *Index of Representation* | | *Index of Urban Underrepresentation* | | *Apportionment Score* | |
	Simple	*Partial*	*Simple*	*Partial*	*Simple*	*Partial*
Total revenue	−.18	−.12	.02	−.09	−.04	−.02
Tax revenue	−.15	.05	.26	.17	.01	−.09
Taxes relative to income	.08	.04	−.06	.01	−.14	.05
Debt	−.24	−.12	.31	.06	.05	−.02
State revenue per capita	−.16	−.07	−.18	−.17	−.10	−.10
Local revenue per capita	−.18	−.09	.04	−.06	−.04	−.19
Federal revenue per capita	−.08	−.19	−.26	−.25	−.03	−.23
State percentage of total revenue	.00	−.06	−.29	−.02	−.13	−.01
Federal percentage of total revenue	.03	−.09	−.36*	−.23	−.04	−.08
Income taxes	.12	.07	.14	.00	.02	.05
Sales taxes	−.14	−.15	−.20	−.20	−.14	−.09
Alcohol and tobacco taxes	.14	.04	.13	−.01	.02	.07
Motor fuel taxes	.22	.08	−.01	.04	.19	.14
Property taxes	.15	.29	.28	.34	.19	.26

Figures are simple and partial correlation coefficients; partial coefficients control for the effects of urbanization, industrialization, income, and education; an asterisk indicates a significant relationship.

If there are evils in state tax and revenue systems, it does not seem likely that reapportionment will correct them. Since the tax policies of well apportioned and malapportioned states cannot be differentiated, it is difficult to support the view that malapportionment is the villain in state tax problems.

CHAPTER VIII

Public Regulatory Policy

TRENDS IN STATE REGULATORY POLICY

STATE REGULATORY POLICY in this study refers to a wide variety of outcomes reflecting public control; they include the numbers and types of governmental units, the sheer quantity of state legislation, certain characteristics of state and local bureaucracies, social control and law enforcement activity, and prison and correctional policy.

There were 91,236 separate governments in the United States in 1962, a significant decline in the total number of governmental units from the 116,807 in 1952. However, as Table VIII-1 indicates, this decline is actually attributable to the consolidation of school districts, since, of all categories of governmental units, only the school districts have declined significantly. Municipalities and special district governments have increased in number, while the number of counties and townships has remained relatively constant, so that, in effect, units of government serving urban populations or providing urban kinds of services are increasing, while non-urban governments are not. The result has been a gradual increase in local governments, if school districts are not considered.

The term "municipality" refers to independent governing units with the legal authority to provide a wide variety of urban services to their residents. The special district, on the other hand, usually provides only one service; it may be independent of other local units, but its jurisdiction is superimposed on the jurisdiction of one or more other units of local government. Approximately 116 million Americans live in 18,000 municipalities. There are also more than 18,000 special district governments today. This represents an upward trend in special district governments since 1942, when only 8,300 special districts were reported. Two-thirds of these special districts governments provide one or another kind of urban service—fire protection, water supply, sewage, hospitals, housing, urban renewal, school buildings, highways, parks and recreation, libraries, and so on. Only about one-third deal with natural resources—soil conservation, irrigation, flood control, and so on. As interesting as these trends may be, it is not growth in the numbers of governmental units, but growth in their size which more adequately reflects increased public control.

The growth of bureaucracy is reflected unmistakably in the increase in the number of government employees, both numerically and in proportion to the population. Total public employees have increased from nearly seven million in 1953 to nearly ten million in 1963. Public employees have increased from 401 per 100,000 population to 467 per 100,000 in ten years. Very often misleading or erroneous statements are made describing the decline of state and local governments and the centralization of government in Washington. Yet every available measure of bureaucracy indicates just the opposite trend. State and local governments are spending more money, employing more people, and undertaking more important responsibilities than ever before in American history. And in recent years state and local governments have grown faster than the federal government. Although the federal government has spent more annually than state and local governments since about 1935, recent increases in state-local spending has reduced the relative superiority of the federal government in this regard. This trend has been discussed in Chapter VII. In addition, Table VIII-1 describes state-local, rather than federal, domination in public employment. While federal employment of civilians has remained at about the same level, 2.4 million, over the ten-year period from 1953 to 1963, state-local employment grew from 4.6 million to 7.1 million in that same period. Even if the nearly three million employees in public education were subtracted, state and local governments employ far more persons than the federal government.

If volume of statutory writing and revision is an index of public control, then it can rightly be said that state governments have never exercised so much formal statutory control as they have in recent years. In the 1951-1953 biennium American state legislation considered over 47,000 bills, but by the 1960-1961 biennium this figure had grown to over 104,000. The total number of state legislative enactments grew from approximately 15,000 to over 33,000 in that same ten-year period. As a society grows more complex and becomes

TABLE VIII-1

Trends in Bureaucracy and Regulatory Policy, 1950-1960

	1950-1953	*1960-1963*
Number of governments, 1952-1962		
Total	116,743	91,185
Counties	3,049	3,043
Municipalities	16,778	17,997
Townships	17,202	17,144
Special districts	12,319	18,323
School systems	67,346	37,019
Number of bills		
Introduced	47,000	104,000
Enacted	15,000	33,000
Government employees, 1953-1963		
Number in thousands		
Total	6,893	9,568
Federal	2,230	2,380
State	1,129	1,775
Local	3,533	5,413
Rate per 100,000 population		
Total	401.3	467.0
Federal	140.8	133.0
State	63.8	83.0
Local	196.7	251.0
Average monthly earnings of all state and local employees, 1953-1963	$295	$457
Urban crime rate, 1952-1961		
Murder and non-negligent manslaughter	5.0	4.7
Robbery	59.6	62.2
Assault	81.5	92.1
Burglary	391.5	576.7
Larceny	187.0	1,438.3
Theft	187.0	248.8
State correctional expenditures, 1951-1961		
Total in millions of $	$211.5	$448.6
Per capita	$2.40	$2.72
Percentage of total state expenditures	1.6	1.7
Policemen per 10,000 population	21.9	25.0
Prisoners present at end of year, 1953-1963		
Numbers		
Total	166,165	213,125
Federal	17,134	23,218
State	149,031	189,907
Rate per 100,000 population		
Total	109	118
Federal	11	13
State	98	105
Executions, 1940-1949 and 1950-1959	1,284	717

U.S. Bureau of the Census, *Statistical Abstract of the United States, 1964* (Washington: Government Printing Office, 1964), passim; and appropriate earlier editions. Council of State Governments, *Book of the States 1962-1963* (Chicago: Council of State Governments, 1964), passim; and appropriate earlier editions.

increasingly urban and industrial, the need for statutory control seems to grow.

Crime rates are the subject of a great deal of popular discussion. Very often they are employed to express the extent of social disorganization or even the effectiveness of law enforcement and social control agencies. Crime rates are based upon the Federal Bureau of Investigation's *Uniform Crime Reports,* but the FBI report is based entirely on figures supplied by state and local police agencies. The FBI has succeeded in establishing a uniform classification of the number of serious crimes per 100,000 people which are known to the police — murder and non-negligent manslaughter, robbery, aggravated assault, burglary, larceny, and theft, including auto theft. But record-keeping is still a serious problem. Official crime statistics are really a function of several factors: the diligence of police in detecting crime, the adequacy of the recording system in tabulating crime, and the amount of crime itself. Only crime rates for urban places go back in time, since only urban police forces were developed enough to keep the necessary records a few years ago. The urban crime rate is a reasonably comparable measure from year to year. It shows a significant increase in non-violent crimes — burglary, larceny, and theft — and only slight changes in crimes involving violence against the person — murder and and non-negligent manslaughter, assault, and robbery.

Increases in social control and law enforcement activity are also revealed by the number of policemen in relation to the population. In 1953 state and local governments employed 21.9 policemen per 10,000 people in the nation; by 1963 not only had the absolute number of policemen grown considerably, but their number in relation to the polulation had grown to 25.0 per 10,000. Significantly more police are needed for social control today than only a few years ago.

Despite greater concern over the problem of human restoration and rehabilitation in correctional institutions, there has been a noticeable increase in the number of prisoners in both state and federal institutions even in the decade 1950-1960. The total prison population increased from 166,165 in 1950 to 213,125 in 1960. This is not only a large absolute increase in prisoners but an increase relative to the nation's population as well. In 1950 there were about 109 prisoners per 100,000 people, compared to 118 prisoners per 100,000 people in 1960.

State expenditures for correction have increased with increases in prison population; these increases in public expenditures for correction have been commensurate with increases in other public expenditures. State correctional expenditures rose from $212 million in 1951 to $489 million in 1961, and per capita correctional expenditures rose from $1.40 to $2.72. Correctional expenditures amounted to only 1.6 per cent of state expenditures in 1951 and only 1.7 per cent in 1961.

ECONOMIC DEVELOPMENT AND PUBLIC REGULATORY POLICY

Economic development has been closely linked in social theory to an increase in the rules which define and regulate the conduct of individuals within a society.[1] Industrialization, increased worker productivity, and wealth are all dependent upon a high degree of specialization in society. The division of labor is the foundation of modern social organization. But what has been taken apart must be put together again: and specialization of men and organizations creates a need for a complex system of coordination in society. Out of interdependence grows a hierarchy of activity and a system of rules which regulates the relationship among men and organizations. Behavior must be ordered and made somewhat predictable if men are to depend on one another.

Corporations, churches, clubs, schools, professional associations, and other large-scale, specialized, formal organizations control segments of our behavior and provide much of the coordination of society. However, government has the task of arbitrating conflicts between these organized groups of people and of maintaining public order in areas outside the control of specialized bureaucracies. As spatially inclusive organizations, governments must maintain order in these areas beyond the control of groups—in parks and playgrounds, on city sidewalks and streets, on the open highway. In order to regulate the relationships among groups and the behavior of individuals outside of groups, governments, among other things, pass laws, maintain organizations to enforce these laws, hire policemen, spend money for public safety, maintain correctional institutions, and occasionally execute people.

Economic development also involves certain dislocations for a society. The process of economic development is uneven; some industries expand, while others contract. Errors of judgment are committed by individuals, firms, and even governments, and they result in unemployment, in the decline of particular industries, and in the impoverishment of particular communities and areas. We have already

[1] See H. H. Gerth and C. Wright Mills, *From Max Weber* (New York: Oxford University Press, 1946), particularly Part VIII; Emile Durkheim, *The Division of Labor in Society,* trans. George Simpson (New York: Free Press, 1964), pp. 256-395. Further references in this chapter to "social theory" or "Weberian theory" are references to these works.

seen that unemployment compensation recipients are more numerous in the more industrial states. Although improvements in human skills are required by a developed society, many individuals are unable to make the necessary improvements, and the ranks of the unemployables grow. The transition from rural to urban life creates further dislocations for some people. Old skills and ways of life are devalued; migration is often accompanied by alienation in the new environment. Rationalization and secularization of value systems, which Weberian theory associates with economic development, very often succeed in undermining traditional values without successfully replacing them. In short, there is good reason to believe that a certain degree of social disorganization is always associated with economic development. Governments, therefore, must devise police and crime policies and correctional and penal policies which reflect the level of economic development.

Weberian theory also postulates that record-keeping is a function of economic and bureaucratic development. Careful record-keeping, which is not a characteristic of underdeveloped nations, is, perhaps, the most important research problem in the comparative study of national governments. Precise comparisons between developed and underdeveloped nations is difficult because underdeveloped nations do not keep the records needed for genuine comparative analysis. This problem is substantially reduced, however, when we are studying states within a highly developed nation. Generally we can rely upon the national government to keep adequate records for all states, regardless of the degree of development in state record-keeping. However, where we must rely upon state agencies for data, or where the federal government itself relies upon state records, the adaquacy of the data is likely to be a function of the levels of economic development in the state. This is particularly true of state data on crime and social control.

In summary, economic development is associated with specialization and differentiation, increased demand for coordination, hierarchies of authority, systems of rules, impersonality, rationalization, and secularization. It is closely associated, too, with changes in both the character and the level of activity in government bureaucracies. Students of comparative national bureaucracies have commented on the increase in laws and regulations, the increased size of public agencies, and the increase in public regularatory activity which are associated with economic development.[2] This chapter explores the relationships

---

[2] Joseph J. Spengler, "Bureaucracy and Economic Development," in Joseph LaPalombara, *Bureaucracy and Political Development*, (Princeton: Princeton University Press, 1963).

between economic development and public regulatory policy in the fifty states; it attempts to ascertain the extent to which differences among the fifty states in the number of governments and laws, in the size of public bureaucracies, in the size and organization of police forces, in the nature of correctional policies, and in the character and extent of public regulating activity, are associated with variations in levels of economic development. The term "public regulatory policy" is used in its broader sense to refer to all of these attributes of state political systems.

LAWS AND GOVERNMENTS IN THE STATES

If economic development is related to an increase in the number of rules which define and regulate the conduct of men, the legislatures of urban industrial states should introduce and enact more laws than the legislatures of rural farm states. Specialization of men and organizations creates a need for a complex system of rules and regulations defining the responsibility of each member of society and the relationships among them. This system of rules is designed to assure uniformity of behavior so that the activities of large numbers of people can be coordinated. For political systems, this seems to imply that economic development will be accompanied by an increase in the quantity of legislation and legislative activity.

The average state legislature considered 2,050 bills in the 1960-1961 biennium and enacted 757 of these into laws. Five states considered over 4,000 bills: California, Connecticut, Florida, Massachusetts, and New York (over 10,000 bills were introduced into the New York legislature); while ten states considered less than 1,000: Idaho, Montana, Nebraska, New Hampshire, North and South Dakota, Utah, Vermont, West Virginia, and Wyoming. Eleven states enacted more than 1,000 laws, including Florida with over 3,000 enactments; while 23 states enacted fewer than 500, including West Virginia's meager 215.

Table VIII-2 indicates that urbanization and industrialization among the fifty states does indeed result in significant increases in the number of bills introduced and enacted in state legislatures. Urbanization appears to be the most influential determinant of legislative activity. While intervening short-term conditions may obscure this relationship in any single legislative session, the average urbanization score of the 11 states which enacted more than 1000 statutes in the 1960-1961 biennium was 72.5. The average urbanization score of the

16 states which enacted between 500 and 1000 laws was 58.7, and the average score for the 23 states enacting fewer than 500 laws was 58.6.

According to the 1962 *Census of Governments,* there were 91,236 governmental units in the United States, with school districts comprising more than one-third (34,678) of this total. The average number of governmental units per state was 1,825; but Illinois had 6,453, while Hawaii had only 21. Thus, there were about 50.8 governments per 100,000 people in the nation: South Dakota had the highest number of governmental units per population ratio, 655, and Hawaii had the lowest, 3.3. The total number of governmental units per population is inversely related to urbanization and industrialization; the rural farm states support more governmental units per population than urban, industrial states.

TABLE VIII-2

**The Relationship between Economic Development
and the Number of Laws and Governments in the States**

	Economic Development			
	Urban-ization	Industrial-ization	Income	Education
Number of bills introduced in state legislatures	.53*	.39*	.28	.04
Number of laws enacted by state legislatures	.40*	.30*	.10	−.03
Total number of governments per 10,000 population	−.39*	−.76*	−.19	−.09
Municipalities and special districts per 10,000 population	−.40*	−.70*	−.16	−.24

Figures are simple correlation coefficients for the fifty states; an asterisk indicates a statistically significant relationship.

But the total figures on governmental units are heavily influenced by the 34,678 school districts in the nation, as well as the 17,144 townships and 3,043 counties. It has already been shown that consolidation of school districts has progressed furthest in the least economically developed states. In recent years the lack of economic resources has been a stimulus for increases in the size of school districts. And, of course, townships and counties are the traditionally rural forms of local government. In contrast, municipalities and special district governments are the governmental units which service urban populations. For that reason it has been decided to separate municipal and special district governments to see if economic development has a separate effect on the proliferation of these types of governmental units.

Throughout the nation in 1962 there were 17,997 municipalities, or approximately 10 per 100,000 people. There were 18,323 special district governments, about 10.2 per 100,000 people. Idaho had 110 municipal and special district governments per 100,000 people; in contrast, Massachusetts had less than one municipal and special district government per 100,000 people. Table VIII-2 indicates that rural farm states support more municipal and special district governments per population than urban industrial states.

In short, local governments in rural farm states are small in scale and encompass fewer people than local governments in urban industrial states. This is true whether we are talking about township and county governments, school districts, or even municipal and special district governments. It may be that this reduction in the scale of political institutions gives rural politics its folksy, personalized flavor, while the large-scale governments, encompassing greater masses of people, help to give political institutions in the urban industrial states their bureaucratic character.

PUBLIC EMPLOYMENT

Recent interest in the problems of economic development in the emerging nations, and interest in comparative public administration, have stimulated inquiry into the role of public bureaucracy in a modern, industrialized, urban society. Weberian theory postulates a relationship between economic development and the specialization, hierarchy of activity, systems of rules, and impersonality which are, of course, the basic characteristics of bureaucuracy. Coordination and control in a complex, highly specialized, and highly interdependent society cannot be accomplished without a large, trained, and organized public bureaucracy. Of course, data collection and measurement problems often make it difficult to devise systematic tests of these Weberian propositions about economic development and bureaucracy across societal and cultural boundaries, but, if these propositions are general in character, they should apply to the fifty states. Urban industrial states should have more extensive and better developed government bureaucracies than rural farm states. Specifically, the economically developed states should have more public employees per 10,000 population, and they should pay these employees more on the average than the underdeveloped states.

The average state had about 326 state and local government employees per 100,000 people in 1961. About 96 of these were state employees, and the remaining 230 were employed by the local governments. In relation to its population, Wyoming employed more people in state and local government than any other state, with 442 state and local government employees per 100,000 people. Hawaii had more state government employees per person than any other state, 216 per 100,000 population; this represented the highest ratio of state to total state-local employees in the nation, 65 per cent.

Table VIII-3 shows the relationships between the measures of economic development and these measures of public employment. These data do not entirely support Weberian theory, in that urbanization and industrialization are *not* shown to be related to the number of public employees per population as we might expect. On the other hand, the income and educational aspects of economic development do correlate significantly with public employment. Within the context of the fifty American states, it appears to be the income and educational attributes of the developed states which permit the development of public administration. All four measures of economic development correlate significantly with the salaries of public employees, yet here again the income and educational attributes of the states are more influential than urbanization or industrialization.

TABLE VIII-3
The Relationship between Economic Development
and State and Local Government Employment

| | Economic Development | | | |
	Urban- ization	Industrial- ization	Income	Education
Total state and local employees per population	.07	−.26	.36*	.61*
State employees per population	−.16	.02	.32*	.36*
State employees as a percentage of total state and local employees	−.15	.16	.22	.21
Average monthly earnings of state and local employees	.41*	.42*	.86*	.58*

Figures are simple correlation coefficients for the fifty states; an asterisk indicates a statistically significant relationship.

CRIME RATES

It has already been suggested that crime rates may measure more than just the frequency of criminal acts. Crime rates may also reflect the diligence of police in detecting crimes and the adequacy of police record-keeping systems. In 1962, according to the FBI, there were 1102 major crimes known to the police per 100,000 people in the nation. The break-down by type of crime is shown in Table VIII-1.

The lowest crime rates were in North Dakota and Mississippi, with 410.4 and 446.4 major crimes per 100,000 people in 1962; the highest crime rates were in California and Nevada, with 2010.7 and 2442.9 major crimes per 100,000 people.

FBI reports on crime are based entirely upon figures supplied by local police, and herein lies a problem. Mississippi's police reports, for example, cover 67 per cent of the state's population living in cities of over 25,000 people, 71 per cent of the population living in cities of less than 25,000 people, but only 28 per cent of the state's rural population — this in a state where over half of the population lives in rural areas. Other omissions from crime statistics in that state stem from the old Mississippi custom of largely ignoring crimes among Negroes, who comprise 42 per cent of the state's population.

Crime rates, therefore, may measure crime, or police diligence, or the adaquacy of police record-keeping. But social theory postulates that all of these phenomena are related to economic development. It has been said that economic development involves certain necessary social dislocations: a certain degree of unemployment appears to be inevitable; the transition from rural to urban life creates a multitude of social problems; social isolation and hostility are frequently by-products of this process; traditional value systems and social control mechanisms are undermined, without their immediate replacement by more relevant values and institutions. All of these conditions are intimately associated with crime. Whether these social dislocations are permanent by-products of economic development or merely an expression of social growing pains, there is still reason to hypothesize that crime itself increases with economic development.

TABLE VIII-4
The Relationship between Economic Development
and Public Regulatory Measures

| | Economic Development | | | |
	Urban-ization	Industrial-ization	Income	Education
State and local employees in police protection per population	.75*	.54*	.64*	.32*
Crime rate: Major crimes per 100,000 population	.61*	.45*	.49*	.38*
Gambling tax revenues as a percentage of total state revenues	.34*	.38*	.34*	.19
Divorce rate: Divorces granted per 10,000 population	.07	.10	.17	.24

Figures are simple correlation coefficients for the fifty states; an asterisk indicates a statistically significant relationship.

But Weberian theory also postulates that professionalization in public employment (which would include police) and concern with record-keeping are both associated with bureaucratic development. Bureaucratic development is, in turn, associated with economic development. Thus, regardless of whether crime rates are measures of crime, of police diligence, or concern for record-keeping, or of some

FIGURE VIII-1

The Fifty States Arranged According to Urbanization and Crime Rates

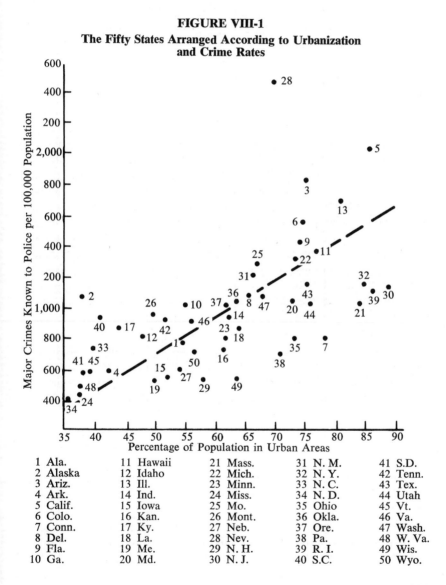

1 Ala.	11 Hawaii	21 Mass.	31 N. M.	41 S.D.
2 Alaska	12 Idaho	22 Mich.	32 N. Y.	42 Tenn.
3 Ariz.	13 Ill.	23 Minn.	33 N. C.	43 Tex.
4 Ark.	14 Ind.	24 Miss.	34 N. D.	44 Utah
5 Calif.	15 Iowa	25 Mo.	35 Ohio	45 Vt.
6 Colo.	16 Kan.	26 Mont.	36 Okla.	46 Va.
7 Conn.	17 Ky.	27 Neb.	37 Ore.	47 Wash.
8 Del.	18 La.	28 Nev.	38 Pa.	48 W. Va.
9 Fla.	19 Me.	29 N. H.	39 R. I.	49 Wis.
10 Ga.	20 Md.	30 N. J.	40 S.C.	50 Wyo.

combination of all of these, there is still reason to expect that crime rates will be positively related to economic development levels. Table VIII-4 tends to confirm this chain of reasoning. Overall, crime rates in the fifty states are positively related to all four measures of economic development, but it is urbanization which provides the most comprehensive explanation of variations in the crime rates. The scattergram for the relationship between urbanization and crime shows that Nevada is the most deviant state; it fails to conform to the urbanization hypothesis by having a much higher crime rate than its degree of urbanization would suggest.

DIVORCE LAWS AND THE REGULATION OF GAMBLING

Two measures reflecting public policy toward gambling and divorce have also been selected for analysis. Both gambling and divorce are highly regulated aspects of social behavior, and both involve public attitudes toward the regulation of private conduct. Rather than categorize the myriad and complex state regulations dealing with these phenomena, it has been decided to measure specific outcomes, that is, state revenue from gambling operations and divorces granted per unit of population. The assumption is that such measures generally reflect the extent of state regulation or suppression of these activities. Of course they also measure the extent to which the public in each state wishes to engage in these activities. But public demands for freedom to engage in these behaviors and public attempts to regulate or suppress them are really opposite sides of the same coin and cannot be logically separated. Thus, our measure of divorces granted per 10,000 population measures both the demand for divorces and the degree to which public regulations reduce the number of divorces granted; our measures of state revenue from gambling operations (including pari-mutuel betting) reflect both the attitude of the state's population toward gambling and the degree to which state law prohibits or discourages gambling.

A total of 25 states reported revenue from gambling or pari-mutuel betting in 1961. The highest amount was, of course, reported in Nevada, which received about 25 per cent of its state revenue from gambling taxes. Twenty-five states reported no revenue from gambling taxes. Despite the large number of states at the bottom of the scale, however, significant correlations have been obtained in Table VIII-4 between the percentage of state revenue derived from gambling taxes and urbanization, industrialization, and income. Apparently economic development alters public attitudes toward gambling and consequently increases the extent to which states will allow this form of recreation and rely on it for public revenue.

Contrary to our expectations, it is not necessarily easier to obtain a divorce in the urban industrial states than in the rural states. The divorce rate in the United States in 1960 was 2.2 divorces per 1,000 persons, down from 2.6 divorces per 1,000 in 1950. The divorce rates in the states ranged from a low of 0.4 in New York to a high of 29.6 in Nevada. There is reason to believe that variations in divorce rates among the states are affected by state law. New York's divorce laws, for example, have been the most stringent in the nation; until very recently adultery was the only legal ground for divorce in that state. It is no surprise, then, that its divorce rate has been the lowest in the nation. On the other hand, Nevada's laws are the most permissive and its legal residence period is the briefest, six weeks. But differences in divorce laws and in divorce rates appear unrelated to urbanism or education, as one might hypothesize. None of the coefficients for the relationships between the four measures of economic development and divorce rates are significant.

POLICE PROTECTION

State, county, and municipal governments are all directly involved in law enforcement. Every state has a central law enforcement agency, sometimes designated the State Police, State Troopers, State Highway Patrol or Texas Rangers. At one time state governors had only the National Guard at their disposal to back up local law enforcement efforts, but the coming of the automobile and intercity highway traffic has led to the establishment in every state of a centralized police system. In addition to patroling the highways, these central agencies provide expert aid and service to local officers and strengthen the arm of the law in sparsely populated regions. Three-fourths of the states have given their central police agencies full law enforcement authority, in addition to highway duties. They may be used to quell riots, cooperate with local authorities in the apprehension of criminals, or even intervene when local authorities have been unable or unwilling to enforce the law. The size and influence of these agencies varies from state to state. State police range in number from a few dozen in Nevada and Alaska to over 3,000 in California. There is no relationship, however, between economic development and the relative size of state police forces. On the whole, state police forces constitute a very small proportion of the total law enforcement effort; law enforcement in the United States is principally a local responsibility.

Historically the county sheriff has been the keystone of law enforcement in the nation. He and his deputies are still the principal enforcement and arresting officers in rural counties and in the unincorporated fringe areas of many urban counties. In addition, the sheriff serves as an executive agent for county and state courts in both civil and criminal matters, and he maintains the county jail for the retention of persons pending trial or sentence or serving short terms of punishment. The sheriff's office is a political one; in every state except Rhode Island he is an elected official. Very often the office of sheriff is a lucrative one. Antiquated fee systems exist in many states under which a sheriff collects a fee for every order, process, warrant, or arrest in which he is involved. Small fortunes can be made by "diligent" sheriffs in one term of office, and, where a sheriff cannot succeed himself, he may alternate the office with his chief deputy in order to prolong his time in office. Constables are elected in most states and perform many of the same functions as sheriffs for rural townships or other subdivisions of the county. Reliance upon the sheriff's office for law enforcement is a characteristic of rural states. Since municipal police forces usually assume the sheriff's law enforcement duties within the boundaries of municipalities, the sheriff's office has seriously atrophied in most urban states; often he is reduced to a process-server for the courts.

Urban police departments are the most important instruments of law enforcement and public safety in the nation today. About two-thirds of the nation's population live in municipalities and depend upon municipal police for protection. City policemen vastly outnumber all the other state and county law enforcement officers combined. The urban police department also does more than merely enforce the law; it engages in a wide range of activity for social control and coordination.

If it is true that economic development requires a large, complex system of public control, we would expect urban industrial states to employ more police per population than rural farm states. Throughout the nation there were 17 state and local employees in police protection per 10,000 population in 1962. This figure ranged from a high of 27 policemen per 10,000 people in Nevada to a low of 9 in South Dakota. Table VIII-4 confirms our expectations that economic development, particularly urbanization, requires greater police control. Urbanization explains over 55 per cent of the variation among the fifty states in policemen per population. Urbanization is the principal determinant of the extent and character of public law enforcement activity.

Urbanization, crime rates, and police protection are all interrelated. The simple coefficient for the relationship between urbanization and crime is .61, and the coefficient for urbanization and police protection is .75. We can expect crime rates and police protection to be associated because both are related to urbanization. And this turns out to be the case; the simple coefficient for the relationship between crime rates and police protection is .65. An increase in the crime rate leads to an increase in police protection (or is it the other way around?). Even if

FIGURE VIII-2

The Fifty States Arranged According to Urbanization and Police Protection

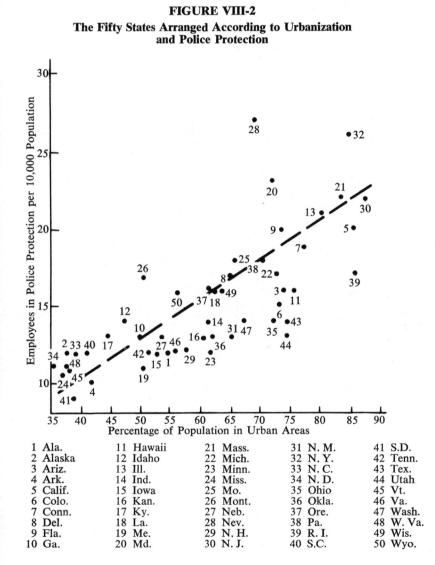

1 Ala.	11 Hawaii	21 Mass.	31 N. M.	41 S.D.
2 Alaska	12 Idaho	22 Mich.	32 N. Y.	42 Tenn.
3 Ariz.	13 Ill.	23 Minn.	33 N. C.	43 Tex.
4 Ark.	14 Ind.	24 Miss.	34 N. D.	44 Utah
5 Calif.	15 Iowa	25 Mo.	35 Ohio	45 Vt.
6 Colo.	16 Kan.	26 Mont.	36 Okla.	46 Va.
7 Conn.	17 Ky.	27 Neb.	37 Ore.	47 Wash.
8 Del.	18 La.	28 Nev.	38 Pa.	48 W. Va.
9 Fla.	19 Me.	29 N. H.	39 R. I.	49 Wis.
10 Ga.	20 Md.	30 N. J.	40 S.C.	50 Wyo.

the effect of urbanization is controlled, there is still a significant relationship between crime rates and police protection. The partial coefficient for this relationship among the fifty states, controlling for the effect of economic development, is a statistically significant .37. In short, crime rates and police protection are independently related. It is no coincidence that Nevada, with the nation's highest crime rate, also employs more policemen per population than any other state.

STATE CORRECTIONAL POLICY

Correctional policies vary markedly among the fifty states. States differ in the number of persons per unit of population committed to prison, in per capita correctional expenditures, in the care and treatment provided offenders, in policies governing the parole of prisoners, in the number of executions carried out, and in many other aspects of penology. Perhaps the explanation for the range among the states of their public policies toward correction lies in the deep division among the American people on correctional philosophy. At least four separate theories of crime and punishment compete for preeminence in guiding public correctional policy. The first is the ancient Judaic-Christian idea of holding the individual personally responsible for his guilty acts and compelling him to pay his debt to society, originally on the basis of an eye for an eye and a life for a life. Another philosophy argues that punishment should be sure, speedy, commensurate with the crime, and sufficiently conspicuous to deter others from committing crimes. Still another consideration in correctional policy is that of protecting the public from law-breakers or habitual criminals by segregating them behind prison walls. Finally there is the theory that law-breakers are partly or entirely victims of social circumstances beyond their control and that society owes them comprehensive treatment in reform and rehabilitation. It is not our task to resolve these profound philosophical differences but merely to examine the socioeconomic conditions which are associated with differences in specific outcomes in correctional policy outcomes.

Over two million Americans each year are prisoners in a jail, police station, juvenile home, or penitentiary. The vast majority are released within one year. There are, however, about a quarter of a million inmates in the prisons administered by state and federal governments in the United States. These prisoners are serving time for serious offenses. Nine-tenths of them have had a record of crime before they committed the act which led to their current imprisonment. About 115,000 are released from these institutions each year, only to be replaced by an even larger number of new prisoners. Despite increased emphasis on rehabilitation, the prison population of the United States increases yearly. New prisons costing $10,000 to $15,000 for each inmate are regularly constructed. New psychological and other treatment facilities are added to prison services, so that the annual cost of operating a correctional system now reaches $2000 per inmate. But penologist Daniel Glaser points out, "Unfortunately there is no convincing evidence that this investment reduces what criminologists call 'recidivism', the offenders return to crime."[3] In short there is no evidence that public correctional policies meet any of the goals of society — protection of the public, deterence to crime, or rehabilitation of the criminal. Nor, adds Glaser, has there been sufficient correctional research to know what the effects of specific prison and parole policies are. It is possible, however, to describe certain characteristics of state correctional policies, even if the effects of these policies remain a mystery, and it is also possible to identify the socioeconomic conditions which are associated with them.

In 1961 the prison population of the United States was 220,329; of these, 23,696 were in federal institutions and 196,633 were in state institutions. This represents about 12.3 prisoners per 10,000 people in the nation. Only three other years in history have found such a large proportion of the population behind bars: 1941, with 12.6 prisoners per 10,000 people; 1940, with 13.2; and 1939, with 13.8. There is considerable variation among the states in prisoner populations. Of course federal prisoners are excluded in considering state prison populations; in 1961 the average state prisoner population was 9.7 per 10,000. New Hampshire, Rhode Island, Massachusetts, and North Dakota imprisoned about 3 persons per 10,000, while Alabama imprisoned 16, Georgia 17 and Maryland 18 per 10,000 population. In short, per capita prison populations vary by as much as 600 per cent among the states.

Differences among the states in prisoner populations may be partly explained by differences in crime rates. Prisoner populations and crime rates among the states are related; the simple coefficient for this relationship is .38. But they also represent differences in sentencing and parole policies. The fact that the statistical probability of a person landing in a state penitentiary is six times greater in some states than in others is more than a result of differences in crime rates. It also reflects differences among the states in correctional philosophy.

It is interesting that the significant socioeconomic condition which

[3] Daniel Glazer, *The Effectiveness of a Prison and Parole System* (New York: Bobbs-Merrill, 1964), p. 4.

correlates with prisoner population turns out to be education. Table VIII-5 shows education to be significantly and inversely correlated with prisoner populations. States with well educated adult populations have lower prisoner populations. We may conclude either that educated populations are more successful in staying out of jail, or that correctional philosophy of a more educated population is more lenient in sentencing and parole, or both.

TABLE VIII-5

**The Relationship between Economic Development
and State Correctional Policy**

| | Economic Development | | | |
	Urban-ization	Industrial-ization	Income	Education
Prisoners per 10,000 population	−.01	−.11	−.11	−.58*
State expenditures for correction, per capita	.32*	.30*	.68*	.58*
State expenditures for correction, per prisoner	.28	.07	.34*	.24
State correctional expenditures relative to income	.06	.06	.36*	.37*
Paroled prisoners as a percentage of all releases	.45*	.30*	.35*	.37*
Public executions, 1950 through 1960	−.19	.13	−.19	−.26

Figures are simple correlation coefficients for the fifty states; an asterisk indicates a statistically significant relationship.

Turning directly to parole policies, in 1960 48,457 prisoners were paroled from state institutions out of a total of 82,166 releases. This means that parolees constituted 59 per cent of all releases. Modern penology with its concern for reform and rehabilitation appears to favor parole releases in lieu of unconditional releases. The function of parole and post-release supervision is (1) to procure information on the parolee's post prison conduct, and (2) to facilitate and graduate the transition between imprisonment and complete freedom by assistance and the enforcement of rules.[4] These functions are presumably oriented toward protecting the public and rehabilitating the offender. The manner in which parole policies are implemented reflects substantial differences among the states in correctional philosophy.

Parole policies in five states — Hawaii, Washington, Colorado, Ohio, and New Hampshire — resulted in over 90 per cent of all releases coming about by means of parole. In contrast, parole in nine states — Missouri, Nebraska, Maryland, Oklahoma, Wyoming, Nevada, South Carolina, Georgia, and Mississippi — is granted to less than 30 per cent

[4] *Ibid.,* chs. 16 and 17.

of all released prisoners. The more extensive use of parole is clearly related to economic development. The urban industrial states with higher income and educational levels release a significantly higher proportion of prisoners on parole than the rural farm states with lower income and educational characteristics.

The most important debate in correctional policy today is the debate over capital punishment. As of 1962, the death penalty had been abolished in eight states—Alaska, Hawaii, Maine, Michigan, Minnesota, North Dakota, Rhode Island, and Wisconsin (although in Michigan, North Dakota, and Rhode Island there were provisions for certain serious exceptions, for example, killing a prison guard). Of the 42 states retaining the death penalty, 23 specified electrocution as the method of execution, 11 specified the gas chamber, 7 specified hanging, and Utah permitted both shooting and hanging. Of these 42 states, however, six did not actually execute anyone from 1950 through 1962: Delaware, Massachusetts, Montana, New Hampshire, South Dakota, and Wyoming. On the other hand, Georgia executed 95 people during this time span. There were a total of 773 state executions between 1950 and 1960, 42 in 1961, and 47 in 1962.

Table VIII-5 indicates that the frequency of capital punishment among the states is not closely related to economic development. However, the frequency of capital punishment is related to per capita prison populations. The simple correlation coefficients for the relationship between willingness-to-imprison and willingness-to-execute is a significant .46. This relationship is independent of any of the effects of economic development. The partial coefficient for the relationship between prison population and executions, controlling for economic development, is a significant .47.

Over $488 million were spent for correctional purposes by the states in 1961. This amounted to about $2.72 per capita for the nation as a whole. State per capita correctional expenditures varied from a high of over $5 in three states (Alaska, Connecticut, and Washington), to a low of less than $1 in Arkansas and Mississippi. All four measures of economic development correlate significantly with per capita state correctional expenditures. It is not surprising that the closest relationship occur between income and correctional expenditures. The income measure has been the most important correlate of all of the per capita public service measures—education, welfare, health, highways, and now correction.

A figure which more directly reflects the state's willingness to invest in the treatment, reform, and rehabilitation of its prisoners is the *per prisoner* correctional expenditure. It seems reasonable to assume that higher per prisoner expenditures mean that a state is at least making a financial effort on behalf of its prisoner population. Per prisoner correctional expenditures ranged from a high of over $8,000 in Massachusetts and Connecticut to a low of $700 in Georgia. The average per prisoner expenditure figure among the states was about $2,500.

Per prisoner expenditures, and presumably the quality of treatment and care for prisoners, is related to income levels in the states. But it is not only the availability of financial resources which leads these states to spend more on their prisoners. If correctional expenditures are considered relative to personal income, it turns out that the states with high levels of income and education spend more on correction even in proportion to their higher incomes. This is not true in education, welfare, and other fields where states with higher incomes are able to provide better services, yet place a lower burden on their incomes. In correctional policy, however, there is some tendency for states with higher income and education to make a greater relative, as well as absolute, effort in the correctional field.

RELATIONSHIPS AMONG REGULATORY VARIABLES

Table VIII-6 is a matrix of simple correlation coefficients, showing all of the relationships among our key regulatory measures.

Crime rates and police protection are closely related. Increases in crime rates are associated with increases in police protection. The simple coefficient for this relationship is .65. Of course, both of these measures are related to economic development, particularly urbanization. But even if the effect of urbanization is controlled, there is still a significant relationship between crime and police protection. The partial correlation coefficient for this controlled relationship is a significant .37.

Gambling revenues are also associated with increases in crime rates and police protection. The simple coefficient for the relationship between gambling revenues and crime rates is a significant .37; and the coefficient for the relationship between gambling and police protection is an even higher .55. This tends to confirm the arguments of opponents of gambling and pari-mutuel betting that these activities lead to an increase in crime and in the cost of police protection. However, since gambling revenue is related to economic development, we expect to find some association between gambling revenue and these two latter variables, simply as a product of the influence of economic development. If the effects of economic development are controlled, the relationships between gambling revenues and crime rates and police

TABLE VIII-6

Relationships among Regulatory Measures

	Policemen Per Population	Crime Rate	Gambling Revenues	Prisoners Per Population	Correctional Expenditures Per Capita	Paroled Releases	Public Executions
Policemen per population	1.00						
Crime rate	.65*	1.00					
Gambling revenues	.55*	.37*	1.00				
Prisoners per population	.12	.38*	-.14	1.00			
Correctional expenditures per capita	.37*	.34*	.12	-.03	1.00		
Paroled as a percentage of all releases	.15	.01	.05	-.30*	.14	1.00	
Public executions	.15	.22	-.02	.46*	-.12	-.03	1.00

Figures are simple correlation coefficients for the fifty states; an asterisk indicates a statistically significant relationship.

protection decline below the accepted levels of significance. The partial coefficients for these controlled relationships are .21 (gambling revenue and crime rates) and .13 (gambling revenue and police protection). Thus gambling itself does not seem to lead to an increase in crime or police protection; these phenomena are associated only because they are all related to economic development.

Crime rates in the states are related to prisoner populations. The simple coefficient for this relationship is a significant .38, and it does not depend upon the effects of economic development. Even if economic development is controlled, an increase in the crime rate is still associated with an increase in the proportion of the population in prison. The partial coefficient for this controlled relationship is a significant .39; controlling for economic development leaves the coefficient virtually unchanged. It is interesting to speculate whether increases in crime cause an increase in prisoners, or whether increased rates of imprisonment cause increases in crime.

As we might expect, increases in correctional expenditures among the states are related to an increase in prisoner population. Correctional expenditures are also associated with crime rates.

Finally we might note that imprisonment and capital punishment are related. The simple coefficient for this relationship is a significant .46. States which imprison a large proportion of their population are the states which make greater use of capital punishment. Apparently education, imprisonment, and capital punishment are all somewhat interrelated. The higher the level of adult education in the states, the smaller the prison population and the fewer the number of public executions. Perhaps more educated populations are better able to avoid prison and execution; more likely, better educated populations hold a correctional philosophy which deemphasizes imprisonment and capital punishment.

Parole is inversely related to imprisonment. The states which rely heavily on imprisonment tend to have restrictive parole policies. This indicates a basic difference in correctional philosophy, one which appears to be related to education. Liberality in parole policy is not associated with crime rates or police protection; there is no evidence that it either increases or reduces crime or the need for policemen.

PARTISANSHIP AND REGULATORY OUTCOMES

Democratic or Republican dominance in state politics does not appear to be an important determinant of regulatory policy. There are, of course, certain associations between partisanship in state government and particular regulatory outcomes. States under Democratic control between 1954 and 1964 were the same states which had fewer governmental units per population, fewer public employees per population, and lower salaries for public employees. These were the same states with more prisoners per population, fewer parolees, and slightly lower correctional expenditures. These associations are shown in the simple correlations in Table VIII-7. However, it is unlikely that partisanship itself has anything to do in bringing about these regulatory outcomes.

TABLE VIII-7

**The Relationships among Economic Development,
Partisanship, and State Regulatory Policy**

| | Democratic Party Control | | | | | |
| | Lower Houses | | Upper Houses | | Governorships | |
	Simple	Partial	Simple	Partial	Simple	Partial
Governments per population	−.47*	−.44	−.41*	−.42	−.30*	−.26
Number of bills introduced	.02	−.09	.03	.03	.03	.07
Number of laws enacted	.23	.13	.23	.20	.24	.26
Public employees	−.35*	.12	−.34*	.03	−.40*	.01
State employees	.08	.28	−.08	.19	−.23	.02
Public employees' salaries	−.32*	.32	−.27	.22	−.44*	.19
Correctional expenditures	−.30*	.27	−.18	.04	−.37*	.16
Policemen	−.04	.19	−.13	.12	−.18	.13
Prisoners	.49*	.51*	.46*	.45*	.35*	.35*
Crime rate	.17	.50*	.11	.44*	−.02	.35*
Gambling revenue	−.06	−.02	−.22	−.21	−.15	.06
Divorce rate	.11	.33	−.03	.10	.06	.25
Parolees	−.36*	−.43*	−.38*	−.39*	−.39*	−.37*

Figures are simple and partial correlation coefficients; partial coefficients control for the effect of urbanization, industrialization, income, and education; an asterisk indicates a statistically significant relationship.

Partisanship is related to economic development, just as regulatory outcomes are related to economic development, particularly urbanization. Of the thirteen regulatory variables listed in Table VIII-7, six are associated with partisanship in the simple coefficients. But four of these six relationships disappear once the effects of economic development are controlled. The partial coefficients indicate that partisanship has no independent effect upon the number of governmental units per population, public employees per population, public employee salaries, or correctional expenditures. The association between partisanship and these outcomes is a product of the effect of economic development.

However, Democratic control of state government remains associated with higher prisoner populations and more restrictive parole policies, even after controlling for economic development. These associations are not dependent on economic development, although it is still doubtful that Democratic control itself causes more people to be locked up in jails. The behavior of the crime rate coefficient is another interesting aspect of Table VIII-7. Holding constant for economic development reveals a significant association between Democratic control of a state government and higher crime rates. Thus, three regulatory outcomes—crime rates, parolees, and prisoner populations—are significantly related to Democratic politics, and these relationships are not a product of economic development.

What is even more surprising is that these relationships between success of the Democratic party and higher crime rates, larger prisoner populations, and fewer parolees, does *not* depend upon the inclusion of the southern states in our analysis. These controlled relationships can be observed in the 39 non-southern states as well as in the fifty states. In spite of these controlled relationships, it is difficult to believe that Democratic politics itself inspires crime or increases prisoner populations. A glance ahead to Chapters IX and X will reveal that these outcomes also remain significantly associated with economic development even after controlling for the system variables—partisanship, participation, and party competition. This makes it even less likely that system variables actually operate to bring about these outcomes.

TABLE VIII-8

The Relationship between Party Competition and State Regulatory Measures, Controlling for the Effect of Economic Development

| | Party Competition | | | | | |
| | Lower Houses | | Upper Houses | | Governorships | |
	Simple	Partial	Simple	Partial	Simple	Partial
Governments per population	−.31*	−.23	−.27	−.22	−.18	−.24
Number of bills introduced	−.09	−.08	−.15	−.10	−.02	.06
Number of laws enacted	.17	.19	.11	.14	.17	.20
Public employees	−.28	.22	−.26	.14	−.24	.21
State employees	.00	.26	.06	.10	−.19	.08
Public employees' salaries	−.42*	.05	−.37*	.15	−.51*	.18
Correctional expenditures	−.25	−.08	−.15	−.10	−.02	.06
Policemen	−.15	.23	−.22	.14	−.25	.16
Prisoners	.39*	.31	.40*	.34	.32*	.32
Crime rate	−.18	.34	−.06	.28	−.10	.29
Gambling revenue	−.12	.14	−.10	.01	−.17	.01
Divorce rate	.13	.33	.03	.16	.02	.23
Parolees	.36*	.29	−.32*	.20	.37*	.29

Figures are simple and partial correlation coefficients; partial coefficients control for the effect of urbanization, industrialization, income, and education; an asterisk indicates a statistically significant relationship.

PARTY COMPETITION AND REGULATORY POLICY

There is no evidence that party competition has any independent effect on state regulatory policy. Table VIII-8, which shows the relationships between our measures of party competition and regulatory outcomes, contains very few significant coefficients. The only regulatory outcomes associated with party competition are the salaries of public employees, prisoners per population, and the proportion of paroled releases. But these relationships are clearly a product of economic development: all of them disappear when economic development is controlled in the partial coefficient. Excluding the southern states from our analysis does not noticeably affect the results of these operations. Clearly, party competition is not an independent determinant of regulatory outcomes.

PARTICIPATION, MALAPPORTIONMENT, AND REGULATORY OUTCOMES

Voter participation is associated with several regulatory outcomes. In the simple coefficients in Table VIII-9, higher voter turnouts are associated with more governmental units per population, more public employees, the salaries of public employees, higher per capita

TABLE VIII-9
The Relationship between Political Participation and State Regulatory Measures,
Controlling for the Effect of Economic Development

| | Voter Participation | | | | | |
| | 1954-1962 Gubernatorial | | 1962 Congressional | | 1958 Congressional | |
	Simple	Partial	Simple	Partial	Simple	Partial
Governments per population	.33*	.38*	.34*	.43*	.33*	.44*
Number of bills introduced	−.02	−.05	.00	−.03	.04	.01
Number of laws enacted	−.20	−.17	−.21	−.20	−.14	−.17
Public employees	.22	−.17	.32*	−.09	.33*	−.13
State employees	.19	−.03	.17	−.13	.27	.04
Public employees' salaries	.35*	−.31	.36*	−.28	.49*	−.30
Correctional expenditures	.31*	−.20	.35*	−.29	.40*	−.21
Policemen	.14	−.18	.16	−.23	.20	−.25
Prisoners	−.50*	−.51*	−.52*	−.57*	−.51*	−.60*
Crime rate	−.03	−.35*	−.02	−.42*	.05	−.37*
Gambling revenues	.15	.06	.17	.07	.16	.03
Divorce rate	−.10	−.26	−.09	−.31	−.04	−.29
Parolees	.40*	.40*	.39*	.37*	.42*	.43*

Figures are simple and partial correlation coefficients; partial coefficients control for the effect of urbanization, industrialization, income, and education; an asterisk indicates a statistically significant relationship.

correctional expenditures, fewer prisoners per population, and a higher proportion of paroled releases. But three of these six associations disappear once economic development is controlled. The relationship between economic development and voter participation really explains the association between participation and public employees, the salaries of public employees, and correctional expenditures. Participation itself appears to have little independent effect on these outcomes.

There are four outcomes which are associated with voter participation, even after controlling for economic development: crime rates (which are not associated in simple coefficients), prisoners, parolees, and governments per population. These relationships remain signifi-

TABLE VIII-10
The Relationship between Malapportionment and State Regulatory Measures, Controlling for the Effect of Economic Development

| | Malapportionment | | | | | |
| | Index of Representation | | Index of Urban Underrepresentation | | Apportionment Score | |
	Simple	Partial	Simple	Partial	Simple	Partial
Governments per population	.21	.19	−.04	.29	.06	.29
Number of bills introduced	.01	.14	.20	.05	.01	.04
Number of laws enacted	−.29	.25	−.10	−.23	−.24	−.24
Public employees	−.12	.10	−.13	.05	−.01	.04
State employees	−.14	−.15	.00	−.01	.09	−.02
Public employees' salaries	−.12	−.03	.24	−.15	.03	−.20
Correctional expenditures	−.27	−.21	.24	.05	.02	−.15
Policemen	−.29	−.21	.20	−.16	−.03	−.10
Prisoners	−.27	.29	−.48*	−.52*	−.40*	−.45*
Crime rate	−.38*	−.28	−.15	−.47*	−.23	−.37*
Gambling revenue	−.22	−.14	.14	−.02	.14	.09
Divorce rate	−.29	−.28	−.26	−.34	−.20	−.27
Parolees	.18	.34	.41*	.37*	.27	.29

Figures are simple and partial correlation coefficients; partial coefficients control for the effect of urbanization, industrialization, income, and education; an asterisk indicates a statistically significant relationship.

cant even after removing the southern states from our analysis. Yet it is not likely that non-participation *causes* crime rates or imprisonment or restrictive parole policies, or even vice versa. The association between participation and these variables does not depend upon economic development, but it probably does depend upon some other intervening condition. This conclusion is buttressed by the fact that, when participation is controlled, coefficients between economic development and crime rates and prisoners remain high. Non-participation, crime, and imprisonment, as well as the educational dropouts and mental failures, are all symptomatic of a general underdevelopment of human capacities.

Crime rates, prisoner populations, and parolees also behave awkwardly in correlation analysis with the measures of malapportionment. On the whole, there is little evidence that the malapportionment of state legislatures significantly affects regulatory outcomes. With the exception of crime rates, prisoner population, and parolees, there are no significant differences in regulatory outcomes between states which are well apportioned and states which are malapportioned. Under these circumstances it is difficult to maintain that malapportionment has any independent effect on regulatory policy. Crime rates, prisoner populations, and parolees continue to be associated with urban underrepresentation and, to a lesser extent, apportionment scores, even after controlling for economic development. This is true even when the southern states are removed from correlation analysis. We are reluctant, however, to conclude that it is malapportionment which brings about these outcomes.

CHAPTER IX

Party Systems and Public Policy

PARTY SYSTEMS AND PUBLIC POLICY

WHILE THE BASIC institutional and legal frameworks of the fifty state governments are quite similar, party systems in the fifty states are remarkably varied. For purposes of analysis, many of the institutional characteristics of state political systems may be treated as constants. However, because states differ considerably with respect to the division of two-party control and the levels of interparty competition, we have an excellent opportunity to observe the effects of differences in party systems upon public policy outcomes. Does the character of the party system have an independent effect upon public policy outcomes, mediating between socioeconomic inputs and these outcomes? Or are policy outcomes determined by socioeconomic conditions without regard to the character of the party system? Does it make any difference in policy outcomes whether it is the Republican or the Democratic party which dominates legislative halls and governors' mansions, or are both parties so subject to socioeconomic forces in the environment that they cannot offer significantly different policy alternatives? Does it make any difference in policy outcomes whether a state has a one-party or two-party style of politics, or do socioeconomic conditions determine policy outcomes regardless of the character of the party system? It is the task of this chapter to summarize our answers to these important questions.

Of course, in assessing the influence of the party system on public policy outcomes, it is necessary to take into account the effects of socioeconomic inputs, since these inputs have already been shown to be related to both party system characteristics and policy outcomes in the states. This chapter will focus upon the effects of the division of two-party control and the level of interparty competition on policy outcomes in all five policy-making areas, while controlling for the effects of the economic development variables. This will enable us to summarize the complex relationships between the characteristics of state party systems (division of two-party control and level of interparty competiton), economic development variables (urbanization, industrialization, income, and education), and public policy outcomes (in education, health and welfare, highways, taxation, and public regulation).

PARTISANSHIP AND PUBLIC POLICY

There are several reasons for believing that Democratic or Republican party success in state politics is *not* predictive of differences in policy outcomes.[1] The American party system is renowned for its decentralized structure. Not only are there two or three separate national organizations within each party—the congressional parties, the parties of the President and presidential candidate, and the parties of the national committees, not to mention splinter caucuses—but each party is also divided into fifty state organizations. These many party organizations are often regarded as devoid of a common ideology and lacking in clear and consistent policy positions. Often state Democratic parties are further apart on policy matters than they are from Republicans. The Minnesota and Mississippi Democratic parties, for example, have little in common except the party label. Variations in state Republican parties may be just as great: certainly the New York and Arizona Republicans are quite different from one another, not to mention the new Alabama Republicans.

Each of these Republican and Democratic state parties is more a product of its state-wide constituency than of any national Democratic of Republican organization. Parties in America are often viewed as brokerage organizations, more inclined to fit their programs to popular demands than to offer significantly different policy alternatives. The Democratic and Republican parties within a state are competing in the

---

[1] The view that the American parties do not offer significantly different policy options is expressed in Pendleton Herring, *The Politics of Democracy* (New York: Norton, 1940), p. 102; E. E. Schattschneider, *Party Government* (New York: Farrar and Rinehart, 1942), p. 92; V. O. Key, Jr., *Politics, Parties, and Pressure Groups*, 4th ed. (New York: Crowell, 1958), ch. 8; and American Political Science Association, Committee on Political Parties, *Toward a More Responsible Two-Party System* (New York: American Political Science Association, 1950).

same vote market, and hence they are led to offer policy positions which are more like each other's than like those of their counterpart parties in different states. Parties in each state tailor policies to local conditions. The result is that the parties do not have any independent effect on state policy outcomes. State parties merely reflect the socio-economic character of their constituencies, as do the policy outcomes.

Nevertheless, several scholars provide us with reasons for challenging this Tweedledee-Tweedledum image of the state parties. Cleavages between the Republican and Democratic parties at the national level have been documented at some length, beginning with Julius Turner's landmark examination of party influence on congressional roll-call votes.[2] Herbert McClosky surveyed the opinions of Democratic and Republican national convention delegates, as well as a national sample of rank-and-file voters, and he found that the parties are "distinct communities of co-believers who diverge sharply on many important issues."[3] More specifically, McClosky found that "Republican and Democratic leaders stand furthest apart on the issues that grow out of their group identification and support—out of the managerial, proprietary and high status connections of the one, and labor, minority, low status and intellectual connections of the other."[4] McClosky did not go on to prove that these leaders act upon their divergent beliefs, but it would be easy to hypothesize from McClosky's study that Democratic or Republican control of a state government would independently affect policy.

Studies of state legislatures have shown Democratic and Republican party majorities in specific states to have opposed each other on a number of important issues.[5] Malcolm Jewell found that on more than half of the non-unanimous roll-call votes in the legislatures of New York, Connecticut, Pennsylvania, Rhode Island, and Massachusetts, the majority of Democrats voted against the majority of Republicans.[6] However, he also found that party majorities did *not* oppose each other on more than half of the non-unanimous roll calls in California, Missouri, and Colorado. William J. Keefe reported that the parties in

---

[2] Julius Turner, *Party and Constituency: Pressures on Congress* (Baltimore: Johns Hopkins University Press, 1951); see also David Truman, *The Congressional Party* (New York: Wiley, 1959); and Duncan MacRae, Jr., *Dimensions of Congressional Voting* (Berkeley: University of California Press, 1958).

[3] Herbert McClosky, *et al.*, "Issue Conflict and Consensus among Party Leaders and Followers," *American Political Science Review*, LIV (1960), 426.

[4] *Ibid.*

[5] For a summary of research dealing with the role of parties in state legislative activity, see Thomas R. Dye, "State Legislative Politics," in Herbert Jacob and Kenneth Vines, eds., *Politics in the American States* (New York: Little, Brown, 1965), pp. 151-206.

[6] Malcolm Jewell, *The State Legislature* (New York: Random House, 1962), p. 52.

Pennsylvania and Illinois differed substantially on questions involving labor, minorities, social legislation, and the role of the government in the economy.[7] On the other hand, the *Legislative System* study obtained mixed results in questioning state legislators about the importance of parties in policy-making. New Jersey legislators thought parties were important; Ohio legislators were divided; but legislators in California and Tennessee thought parties exercised little or no influence.[8]

The evidence seems to support the view that the parties differ on policy questions only in those states in which the parties represent separate socioeconomic constituencies.[9] Party conflict over policy questions is most frequent in those states in which Democratic legislators represent central-city, low-income, ethnic, and racial constituencies, and Republican legislators represent middle-class, suburban, small-town, and rural constituencies. In these states, the parties clash over the major social and economic issues which divide the national parties. Party conflict on these policy questions is much less frequent in the rural states with their more homogeneous populations.

The existence of party conflict over policy questions *within* certain states does not necessarily mean that throughout the fifty states a Democratic- or Republican-controlled state government will be predictive of specific policy outcomes. Which party enjoys a majority in the legislature or occupies the governor's chair may make considerable difference in one state, but throughout the fifty states the Republican and Democratic parties may still not offer consistent policy alternatives which permit us to predict policy outcomes on the basis of which party dominates a state government.

THE INDEPENDENT EFFECT OF PARTISANSHIP

If the policy choices of predominantly Democratic states are significantly different from the policy choices of predominantly Republican states, and if these differences in policy can be traced to the effect of Democratic and Republican party control, then we can

[7] William J. Keefe, "Comparative Study of the Role of Political Parties in State Legislatures," *Western Political Quarterly,* IX (1956), 535-41.
[8] John C. Wahlke, Heinz Eulau, William Buchanan, and Leroy L. Ferguson, *The Legislative System* (New York: Wiley, 1962), p. 425.
[9] Duncan MacRae, Jr., "The Relation between Roll Call Votes and Constituencies in the Massachusetts House of Representatives," *American Political Science Review,* XLVI (1952), 1046-55; Thomas R. Dye, "A Comparison of Constituency Influences in the Upper and Lower Chambers of a State Legislature," *Western Political Quarterly,* XIV (1961), 473-80; and Thomas A. Flinn, "Party Responsibility in the States: Some Causal Factors," *American Political Science Review,* LVIII (1964), 60-71.

conclude that partisanship does independently effect policy outcomes. But if there are no policy differences between Democratic and Republican states, or if the differences which exist can be traced to the effect of some intervening variable other than partisanship, then we must conclude that partisanship has little or no independent effect on policy outcomes.

Our measures of Democratic and Republican party fortunes center upon control of those institutions charged with formal responsibility for state policy-making—the governorships and the upper and lower houses of the state legislatures. As we explained in Chapter III, all measures are expressed in Democratic percentages. Democratic control of the upper and lower houses of state legislatures is measured by the percentages of all seats in those houses won by Democrats from 1954 through 1962. Democratic influence in governor's chairs is measured by the average Democratic percentage in gubernatorial elections between 1954 and 1962. While partisanship is expressed in Democratic percentages, we need only reverse the signs of any coefficients obtained with the Democratic measures in order to observe the effect of Republican control.

Economic development variables have already been shown in Chapter III to be related to Democratic and Republican party control in state politics. The 11 southern states as a group rank considerably below national standards in their levels of economic development, particularly in income and the educational level of the adult population. Because of the Democratic party's historically preeminent role in the South, which was reflected in its success in the state legislatures and governorships in the period from 1954 to 1964, Democratic control of a state government correlates inversely with income and educational levels among the fifty states. In addition, throughout the five policy-oriented chapters, we observed many significant correlations between the income and educational measures and a large number of policy outcomes. Thus, Democratic party control and Republican party control are likely to be associated with some policy outcomes, if only because both policy outcomes and party fortunes are linked to economic development. Our task therefore is to sort out the effects of partisanship from the effects of economic development.

Simple and partial correlation analysis is again employed to show the relationships between a political system variable and policy outcomes while controlling for the effects of economic development. In the simple coefficients in Table IX-1, which do not control for the effects of economic development, Democratic fortunes in state government appear to be linked to as many as 31 of the 54 policy outcomes listed there. In the field of education, the Democratic party's control of a state government is associated with lower per pupil expenditures, fewer male teachers, poor pupil-teacher ratios, more dropouts and mental failures, and increased state participation in educational finance. In the welfare field, Democratic party fortunes are associated with greater state participation, lower benefit levels, and increased numbers of recipients. Democratic control among the fifty states is also correlated with lower highway expenditures, more highway fund divisions, fewer public employees, more prisoners, and fewer parolees. Finally, Democratic control is associated with lower taxes and revenues per capita, as well as increased state proportions of total state-local revenue. Of course, Republican control is associated with these policy outcomes to the same degree but in the opposite fashion.

The problem, of course, is determining the extent to which the relationships between Democratic control and these various policy outcomes is simply a product of Democratic dominance in the states with lower income and educational levels. Partial coefficients can control for the effects of income and education as well as the other economic development variables. And the partial coefficients in Table IX-1 indicate that a great deal of the association between partisanship and public policy is a product of economic development.

In the field of education, partisanship has no independent effect upon per pupil expenditures, average teachers' salaries, or male teachers. However, even after controlling for economic development, significant associations remain for pupil-teacher ratios, dropout rates, mental failures, size of the school districts, and state financial participation. The coefficients for these relationships are considerably lowered when economic development is controlled, but they still remain above the accepted levels of significance. However, even in view of these controlled relationships, it is difficult to believe that domination by the Democratic party brings about higher pupil-teacher ratios and more dropouts and mental failures. The concentration of southern states among the most Democratic states accounts for these particular relationships. If the southern states are removed from the correlations, there is no association between party affiliation and pupil-teacher ratios, dropouts, or mental failures.

With regard to size of the school districts and state and federal financial participation in education, however, it seems more likely that Democratic politics may be independently associated with these educational outcomes. The high correlations between Democratic control and state participation are only slightly affected by controlling for economic development. And perhaps the most interesting feature among the education variables in Table IX-1 is the way in which controlling for economic development increased the correlation between Democratic success and federal financial participation in education. Furthermore, these relationships remain strong even when the southern states are excluded from the correlations.

In the welfare field, almost all of the association between partisanship and public policy disappears once economic development is controlled. Ten welfare variables are associated with partisanship before economic development is controlled, but all of these relationships disappear in the partial cofficients, except for the OAA and ADC

TABLE IX-1

The Relationship between Democratic Party Control and State Policy Outcomes, Controlling for the Effect of Economic Development

| | Democratic Party Control | | | | | |
| | Lower Houses | | Upper Houses | | Governorships | |
	Simple	Partial	Simple	Partial	Simple	Partial
Education						
Per pupil expenditures	−.47*	−.06	−.43	.06	−.58*	−.18
Average teachers' salaries	−.23	.27	−.20	.05	−.42*	.02
Teachers with B.A.	.62*	.67*	.60	.71*	.41*	.45*
Teachers with M.A.	−.15	.06	−.12	.16	−.24	.04
Male teachers	−.49*	−.25	−.48*	−.21	−.58*	−.29
Pupil-teacher ratios	.72*	.50*	.67*	.44*	.72*	.51*
Dropout rate	−.69*	−.55*	−.66*	−.46*	−.64*	−.34
Mental failures	.71*	.42*	.64*	.39*	.74*	.56*
Size of school districts	.64*	.49*	.52*	.36*	.44*	.22
State participation	.68*	.61*	.63*	.53*	.55*	.41*
Federal participation	.27	.60*	.29	.51*	.18	.38*
Welfare						
Per capita welfare expenditures	.01*	−.08	.06	.02	−.12	−.23
Per capita health expenditures	−.10	.20	−.23	.02	−.13	.27
State participation in welfare	.37*	.26	.38*	.28	.33*	.19
State participation in health	−.15	−.18	−.07	−.13	−.13	−.26
Federal participation in welfare	.44*	.07*	.47*	.02	.47*	−.13
Unemployment benefits	−.51*	−.13	−.51*	−.11	−.53*	−.00
OAA benefits	−.65*	−.49*	−.64*	−.44*	−.59*	−.28
ADC benefits	−.64*	−.55*	−.65*	−.47*	−.68*	−.44*
Blind benefits	−.50*	−.26	−.51*	−.23	−.53*	−.14
General assistance benefits	−.45*	−.26	−.51*	−.32	−.45*	−.07
OAA recipients	.38*	.13	.42*	.20	.30*	−.04
ADC recipients	.39*	.10	.39*	.13	.15	−.30
Unemployment recipients	−.20	−.26	−.26	−.29	−.19	−.07
General assistance cases	−.32*	−.32	−.29	−.22	−.30*	−.20

TABLE IX-1 — Continued

| | Democratic Party Control | | | | | |
| | Lower Houses | | Upper Houses | | Governorships | |
	Simple	*Partial*	*Simple*	*Partial*	*Simple*	*Partial*
Highways						
Per capita highway						
expenditures	−.54*	−.33	−.49*	−.37*	−.37*	−.15
State participation	−.44*	−.21	−.37*	−.23	−.31*	−.13
Federal participation	−.26	.19	−.16	.01	−.14	.04
Funds from highway users	.11	−.11	.03	−.20	.10	−.14
Highway fund diversion	.30*	.21	.25	.21	.32*	.36
Rural-urban distribution	.05	.06	.07	.02	.25	.26
Public Regulation						
Governments per						
population	−.47*	−.44*	−.41*	−.42*	−.30*	−.26
Number of bills introduced	.02	−.09	.03	.03	.03	.07
Number of laws enacted	.23	.13	.23	.20	.24	.26
Public employees	−.35*	.12	−.34*	.03	−.40*	−.01
State employees	−.08	.28	−.08	.19	−.23	−.02
Public employees' salaries	−.32*	−.32	−.27	−.22	−.44*	.19
Correctional expenditures	−.30*	.27	−.18	.04	−.37*	.16
Policemen	−.04	.19	−.13	.12	−.18	.13
Prisoners	.49*	.51*	.46*	.45*	.35*	.35*
Crime rate	.17	.50*	.11	.44*	.02	.35*
Gambling revenue	−.06	−.02	−.22	−.21	−.15	−.06
Divorce rate	.11	.33	−.03	.10	.06	.25
Parolees	−.36*	−.43*	−.38*	−.39*	−.39*	−.37*
Taxation						
Total revenue per capita	−.46*	.18	−.46*	.09	−.53*	.04
Total taxes per capita	−.57*	−.29	−.60*	−.32	−.62*	−.21
Debt	−.03	.17	−.01	.28	−.15	.12
State percentage of						
total revenue	.54*	.53*	.55*	.47*	.42*	.29
Federal percentage of						
total revenue	.20	.39*	.26	.35*	.23	.27
Income taxes	−.06	.18	.01	.22	−.17	.00
Sales taxes	.12	.06	.07	−.09	.19	.06
Alcohol and tobacco taxes	.04	−.08	.04	−.07	.19	.13
Motor fuel taxes	−.26	−.37	−.17	−.27	−.11	−.24
Property taxes	−.68*	−.64*	−.64*	−.54*	−.52*	−.36*

Figures are simple and partial correlation coefficients; partial coefficients control for the effect of urbanization, industrialization, income, and education; an asterisk indicates a significant relationship.

benefit measures. And these two relationships disappear when the southern states are dropped from the correlations. Democratic politics does not itself bring about lower welfare benefits or more welfare recipients, as the simple coefficients suggest. These associations were obviously a product of the relationships between both Democratic politics and economic underdevelopment.

Partisanship does appear to have some independent effect upon state highway expenditures. Republican states spend more on highways than Democratic states even after controlling for the effects of economic development and for the influence of the southern states.

Partisanship has no independent effect on 9 of the 13 state regulatory policies. However, control by the Democratic party correlates significantly with increases in the size of governments, prisoner populations, crime rates, and decreases in parole releases, even after economic development is controlled. Inclusion of the southern states in the ranks of the most Democratic states does *not* explain these relationships; they also occur when the non-southern states are considered separately. We are reluctant to conclude that it is Democratic party domination which brings about crime and incarceration. Yet here there is a relationship which is independent of the effects of economic development.

In the field of taxation a great deal of the association between partisanship and tax and revenues disappears once economic development is controlled. There appears to be no independent relationship between Democratic or Republican control of a state government and tax and revenue levels or the types of taxes relied upon for revenue. On the other hand, significant relationships between Democratic politics and increased state and federal financial participation can still be observed even after economic development is controlled. This means that Republican politics is significantly related to increased financial reliance upon local governments. The fact that significant correlations can be observed between Democratic party control and increased federal participation in education, welfare, and revenue, even after controlling for economic development, strongly suggests that Democratic-controlled state governments may indeed be more inclined toward, and successful in, obtaining federal money than Republican state governments.

SOME CONCLUSIONS ABOUT PARTISANSHIP

In summary, a great deal of the association between partisanship and public policy is really a product of the influence of economic development variables. On the other hand, relationships between economic development and policy outcomes do *not* depend upon the influence of Democratic or Republican party success. Table IX-2 summarizes the effect of economic development on policy outcomes. In all, 49 out of the 54 summary policy variables are related in simple coefficients to one or more of the economic development indices. But perhaps even more interesting are the relationships revealed in the partial coefficients. The partial coefficients in Table IX-2 describe the relationships between economic development and policy outcomes while controlling for all three measures of party affiliation, and we should note the large number of significant partial coefficients. For the most part, holding constant for party affiliation does *not* lower the correlations between economic development and policy outcomes. Comparing the partial coefficients in Table IX-2 with those in Table IX-1 suggests that, on the whole, economic development is more influential in indepedently shaping policy outcomes than party affiliation.[10]

Of course we have been willing to attribute to party affiliation an independent influence upon state and federal financial participation in education, welfare, and overall revenue. Democratic control of a state government is independently related to increases in state and federal financial participation, and Republican control of a state government is independently related to increased financial reliance upon local governments. Our willingness to attribute these outcomes to the effects of party affiliation is supported by the partial coefficients in Table IX-2. If party affiliation is controlled, the relationships between economic development and the several mesures of state and federal financial participation and reliance upon property taxation are seriously affected. Holding constant for party affiliation noticeably reduces the coefficients for these relationships. This tends to confirm our conclusion that Republican and Democratic control of a state government does have an effect upon the degree to which the state and federal governments are relied upon to supply revenue in contrast to reliance upon local governments. This conclusion fits neatly with the results of opinion surveys which show that Republican leaders tend to stress local government in contrast to centralization at the state or federal levels of government.

On the whole, however, Democratic or Republican control of a state government is not a good predictor of state policy outcomes. The fifty separate Democratic parties are quite different from one another, as are the fifty Republican parties. Neither Democrats nor Republicans offer consistent programs for state governments from state to state.

[10] The partial coefficients in Table IX-2 control for the effect of three partisanship measures, while the partial coefficients in Table IX-1 control for the effect of four socio-economic measures. In other words, we are comparing third-order partial coefficients with fourth-order partial coefficients. This is only a slight computational imbalance, and it is extremely unlikely that the contrasting results are a product of this imbalance. The analysis in Chapter XI confirms these results. This slight imbalance occurs in comparisons of partial coefficients in both this chapter and Chapter X.

TABLE IX-2
The Relationship between Economic Development and State Policy Outcomes, Controlling for the Effect of Partisanship

State Policy Measures	Urbanization Simple	Urbanization Partial	Industrialization Simple (Economic Development)	Industrialization Partial	Income Simple	Income Partial	Education Simple	Education Partial
Education								
Per pupil expenditures	.51*	.53*	.36*	.45*	.83*	.77*	.59*	.37*
Average teachers' salaries	.69*	.70*	.64*	.70*	.88*	.90*	.57*	.48*
Teachers with B.A.	.42*	.63*	.60*	.72*	.11	.61*	-.04	.44*
Teachers with M.A.	.54*	.54*	.42*	.44*	.55*	.54*	.42*	.37*
Male teachers	.48*	.47*	.26	.32	.63*	.45*	.63*	.43*
Pupil teacher ratios	-.13	-.27	-.19	.26	-.43*	.33*	-.50*	-.06
Dropout rates	-.40*	-.47*	-.09	.08	-.54*	.39*	-.60*	-.31*
Mental failures	-.05	.12	.13	.17	-.46*	.37*	-.70*	-.46*
Size of school districts	.06	.06	.26	.21	-.18	.11	-.37*	-.07
State participation	-.10	-.06	.18	.17	-.30*	.17	-.35*	.06
Federal participation	-.36*	-.37*	-.08	-.11	-.32*	.14	-.27	.28
Welfare								
Per capita welfare expenditures	.19	.18	.07	.07	-.01	-.07	-.07	.03
Per capita health expenditures	.45*	.38*	.39*	.36*	.56*	.58*	.42*	.47*
State participation in welfare	-.11	-.05	-.15	-.17	-.35*	-.18	-.17	.07
State participation in health	-.30*	-.35*	-.07	-.05	-.08	-.18	-.15	-.29
Federal participation in welfare	-.43*	-.38*	-.35*	-.40*	-.82*	-.76*	-.59*	-.44*
Unemployment benefits	.55*	.56*	.30*	.38*	.80*	.72*	.67*	.51*
OAA benefits	.49*	.56*	.15	.25	.63*	.45*	.61*	.35*
ADC benefits	.51*	.56*	.26	.34	.74*	.59*	.55*	.21
Blind benefits	.59*	.62*	.28	.34	.71*	.58*	.64*	.47*
General assistance	.58*	.57*	.39*	.45*	.76*	.68*	.43*	.22
OAA recipients	-.22	-.17	-.26	-.30	-.55*	-.45*	-.35*	-.19
ADC recipients	-.15	-.21	.16	.10	-.30*	-.25	-.42*	.38*
Unemployment recipients	.39*	.36*	.69*	.72*	.58*	.56*	.23	.14
General assistance cases	.38*	.40*	.34*	.40*	.40*	.41*	.25	.06

	1	2	3	4	5	6	7	8
Highways								
Per capita highway expenditures	-.37*	-.48*	-.51*	-.54*	.02	-.31	.04	.13
State participation	-.30*	-.27	.05	-.07	-.15	-.07	-.04	-.05
Federal participation	-.45*	.45*	-.42*	-.38*	-.10	-.21	.23	.15
Funds from highway users	-.04	-.08	-.20	-.25	-.32*	-.36*	-.26	-.25
Highway fund diversion	.42*	.52*	.29	.29	-.07	.32	-.06	.20
Rural-urban distribution	-.35*	-.29	-.45*	-.43*	-.38*	-.33*	-.07	-.05
Public Regulation								
Governments per population	-.39*	-.46*	-.76*	-.81*	-.19	-.52*	-.09	-.22
Number of bills introduced	.53*	.59*	.39*	.42*	.28	.36*	.04	-.07
Number of laws enacted	.40*	.56*	.30*	.31*	.10	.31	-.03	.16
Public employees	.07	-.01	-.26	-.30	.36*	.45*	.61*	.51*
State employees	-.16	-.27	.02	-.02	.32*	.13	.36*	.38*
Public employees' salaries	.41*	.39*	.42*	.48*	.83*	.82*	.58*	.47*
Correctional expenditures	.32*	.33	.30*	.36*	.69*	.69*	.58*	.51*
Policemen	.75*	.71*	.54*	.51*	.64*	.67*	.32*	.31
Prisoners	-.01	-.01	.11	.06	-.11	.15	-.58*	-.29
Crime rate	.61*	.60*	.45*	.40*	.49*	.63*	.38*	.55*
Gambling revenue	.34*	.23	.38*	.33	.34*	.29	.19	.16
Divorce rate	.07	.03	.10	.20	.17	.22	.24	.30
Parolees	.45*	.41*	.30*	.33	.35*	.15	.37*	.03
Taxation								
Total revenue per capita	.30*	.21	.03	.02	.64*	.48*	.75*	.64*
Total taxes per capita	.59*	.63*	.23	.29	.76*	.63*	.74*	.58*
Debt	.61*	.62*	.54*	.55*	.59*	.65*	.37	.37
State percentage of total revenue	-.28	-.29	-.08	-.16	-.34*	-.10	-.24	-.09
Federal percentage of total revenue	-.59*	-.56*	-.32*	-.32	-.33*	-.22	-.07	-.10
Income taxes	-.05	-.07	-.02	-.02	.20	.17	.19	.14
Sales taxes	-.03	-.06	-.19	-.01	-.15	-.08	-.19	-.11
Alcohol and tobacco taxes	-.10	-.04	-.01	.04	-.10	.00	-.22	-.17
Motor fuel taxes	-.32*	-.29	-.35*	-.30	-.27	-.43*	-.10	-.27
Property taxes	.36*	.31	-.11	-.06	.32*	.00	.43*	-.09

Figures are simple and partial correlation coefficients; partial coefficients control for the effects of three measures of partisanship; an asterisk indicates a significant relationship.

Instead, the state parties are more products of their constituencies than they are molders of them. Socioeconomic conditions in a state appear to be much more influential in determining policy outcomes than the party which is in control of the state government. Socioeconomic conditions mold the parties and determine public policy, and it is difficult to discover any independent effect of party affiliation upon public policy.

Party conflict may have an important bearing on policy questions within certain states. We have already cited literature which describes conflicting policy positions of the parties in certain urban industrial states. But in a great many states party conflict over policy questions is missing. And even in urban states a large number of questions before the legislatures are decided by unanimous votes or by votes in which a majority of both parties are in agreement. In short, many policy outcomes in state government are not party issues. Democratic or Republican control of state government is certainly not as good a predictor of policy outcomes as are the measures of economic development.

PARTY AFFILIATION AND PARTY COMPETITION

Some additional understanding of the relationships between party control of a state government and public policy outcomes can be obtained by contrasting the policy choices of the states, classified by their degree of Republican or Democratic control. In certain important policy dimensions, strong Democratic and strong Republican states resemble each other more than they resemble states under divided control. For example, per pupil expenditures and average teachers' salaries in both strong Republican and strong Democratic states are lower than in states under divided party control. Welfare benefits are lower in both strong Republican and strong Democratic states than in divided states. The same resemblance between strong Republican and strong Democratic states in contrast to divided states can be observed in welfare benefits, welfare recipients, highway expenditures, and per capita tax and revenue levels. In short, divided party control seems to be more closely associated with these policy outcomes than Republican or Democratic party control.

These findings suggest that interparty competition itself is more closely associated with policy outcomes than partisanship. Since the one-party Democratic and one-party Republican states resemble each other in policy outcomes more than they resemble the two-party states, it seems appropriate to inquire whether the existence of party competition is a determinant of policy outcomes.

PARTY COMPETITION AND PUBLIC POLICY

The relationship between economic development and state party systems has already been established in the literature on American state politics. Golembiewski, in a study of the relationships between a variety of socioeconomic factors and state party systems, reported statistically significant correlations between urbanism, income, and industrialization and several measures of party competition among the fifty states.[11] Ranney and Kendall, Key, and Schlesinger have also implied that one or more of the measures of economic development correlate closely with party competition in the American states.[12]

This linkage has been reconfirmed in the figures presented in Chapter III. Party competition in state legislatures is measured by one minus the percentage of seats in each house held by the majority party, whether Republican or Democratic, between 1954 and 1964. Party competition in gubernatorial elections is measured by one minus the average margin of victory posted by the winning candidates, whether Republican or Democratic. Legislative competition scores range from 49 (1 − 51 per cent) in the Pennsylvania and Illinois lower houses (most competitive), to 0 (1 − 100 per cent) in the houses and senates of Arkansas, Alabama, Louisiana, Mississippi, and South Carolina (least competitive). Gubernatorial competition scores range from 48 (1 − 52 per cent) in Illinois, Iowa, Delaware, Wyoming, Massachusetts, Montana, New York, Michigan, New Jersey, Minnesota, and Washington (most competitive), to under 10 (1 − 90 per cent) in Louisiana, Georgia, Mississippi, and South Carolina. In Chapter III these competition scores have been shown to be significantly related to income, education, and urbanization.[13]

The linkage between system characteristics and policy outcomes in American state politics is *not* so well established in the literature. In the most thorough study of this relationship to date, Dawson and

[11] Robert T. Golembiewski, "A Taxonomic Approach to State Political Party Strength," *Western Political Quarterly,* XI (1958), 494-513.

[12] Austin Ranney and Wilmoore Kendall, "The American Party System," *American Political Science Review,* XLVIII (1954), 477-85; Joseph A. Schlesinger, "A Two-Dimensional Scheme for Classifying States According to the Degree of Inter-Party Competition," *American Political Science Review,* XLIX (1955), 1120-28; and V. O. Key, Jr., *American State Politics* (New York: Knopf, 1956), p. 99.

[13] See Chapter III, p. 58.

Robinson cite only the work of V. O. Key, Jr. and Duane Lockard as relevant research in state politics on the impact of system characteristics on policy outcomes.[14] In his *Southern Politics,* Key finds that states with loose multifactional systems and less continuity of competition tend to pursue conservative politics on behalf of upper socioeconomic interests.[15] In states with cohesive and continuous factions more liberal policies are pursued on behalf of less affluent interests. Duane Lockard observed among the six New England states that the two-party states (Massachusetts, Rhode Island, and Connecticut), in contrast to the one-party states (Maine, New Hampshire, and Vermont), received a larger portion of their revenue from business and death taxes, spent more on welfare services such as aid to the blind, the aged, and dependent children, and were better apportioned.[16] Neither of these studies, however, attempted systematically to hold constant for the impact of economic development while observing these different policy outcomes. It was Dawson and Robinson who first attempted to sort out the influence of party competition on policy outcomes from the influence of economic development. The focus of the Dawson and Robinson study was upon welfare policy outcomes, which were defined to include the percentage of state revenue from death and gift taxes, per capita state revenue, per pupil expenditures, average assistance payments to the blind, the aged, and dependent children, and average unemployment compensation payments. Rank order correlation coefficients among 46 states showed that both party competition and income, urbanization, and industrialization were related to these policy outcomes. When party competition was held constant, wealth continued to correlate closely with policy outcomes. However, when wealth was held constant, party competition did *not* appear to be related to policy outcomes. The authors concluded that "interparty competition does not play as influential a role in determining the nature and scope of welfare policies as earlier studies suggested. The level of public social welfare programs in the American states seems to be more a function of socio-economic factors, especially per capita income."[17] In short, party competition has been found to have little independent effect on welfare policies; whatever correlations do exist

[14] Richard E. Dawson and James A. Robinson, "Interparty Competition, Economic Variables, and Welfare Policies in the American States," *Journal of Politics,* II (1963), 265-89.
[15] V. O. Key, Jr., *Southern Politics in State and Nation* (New York: Knopf, 1951), pp. 298-314.
[16] Duane Lockard, *New England State Politics* (Princeton: Princeton University Press, 1959), pp. 320-40.
[17] Dawson and Robinson, p. 289.

between welfare policies and competition, they are merely a product of the relationship between economic development and competition, and economic development and welfare.

Table IX-3 shows the relationship between party competition and 54 separate measures of education, welfare, highway, tax, and regulatory policies in the fifty states. In the simple coefficients, which do *not* control for the effects of economic development variables, party competition appears closely related to a number of important policy outcomes. States with a high degree of party competition tend to spend more money per pupil for public schools, pay higher teachers' salaries, attract more male teachers, enjoy lower pupil-teacher ratios, have fewer dropouts and mental failures, have larger school districts, and raise more school revenue from local rather than from state or federal sources. These same states tend to pay more liberal welfare benefits, and tend to rely more on local welfare monies than on state or federal sources. States with competitive parties also tend to raise more total revenue per capita and more tax revenues, and they also tend to rely more on local than on state sources of revenue. In all, 26 of the 54 policy measures are significantly associated with party competition in simple coefficients. Party competition has been found to be unrelated to 38 policy measures, including per capita health and welfare expenditures and finance, public employment, police and correctional policy, and the relative reliance placed upon income, sales, alcohol and tobacco, and motor vehicle taxes as sources of state revenue.

However, when the effects of economic development are controlled in the partial correlation coefficients, almost all of the association between party competition and policy disappears. Of the 26 statistically significant correlations shown in simple coefficients, 24 of these fall below accepted significance levels, once urbanization, industrialization, income, and education are controlled. In short, party competition has *no apparent independent effect* on 52 of the 54 policy outcomes investigated.

The only apparently independent effect of party competition on policy outcomes is the effect on dropout rates and mental failures. Yet even these relationships disappear when the southern states are removed from the correlations. In order to provide a check upon our findings that party competition has little independent effect on policy outcomes and that its association with these outcomes is merely a product of the intervening impact of economic development, the relationship between economic development and policy outcomes has been observed in Table IX-4, while controlling for the combined effects of three measures of party competition. The simple coefficients in Table IX-4, which do *not* control for party competition, summarize many strong relationships described in earlier chapters between economic development and a variety of policy outcomes. Of the 54 measured policy outcomes, 49 are significantly associated with at least one of the measures of economic development.

But the most striking comparison between Tables IX-4 and IX-3 is in the partial coefficients. The significant relationships between socioeconomic variables and policy outcomes *do not disappear* when the effect of party competition is controlled. For the most part, the partial coefficients in Table IX-4, unlike those in Table IX-3, continue

TABLE IX-3

The Relationship between Party Competition and State Policy Outcomes, Controlling for the Effect of Economic Development

| | Party Competition | | | | | |
| | Lower Houses | | Upper Houses | | Governorships | |
	Simple	Partial	Simple	Partial	Simple	Partial
Education						
Per pupil expenditures	.51*	.08	.48*	.00	.59*	.08
Average teachers' salaries	.36*	.11	.35*	.18	.50*	.12
Teachers with B.A.	−.38*	−.34	−.39*	−.34	−.32*	−.34
Teachers with M.A.	.16	.16	.13	.22	.35*	.05
Male teachers	.50*	.14	.41*	.03	.57*	.22
Pupil-teacher ratios	−.55*	−.21	−.50*	−.15	−.64*	−.34
Dropout rates	−.74*	−.53*	−.67*	−.40*	−.62*	−.38*
Mental failures	−.64*	−.37*	−.57*	−.36*	−.75*	−.63*
Size of school districts	−.51*	−.34	−.37*	−.18	−.43*	−.29
State participation	−.50*	−.31	−.42*	.21	−.47*	−.34
Federal participation	−.24	−.30	−.26	−.34	−.14	−.34
Welfare						
Per capita welfare expenditures	.01	−.12	.00	−.00	−.03	−.01
Per capita health expenditures	.20	.11	.27	.01	.20	.26
State participation in welfare	−.33*	−.20	−.30*	−.12	−.36*	−.17
State participation in health	.10	.06	.06	−.00	−.06	−.11
Federal participation in welfare	−.48*	.02	−.50	−.08	−.52	−.17
Unemployment benefits	.52*	.05	.51*	.04	.52*	.11
OAA benefits	.60*	.01	.57*	.02	.55*	.02
ADC benefits	.65*	.04	.60*	.03	.69*	.07
Blind benefits	.61*	.11	.59	−.11	.53	−.02
General assistance	−.56*	.16	−.51*	−.09	−.53	−.05
OAA recipients	.32*	.07	.34*	.09	.48*	.12
ADC recipients	.28	−.06	.27	−.06	.17	−.02
Unemployment recipients	−.17	−.13	−.22	−.20	−.30*	−.16
General assistance cases	−.32*	−.24	−.27	−.14	−.30*	−.12

TABLE IX-3 — Continued

| | Party Competition | | | | | |
| | Lower Houses | | Upper Houses | | Governorships | |
	Simple	Partial	Simple	Partial	Simple	Partial
Highways						
Per capita highway						
expenditures	−.20	.15	−.18	.10	−.25	−.05
State participation	.18	.06	.15	−.01	.09	.00
Federal participation	−.13	.02	−.10	−.02	−.08	−.09
Funds from highway users	.18	−.19	.05	−.11	.09	−.23
Highway fund diversion	.19	.20	.14	.18	.21	.23
Rural-urban distribution	.12	.08	.12	.04	.36*	.34
Public Regulation						
Governments per						
population	.31*	−.23	−.27	−.22	−.18	−.24
Number of bills introduced	−.09	−.08	−.15	−.10	−.02	.06
Number of laws enacted	.17	.19	.11	.14	.17	.20
Public employees	−.28	.22	−.26	.14	−.24	.21
State employees	.00	.26	.06	.10	−.19	.08
Public employees' salaries	−.42*	.05	−.37*	.15	.51*	.18
Correctional expenditures	−.25	.08	−.15	−.10	−.02	.06
Policemen	−.15	.23	−.22	.14	−.25	.16
Prisoners	.39*	.31	.40*	.34	.32*	.32
Crime rate	−.18	.23	−.06	.28	−.10	.29
Gambling revenue	−.12	.14	−.10	.01	−.17	.01
Divorce rate	.13	.33	.03	.16	.02	.23
Parolees	.36*	.29	.32*	.20	.37*	.29
Taxation						
Total revenue per capita	.40*	.19	.40	.13	.47	.16
Total taxes per capita	.52*	.03	.53*	.02	.59	.07
Debt	.22	.02	.24	.01	.21	.02
State percentage of						
total revenue	−.53*	−.34	−.47*	−.30	−.44*	−.28
Federal percentage of						
total revenue	−.25	−.21	−.25	−.14	−.26	−.24
Income taxes	.12	.05	.10	.03	.18	.01
Sales taxes	.22	.13	.22	.15	.15	.00
Alcohol and tobacco taxes	.15	.04	.10	.02	.16	.02
Motor fuel taxes	−.15	−.06	−.05	−.03	−.10	−.10
Property taxes	−.61*	−.34	−.52*	−.31	−.48*	−.32

Figures are simple and partial correlation coefficients; partial coefficients control for the effect of urbanization, industrialization, income, and education; an asterisk indicates a significant relationship.

to identify statistically significant relationships even after controlling for the effect of party competition. Of the 49 policy variables for which significant simple correlations are obtained in Table IX-4, 45 remain significantly related to one or more socioeconomic variables, even after party competition is controlled. Controlling for party competition does *not* seriously affect the relationships between economic development

TABLE IX-4

The Relationship between Economic Development and State Policy Outcomes, Controlling for the Effect of Party Competition

State Policy Measures	Economic Development							
	Urbanization		Industrialization		Income		Education	
	Simple	Partial	Simple	Partial	Simple	Partial	Simple	Partial
Education								
Per pupil expenditures	.51*	.44*	.36*	.36*	.83*	.73*	.59*	.35*
Average teachers' salaries	.69*	.66*	.64*	.66*	.88*	.85*	.57*	.39*
Teachers with B.A.	.42*	.64*	.60*	.71	.11	.53*	-.04	.28
Teachers with M.A.	.54*	.52*	.42*	.38*	.55*	.49*	.42*	.30
Male teachers	.48*	.43*	.26	.25	.63*	.42*	.63*	.39*
Pupil-teacher ratios	-.13	.09	-.19	-.11	-.43*	-.39*	-.50*	-.11
Dropout rate	-.40*	.30	.09	-.21	.54*	.18	-.60*	.24
Mental failures	-.05	.30	.13	.38*	-.46*	.10	-.70*	.41*
Size of school districts	.06	.23	.26	.35*	-.18	.20	-.37*	-.27
State participation	-.10	.06	.18	.27	-.30*	.16	.35*	.50*
Federal participation	-.36*	-.35*	-.08	-.08	-.32*	.14	-.27	.27
Welfare								
Per capita welfare expenditures	.19	.21	.07	-.09	-.01	.01	-.07	.11
Per capita health expenditures	.45*	.38*	.39*	.38*	.56*	.57*	.42*	.42*
State participation in welfare	-.11	-.16	-.15	-.13	-.35*	-.15	-.17	.13
State participation in health	-.30*	-.35*	-.07	-.12	-.08	-.15	-.15	-.19
Federal participation in welfare	-.43*	-.31	-.35*	-.35*	-.82*	-.74*	-.59*	-.39*
Unemployment benefits	.55*	.47*	.30*	.31	.80*	.71*	.67*	.50*
OAA benefits	.49*	.41*	.15	.13	.63*	.41*	.61*	.35*
ADC benefits	.51*	.46*	.26	.27	.74*	.52*	.55*	.12
Blind benefits	.59*	.55*	.28	.32	.71*	.55*	.64*	.32*
General assistance	.58*	.54*	.39*	.45*	.76*	.65*	.43*	.08
OAA recipients	-.22	-.07	-.26	-.20	-.55*	-.35*	-.35*	-.10
ADC recipients	-.15	-.09	.16	.16	-.30*	-.23	-.42*	-.37*
Unemployment recipients	.39*	.32	.69*	.67*	.58*	.51*	.23	-.07
General assistance cases	.38*	.32	.34*	.35*	.40*	.27	.25	-.03

Highways								
Per capita highway expenditures	-.37*	-.49*	-.51*	-.58*	.02	-.21	.04	.27
State participation	-.30*	-.27	.05	-.04	-.15	-.09	-.04	.07
Federal participation	-.45*	-.50*	-.42*	-.42*	-.10	-.19	.23	.22
Funds from highway users	.04	.00	.20	-.17	-.32*	-.36*	.26	-.30
Highway fund diversion	.42*	.52*	.29	.33	-.07	.29	.06	.13
Rural-urban distribution	-.35*	-.30	-.45*	-.40*	-.38*	-.24	-.07	.17
Public Regulation								
Governments per population	-.39*	-.51*	-.76*	.81*	-.19	-.47*	-.09	-.11
Number of bills introduced	.53*	.53*	.39*	.41*	.28	.33	.04	.02
Number of laws enacted	.40*	.48*	.30*	.32	.10	.29	-.03	.14
Public employees	.07	-.02	.26	-.30	.36*	.12	.61*	.59*
State employees	-.16	-.25	.02	-.05	.32*	.15	.36*	.39*
Public employees' salaries	.41*	.35*	.42*	.42*	.83*	.77*	.58*	.37*
Correctional expenditures	.32*	.21	.30*	.24	.69*	.62*	.58*	.50*
Policemen	.75*	.72*	.54*	.53*	.64*	.66*	.32*	.26
Prisoners	-.01	.14	.11	.60	-.11	.20	-.58*	-.37*
Crime rate	.61*	.61*	.45*	.43*	.49*	.58*	.38*	.46*
Gambling revenue	.34*	.30	.38*	.35*	.34*	.33	.19	.20
Divorce rate	.07	.06	.10	.06	.17	.26	.24	.42*
Parolees	.45*	.39*	.30*	.30	.35*	.14	.37*	.01
Taxation								
Total revenue per capita	.30*	.16	.03	-.05	.64*	.48*	.75*	.67*
Total taxes per capita	.59*	.52*	.23	.19	.76	.60*	.74*	.58*
Debt	.61*	.58*	.54*	.55*	.59*	.60*	.37*	.22
State percentage of total revenue	-.28	-.17	-.08	-.07	-.34*	-.03	.24	.16
Federal percentage of total revenue	-.59*	-.55*	-.32*	-.30	-.33*	-.20	-.07	.14
Income taxes	-.05	-.10	.02	-.01	.20	.12	.19	.10
Sales taxes	-.03	.11	-.19	.01	-.15	-.04	.19	-.08
Alcohol and tobacco taxes	-.10	-.07	-.01	.00	-.10	.00	-.22	-.14
Motor fuel taxes	-.32*	-.35*	-.35*	-.36*	-.27	-.47*	-.10	-.27
Property taxes	.36*	.15	-.11	-.17	.32*	-.06	.43*	.06

Figures are simple and partial correlation coefficients, partial coefficients control for the effect of three measures of party competition; an asterisk indicates a significant relationship.

and educational expenditures, teacher preparation, salary levels, the proportion of male teachers, pupil-teacher ratios, welfare benefit levels, or state and local government revenues or tax receipts. Controlling for party competition has some effect on the relationships between economic development and dropout rates, the state participation in highway finance, the state proportion of total revenue receipts, and reliance upon property taxation. In short, while party competition has little independent effect on policy outcomes after economic development is controlled, economic development continues to have considerable independent effect on policy outcomes after party competition is controlled. These operations suggest that party competition does not play as influential a role on determining policy outcomes as the level of economic development.

SOME CONCLUSIONS ABOUT PARTY COMPETITION IN THE STATES

Economic development in the American states is related to party competition and to many policy outcomes, but party competition itself appears to have little independent effect on policy outcomes. Differences in the policy choices of competitive and non-competitive states turn out to be largely a product of differences in levels of economic development rather than a direct product of party competition. Economic development—urbanization, industrialization, income and education—is more influential in determining policy outcomes than party competition. Most of the association between party competition and policy outcomes is merely a product of the relationships between economic development and party competition, and economic development and policy outcomes.

Of course, these conclusions are predicted on results obtained from analyzing selected measures of state policy in five separate fields —education, welfare, highways, taxation, and public regulation. Conceivably, party competition may have a more direct effect on some policy outcomes which have not been investigated. However, expenditures for welfare and education, the liberality of welfare benefits, teachers' salaries, the quality of public education, and the tax and revenue structure are certainly among the most important decisions that states must make. And party competition seems to have little impact on the outcome of these decisions.

Returning to the conceptual framework set forth at the beginning of this paper, an important system variable, party competition, has been shown to have little independent effect on a variety of policy outcomes.

This suggests that the linkage between socioeconomic inputs and policy outcomes is an unbroken one, and that characteristics of political systems do not independently influence policy outcomes. Political systems are, by definition, the structure and processes which function to make public policy, but these systems do not so much mediate between societal requirements and public policy as they reflect societal requirements in public policy. Political system characteristics are much less important than socioeconomic inputs in determining policy outcomes.

Where does this leave the study of political system variables in the American states? It is still important to know what goes on in the little black box. Understanding the functional interrelatedness of system variables is important regardless of the impact of these variables on policy outcomes, because we want to know *how* a political system goes about transforming socioeconomic inputs into policy outcomes. The way in which a society authoritatively allocates values may be an even more important question than the outcomes of these value allocations.

All that we have shown here is that party competition in the American states does not seem to have a measurable impact on certain policy outcomes, once socioeconomic variables are controlled. This is not to say that party competition does not vitally affect state political systems or processes. Quantification, regardless of its degree of sophistication, necessitates a simplification of very complex processes. Perhaps the influence of party competition on policy outcomes is so subtle and diverse that it defies quantification. Certainly we need more refined analysis of the relationships between socioeconomic conditions, political system characteristics, and policy outcomes. But the operations we have performed at least succeed in challenging the easy assumptions and simple generalizations about the effect of party competition on public policy.

CHAPTER X

Electoral Systems and Policy Outcomes

ELECTORAL SYSTEMS AND POLICY OUTCOMES

IN CONSTRUCTING OUR MODEL for the analysis of policy outcomes in Chapter I, we questioned whether or not differences among the states in policy choices could be attributed to the independent effect of system characteristics. Our definition of system characteristics includes voter participation and legislative malapportionment as attributes of state electoral systems. Do these system characteristics mediate between socioeconomic inputs and policy outcomes, or are policy outcomes determined by socioeconomic conditions without regard to these electoral system characteristics? To state the problem in operational language: Are the policy choices of states with one type of electoral system any different from the policy choices of states with another type of electoral system, and can these differences in policy choices be attributed to differences in electoral system characteristics? The purpose of this chapter is to explore the complex relationships between electoral system characteristics, economic development variables, and public policy outcomes.

VOTER TURNOUT AND PUBLIC POLICY

Popular participation in the political system is the very definition of democracy. There are many ways for individuals to participate in politics. They may belong to political clubs or to organizations which support specific policy positions or endorse candidates; they may contribute money or buy tickets in a campaign; they may write letters to public officials or to newspapers; they may engage in political discussions; they may work for one of the parties or candidates; or, in a passive sense, they may follow an issue or a campaign in the mass media. But for most Americans, voting is the most common form of participation in the political system.

Voting requires an individual to make not one but two decisions. He must choose between rival parties or candidates, and he must choose whether or not to cast his vote at all. The second decision is just as important as his selection of parties or candidates, because his selection is not effective unless it is expressed at the polls. Decisions about whether or not to vote can clearly influence the outcomes of elections. Non-voting is widespread; even in presidential elections generally less than two-thirds of the adult population go to the polls.

Voter participation is highly valued in American political theory. Popular control of government, control of leaders by followers, is not possible if the citizenry is politically inert. It is difficult to demonstrate that a government is truly representative if only a small portion of the population has participated in its selection. A high voter turnout in a free society indicates that the people believe they have an important stake in the outcome of an election and that they feel that they can personally influence that outcome. Non-voting may indicate that the public feels that nothing important is decided through the electoral process. Or non-voting may suggest the alienation of the general public from the political system — and a belief that voting cannot influence the course of political events. Democratic theory, then, places a high value on voter turnout, and a good deal of effort is expended on exhortations to vote. The value of popular participation in government, and indeed the value of democratic government itself, is essentially a subject for normative inquiry. Such a topic deals with deeply held value preferences about the way societies should be governed. But questions about the effect of popular participation on public policy can be approached through empirical inquiry. Of course, empirical studies can in no way demonstrate the moral value of the principle that "every citizen should exercise his right to vote." But systematic comparative analysis can help us to understand the effects of high or low voter turnouts on public policy outcomes.

Are policy outcomes in states with consistently high voter turnouts significantly different from policy outcomes in states with low voter turnout, and can these policy differences be traced to the effect of the voter turnout? There is some reason to believe that participation levels may affect policy outcomes. Non-voting does not occur uniformly throughout all segments of the population. National surveys conducted by the University of Michigan Survey Research Center show the following percentages of non-voting for various groups within the national population in the 1960 presidential election:[1]

Group Characteristic	*Percent* *Non-voting*
Education	
Grade School	33%
High School	19
College	10
Occupation	
Professional and Managerial	12
Other White Collar	16
Skilled and Semiskilled	22
Unskilled	32
Farm Operators	23
Community	
Metropolitan Area	17
Towns and Cities	37
Rural Areas	59
Race	
White	19
Negro	46

All available evidence indicates that lower socioeconomic groups exhibit less interest in politics, have a lower sense of political efficacy, and have lower voting rates.

Let us assume, then, that a low voter turnout means that people at lower socioeconomic levels have not participated. The lower the voter turnout, the more overrepresented we may expect higher socioeconomic groups to be among those going to the polls. The higher the voter turnout, the greater the representation of the lower socioeconomic groups among the voters. Because of this disproportionate representation of higher and lower socioeconomic groups among voters and non-voters, we can expect the outcome of elections to be affected by voter turnout levels. And, of course, the presumption is that the outcome of elections has some influence on the outcome of public policy issues.

In summarizing the effect of political participation on policy outcomes, the measures of participation which are described in Chapter III are employed. The most important measure is the average voter

[1] Fred I. Greenstein, *The American Party System and the American People* (Englewood Cliffs, N.J.: Prentice-Hall, 1963), pp. 24-25.

turnout (votes cast as a percentage of the voting-age population) in gubernatorial elections between 1954 and 1962 inclusively. This is the only available measure of voter turnout in elections for state officials. Ideally we would also wish to examine election returns for all 5,000 state legislative seats in the nation over a ten-year period, but these returns are not yet readily available to scholars. As a check upon our reliance on gubernatorial elections, however, two additional voter participation measures have been added. These are voter turnout rates in two off-year congressional elections, 1962 and 1958. Our assumption is that voter participation rates among the states vary uniformly in federal and state elections; states which have higher participation rates in federal elections are likely to have higher participation rates in state elections.

Fifty-four policy outcome measures are employed here to summarize the impact of political participation. These measures reflect state policy in the fields of education, health and welfare, highways, public regulation, and taxation. The meaning and importance of each of these measures is described in the earlier policy-oriented chapters from which they have been drawn.

THE INDEPENDENT EFFECT OF VOTER PARTICIPATION LEVELS

Only if the policy choices of states with high voter turnouts are significantly different from the policy choices of states with low voter turnout, and if these policy differences can be traced to voter turnout levels rather than to socioeconomic conditions, can we say that participation independently affects policy outcomes. Simple correlation coefficients can tell us the extent to which differences in policies among the fifty states are associated with differences in political participation, but they do not deal with the possibility that some other intervening variable and not participation might account for these policy differences. In other words, in order to assess the influence of participation on policy outcomes, it is necessary to control for the effects of socioeconomic variables.

Table X-1 shows the relationship between political participation and the 54 measures of policy in education, welfare, highways, regulation, and taxation in the fifty states. As we might expect, there is a great deal of association between participation levels and policy outcomes. Thirty out of the 54 selected policy outcomes are significantly associated with participation levels in simple correlation coefficients. These simple coefficients, of course, do *not* control for the effect of economic development. In the field of education higher voter participation in the states is associated with higher per pupil expenditures, higher teachers' salaries, better teacher preparation, more male teachers, lower pupil-teacher ratios, lower dropout rates and mental failures, smaller school districts, and less financial participation by the state. In the welfare field, higher participation is associated with higher welfare benefit levels, smaller numbers of welfare recipients, larger numbers of recipients of unemployment compensation, and less federal financial aid. In the field of highway policy, greater participation is associated with

TABLE X-1

The Relationship between Political Participation and State Policy Outcomes, Controlling for the Effect of Economic Development

| | Voter Participation | | | | | |
| | 1954-1962 Gubernatorial | | 1962 Congressional | | 1958 Congressional | |
State Policy Measures	*Simple*	*Partial*	*Simple*	*Partial*	*Simple*	*Partial*
Education						
Per pupil expenditures	.49*	.18	.58*	.08	.58*	−.05
Average teachers' salaries	.35*	−.16	.42*	−.17	.44*	−.26
Teachers with B.A.	−.37*	−.37	−.43*	−.50	−.38*	−.44
Teachers with M.A.	.31*	.11	.25	−.05	.34*	.06
Male teachers	.49*	.22	.63*	.32	.61*	.31
Pupil-teacher ratios	−.63*	−.30	−.70*	−.39	−.65*	−.32
Dropout rate	−.66*	−.53*	−.68*	−.49*	−.71*	−.49*
Mental failures	−.73*	−.63*	−.78*	−.63*	−.77*	−.60*
Size of school districts	−.45*	−.29	−.53*	−.41*	−.46*	−.28
State participation	−.46*	−.31	−.56*	−.46*	−.48*	−.33
Federal participation	−.26*	−.21	−.24	−.28	−.14	−.34
Welfare						
Per capita welfare expenditures	.06	−.15	.04	.07	.03	.14
Per capita health expenditures	.07	−.29	.17	−.03	.18	−.30
State participation in welfare	−.24	−.02	−.30	−.08	−.26	−.01
State participation in health	.09	.05	.07	.09	.07	.11
Federal participation in welfare	−.46*	−.06	−.54*	.00	−.62*	−.03
Unemployment benefits	.43*	−.04	.55*	.02	.58*	−.02
OAA benefits	.54*	−.02	.67*	.06	.63*	.02
ADC benefits	.64*	.02	.74*	.08	.73*	.06
Blind benefits	.50*	.04	.60*	.12	.57*	.04
General assistance benefits	.47*	.04	.52*	.07	.00*	.01
OAA recipients	−.40*	−.13	−.37*	−.02	−.46*	−.10
ADC recipients	−.10	.23	−.17	.22	−.19	.26
Unemployment recipients	.30*	.24	.31*	.23	.34*	.26
General assistance cases	.37*	.30	.34*	.09	.34*	.23

TABLE X-1 – Continued

| | Voter Participation | | | | | |
| | 1954-1962 Gubernatorial | | 1962 Congressional | | 1958 Congressional | |
State Policy Measures	Simple	Partial	Simple	Partial	Simple	Partial
Highways						
Per capita highway expenditures	.27	.03	.35*	.15	.33*	.11
State participation	.02	.10	.02	.12	−.04	.13
Federal participation	.23	−.20	.08	−.17	.12	−.09
Funds from highway users	−.05	.20	−.02	.12	−.14	.17
Highway fund diversion	−.20	−.15	−.19	−.13	−.22	−.21
Rural-urban distribution	−.19	−.13	−.17	−.08	−.12	−.03
Public Regulation						
Governments per population	.33*	.38*	.34*	.43*	.33*	.44*
Number of bills introduced	−.02	−.05	.00	−.03	.04	.01
Number of laws enacted	−.20	−.17	−.21	−.20	−.17	−.17
Public employees	.22	−.17	.32*	−.09	.33*	−.13
State employees	.19	−.03	.17	−.13	.27	.04
Public employees' salaries	.35*	−.31	.36*	−.28	.49*	−.30
Correctional expenditures	.31	−.20	.35*	.29	.40*	−.27
Policemen	.14	−.18	.16	.23	.20	−.25
Prisoners	−.50*	−.51*	−.52*	−.57*	−.51*	−.60*
Crime rate	−.03	−.35*	−.02	−.42*	.05	−.37
Gambling revenue	.15	.06	.17	.07	.16	.03
Divorce rate	−.10	−.26	−.09	−.31	.04	−.29
Parolees	.40*	.40*	.39*	.37*	.42*	.43*
Taxation						
Total revenue per capita	.39*	−.09	.50*	−.09	.55*	−.07
Total taxes per capita	.52*	.14	.59*	.15	.63*	.12
Debt	.11	−.13	.13	−.19	.16	−.21
State percentage of total revenue	−.42*	−.30	−.48*	−.34	−.40*	−.23
Federal percentage of total revenue	−.23	−.25	−.20	−.20	−.18	−.14
Income taxes	.08	−.10	.07	−.07	.11	−.07
Sales taxes	−.03	.13	−.14	.03	−.10	.10
Alcohol and tobacco taxes	−.21	−.08	−.19	−.04	−.20	−.04
Motor fuel taxes	.15	.04	.20	.12	.06	.05
Property taxes	.50*	.32	.48*	.29	.51*	.31

Figures are simple and partial correlation coefficients; partial coefficients control for the effect of urbanization, industrialization, income, and education; an asterisk indicates a significant relationship.

increased highway expenditures. States with higher participation rates have more local governments per population, require more public employees, pay higher salaries for public employees, and have higher correctional expenditures. Finally, voter turnout is also associated in simple coefficients with total revenue per capita, tax revenue per capita, the state proportion of total revenue, and reliance upon property taxation for state-local revenue.

Further analysis reveals, however, that most of these associations between voter participation and policy outcomes are a product of the effect of economic development. The most striking feature in Table X-1 is the disappearance of significant correlations once economic development is controlled. When the combined effect of urbanization, industrialization, income, and education is controlled in the partial correlation coefficients, most of the associations between political participation and public policy disappear. Of the 30 significant correlations shown in the simple coefficients, all but six fall below accepted levels of significance once the effects of economic development are controlled. Thus, most of the associations between participation levels and policy outcomes are really a product of the relationships between both of these sets of variables and economic development. Political participation, then, has no apparent *independent* effect on 48 of the 54 policy variables selected for analysis.

Voter participation appears independently related only to dropout rates, mental failures, prisoners' crime rates, and parolees. The relationship with governments per population disappears if the southern states are removed, but these other relationships do not. It is interesting that political alienation, as expressed in non-voting, is independently related to these indices of social disorganization: it is not likely that non-voting causes dropouts, crime, or imprisonment, but there are relationships here which do not depend upon economic development.

Our evidence seems to support the conclusion that levels of political participation in state politics have little independent effect on policy outcomes and that the associations between participation and policy outcomes is merely a product of the effects of economic development. In order to provide a check upon this conclusion, the relationship between economic development and policy outcomes has been observed while controlling for the combined effects of the three measures of political participation. If political participation independently influences policy outcomes, the coefficients between economic development and policy outcomes should be lowered when the effects of political participation are controlled. However, if controlling for participation does *not* lower the coefficients between economic development and policy outcomes, then we can reaffirm our conclusion that levels of political participation have little independent effect on state policy outcomes.

The simple coefficients in Table X-2 summarize what has been reported in earlier chapters about the relationships between economic development and policy outcomes. Forty-eight of the 54 selected policy measures are significantly associated with at least one of the measures of economic development. But the most important characteristic of Table X-2 is that the relationships between economic development variables and policy outcomes *do not disappear* when the effect of political participation is controlled. The partial coefficients in Table X-2 control for the effect of all three participation measures. For the most part, these partial coefficients continue to indentify statistically significant relationships between economic development and policy outcomes even after controlling for the participation measures. Therefore, the effects of economic development on policy outcomes are independent of the effects of political participation. Controlling for participation has some effect on the relationships between economic development and state participation in education, highways, revenue collection, and reliance upon property taxation. But, on the whole, the effects of economic development on policy outcomes appear to be independent of the effects of political participation.

SOME CONCLUSIONS ABOUT POLITICAL PARTICIPATION

Levels of political participation among the states are a function of levels of economic development, just as many policy outcomes seem to be a function of economic development levels. But differences among the states in participation levels do not appear to have much *independent* effect upon policy outcomes. Differences in public policies between states with high and low participation turn out to be a product of differences in economic development. Certainly political participation does not play as influential a role in determining policy outcomes as economic development. In terms of our original model for analyzing policy outcomes, another system variable has been shown to have little independent effect on policy outcomes, and socioeconomic inputs have been shown to affect policy more directly than an important system characteristic.

Of course the same caveats made throughout this study are applicable to our findings regarding political participation. Less than one hundred policy measures in all were employed in this study, and the summary tables deal with only 54 of the more important policy measures. Conceivably, participation may have a more observable effect on some other policy outcomes not investigated. Yet few would quarrel with our contention that the activities of state governments in

TABLE X-2

The Relationship between Economic Development and State Policy Outcomes,
Controlling for the Effect of Political Participation

State Policy Measures	Urbanization		Industrialization		Income		Education	
	Simple	Partial	Simple	Partial	Simple	Partial	Simple	Partial
Education								
Per pupil expenditures	.51*	.43*	.36*	.35*	.83*	.72*	.59*	.31
Average teachers' salaries	.69*	.64*	.64*	.66*	.88*	.86*	.57*	.38*
Teachers with B.A.	.42*	.56*	.60*	.69*	.11	.48*	-.04	.24
Teachers with M.A.	.54*	.48*	.42*	.40*	.55*	.46*	.42*	.27
Male teachers	.48*	.41*	.26	.23	.63*	.36*	.63*	.36*
Pupil-teacher ratios	-.13	.03	-.19	-.33	-.43*	-.05	-.50*	-.20
Dropout rate	-.40*	-.32	-.09	-.24	-.54*	-.13	-.60*	-.39*
Mental failures	-.05	.21	.13	.30	-.46*	.04	-.70*	-.50*
Size of school districts	.06	.19	.26	.33	-.18	.15	-.37*	-.15
State participation	-.10	.12	.18	.24	-.30*	.05	-.35*	-.11
Federal participation	-.36*	-.43*	-.08	-.10	-.32*	.03	-.27	.15
Welfare								
Per capita welfare expenditures	.19	.19	.07	-.07	-.01	-.04	-.07	.09
Per capita health expenditures	.45*	.38*	.39*	-.36*	.56*	.56*	.42*	.36*
State participation in welfare	-.11	-.06	-.15	-.14	-.35*	-.28	-.17	-.01
State participation in health	-.30*	-.35*	-.07	-.07	-.08	-.16	-.15	-.24
Federal participation in welfare	-.43*	-.30	-.35*	-.33	-.82*	-.65*	-.59*	-.25
Unemployment benefits	.55*	.47*	.30*	.26	.80*	.62*	.67*	.42*
OAA benefits	.49*	.42*	.15	-.10	.63*	.35*	.61*	.35*
Blind benefits	.59*	.55*	.28	.26	.71*	.52*	.64*	.43*
General assistance	.58*	.53*	.39*	.38*	.76*	.65*	.43*	.16
OAA recipients	-.22*	-.10	-.26	-.23	-.55*	-.37*	-.35*	-.08
ADC recipients	-.15	-.09	.16	.20	-.30*	-.22	-.42*	-.37*
Unemployment recipients	-.39*	.33	.69*	.70*	.58*	.52*	.23	.00
General assistance cases	.38*	.35*	.34*	.33	.40*	.26	.25	.07
ADC benefits	.51*	.46*	.24	.24	.24	.44*	.55*	.10

Highways								
Per capita highway expenditures	−.37*	−.51*	−.51*	−.59*	.02	−.31	.36*	.20
State participation	−.30*	−.28	−.05	−.07	−.15	−.13	.04	.01
Federal participation	−.45*	−.55*	.42*	−.15*	−.10	−.33	.23	.13
Funds from highway users	−.04	.20	.20	−.18	−.32*	−.30	.26	−.19
Highway fund diversion	.42*	.49*	.29	.30	.07	.26	.06	.10
Rural-urban distribution	−.35	−.36*	−.45*	−.46*	−.38*	−.47*	.07	.04
Public Regulation								
Governments per population	−.39*	−.50*	−.76*	−.84*	−.19	−.56*	−.09	−.13
Number of bills introduced	.53*	.55*	.39*	.39*	.28	.34	.04	−.15
Number of laws enacted	.40*	.48*	.30*	.32	.10	.31	.03	.09
Public employees	.07	−.07	−.26	−.37*	.36*	−.04	.61*	.52*
State employees	−.16	−.32	.02	−.05	.32*	−.04	.36*	.20
Public employees' salaries	.41*	.28	.42*	.40*	.83*	.74*	.58*	.35*
Correctional expenditures	.32*	−.18	.30*	.33	.69*	.55*	.58*	.44*
Policemen	.75*	.72*	.54*	.52*	.64*	.67*	.32*	.22
Prisoners	−.01	.11	.11	.16	−.11	−.32	−.58*	−.38*
Crime rate	.61*	.59*	.45*	.42*	.49*	.57*	.38*	.41*
Gambling revenue	.34*	.35*	.38*	.39*	.34*	.39*	.19	.14
Divorce rate	.07	.07	.10	.10	.17	.29	.24	.33
Parolees	.45*	.41*	.30*	.30	.35*	.14	.37*	.02
Taxation								
Total revenue per capita	.30*	.11	.03	.10	.64*	.35*	.75*	.58*
Total taxes per capita	.59*	.54*	.23	.18	.76*	.54*	.74*	.54*
Debt	.61*	.57*	.54*	.52*	.59*	.61*	.37*	.23
State percentage of total revenue	−.28	−.27	−.08	−.09	−.34*	−.22	.24	−.05
Federal percentage of total revenue	−.59*	−.61*	−.32*	−.32	−.33*	−.34	−.07	.02
Income taxes	.05	−.13	.02	−.24	.20	.11	.19	.14
Sales taxes	−.03	.10	−.19	.06	−.15	−.05	.19	−.11
Alcohol and tobacco taxes	−.10	−.04	−.01	.03	−.10	.08	−.22	−.13
Motor fuel taxes	−.32*	−.30	−.35*	−.35*	−.27	−.33	−.10	−.09
Property taxes	.36*	.19	−.11	−.17	.32*	.02	.43*	.20

Figures are simple and partial correlation coefficients; partial coefficients control for the effects of three measures of political participation; an asterisk indicates a significant relationship.

the field of education, health and welfare, highways, public safety, and taxation are important matters of public concern. And political participation does not seem to affect the outcome of these activities.

It is important to remember, however, that we are dealing with the effect of participation on policy outcomes. Our finding that participation levels do not directly affect policy outcomes does not mean that participation levels cannot vitally affect other political system variables. Certainly there is reason to believe, for example, that the drive to increase Negro voter registration throughout the South will affect political processes and even perhaps the structure of power in that region. Important social as well as political consequences may result from increased Negro voting, but there is no evidence that increased Negro voting will provide more educational expenditures, more liberal welfare benefits, increased or decreased tax levels, or other large-scale transformations in public policy. Negroes will eventually play a more important role in the political systems of the southern states as a result of increased voter participation, but in general they will respond to socioeconomic conditions in these states in much the same fashion as whites do. They will find the economic development of the South to be just as great an influence on what they can do in providing public service as it has been on white policy-makers. Negro voter registration, no matter how important an influence it may be on political events in Alabama and Mississippi, will not in itself solve the problems of economic underdevelopment in these states. Thus, in the long run, urbanization, industrialization, income, and education in the South, as well as in the rest of the nation, will have a greater impact on policy outcomes than increased Negro, or white, political participation.

It is also important to remember that these findings about participation and policy outcomes in no way reflect upon the moral imperatives in democratic theory about popular participation. In terms of our fundamental value commitments, it may even be more important *how* policy outcomes are made than *what* these policy outcomes are. The normative obligation of every citizen in a democracy to participate in public policy-making is as important as it ever was. These findings about participation and policy outcomes in no way alter our moral commitments to guarantee to every person an opportunity to participate in politics, particularly at the polls.

MALAPPORTIONMENT AND PUBLIC POLICY

Commentators on state politics have often implied that malapportionment seriously affects the policy choices of state legislatures. In the literature on state politics it is frequently argued that there are important policy differences between urban and rural constituencies and that malapportionment, by overrepresenting rural interests, grants them a real advantage in policy-making.[2] It is frequently predicted that reapportionment on a population basis will bring about noticeable shifts in many state policies.[3]

Malapportionment of state legislatures has been successfully challenged on the grounds that it denies to citizens equal protection of the laws.[4] This challenge is essentially a moral one, stemming from deeply held values about political equality.[5] The merits of this type of challenge do not lend themselves to empirical verification. However, statements about the effect of malapportionment on public policy and predictions about the policy consequences of reapportionment can be tested empirically. Such tests, of course, in no way reflect upon the moral quality of the proposition "as nearly as practicable one man's vote should be equal to another's."[6] But they can help us to know what to expect in the way of policy changes in the wake of reapportionment. In the past, proponents of reapportionment have been very enthusiastic about its expected consequences. Having attributed a lack of party competition, unfair distribution of state funds, conservative tax policies, unprogressive educational policies, and penny-pinching welfare policies to rural overrepresentation, they naturally expect to see these conditions changed by reapportionment. Court-ordered reapportionment is viewed as a source of strength for state legislatures, rather than an infringement of a heretofore exclusive perogative of these bodies. Reapportionment, it is said, will help states come to grips with important domestic problems in the nation and reassume their rightful place in our federal system.

[2] See Charles Adrian, *State and Local Governments* (New York: McGraw-Hill, 1960), pp. 306-7; Daniel Grant and H. C. Nixon, *State and Local Governments in America* (Boston: Allyn and Bacon, 1963), pp. 204-5; Richard Frost, "On Derge's Metropolitan and Outstate Legislative Delegations," *American Political Science Review,* LIII (1959), 792-95; Commission on Intergovernmental Relations, *A Report to the President for Transmittal to Congress* (Washington: Government Printing Office, 1955), p. 39; Malcolm Jewell, *The State Legislature* (New York: Random House, 1962), pp. 30-33; and V. O. Key, Jr., *American State Politics: An Introduction* (New York: Knopf, 1956), pp. 76-77.

[3] See "After Redistricting Decision—Where States May See Changes in Taxes, Welfare, Highways," *U. S. News and World Report,* July 6, 1964, pp. 34-36; and "A New Charter for State Legislatures," *Time,* June 26, 1964, pp. 22-23.

[4] *Baker* v. *Carr,* 369 U.S. 186 (1962); *Reynolds* v. *Sims,* 84 S. Ct. 1362 (1964).

[5] For example: "The conception of political equality from the Declaration of Independence to Lincoln's Gettysburg Address, to the Fourteenth, Fifteenth, Seventeenth, and Nineteenth Amendments can mean only one thing—one person, one vote." *Gray* v. *Sanders,* 83 S. Ct. 801 (1963).

[6] *Westberry* v. *Sanders,* 84 S. Ct. 526 (1964), p. 530.

In contrast, a few scholars have sounded a note of caution regarding the expected consequences of reapportionment. On the basis of roll-call analysis in the Missouri and Illinois legislatures, David Derge concluded that metropolitan legislators and non-metropolitan legislators seldom lined up to oppose each other in unified voting blocs.[7] It is difficult to see how reapportioning legislatures to reduce rural over-representation will have much effect on policy-making, if we accept Derge's conclusions that only infrequently do rural-urban divisions influence legislative decisions anyway. Duane Lockard also entered a caveat about the consequences of malapportionment. With specific reference to conditions in Massachusetts and Connecticut, he asked: "Do states with fair apportionment respond to urban appeals more readily? If anyone has made a systematic study of this, I am unaware of it, but limited evidence does not seem to indicate that the states with fair apportionment are any more considerate of urban problems than the states with malapportionment."[8] Herbert Jacob was equally skeptical of the consequences of malapportionment. He computed rank order correlation coefficients for the relationship between malapportionment and party competition, highway fund distributions, and certain welfare expenditures for the fifty states. On the basis of low coefficients, he concluded "it is improbable that it [reapportionment] will substantially invigorate state governments or dissolve the stalemates which sap public confidence in them."[9]

Our task here is systematically to examine the impact of malapportionment on public policy in all fifty states. If the policy choices of malapportioned legislatures are noticeably different from the policy choices of well apportioned legislatures, and these differences in policies can be traced to malapportionment rather than some other condition, then reapportionment can be expected to have a significant impact on state policies. However, if the policy choices of well apportioned and malapportioned legislatures do not differ significantly, or if the differences which do occur are the product of some condition other than malapportionment, then more caution is warranted regarding the political changes which reapportionment may bring.

Our measures of malapportionment are explained in Chapter III. They include the index of representation, which is the theoretical minimum percentage of a state's population that can elect a majority of

[7] David Derge, "Metropolitan and Outstate Alignments in the Illinois and Missouri Legislative Delegations," *American Political Science Review,* LIII (1958), 1051-65.
[8] Duane Lockard, *The Politics of State and Local Government* (New York: Macmillan, 1963), p. 319.
[9] Herbert Jacob, "The Consequences of Malapportionment: A Note of Caution," *Social Forces,* XLIII (1964), 261.

each house; the degree of urban underrepresentation, which is the ratio of the size of a single-member constituency in the largest county compared to the average size of a single-member constituency in the state; and the apportionment score, which is the degree to which the populations of the states' legislative constituencies approach a normal curve. Each of these measures depicts a slightly different aspect of malapportionment and each results in a slightly different ranking of states.[10] The first measure focuses on the minimum proportion of a state's population which can control the legislature, the second measure focuses on urban underrepresentation, and the third focuses on the degree to which a state's apportionment schedule approaches the statistical concept of normality. In the analysis to follow we shall evaluate the political relevance of each of these measures.

THE INDEPENDENT EFFECT OF MALAPPORTIONMENT ON POLICY OUTCOMES

Table X-3 shows the relationship between malapportionment and 54 separate measures of policies in education, welfare, highways, public regulation, and taxation in the fifty states. Perhaps the most striking feature of Table X-3 is that *none* of the coefficients reported there are very high. For the most part, variations in public policy among the states are *not* associated with malapportionment.

In the field of education, we can hypothesize that malapportionment results in lower per pupil expenditures, lower teachers' salaries, and higher pupil-teacher ratios, which in turn mean lower teacher qualification, higher dropout rates, and more selective service mental failures. The signs of the coefficients in Table X-3 tend to bear out these relationships, but few of the coefficients obtain at a level of significance which would merit much confidence in these hypotheses. None of the coefficients under the index of representativeness or the apportionment score are statistically significant. This helps confirm our suspicion that malapportionment in its technical aspects has no policy relevance. Urban underrepresentation is slightly related to higher pupil-teacher ratios, higher dropout rates and increased state and federal participation in public school finance. Yet these relationships are not close enough to warrant predictions about changes in these policies once urban areas are given more representation. Per pupil school expenditures seem to decline with malapportionment, yet this

[10] The simple correlation coefficients between these three measures are as follows: index of representativeness and urban underrepresentation: .45; index of representativeness and apportionment score: .50; urban underrepresentation and apportionment score: .70.

relationship is clearly a product of the fact that per pupil expenditures are lower in the rural, less wealthy, agricultural states; once socioeconomic variables are controlled in partial coefficients, the relationship between pupil expenditures and malapportionment disappears. Likewise the relationship between low teachers' salaries and malapportionment also disappears once socioeconomic variables are controlled.

Few policy variables in the welfare field appear related to malapportionment. The closest relationship is between urban underrepresentation and state participation in the provision of health and hospital

TABLE X-3

The Relationship between Malapportionment and State Policy Outcomes, Controlling for the Effect of Economic Development

| | Malapportionment | | | | | |
| State Policy Measures | Index of Representation | | Index of Urban Underrepresentation | | Apportionment Score | |
	Simple	Partial	Simple	Partial	Simple	Partial
Education						
Per pupil expenditures	.12	.06	.36*	.12	.09	.15
Average teachers' salaries	−.29	−.20	.30*	−.17	.01	−.28
Teachers with B.A.	−.24	−.19	−.13	−.29	−.12	−.24
Teachers with M.A.	−.07	.10	.14	.07	.10	−.04
Male teachers	−.22	−.09	.15	.01	.01	−.10
Pupil-teacher ratios	−.11	−.23	−.31*	−.41*	−.15	−.21
Dropout rate	.06	.29	.37*	.54*	.15	.29
Mental failures	−.09	−.27	−.15	−.27	−.16	−.14
Size of school districts	−.24	−.31	−.10	−.20	−.13	−.15
State participation	−.25	−.34	−.32*	−.43*	−.23	−.28
Federal participation	−.06	−.13	−.33*	−.39*	−.07	−.18
Welfare						
Per capita welfare expenditures	.02	.07	.03	.03	−.19	−.07
Per capita health expenditures	−.09	.00	.30*	.09	−.10	.04
State participation in welfare	−.12	−.17	−.26	−.11	−.08	−.05
State participation in health	.10	.06	.34*	.31	.17	.18
Federal participation in welfare	.08	.02	.36*	.24	.13	.09
Unemployment benefits	.17	−.02	.30*	.09	.13	.03
OAA benefits	−.01	.07	.37*	.04	.01	.06
ADC benefits	.12	.11	.49*	.06	.14	.09
Blind benefits	−.08	.16	.32*	.09	.01	.02
General assistance	.03	.19	.51*	.18	.17	.16
OAA recipients	.15	.08	−.15	.04	−.19	−.04
ADC recipients	.01	−.03	−.11	−.14	−.08	−.06
Unemployment recipients	−.11	.02	.41*	.18	.29	.23
General assistance cases	.05	−.19	−.33*	−.08	−.19	−.17

TABLE X-3—Continued

State Policy Measures	Index of Representation		Malapportionment Index of Urban Underrepresentation		Apportionment Score	
	Simple	Partial	Simple	Partial	Simple	Partial
Highways						
Per capita highway expenditures	.05	−.01	−.06	.16	.04	.04
State participation	−.29	−.04	−.22	−.19	−.08	−.18
Federal participation	.08	.04	−.11	.04	.15	.13
Funds from highway users	.23	.22	.15	−.05	.10	.00
Highway fund diversion	−.29	−.03	−.17	−.32	−.21	−.20
Rural-urban distribution	.06	−.03	−.37*	−.18	−.10	−.05
Public Regulation						
Governments per population	.21	.19	.04	.29	.06	.29
Number of bills introduced	.01	.14	.20	.05	.01	.04
Number of laws enacted	.29	.25	−.10	.23	−.24	−.24
Public employees	−.12	.10	−.13	.05	−.01	.04
State employees	−.14	−.15	.00	.01	.09	−.02
Public employees' salaries	.12	.03	.24	−.15	.03	−.20
Correctional expenditures	−.27	−.21	.24	.05	.02	−.15
Policemen	−.29	−.21	.20	−.16	−.03	−.10
Prisoners	−.27	−.29	−.48*	−.52*	−.40	−.45*
Crime rate	−.38*	−.28	−.15	−.47*	−.23	−.37*
Gambling revenue	−.22	−.14	.14	−.02	.14	.09
Divorce rate	−.29	−.28	−.26	−.34	−.20	−.09
Parolees	.18	.34	.41*	.37*	.27	.29
Taxation						
Total revenue per capita	−.18	−.12	.02	−.09	−.04	−.02
Total taxes per capita	−.15	.05	.26	.17	.01	−.09
Debt	−.24	−.12	.31	.06	.05	−.02
State percentage of total revenue	.00	−.06	−.29	−.02	−.13	−.01
Federal percentage of total revenue	.03	−.09	−.36*	−.23	−.04	−.08
Income taxes	.12	.07	.14	.00	.02	.05
Sales taxes	−.14	−.15	−.20	−.20	−.14	−.09
Alcohol and tobacco taxes	.14	.04	.13	−.01	.02	.07
Motor fuel taxes	.22	.08	−.01	.04	.19	.14
Property taxes	.15	.29	.28	.34	.19	.26

Figures are simple and partial correlation coefficients; partial coefficients control for the effect of urbanization, industrialization, income and education; an asterisk indicates a significant relationship.

services. Yet urban underrepresentation accounts for only 11 per cent of the total variation among the states in the extent of their participation in the health field. The level of payments to recipients of unemployment compensation, old age assistance, aid to dependent children, and aid to the blind appears to be slightly related to urban underrepresentation on the basis of simple coefficients. These coefficients disappear, however, once socioeconomic variables are controlled. In short, the relationship between urban representation and welfare policies among the fifty states is a product of intervening socioeconomic variables. There is no evidence that reapportionment will bring any noticeable liberalization of welfare policies.

One of the most frequent complaints about malapportionment is that it leads to discrimination against urban areas in the distribution of state funds. It turns out that there is a significant association between urban underrepresentation and discrimination against urban areas in highway fund allocations; the simple coefficient (−.37) indicates that an increase in urban representation is associated with a decrease in the proportion of highway funds going to rural areas. However, when economic development is controlled, even this association disappears. In fact there are no significant partial correlations between malapportionment and highway policies. The only measures of public regulation which remain significantly related to urban underrepresentation after economic development is controlled are prisoner populations, crime rates, and parolees.

None of the relationships between malapportionment and the eight selected tax policies are statistically significant. It is doubtful, for example, that reapportionment will bring higher tax levies. Neither total state and local taxes per capita nor total state revenues per capita are significantly related to apportionment. While federal grants constitute a larger share of the revenue of malapportioned states, this is merely a product of the fact that these states tend to be less wealthy; the relationship between federal support and malapportionment disappears when socioeconomic variables are controlled. State revenues are a larger share of total revenues in malapportioned states, but this relationship also appears as a product of socioeconomic variables rather than malapportionment itself. Certainly there is no evidence that reapportionment will bring about any substantial changes in state tax structures.

It is interesting to note that the few significant policy correlations which have been obtained in this study are obtained with David and Eisenberg's index of urban underrepresentation. This index measures the degree to which a particular political interest is affected by malapportionment rather than the existence of malapportionment in the technical sense. The failure to obtain any significant policy correlates with the index of representativeness suggests that the theoretical minimum population which *could* control a legislature is not a relevant political variable. Nor does the extent to which the population of legislative districts approach a normal statistical curve, as measured by the Schubert and Press apportionment score, appear to be a politically relevant variable. Schubert and Press rebuked earlier scholars for their technically unsophisticated measures of malapportionment ("the difference in the costs for the computation of precise and crude indices is . . . minimal").[11] Yet it turns out that David and Eisenberg with their less sophisticated measure came closer to identifying the relevant political aspect of malapportionment than Schubert and Press. For malapportionment becomes relevant only when it operates to discriminate against specific political interests in a state.

It is possible to construct one final check upon the finding that malapportionment has little independent effect on policy outcomes. Partial correlation coefficients can be computed for the relationships between economic development variables and policy outcomes while controlling for the effects of malapportionment. If malapportionment independently influences policy outcomes, the coefficients between economic development and policy outcomes should be noticeably lowered when the effects of the three measures of malapportionment are controlled. If controlling for malapportionment does not lower these coefficients, it will reconfirm our finding that malapportionment has little independent effect on policy outcomes.

Table X-4 tends to confirm our findings that malapportionment does not substantially affect policy outcomes. The simple coefficients in that table are the same coefficients shown earlier; they summarize the relationship between economic development and policy outcomes. But the important feature of Table X-4 is that these relationships between economic development and public policy are *not* seriously affected when malapportionment is controlled. The partial coefficients, which control for the combined effects of all three measures of malapportionment, continue to identify statistically significant relationships between economic development and public policy. The only policy variables for which significant correlations with economic development disappear after malapportionment is controlled are federal participation in education, highway-user revenues, state employees per population, and the state percentage of total revenue. On the whole, controlling for the effects of malapportionment does *not* seriously alter the relationships between economic development and policy outcomes in education, welfare, highways, public morality, and taxation.

[11] Glendon Schubert and Charles Press, "Measuring Malapportionment," *American Political Science Review,* LVIII (1964), 311.

TABLE X-4

The Relationship between Economic Development and State Policy Outcomes, Controlling for the Effect of Malapportionment

State Policy Measures	Economic Development							
	Urbanization		Industrialization		Income		Education	
	Simple	Partial	Simple	Partial	Simple	Partial	Simple	Partial
Education								
Per pupil expenditures	.51*	.37*	.36*	.16	.83*	.79*	.59*	.61*
Average teachers' salaries	.69*	.57*	.64*	.51*	.88*	.84*	.57*	.59*
Teachers with B.A.	.42*	.45*	.60*	.68*	.11	.10	−.04	−.10
Teachers with M.A.	.54*	.52*	.42*	.87*	.55*	.54*	.42*	.39*
Males teachers	.48*	.38*	.26	.11	.63*	.57*	.63*	.62*
Pupil-teacher ratios	−.13	−.02	−.19	.38*	−.43*	−.38*	−.50*	−.54*
Dropout rate	−.40*	.80	−.09	−.32	−.54*	−.47*	−.60*	−.65*
Mental failures	−.05	−.04	.13	.20	−.46*	−.51*	−.70*	−.73*
Size of school districts	.06	.00	.26	.26	.18	−.29	−.37*	−.45*
State participation	−.10	−.07	.18	.30	−.23	−.21	.35*	−.41*
Federal participation	−.36*	−.27	−.08	.08	−.32*	.18	−.27	.10
Welfare								
Per capita welfare expenditures	.19	.16	.07	.07	−.01	.05	−.07	.16
Per capita health expenditures	.45*	.41*	.39*	.36*	.56*	.57*	.42*	.41*
State participation in welfare	−.11	−.04	−.15	.34	−.35*	−.35*	−.17	−.20
State participation in health	−.30*	−.52*	−.07	−.08	−.08	−.29	−.15	−.19
Federal participation in welfare	−.43*	−.32	−.35*	−.19	−.82*	−.80*	−.59*	−.59*
Unemployment benefits	.55*	.43*	.30*	.10	.80*	.75*	.87*	.67*
OAA benefits	.49*	.37*	.15	−.05	.63*	.57*	.61*	.71*
ADC benefits	.51*	.43*	.26	.08	.74*	.74*	.55*	.67*
Blind benefits	.59*	.53*	.28	.15	.71*	.69*	.64*	.74*
General assistance	.58*	.47*	.39*	−.20	.76*	.71*	.43*	.49*
OAA recipients	−.22	−.12	−.26	.14	−.55*	−.50*	−.35*	.27
ADC recipients	−.15	−.11	.16	.26	−.80*	−.28	−.42*	−.42*
Unemployment recipients	.39*	.22	.69*	.58*	.58*	.41*	.23	.12
General assistance cases	.38*	.30	.34*	.25	.40*	.36*	.25	.20

Highways							
Per capita highway expenditures	−.37*	−.36*	−.51*	−.54*	.02	.04	.39*
State participation	−.30*	−.38*	−.05	.04	.15	−.04	.13
Federal participation	−.45*	−.41*	−.42*	−.41*	−.10	.23	.24
Funds from highway users	−.04	.17	−.20	−.01	−.32*	−.26	−.17
Highway fund diversion	.42*	.43*	.29	.30	.07	−.06	−.11
Rural-urban distribution	−.35*	−.18	−.45*	−.35*	−.38*	−.07	−.01
Public Regulation							
Governments per population	−.39*	−.32	.76*	−.78*	.19	−.09	.16
Number of bills introduced	.53*	.51*	.39*	.35*	.28	.04	.03
Number of laws enacted	.40*	.37*	.30*	.28	.10	−.03	−.06
Public employees	.07	.11	−.26	−.29	.36*	.61*	.62*
State employees	−.16	.25	.02	−.05	.32*	.36*	.30
Public employees' salaries	.41*	.28	.42*	.30	.83*	.58*	.60*
Correctional expenditures	.32*	.10	.30	.07	.69*	.58*	.58*
Policemen	.75*	.67*	.54*	.41*	.64*	.32*	.26
Prisoners	−.01	.12	.11	.33	−.11	−.58*	−.33
Crime rate	.61*	.63*	.45*	.46*	.49*	.38*	.37*
Gambling revenue	.34*	.24	.38*	.26	.34*	.19	.08
Divorce rate	.07	.14	.10	.19	.17	.24	.23
Parolees	.45*	.42*	.30*	.20	.35*	.37*	.28
Taxation							
Total revenue per capita	.30*	.23	.03	−.07	.64*	.75*	.76*
Total taxes per capita	.59*	.48*	.23	.03	.76*	.74*	.78*
Debt	.61*	.47*	.54*	.38*	.59*	.37*	.24
State percentage of total revenue	−.28	−.17	−.08	.08	−.34*	−.24	−.22
Federal percentage of total revenue	−.59*	−.50*	−.32*	−.16	.33*	−.07	−.04
Income taxes	.05	−.09	.02	.04	.20	.19	.23
Sales taxes	−.03	.08	−.19	.08	−.15	−.19	−.20
Alcohol and tobacco taxes	−.10	−.13	−.01	−.14	−.10	−.22	−.20
Motor fuel taxes	−.32*	−.23	−.35*	−.31	−.27	−.10	−.09
Property taxes	.36*	.24	−.11	.24	.32*	.43*	.46*

Figures are simple and partial correlation coefficients; partial coefficients control for the effects of three measures of malapportionment; an asterisk indicates a significant relationship.

SOME CONCLUSIONS ABOUT MALAPPORTIONMENT

On the whole, the policy choices of malapportioned legislatures are not noticeably different from the policy choices of well apportioned legislatures. Most of the policy differences which do occur turn out to be a product of socioeconomic differences among the states rather than a direct product of apportionment practices. Relationships which do appear between malapportionment and public policy are so slight that reapportionment is not likely to bring about any significant policy changes. Of course these conclusions are predicted on results obtained from analyzing selected measures of public policy in five separate fields — education, welfare, highways, taxation and public regulation. Conceivably malapportionment could have a more direct effect on some area of policy-making that has not been investigated. However, expenditures for welfare and education, the liberality of welfare benefits, teachers' salaries, the quality of public education, the distribution of highway funds, the tax burden, the revenue structure, and the extent of state participation in education, health, welfare, and highways are certainly among the most important issues in state politics. And apportionment practices seem to have little impact on the outcomes of these issues.

How can we account for the bitter political battles fought over reapportionment in many states if malapportionment really has little effect on public policy? Perhaps the explanation lies in the distinction between the potential for power and the exercise of power. Certainly malapportionment overweights rural representation in legislatures. Malapportionment may actually give rural legislators a potential for power over their urban counterparts, but, if they do not vote together with a high degree of unity to oppose urban interests on actual questions of public policy, their power may be more hypothetical than real. Legislative control can change hands and still leave policies unchanged if there are few policy differences between those placed in power and those dispossessed. Suburban voters, for example, may be just as conservative as rural voters whose voice they may replace. In addition, divisions other than rural-versus-urban may characterize much of the legislative process: divisions between the parties, between a governor's supporters and his opponents, between various economic interests and organized groups, between liberals and conservatives, between labor and management, between regions of a state and so forth. Reapportionment could change the distribution of power between rural and urban constituencies and yet have so subtle an effect on these other divisions that few policy changes would result. In short, even if rural-urban divisions are affected by reapportionment, these divisions are only one of many types of legislative divisions.

These conclusions need not moderate enthusiasm for reapportionment. The moral case for equality of representation is as compelling as it ever was. The impact of reapportionment on public policy, however, may be somewhat less sweeping than many have expected.

CHAPTER XI

Economic Development, State Politics, and Public Policy

THE EXPLANATION OF POLICY OUTCOMES

THIS BOOK IS CONCERNED with policy outcomes in American state politics. We are interested in what the states *do* in education, health and welfare, highways, taxation, and public regulation. Much of the book has been devoted to the description of policy outcomes, but its central task is one of explanation.

At the outset we constructed an analytic model to help portray the relationships between policy outcomes and the forces which shape them. Policy outcomes are conceptualized as the product of forces brought to bear upon a system, causing it to make particular responses. The political system is defined as that group of interrelated structures and processes which functions to allocate authoritatively values in society. Environmental characteristics, particularly economic development, are considered to generate inputs which are directed into the political system in the form of demands and support. Policy outcomes are viewed as the value commitments of the political system and the end product of political activity.

The task of policy research is seen as the investigation of the linkages between environmental inputs, political system characteristics, and policy outcomes. Our model has hypothesized several explanatory linkages. First of all, it posits that socioeconomic conditions help to shape the character of state political systems. Secondly, it suggests that socioeconomic conditions help to determine policy outcomes in the states. Finally, it raises the question of whether or not political system characteristics in the states independently influence policy outcomes. Two configurations of linkages have been suggested: in one the political system characteristics have an important independent effect on policy outcomes by mediating between socioeconomic conditions and these outcomes; in the other socioeconomic variables directly influence public policy without being mediated by system variables.

Our policy research has been designed to test these explanatory linkages against data derived from the fifty states; to explore the relationships between socioeconomic variables and political system characteristics, between socioeconomic variables and policy outcomes, and between political system characteristics and policy outcomes; and especially to test if political system characteristics can be shown to influence policy outcomes once the effects of socioeconomic variables are controlled. Do the characteristics of these systems have any distinct influence on policy outcomes, separate from the influence of socioeconomic development?

A model is only a representation of reality; it is never completely congruent with real world conditions. Moreover research operations are never completely congruent with our models of political life. This gap between the language of explanation and the language of research has been discussed in Chapter II. It seems that we must learn to live with discontinuities between the real world of politics, our explanatory model of political life, and our research operations.

For example, it is inevitable that, in the process of simplifying reality, we must reduce the number of variables which we can consider to be relevant to the formation of public policy. It is not possible to consider *all* of the environmental forces which may conceivably influence policy outcomes, nor is it possible to consider all of the possible variations in political system characteristics which may conceivably affect policy outcomes. On the basis of both theoretical reasoning and earlier empirical research, four economic development variables have been selected for inclusion in our model—urbanization, industrialization, income, and education, and four system characteristics have also been selected—the division of two-party control, the level of interparty competition, the level of voter participation, and the degree of malapportionment. Finally, a wide variety of policy outcomes in the fields of education, health and welfare, highways, taxation, and public regulation have been chosen for analysis. In short, our model has been operationalized by the selection of specific measures of socioeconomic development, political system characteristics, and policy outcomes.

EVALUATING AN EXPLANATORY MODEL

Let us begin to evaluate our explanatory model by trying to summarize its powers of explanation. To what extent can policy differences among the states be explained by reference to the model? Operationally speaking, the question becomes: How much of the total variation in state policies can be attributed to all of the economic development variables and political system characteristics considered together?

Multiple correlation analysis can show the extent to which variations among the states on each policy measure can be explained by all of the economic and political factors included in our model. Multiple correlation coefficients can range from .00, indicating that the factors in our model have failed to explain any variation in policy outcomes among the states, to 1.00, indicating that the factors in our model, considered together, have succeeded in explaining all of the policy differences among the states.

Multiple correlation coefficients for 54 key policy variables are shown in the left-hand column of Table XI-1. These coefficients summarize the total effect of the four measures of economic development and four political system variables on each policy outcome. In other words, these coefficients summarize the explanatory power of urbanization, industrialization, income, education, partisanship, party competition, voter participation, and malapportionment, considered together.

The summary coefficients presented in Table XI-1 show that our model possesses very substantial explanatory power. Of course, the question of what is or is not a satisfactory level of explanation is always a very subjective one. But it seems safe to conclude that our model has turned out to be a very powerful tool in policy analysis. A multiple coefficient of .71 or above indicates that more than half of the total variation among the states on a policy measure has been explained by our model. A majority of our key policy measures are above that level of explanation, and many others are quite near to it. This means that our model succeeds in explaining most of the variation among the fifty states in important policy outcomes in education, health and welfare, highways, taxation, and public regulatory activity.

While multiple coefficients can summarize the overall explanatory power of our model, they do not deal with the specific linkages in our model among public policy, economic development, and state politics. Let us turn now to a brief summary of the linkages which have been revealed in the analysis of data derived from the fifty states.

ECONOMIC DEVELOPMENT AND POLITICAL SYSTEMS

In order to understand the effects of political system characteristics on policy outcomes, it is important to keep in mind the relationships between economic development and political system variables. For example, success of the Democratic or Republican party in the fifty states has been shown in Chapter III to be related to income and educational levels in the states. Republicans are more successful in the wealthier states with better educated adult population, while poorer states are heavily Democratic. Of course this relationship is strongly influenced by the inclusion of the 11 southern states. If the southern states are removed from analysis, success of the Democratic party is more closely related to industrialization in the states.

Correlation analysis in Chapter III has also confirmed the findings of several other scholars that interparty competition in the fifty states is closely related to economic development. One-party Democratic and one-party Republican states tend to have lower income and educational attributes than two-party states. Voter participation rates in the states are also related to levels of economic development. If voting turnouts in gubernatorial and congressional elections are indicators of general political participation, then political participation is measurably greater in states with higher income and educational levels.

Malapportionment of state legislatures is the final political system characteristic to be considered. There is a slight tendency for rural farm states to undervalue votes in larger urban areas; this is not true of urban industrial states.

In short, economic development affects political system characteristics as well as policy outcomes. Thus, in order to sort out the independent effect of system characteristics on policy outcomes, it is necessary to control for the effect of economic development.

ECONOMIC DEVELOPMENT AND POLICY OUTCOMES

Let us now summarize the linkages which have been observed between economic development and policy outcomes in education, health and welfare, highways, taxation, and public regulation.

Variations in educational policy outcomes are closely related to differences among the states in economic development. The range of variation among the states in per pupil expenditures is very wide; some states spend over two-and-one-half times more than other states on the education of each child. These differences in educational expenditures among the states are closely related to differences in wealth. Educa-

TABLE XI-1

A Comparison of the Effects of Economic Development Variables and Political System Variables on Policy Outcomes in the American States

	Total Effect of Economic Development and Political System Variables	Total Effect of Economic Development Variables	Total Effect of Political System Variables	Effect of Economic Development Variables, Controlling for Political System Variables	Effect of Political System Variables, Controlling for Economic Development Variables
Education					
Per pupil expenditures	.86	.85	.58	.61	.04
Average teachers' salaries	.91	.90	.43	.78	.05
Teachers with B.A.	.85	.70	.64	.54	.47
Teachers with M.A.	.64	.60	.33	.34	.08
Male teachers	.73	.70	.56	.32	.10
Pupil-teacher ratios	.80	.70	.74	.24	.30
Dropout rate	.91	.82	.79	.54	.48
Mental failures	.88	.79	.81	.32	.39
Size of school districts	.69	.52	.67	.05	.28
State participation	.74	.49	.70	.13	.41
Federal participation	.74	.50	.37	.48	.40
Welfare					
Per capita welfare expenditures	.52	.41	.41	.12	.12
Per capita health expenditures	.57	.42	.40	.18	.16
State participation in welfare	.52	.41	.40	.17	.16
State participation in health	.57	.42	.40	.18	.16
Federal participation in welfare	.85	.85	.54	.62	.04
Unemployment benefits	.85	.84	.57	.60	.07
OAA benefits	.82	.74	.69	.37	.27
ADC benefits	.87	.80	.75	.44	.35
Blind benefits	.82	.78	.63	.43	.13
General assistance benefits	.86	.81	.66	.54	.24
OAA recipients	.62	.59	.41	.25	.05
ADC recipients	.66	.55	.50	.25	.20

Unemployment recipients	.78	.76	.43	.52	.09
General assistance cases	.55	.43	.44	.14	.14
Highways					
Per capita highway expenditures	.81	.75	.64	.40	.10
State participation	.56	.48	.34	.22	.10
Federal participation	.65	.65	.39	.35	.00
Funds from highway users	.50	.42	.18	.23	.09
Highway fund diversion	.59	.51	.31	.29	.12
Rural-urban distribution	.55	.52	.41	.16	.04
Public Regulation					
Government per population	.87	.83	.53	.66	.27
Number of bills introduced	.59	.57	.28	.29	.04
Number of laws enacted	.53	.48	.23	.25	.06
Public employees	.75	.73	.46	.46	.07
State employees	.65	.54	.25	.39	.19
Public employees' salaries	.88	.86	.44	.72	.12
Correctional expenditures	.78	.72	.34	.56	.19
Policemen	.80	.79	.26	.62	.38
Prisoners	.67	.27	.60	.14	.41
Crime rate	.77	.63	.28	.57	.33
Gambling revenue	.45	.40	.22	.17	.04
Divorce rate	.64	.37	.26	.24	.17
Parolees	.45	.49	.42	.28	.22
Taxation					
Total revenue per capita	.84	.81	.51	.61	.12
Total taxes per capita	.89	.87	.61	.66	.16
Debt	.71	.67	.40	.40	.07
State percentage of total revenue	.68	.40	.60	.17	.36
Federal percentage of total revenue	.71	.64	.39	.42	.17
Income taxes	.42	.32	.16	.15	.09
Sales taxes	.45	.33	.25	.15	.10
Alcohol and tobacco taxes	.40	.35	.25	.11	.05
Motor fuel taxes	.53	.38	.28	.23	.17
Property taxes	.80	.58	.73	.23	.46

tional effort, or the proportion of personal income in a state spent for education, is also related to wealth, although in a different fashion. Wealthier states actually spend less in relation to personal income than poorer states, yet they are still able to spend considerably more dollars for the education of each child. Wealth, expressed in terms of median family income, also explains most of the differences among the states in average teachers' salaries, teacher-pupil ratios, and the male proportion of teachers.

It is not wealth but the educational level of the adult population which is the single most important determinant of high school dropouts and selective service mental failures among the states. Once adult educational levels are controlled, dropout rates and mental failures appear unaffected by school expenditures, teachers' salaries, or teacher-pupil ratios. It is the educational level of adults rather than the public schools *per se* which seems to be the most important influence on the child.

Economic development also affects the organization and financing of state school systems. Centralization of educational administration within each state appears to be in part a function of the state's degree of economic development; centralization has proceeded further in the less economically developed states. School districts are larger in the poorer states, and the state government rather than the local school district carries a larger share of the cost of public education in these states. Although the federal government carries only a small share of the cost of public schools, federal aid is relatively more important in the poorer states. When economic development is controlled, state and federal participation in school finance does not appear to be related to increased pupil expenditures. Instead, state and federal participation appear to be a substitute for local support rather than a stimulant to school expenditures. Finally, economic development, together with the racial characteristics of the population, help to explain progress toward desegregation in 11 southern states.

The federal government plays a much greater role in the health and welfare field than in the field of education. The Great Depression did a great deal to alter public policy in the welfare field, and the national Social Security Act provides the basic framework for state as well as federal welfare policy. The states still spend roughly $2 in public assistance for every $1 spent by the federal government, and the states continue to exercise major responsibilities in the determination of health and welfare policy, but, in order to understand health and welfare policy, it is necessary to account for the effect of federal policy. The impact of levels of economic development in the states is directly reflected in welfare benefits. Benefits per recipient vary among the states by as much as 200 per cent, and these variations are quite closely related to income levels in the states. Income levels have influenced benefits in both wholly state-financed programs and also in the federal grant-in-aid programs. Federal participation does not entirely equalize benefit levels.

The effect of federal welfare policy is more obvious in figures reflecting the numbers of recipients receiving public assistance. In those programs receiving federal aid, poorer states provide assistance to more persons per population than richer states. But in general assistance programs, which are *not* federally aided, richer states provide assistance to more people than poorer states. Undoubtedly it is federal policy which leads poorer states to provide smaller amounts of money to larger numbers of people. With regard to unemployment compensation, the number of recipients is closely related to levels of industrialization in the states.

Health care is not as closely related to levels of economic development in the states as we might expect. Economic development is important in determining measures of private health care—physicians per population and hospital insurance—but it is not related to variations among the states in public hospital facilities or death rates.

The effects of federal policy are also visible in state health and welfare expenditure levels. Per capita welfare expenditures do not correlate with the measures of economic development, and this can be attributed to the effect of federal participation in welfare financing. The federal government provides about half of the funds spent on public assistance, but federal percentages of total public assistance expenditures decline with increases in state income levels. This means that federal policy offsets the effects of economic underdevelopment in the poorer states so that per capita welfare expenditures do not reflect income levels in the states. Poorer states still must spend a larger proportion of their personal incomes on health and welfare than richer states.

Reliance upon state-local welfare funds, in contrast to reliance upon federal funds, is associated with higher benefit levels but lower numbers of welfare recipients. Federal money does not operate to increase state welfare expenditures so much as it operates to offset the effects of lower economic development levels on state welfare efforts.

While the effect of federal highway activity has been to promote uniformity among the fifty states in highway policy, there are still significant differences among the states on a wide variety of highway outcomes. In 1961, per capita highway expenditures varied more than

300 per cent from the lowest to the highest state. Variations in these expenditures are related to urbanization and industrialization in the states; highway expenditures are significantly higher in the rural agricultural states. Not only do the rural farm states spend more per capita on highways, but they also spend more in relation to their income and more in relation to total public expenditures.

Federal funds for highway construction are channeled through state highway departments and these funds account for about 30 per cent of all state highway expenditures. Per capita amounts of federal highway aid to the states and the proportions of state highway funds from the federal government vary inversely with economic development. The impact of federal highway aid is greater in the rural farm states. Furthermore, the availability of federal highway funds is positively related to increased state highway expenditures. Discrimination against urban areas in state highway finance is characteristic of most states. However, this discrimination is more flagrant in rural farm states than in urban industrial states. Discrimination against cities in direct state expenditures and in state grants for local roads is more pronounced in rural states.

Interests favorable toward highway construction have generally favored the organization of independent highway commissions in the states and the earmarking of highway-user revenues for spending on highways only. While there is no empirical evidence that highway programs under independent commissions are more favored than those under direct gubernatorial control, the diversion of highway-user revenue to non-highway purposes does correlate with lower highway expenditures. Urban industrial states are more likely to divert highway-user revenue than rural farm states.

Local governments have come to rely increasingly on state funds even for their local roads. State expenditures account for almost 80 per cent of state-local expenditures throughout the nation, but this degree of centralization in highway finance varies from state to state. Local highway efforts are slightly more important in the urban states.

There is little doubt that the ability of states to raise revenue is a function of their level of economic development. Both tax revenues and total revenues per capita are closely related to wealth, as is the ability to carry larger per capita debt levels. Tax burdens, or the percentage of personal income devoted to taxes, is a function of industrialization. The greater the degree of industrialization, the lower the tax burden. There is some relationship between high tax burdens and high tax levels, but there are some states which are in the enviable position of having high tax levels with low tax burdens. The industrial resources of these states are such that they can collect high per capita taxes yet not take a very large share of personal income. In contrast, in some very poor, rural, non-industrial states, low per capita taxes and presumably low public service levels are still accompanied by high tax burdens.

Local governments tend to play a greater role in the financial structure of urban high-income states, while state governments collect a greater proportion of total revenue in rural low-income states. Overall, federal financial support of state and local governments is inversely related to economic development levels. Current federal aid formulas insure that states at lower levels of economic development receive larger proportions of their revenue from the federal government.

Surprisingly, we have found that urban industrial states rely more upon regressive property taxes in their total state-local financial structures than rural farm states. This is not to say that economic development leads to regressivity. But local governments, with their reliance upon property taxes, provide more governmental services and collect more taxes in urban states than in rural states. If only state tax sources are considered, there is no significant relationship between economic development and reliance upon sales or income taxes, which suggests that at the state level progressivity or regressivity in taxation is not a function of economic development.

The legislatures of urban industrial states introduce and enact more laws than the legislatures of rural farm states. Thus, it appears that the sheer quantity of the legislative outputs of a state is a function of economic development. The quantity of governmental units is also related to economic development, but in the reverse fashion. Rural farm states have more governmental units per person than urban industrial states. An increase in income and education is linked to an increase in the number of public employees per population and to their average monthly earnings; this suggests that the level and quality of public service is also a function of economic development.

Crime rates and police protection are related to urbanization; an increase in urbanization leads to an increase in both of these variables. State correctional policies, including prisoner populations, correctional expenditures per capita and per prisoner, and reliance upon parole, are all related to one or another measure of economic development.

In short, there are many significant linkages between economic development and policy outcomes in the states. Multiple coefficients which show the total effect of urbanization, industrialization, income, and education on 54 key policy outcomes can be found in the second column of Table XI-1.

THE FEDERAL EFFECT

The only modification in our model which is suggested by our correlations between economic inputs and policy outcomes involves the intervening effect of federal policy. Our original model has implied that the fifty states can be viewed as separate political systems, but the policies of the federal government are so influential in shaping state policy outcomes that some recognition must be given to the character of American federalism today.

American federalism no longer means that the functions of the national government and the functions of the state governments are separate and distinct. Empirically, there never was a time when state governments exercised exclusive responsibilities in education, welfare, or roads, although the belief in such a separation was widespread.[1] Both the national and state governments share responsibility for public policy in all of the fields under study. The role of each level of government varies, depending upon the field; federal policy, for example, is more important in shaping outcomes in welfare than in education. But it is difficult to treat the fifty American states as separate political systems, even from an analytic standpoint.

The way in which the states respond to economic development inputs depends in considerable measure on the posture of the federal government. Occasionally the effect of federal policy is to offset the impact of levels of economic development on state policy outcomes. A notable example of this effect occurs in per capita welfare expenditures. In other areas federal policy appears to accentuate policy differences among the states. For example, federal highway aid to rural states strengthens rural-urban differences in per capita highway expenditures. Thus, state political systems are conditioned by their place in the American federal system.

The federal government cannot be conceptualized as a constant element in the environment of the fifty state political systems, because federal policy does not impinge upon the states in a uniform fashion. The policies of the federal government impinge very unevenly upon the states; federal activities have a different impact on policy outcomes

[1] See Morton Grodzins, "The Federal System," in *Goals for Americans* (Englewood Cliffs, N.J.: Prentice-Hall, 1960); Daniel J. Elazar, *The American Partnership* (Chicago: University of Chicago Press, 1962); and William H. Riker, *Federalism* (Boston: Little, Brown, 1964).

from state to state. Perhaps it would be better to reconstruct our model so that we can consider federal policy as a separate kind of input variable, distinct from socioeconomic variables yet not a part of the state political system.

POLITICAL SYSTEMS AND POLICY OUTCOMES

Finally, let us summarize our findings regarding linkages between political system variables and policy outcomes. Much of the literature in state politics implies that the division of the two-party vote, the level of interparty competition, the level of voter participation, and the degree of malapportionment in legislative bodies all independently influence public policy. Moreover, at first glance the fact that there are obvious policy differences between states with different degrees of party competition, Democratic dominance, and voter participation lends some support to the notion that these system characteristics influence public policy. The multiple coefficients presented in the third column in Table XI-1 summarize the effect of these four variables.

However, partial correlation analysis reveals that these sysem characteristics have relatively little *independent* effect on policy outcomes in the states. Economic development shapes both political systems and policy outcomes, and most of the association that occurs between system characteristics and policy outcomes can be attributed to the influence of economic development. Differences in the policy choices of states with different types of political systems turn out to be largely a product of differing socioeconomic levels rather than a direct product of political variables. Levels of urbanization, industrialization, income, and education appear to be more influential in shaping policy outcomes than political system characteristics.

On the whole, the analysis in Chapter IX has indicated that Democratic or Republican control of a state government is not as good a predictor of its policy outcomes as is its levels of economic development. The fifty separate Democratic parties in the states are quite different from one another, as are the Republican parties. These state parties are a product of their constituencies. The policy positions of each are shaped by socioeconomic conditions within their respective states. Within particular states the parties may differ over certain issues, but throughout the fifty states Democratic or Republican control of the state government does not produce consistent policy outcomes. When the effects of socioeconomic variables are controlled and when the southern states are dropped from the correlations, a great deal of the association between policy outcomes and Democratic or Republican party strength in the state governments disappears. But when the measures of the strength of the Democratic or Republican party are controlled, there is relatively little change in the correlations between socioeconomic variables and policy outcomes. This justifies our inference that partisanship has little independent effect on policy outcomes.

When the same tests are applied to measures of party competition in the states, similar results are obtained. Economic development in the American states is related to party competition and to many policy outcomes, but party competition itself appears to have little independent effect on policy outcomes. Differences in the policy choices of competitive and non-competitive states turns out to be a product of differences in economic development rather than a direct product of party competition. When the effects of economic development are controlled, most of the association between party competition and policy outcomes disappears. But the association between economic development and policy outcomes remains strong, even after controlling for the effects of party competition. We can only conclude that party competition is much less important than economic development in shaping policy outcomes.

Similarly, there is little empirical evidence that increased voter participation *independently* affects policy outcomes in the states. When the effects of economic development are controlled, as in the analysis in Chapter X, most of the association between voter participation and policy outcomes disappears. But the association between economic development and policy outcomes remains strong even after controlling for voter participation—strong evidence that economic development is more influential in shaping policy outcomes in the states than the level of political participation.

Malapportionment is another political system variable which appears to have little independent effect on policy outcomes in the states. On the whole, the policy choices of malapportioned legislatures are not noticeably different from the policy choices of well apportioned legislatures. Policy differences which do occur turned out to be a product of socioeconomic differences among the states and not a direct product of apportionment practices. Certainly malapportionment gives more weight to the political influence of rural voters. And reapportionment may noticeably affect the style and character of state politics. But there is no empirical evidence that reapportionment will bring about any substantial changes in state programs in education, welfare, highways, taxation, or the regulation of public morality. In terms of our original model for analyzing policy outcomes in the American states, we have been unable to produce much evidence in Chapters IX and X to support the existence of an explanatory linkage between political system characteristics and policy outcomes.

However, one further set of operations will test our belief that the character of political systems is less important than economic development in shaping public policy. Thus far, we have considered the effect of each political variable separately. We have not yet observed the combined effects of all of our political variables on public policy. Yet we know that these political variables are somewhat interrelated. The question remains whether or not all of the political system characteristics considered together may not turn out to be very influential in shaping public policy.

We want to know how much of the variation in public policy can be explained by *all* of the political system characteristics at once, while controlling for *all* of the socioeconomic variables at once. Then we want to compare this with the variations in public policy which can be explained by *all* of the socioeconomic variables while controlling for *all* of the political factors. The only way to do this is with multiple-partial correlation coefficients. These statistics permit us to compare the influence of all of our economic development variables with the influence of all the political system characteristics.[2]

In Table XI-1 the multiple-partial coefficients in the fourth column from the left show us the explanatory power of all of the economic development variables while controlling for all of the political system variables. The multiple-partial coefficients in the fifth column show the explanatory power of all of the political system variables while controlling for all of the economic development variables. By comparing the size of the coefficients in these two columns we can compare the

[2] In order to combine all of the political system characteristics, one measure of each political variable has been selected for inclusion in the multiple and multiple-partial correlation analysis in this chapter. In earlier chapters three measures of each of the four political variables (twelve measures in all) were employed. But in order to balance the computations of multiple-partials in this chapter, only four political measures are employed in comparisons with the four socioeconomic measures. This insures that our results are not a product of imbalances in our comparisons. An attempt has been made to select the most influential measure of each of the four political variables. Our choice is as follows: *partisanship* — the percentage of the total seats in the lower house held by Democrats from 1954 to 1964; *party competition* — one minus the percentage of total seats in the lower house held by the majority party from 1954 to 1964; *voter participation* — the average percentage of eligible voters casting votes in gubernatorial elections between 1954 and 1964; *malapportionment* — David and Eisenberg's score for the value of a vote cast in the largest urban counties. Thus, in Table XI-1 all references to political system variables are references to these four measures. Of course, references to economic development variables are references to the measures of urbanization, industrialization, income, and education described in Chapter II.

effects of all the economic development variables while controlling for all the political system variables, with the effects of all the political variables while controlling for all the economic development variables.

Again the evidence seems conclusive: economic development variables are more influential than political system characteristics in shaping public policy in the states. The multiple and multiple-partial correlation analysis presented in Table XI-1 confirms the results of our simple and partial correlation analysis presented in earlier chapters. Forty-seven of the 54 key policy variables listed are more closely related to economic variables than to political variables. These are the policy outcomes for which the coefficients in the fourth column are larger than the coefficients in the fifth column. For these 47 policy outcomes the effects of all economic variables under controlled conditions are greater than the effects of all political variables under controlled conditions.

There are only seven policy outcomes which appear to be more influenced by political variables than by economic variables. These are pupil-teacher ratios, dropout rates, the size of school districts, prisoners per population, reliance upon state government for school revenue, reliance upon state government for total revenue, and reliance upon property taxation. It is interesting that four of the seven outcomes have to do with reliance upon local government *vis à vis* state government — in taxation, public expenditures, and presumably public service. These policies are discussed at length in earlier chapters. Political conditions in the states may not *cause* or *bring about* these outcomes, but there is an association between political conditions in the states and these outcomes which is not merely a product of the intervening impact of economic development. Thus, there are some significant exceptions to our conclusions that economic variables are more influential in determining policy outcomes than political system characteristics.

We are not really justified in concluding from this study that political variables do not have *any* impact on public policy in the states. We can only say that partisanship, party competition, participation, and malapportionment do not appear to be as influential as economic development in determining most of the policy outcomes we have mentioned.

It may be that the measures we have employed are too crude to reveal the real impact of political variables on state activities. Perhaps the effect of politics on policy outcomes is too subtle to be revealed in quantitative analysis. It should be pointed out, however, that the economic development variables we employed were just as crude as the political variables we used, yet the crudely measured economic variables were found to be related to policy outcomes while the crudely measured political variables were not. In other words, we can observe the effects of economic development on public policy using very rough measures in quantitative analysis, yet we can not see the effects of political variables under similar circumstances.

Another caveat which we should take into account here is that there may be political variables other than partisanship, party competition, participation, and malapportionment which affect policy outcomes. Studies involving political variables which are not included in our model may reveal that important policy outcomes are independently influenced by other political variables. For example, it may be that differences among state populations in their political values and attachments can be shown to influence policy outcomes significantly even after controlling for the effects of economic development. However, we have already pointed out that a great deal of the literature in political science asserts that the variables included in our model *are* influential political variables. Moreover, throughout the text we presented a great deal of a priori reasoning to the effect that these political variables should influence policy outcomes. It is hardly appropriate now to say that we have been knocking down "straw men". Our findings at least warn political scientists against making simple generalizations about the policy consequences of partisanship, party competition, participation, and malapportionment.

SOME REFLECTIONS ON POLICY RESEARCH

Political scientists may feel uncomfortable with our findings that certain political variables do not count for much in shaping public policy. How far can this sort of proposition be generalized? Can we hypothesize that the structure of *national* political systems is not really relevant to their policy outputs? Can we say that policy outcomes in nations at the same level of economic development will be similar, regardless of their ideological orientation or type of political organization? Of course we know that, in response to economic development, political systems move toward specialization, hierarchy, and impersonality and acquire other characteristics of modern bureaucracy. But whether a modernized, bureaucratic structure happens to be parliamentary or presidential may not have any relevance for policy outcomes. Furthermore, democratic and non-democratic nations at the same levels of economic development may undertake the same types and levels of government activities. And if one classifies an economic enterprise as a system variable rather than a policy outcome, it may be that socialist and capitalist nations at the same levels of economic development pursue similar domestic policies.

Perhaps differences in the character of state political systems are relatively slight in comparison with differences in the character of national political systems, and it will be easier to discern the influence of political system variables on policy outcomes in cross-national studies. On the other hand, the hypothesis that system variables do *not* independently affect the policy choices of national governments certainly merits investigation.

One of the very few systematic studies to examine the relationship between system variables and policy outcomes is Phillips Cutright's study of social security programs in 76 nations.[3] Interestingly, Cutright's findings parallel those in this study. In spite of very great differences among nations in ideological orientation and type of political system, social security policy outcomes are closely related to levels of economic development. Similar social security programs are found in democratic and non-democratic governments with the same levels of economic development. The Cutright findings clearly suggest that policy outcomes are more closely related to economic development inputs than to political system characteristics.

The fact that there are very few studies of policy outcomes in comparative national politics is evidence of the preoccupation of political scientists with system variables. There have been comparative studies which have highlighted differences in the political life of individuals living under democratic or totalitarian governments, but very little comparative research on educational outcomes, welfare services, health programs, highway programs, taxation or expenditure policies, or correctional policies under these contrasting systems of government. Such study of the outputs of national governments has been discouraged by a serious lack of data on the policies and programs of national governments. The bases of most cross-cultural data emphasize political system variables and socioeconomic input variables. Very little information is provided about the activities of national governments — about national budgets, expenditure patterns, educational programs, welfare benefits, health services, transportation policy, care of the aged, and so on.

[3] Phillips Cutright, "Political Structure, Economic Development, and National Social Security Programs," *American Journal of Sociology,* LXX (1965), 537-50; and U.S. Department of Health, Education, and Welfare, Social Security Administration, *Social Security Programs Throughout the World 1961* (Washington: Government Printing Office, 1961).

This preoccupation of political science with political system variables had led to considerable myopia regarding policy outcomes. Very few political scientists have been saying what Dawson and Robinson said in 1962: "We begin with the assumption that public policy is the major dependent variable which political science seeks to explain."[4] Since few scholars have devoted very much attention to the substance of public policy, it has been very easy to *assume* that system characteristics independently influence policy outcomes.

Political science has been guilty of viewing political life as a closed system. Specifically, political scientists have developed modes of analysis which lead them to account for what happens in a political system solely in terms of its internal activities. For example, the outcome of a battle over state labor legislation is usually explained by referring to the activities of labor and management interest groups, the mechanization of or folkways in the state legislature, the power of the governor, and so on. Rarely do we penetrate to the economic forces which give rise to the issue in the first place and which more often than not determine its outcome. We explain the outcome of battles over educational policy in terms of the activities of the National Education Association or the United States Office of Education, of the relations between the state education departments, governors, and legislatures, of the position of the Catholic hierarchy, of the political strength of taxpayers' organizations, and so on. Yet policy outcomes in the field of education may be fundamentally a product of our level of wealth, urbanization, and industrialization.

Everybody recognizes that environmental variables are operative, but these variables are often slighted, and occasionally ignored, in specific explanations. Explanations are usually couched in terms of activities which occur within the political system. Political science does not lack descriptions of what goes on *within* political systems; what it does lack is a clear picture of the linkages between political activity, environmental variables, and public policy. How do political demands develop out of environmental conditions? How are these demands made manifest and communicated? How does the political system adopt itself to these demands? How is the substance of public policy affected by these demands?

We do not mean to imply in this discussion that the study of political system variables is not an important undertaking. It is still vitally important that we understand what goes on in the little black

---

[4] Richard E. Dawson and James A. Robinson, "Inter-Party Competition, Economic Variables, and Welfare Policies in the American States," *Journal of Politics,* XXV (1963), 265.

box labeled political system. Finding a correlation between cigarette-smoking and the incidence of cancer does not in itself increase our understanding of the functioning of human cells: we still want to know *how* cancerous cells are formed and how they behave. So also, finding a correlation between industrialization and protection against unemployment does not in itself increase our understanding of the functioning of political systems: we still want to know *how* a political system goes about transforming socioeconomic inputs into policy outcomes. In this study we suggest only that certain political variables have no measurable impact on policy outcomes in the states, which is not to say that party competition, political participation, malapportionment, or other system variables do not vitally affect state governmental systems and political processes.

The *way* in which a society authoritatively allocates values may be an even more important question than the outcomes of these value allocations. Our commitments to democratic processes are essentially commitments to a mode of decision-making. The legitimacy of the democratic form of government has never really depended upon the policy outcomes which it is expected to produce; rather, it is based upon the assertion that this mode of decision-making maximizes opportunities for the individual's participation in the formation of public policy. Such decision-making is consistent with the values in Western civilization which stress the dignity and worth of the individual. Even if it were shown that democratic and totalitarian governments provide the same health care to their constituents, this would not reflect adversely on the moral quality of democratic government. Support for any political system comes not only from its success in producing satisfying outputs but also from the deeply-rooted attachment of its supporters to the system itself.

American political science has tended to emphasize the support a system receives as a product of commitments to the character of the system itself. These commitments are certainly important to any political system, but what consequences do policy outcomes have for the level of support accorded to a political system? Which demands must be satisfied in order to maintain enough support to enable the system to persist? How long can attachments to the system provide the necessary support for a political system in the face of unsatisfying outcomes? These and similar questions lie behind the need for future research on policy outcomes.

Our final comments concern the implications of policy research for political reform. Proponents of reform in state politics have extolled the virtues of high levels of party competition, increased voter participation, and equitable apportionment of state legislatures. These system characteristics are highly valued in the literature on American politics. And yet we have concluded that they have little independent effect on state policy outcomes. Where does this leave proponents of reform?

The answer, of course, is that our findings in no way reflect upon our value commitments to political reform. The normative arguments on behalf of party competition, voter participation, and reapportionment are as compelling as they ever were; they stem from deeply held values about political equality and popular participation in government. Our empirical model has been designed to explain political life, not to provide a guide for political reform. By choosing to employ an empirical model we have committed ourselves to the task of explanation rather than recommendation.

Only insofar as reform arguments involve predictions about the policy consequences of particular reforms can they be tested empirically. Such tests in no way reflect upon the moral quality of the reforms themselves, but they help us to know what, if any, policy changes may be expected in the wake of reform. They warn us not to be overly optimistic about the policy changes which can be expected from reapportionment, from the growth of two-party government in the South, or from an increase in Negro voter participation. A reapportioned legislature is likely to be circumscribed by the same economic facts-of-life that faced its malapportioned predecessor: perhaps policy demands will manifest themselves somewhat differently *within* a reapportioned legislature, but there is no evidence that reapportionment will produce any different policy outcomes. A two-party South must cope with the same economic underdevelopment that the one-party South has faced for so many years: an increase in party competition *per se* is not a substitute for economic growth in the Southern region. Economic growth rather than party competition will be the most significant factor in improvements in state education, welfare, highways, and tax programs. Negroes will come to play a more important role in the political systems of many states as a result of increased voter registration, but they will find that economic development will define what they can provide in the way of public services as it has defined it for white policy-makers.

Yet there is no reason why these findings should affect our enthusiasm for reform. Our moral commitments to insure and encourage popular participation in the political life of the nation do not depend upon empirical evidence that increased participation affects the content of public policy.

APPENDIX

Descriptions of Variables and Sources

No.	Description	Source
1	Percentage of population living in urban areas, 1960	*U.S. Census of Population, 1960*
2	One minus the percentage of the work force in farming, fisheries, and forestry, 1960	*U.S. Census of Population, 1960*
3	Median family income in dollars, 1959	*U.S. Census of Population, 1960*
4	Median school year completed by population over 25 years old, 1960	*U.S. Census of Population, 1960*
5	Percentage of membership of lower house, 1954-1964, which is Democratic	*U.S. Statistical Abstract, 1963,* p. 380
6	Percentage of membership of upper house, 1954-1964, which is Democratic	*U.S. Statistical Abstract, 1963,* p. 380
7	Average Democratic percentage in elections for governor, 1954-1964	*U.S. Statistical Abstract, 1963,* p. 379
8	Percentage of membership of lower house, 1954-1964, from majority party	*U.S. Statistical Abstract, 1963,* p. 380
9	Percentage of membership of upper house, 1954-1964, from majority party	*U.S. Statistical Abstract, 1963,* p. 380
10	Average winning percentage in elections for governor, 1954-1964	*U.S. Statistical Abstract, 1965,* p. 379

No.	Description	Source
11	Dauer and Kelsay index of representativeness: percentage of state population which could elect majority of legislators, 1955	Paul T. David and Ralph Eisenberg, *Devaluation of the Urban and Suburban Vote* (Charlottesville: Bureau of Public Administration, University of Virginia, 1961), p. 5
12	David and Eisenberg value of vote in largest counties, 1960	David and Eisenberg, p. 15
13	Press and Schubert apportionment score, 1962	"Measuring Malapportionment," *American Political Science Review, LVIII* (1964), p. 969
14	Votes cast for governor, 1954-1964, as percentage of voting-age population in 1962	*U.S. Statistical Abstract, 1963,* p. 379
15	Votes cast for U.S. Representative in 1962, as percentage of voting-age population in 1962	*U.S. Statistical Abstract, 1963,* p. 382
16	Votes cast for U.S. Representative in 1958, as percentage of voting-age population in 1958	*U.S. Statistical Abstract, 1963,* p. 382
17	Per pupil expenditures in average daily attendance, 1961	U.S. Office of Education, *Statistics of State School Systems, 1961-1962,* p. 71
18	Educational expenditures as a percentage of personal income, 1960	*U.S. Statistical Abstract, 1963,* pp. 115, 320
19	School revenue from state as percentage of total school revenue, 1961	U.S. Office of Education, *Statistics of State School Systems, 1961-1962,* p. 54
20	Average annual salary per instructional staff, 1961	U.S. Office of Education, *Statistics of State School Systems,* pp. 26-27
21	Male school teachers as percentage of total, 1963	National Education Association, *Rankings of the States, 1964*
22	Education expenditures of state and local governments, as percentage of total state and local expenditures, 1961	*U.S. Statistical Abstract, 1963,* p. 424
23	Average size of school districts, in number of pupils, 1961	U.S. Office of Education, *Statistics of State School Systems, 1961-1962,* pp. 5-6
24	Pupil-teacher ratio: enrollment per total instructional staff, 1961	U.S. Office of Education, *Statistics of State School Systems, 1961-1962,* pp. 33-34

No.	Description	Source
25	Percentage of elementary teachers with B.A. degree or above, 1961	National Education Association, *Financing the Public Schools 1960-1970,* p. 120
26	Percentage of secondary teachers with M.A. degree or above, 1961	National Education Association, *Financing the Public Schools 1960-1970,* p. 120
27	High school graduates in 1963, as percentage of ninth graders in 1959	National Education Association, *Ranking of the States, 1964*
28	Selective service examinees disqualified for failing mental test, 1962	*U.S. Statistical Abstract, 1963,* p. 269
29	School revenue from federal government as percentage of total school revenue, 1961	U.S. Office of Education, *Statistics of State School Systems, 1961-1962,* p. 54
30	Per capita educational expenditures of state and local governments, 1961	*U.S. Statistical Abstract, 1963,* p. 424
31	Unemployment compensation, average weekly payment per recipient, 1961	*U.S. Statistical Abstract, 1962,* p. 292
32	Old age assistance, average monthly payment, 1961	*U.S. Statistical Abstract, 1962,* p. 299
33	Aid to dependent children, average monthly payment per family, 1961	*U.S. Statistical Abstract, 1962,* p. 299
34	Aid to the blind, average monthly payment, 1961	*U.S. Statistical Abstract, 1962,* p. 299
35	Medical assistance for aged, Kerr-Mills, average monthly payment, 1962	*U.S. Statistical Abstract, 1963,* p. 308
36	General assistance, average payment per case, 1961	*U.S. Statistical Abstract, 1962,* p. 299
37	Old age assistance, recipients per 100,000 population, 1961	*U.S. Statistical Abstract, 1962,* p. 298
38	Aid to dependent children, recipients per 100,000 population, 1961	*U.S. Statistical Abstract, 1962,* p. 298
39	Unemployment compensation, recipients per 100,000 population, 1961	*U.S. Statistical Abstract, 1962,* p. 292
40	Aid to the blind, recipients per 100,000 population, 1961	*U.S. Statistical Abstract, 1962,* p. 298
41	Aid to the disabled, recipients per 100,000 population, 1961	*U.S. Statistical Abstract, 1962,* p. 298
42	General assistance cases per 100,000 population, 1961	*U.S. Statistical Abstract, 1962,* p. 298

No.	Description	Source
43	Deaths of infants under one year old per 1,000 live births, 1961, white	*U.S. Statistical Abstract, 1963,* p. 67
44	Deaths of infants under one year old per 1,000 live births, 1961, non-white	*U.S. Statistical Abstract, 1963,* p. 67
45	Physicians per 10,000 population, 1961	*U.S. Statistical Abstract, 1963,* p. 74
46	Hospital beds per 10,000 population, 1961	*U.S. Statistical Abstract, 1963,* p. 81
47	Patients in public mental hospitals per 100,000 population, 1960	*U.S. Statistical Abstract, 1963,* p. 85
48	Patients in public institutions for mentally retarded per 100,000 population, 1960	*U.S. Statistical Abstract, 1963,* p. 85
49	Percentage of population covered by hospitalization insurance, 1961	*U.S. Statistical Abstract, 1963,* p. 480
50	Per capita expenditures of state-local governments for public welfare, 1961	*U.S. Statistical Abstract, 1963,* p. 424
51	Per capita expenditures of state-local governments for health and hospitals, 1961	*U.S. Statistical Abstract, 1963,* p. 424
52	Welfare expenditures as percentage of total state-local expenditures, 1961	*U.S. Statistical Abstract, 1963,* p. 424
53	Health and hospital expenditures as percentage of total state-local expenditures, 1961	*U.S. Statistical Abstract, 1963,* p. 424
54	Per capita state expenditures for welfare, 1961	*U.S. Statistical Abstract, 1963,* p. 428
55	Per capita state expenditures for health and hospitals, 1961	*U.S. Statistical Abstract, 1963,* p. 428
56	Per capita community chest donations, 1961	*U.S. Statistical Abstract, 1962,* p. 306
57	State expenditures as a percentage of total state-local expenditures for welfare, 1961	*U.S. Statistical Abstract, 1963,* p. 428
58	State expenditures as a percentage of total state-local expenditures for health and hospitals, 1961	*U.S. Statistical Abstract, 1963,* p. 428
59	Per capita federal grants to state-local governments for health, welfare, and related activities, 1961	*U.S. Statistical Abstract, 1962,* p. 277
60	Federal percentage of public assistance funds, 1961	*Social Security Bulletin, 1959-1961,* p. 104

No.	*Description*	*Source*
61	Total state and local expenditures for welfare as percentage of total personal income	*U.S. Statistical Abstract, 1963,* p. 424
62	Per capita state-local expenditures for highways, 1961	*U.S. Statistical Abstract, 1963,* p. 424
63	Percentage of total state-local expenditures for highways, 1961	*U.S. Statistical Abstract, 1963,* p. 424
64	State-local expenditures for highways in relation to personal income, 1961	*U.S. Statistical Abstract, 1963,* p. 424
65	Per capita state expenditures for highways, 1961	*U.S. Statistical Abstract, 1963,* p. 429
66	State expenditures as a percentage of total highway expenditures, 1961	*U.S. Statistical Abstract, 1963,* p. 429
67	Percentage of state highway funds from motor fuel taxes, 1961	*U.S. Statistical Abstract, 1963,* p. 563
68	Percentage of state highway funds from federal government, 1961	*U.S. Statistical Abstract, 1963,* p. 563
69	Per capita highway funds from federal government, 1961	*U.S. Statistical Abstract, 1963,* p. 563
70	Percentage of state disbursements for local roads and streets going to county and township roads rather than municipal streets, 1961	U.S. Department of Commerce, Bureau of Public Roads, *Highway Statistics, 1962,* pp. 37-38
71	Discrimination against urban areas in state highway expenditures, 1957-1959 average	Philip H. Burch, *Highway Revenue and Expenditure Policy in the United States* (New Brunswick: Rutgers University Press, 1962), p. 166
72	Percentage of state highway funds granted to localities, 1961	*U.S. Statistical Abstract, 1963,* p. 563
73	Highway revenue diversion percentages, 1959	U.S. Department of Commerce, Bureau of Public Roads, *Highway Statistics, 1959,* pp. 37-38
74	Total highway mileage, 1961	*U.S. Statistical Abstract, 1963,* p. 577
75	Automobile registration, persons per vehicle, 1961	*U.S. Statistical Abstract, 1963,* p. 569
76	Designated mileage in interstate highway system, 1961	*U.S. Statistical Abstract, 1963,* p. 558
77	Mileage in federal primary system, 1961	*U.S. Statistical Abstract, 1961,* p. 558
78	Total state and local revenues per capita, 1961	*U.S. Statistical Abstract, 1963,* p. 423

No.	Description	Source
79	Total state and local tax revenues per capita, 1961	*U.S. Statistical Abstract, 1963,* p. 423
80	Total state and local tax revenues per $1,000 of personal income, 1961	*U.S. Statistical Abstract, 1963,* p. 423
81	State revenues per capita, 1961	*U.S. Statistical Abstract, 1963,* p. 423
82	Local revenues per capita, 1961	*U.S. Statistical Abstract, 1963,* pp. 423, 428
83	State revenue as a percentage of total state-local revenues, 1961	*U.S. Statistical Abstract, 1963,* pp. 423, 428
84	Per capita total state-local revenue from federal government, 1961	*U.S. Statistical Abstract, 1963,* p. 423
85	Federal revenues as a percentage of total state-local revenues, 1961	*U.S. Statistical Abstract, 1963,* p. 423
86	Income tax revenues as a percentage of total state-local revenues, 1961	*U.S. Statistical Abstract, 1962,* p. 428
87	Sales tax revenues as a percentage of total state tax revenues, 1961	*U.S. Statistical Abstract, 1962,* p. 428
88	Alcohol and tobacco tax revenues as a percentage of total state tax revenues, 1961	*U.S. Statistical Abstract, 1962,* p. 428
89	Motor fuel and motor vehicle license taxes as a percentage of total state revenues, 1961	*U.S. Statistical Abstract, 1962,* p. 428
90	Property taxes as a percentage of total state-local tax revenue	*U.S. Statistical Abstract, 1963,* p. 423
91	Per capita total state-local debt outstanding, 1961	*U.S. Statistical Abstract, 1963,* p. 425
92	Per capita state personal income, 1961	Council of State Governments, *Book of the States, 1962-1963,* pp. 56-57
93	Number of bills introduced in state legislature, 1960-1961	Council of State Governments, *Book of the States, 1962-1963,* pp. 56-57
94	Number of bills enacted by state legislature, 1960-1961	Council of State Governments, *Book of the States, 1962-1963,* pp. 56-57
95	Governments per 100,000 population, 1962	*U.S. Statistical Abstract, 1963,* p. 415
96	Municipalities and special districts per 100,000 population, 1962	*U.S. Statistical Abstract, 1963,* p. 415
97	Total state-local government employees per 100,000 population, 1961	*U.S. Statistical Abstract, 1962,* p. 432
98	State employees per 10,000 population, 1961	*U.S. Statistical Abstract, 1962,* p. 432

No.	Description	Source
99	State employees as percentage of total state-local employees, 1961	*U.S. Statistical Abstract, 1962,* p. 432
100	Average monthly earnings of state-local employees, 1962	*U.S. Statistical Abstract, 1963,* p. 440
101	Percentage of population which is white, 1960	*U.S. Statistical Abstract, 1963,* p. 30
102	Divorce rate: divorces granted per 1,000 population, 1960	*U.S. Statistical Abstract, 1963,* p. 69
103	Prisoners per 10,000 population, 1961	*U.S. Statistical Abstract, 1963,* p. 164
104	Crime rates: major crimes known per 10,000 population, 1962	National Education Association, *Rankings of the States, 1964,* p. 52
105	Pari-mutuel and gambling receipts as percentage of total state revenues, 1962	U.S. Bureau of Census, *Compendium of State Government Finance, 1962,* p. 12
106	Death penalty: no death penalty death penalty, no executions — number of executions, 1950-1960	*U.S. Statistical Abstract, 1963,* p. 168
107	Per capita state expenditures for correction, 1961	*U.S. Statistical Abstract, 1963,* p. 428
108	Total state expenditures for correction as percentage of total personal income, 1961	*U.S. Statistical Abstract, 1963,* p. 428
109	Total state-local employees in police protection per 10,000 population, 1962	*U.S. Statistical Abstract, 1963,* p. 428
110	State correctional expenditures per prisoner, 1961	*U.S. Statistical Abstract, 1963,* pp. 164, 428
111	Parole prisoners as percentage of all releases	Council of State Governments, *Book of the States, 1962-1963,* pp. 428-29

INDEX

Printed in U.S.A.